CONTENTIOUS CURRICULA

PRINCETON STUDIES
IN CULTURAL SOCIOLOGY

─────────── EDITORS ───────────

Paul J. DiMaggio

Michèle Lamont

Robert J. Wuthnow

Viviana A. Zelizer

CONTENTIOUS CURRICULA

AFROCENTRISM AND CREATIONISM
IN AMERICAN PUBLIC SCHOOLS

Amy J. Binder

PRINCETON UNIVERSITY PRESS   PRINCETON AND OXFORD

Copyright © 2002 by Princeton University Press
Published by Princeton University Press, 41 William Street,
Princeton, New Jersey 08540
In the United Kingdom: Princeton University Press,
3 Market Place, Woodstock, Oxfordshire OX20 1SY
All Rights Reserved

Second printing, and first paperback printing, 2004
Paperback ISBN 0-691-11790-X

*The Library of Congress has cataloged the cloth edition of
this book as follows*

Binder, Amy J., 1964–
Contentious curricula : afrocentrism and creationism in American
public schools / Amy J. Binder.
p. cm. — (Princeton studies in cultural sociology)
Includes bibliographical references and index.
ISBN 0-691-09180-3 (alk. paper)
1. Curriculum change—United States. 2. Social movements—
United States. 3. Afrocentrism—Study and teaching—United States.
4. Creationism—Study and teaching—United States. I. Title.
II. Series.
LB1570 .B52 2002
375'.001'0973—dc21   2001058001

British Library Cataloging-in-Publication Data is available

This book has been composed in Sabon

Printed on acid-free paper. ∞

pup.princeton.edu

Printed in the United States of America

10   9   8   7   6   5   4   3   2

Contents

Preface

THIS IS A book about two groups of citizens who, in the last twenty years of the twentieth century, felt increasingly estranged from the routine curricula taught in American public schools, and who tried to do something about their sense of alienation. Members of these groups despaired that their children marched into school, day after day, only to be fed a 'propagandistic' meal of 'half-truths' and 'outright lies.' They agonized over the thought that students were suffering diminished self-esteem and underachieving academically as a consequence of receiving these state-approved falsehoods. Parents and others active in these causes feared that their values, and their children's very personhood, were being stripped away by arrogant teachers and administrators in oppressive educational systems. Who were these challengers? On one side of the social spectrum were Afrocentrists—African Americans critical of what they called the Eurocentric emphasis in social studies and history classes, in particular—and on the other side of the social universe were creationists—Christian conservatives troubled by the teaching of evolution in science classes. Finding themselves on the margins of mainstream American thought and politics, these two groups of Americans fought back against what they considered to be an oppressive institution. This is an account of the challenges they presented to American public school systems.

If this is a study of two groups confronting American schools, it is also an examination of how the public education system responded to these two sets of challengers, and of the outcomes of those challenges. Schools, as we know from personal experience and from decades of academic research into their many details as formal and informal organizations, are places with complex and multiple responsibilities, with both the obligation to respond to their unique constituents and the mandate to deliver a credible, recognizable, and, foremost, legitimate, educational product to all of their diverse patrons. Because schools are so often contradictory and complex, and because they have limited funds and personnel, the multiple tasks and responsibilities of education systems land their decision makers in a breathtaking web of conflict when it comes to determining *how* to educate children, *whom* to prioritize as educable students, and *what* to teach at any particular time, in any particular school system. Conflict is ever present in school systems around such issues, complicating educators' efforts to reach consensus on preferred activities and goals.

One of the most trying issues educators confront is what to do when challenged by outsiders—like Afrocentric or creationist groups. Challengers often come from factions of a school system's constituency, whose members believe that some activity occurring in classrooms is not fair, academically defensible, or otherwise beneficial to children. School officials face colliding demands when challenges occur, and ask themselves whether they should allow outsiders into educational decision-making circles since, after all, public schools are community organizations, largely paid for by the very "clients" who are demanding change? Or, should schools attempt to fortify their boundaries against intrusion, since these "outsiders" may be composed of only a minority of the school system who represent non-mainstream opinion, and since schools are responsible for teaching a standard set of substantive facts and specific pedagogical processes? Do schools take route A at one time and route B at another, depending on the identity of the challenger movement and the type of changes being proposed? How do schools know when to use one alternative or the other?

These are important questions—both about schools, in particular, and about large social institutions, generally. And because they are important questions, with significant consequences for understanding contentious challenges in the wider world, they are best answered using a varied set of tools from a number of sociological fields. In this book, I will combine insights from educational research, the study of social movements, and organizational theory in an effort to capture the cultural, political, and structural elements of these battles, and to provide an explanation for why these struggles proceeded as they did.

Studying Marginal Challenges

But why these specific challenges, of all the school reform battles going on in the past two decades? The 1980s and 1990s were a strangely placid time for large-scale politics and social activism in the United States, affected by a conservative political environment beginning with the Reagan-Bush era and continuing through the economic prosperity of the Clinton presidency. But they were a time of foment, as well, among smaller groups from both the Left and the Right who felt disaffected from politics as usual. Although they, by no means, came close to representing the majority of U.S. citizens, clusters of the disaffected expressed alienation from "the way of the world" in those years. This was particularly true for those who felt, on the one hand, that their ethnic / racial / gender / sexual group was socially underappreciated, or politically and economically oppressed; and those, on the other hand, who felt that America had lost its way by catering to those very groups who had become "too radicalized," or too

"politically correct," in their claims of oppression.[1] Many of these complaints on both the Right and Left took place at the local level, rather
than on a national stage, and often these were in schools. Members of the
alienated demanded increased representation in the day-to-day activities
of school life, such as in the right to post the Ten Commandments in
their school rooms, or the right to have their African American children
schooled in Ebonics.[2]

In choosing to study Afrocentric and creationist challenges to American
schools, I made a choice to look more closely at this disaffection, to focus
on the storm beneath the calm, as sociologists are often wont to do. Call
it an occupational hazard, call it a desire to see what the underdog is up
to—whoever those underdogs are, and whatever our sympathies for their
particular assertions of dispossession. I decided to look at these two self-
proclaimed disenfranchised groups because they presented such a fine
comparison—they were on opposite sides of the sociopolitical continuum,
and both despised the center; they felt disenfranchised, but both found
ways to exert some power in their school systems. They were, above all,
expressive challengers: impassioned, worried about their children, and
concerned about the future of their country.

Among those whose work is a model for synthesizing vast theoretical
literatures and massive amounts of archival data (not to mention work
that concerns discourses about children), I have turned to Nicola Beisel
again and again for fresh intellectual insights, emotional support, and an
invaluable friendship. Although our work departs from each other's in
significant ways, it would be good for my ego to think that there are
similarities, too. Nicki's research has long represented for me an example
of the highest form to aim for. She was my advisor during the dissertation
phase of this project (and before), and has been a trusted friend, confidant,
and teacher to this day. She is much loved and respected.

I owe an enormous amount of gratitude to the two other fine human
beings on my dissertation committee: Art Stinchcombe and Christopher
(Sandy) Jencks. Imposing figures on paper, these two very decent people
were generous with their time and their astoundingly smart ideas. Having
a quantitative sociologist who expressed skepticism about the precision
of cultural sociology and interpretive methods (as Sandy did) was the
right kind of challenge for working out my ideas. It wasn't easy, but it
was rewarding. Art, a prodigious critic, frequently amazed me with the
depth of his knowledge and his feel for data and theory. I often left his
office both in a giddy daze and with a slightly upset stomach—these were
reactions to being in the presence of deep sociological wisdom. The memory of the day Art wrote the word "stunning" on my dissertation theory

chapter is a recollection I'll take to the grave. I know that in this business one shouldn't need such external validation, but I confess, it's nice when you can get it.

Many others across the country have read pieces of this manuscript and have been generous with their comments. Doug McAdam has been critical and kind in his commentary, offering constructive criticism at a key point in my thinking about this project. He is deservedly renowned for being not only a good guy (I speak here of his magnanimity), but also a very wise guy. The participants in his political sociology workshop at Stanford, 2000–2001, were also helpful in pointing out key books to read and ideas to think about as I developed the manuscript. I am also extremely fortunate to have had Paul DiMaggio read the first draft of this manuscript— I cannot think of a person who could have provided a sharper eye for catching the errors I made in both logic and articulation. Although Paul can't be faulted for any weaknesses in the book that remain, he can be credited with bringing the argument to a much higher level.

Other readers and commentators include Mitchell Stevens, a treasured friend and colleague; Scott Davies, a comrade in studying education reform from a social movements perspective; Michèle Lamont, an early trusted outside advisor; Jim Rosenbaum, an early trusted inside advisor; my colleagues Jon Miller, Barry Glassner, and Kelly Musick at USC; Rhys Williams, an ASA friend and trusted reader; Marie-Laure Djelic, a happy encounter at Stanford; Meredith Phillips, Bethany Bryson, Michael Olneck, Michael Foley, Marc Ventresca, Larry Cuban, Walter Powell, Greg Stanczak, Wendy DeBoer, and reviewers and editors of *Sociology of Education, American Sociological Review,* and the *American Journal of Sociology.* Thanks to John Meyer for hosting this invisible visiting scholar at Stanford during her year off. I would also like to express gratitude to Ian Malcolm, who shepherded the manuscript through the editorial process at Princeton University Press, and to Linda Truilo for her careful reading of the manuscript and her insightful comments.

The people I interviewed out in the field were very kind to give me their time and energy—often more than once. It never ceased to amaze me that busy people, important people, would be so generous with a novice researcher. I learned a great deal from them. I have tried to treat their observations with the care and precision they deserve. I thank especially Kevin Padian, Linda Biemer, Virginia Sanchez-Korrol, Betsy Hammond, Bill Loftus, and Murdell McFarlin for volunteering to read sections of this manuscript several years after our initial interviews.

I thank the heavens—or the entrepreneurs responsible—for the Lexis-Nexis database, and for Northwestern's, University of Southern California's, and Stanford's decisions to provide the database service free-of-charge to their research communities. I am also grateful for the solid reporting that was done in the local newspapers that I used in each of the cases: The *Atlanta Journal-Constitution*, *New York Times*, *Washington Post*, *New Orleans Times-Picayune*, *Kansas City Star*, *San Diego Union Tribune*, and *Los Angeles Times*.

I also would like to acknowledge three sources of income over the past five years, which allowed me to write for long stretches of time, undeterred by teaching, teaching assisting, and / or research assisting. As a doctoral student, I received a dissertation fellowship from Northwestern University, which paid for a year of nonteaching, nonresearch-assistant writing time. Without it, I would have been slogging away on the dissertation much longer and less happily. I would also like to thank the Spencer Foundation and its Small Grants program, which allowed me to buy out teaching for one semester during my third year of assistant professorship at USC. The data presented, the statements made, and the views expressed are solely my responsibility. USC also facilitated this project with both research monies and its generous post-review semester leave for junior faculty—a real gift for research.

I would like to thank the publishers of the following ariticles or chapters of mine for permission to draw on these papers for use in this book: "Friend and Foe: Boundary Work and Collective Identity in the Afrocentric and Multicultural Curriculum Movements in American Public Education," in *The Cultural Territories of Race: Black and White Boundaries*, ed. Michèle Lamont (Chicago: University of Chicago Press and New York: Russell Sage Foundation, 1999) (used in chapter 1); "Why Do Some Curricular Challenges 'Work' While Others Do Not? The Case of Three Afrocentric Challenges: Atlanta, Washington, D.C., and New York State," *Sociology of Education* 73 (2000): 69–91 (used in chapter 4); and "Identity Trouble in Sacrosanct Battles: When the Elite and Grassroots Confront Each Other in Creationist Challenges to Schools," *Religion and Education* (Fall 2001) (used in chapter 6).

Finally, I thank my family and friends, who provide emotional and intellectual grounding. Among those who have been key to the process of writing are Paul Lerner, Linda Millon, Beth Porter, Timothy Self, Charlotte Siegel, and Jenny Wolfe-Binder. My mother Lois Binder—at the very center of this network (always)—is to whom I owe it all.

One

Introduction to Afrocentrism and Creationism, Challengers to Educational "Injustice"

In 1988, the District of Columbia public school system found itself perched on the edge of a controversy that would bedevil it for the next ten years. Although the issue would ebb and flow as the decade wore on, one superintendent lost his job over the controversy, and a great deal of ink was spilled, and vitriol expressed, in the local media over the strengths and weaknesses of the proposed plan. All of this discussion was activated by a proposal to infuse "African-centered" materials and methods of instruction into the local public school curriculum. The people who advanced the proposal argued that the district's curriculum was biased toward European knowledge and Western styles of teaching, and that this bias was harmful to the self-esteem and performance of African American school children. Proponents of Afrocentrism also complained that their views were not being represented within the district's official decision-making bodies, and that they were being denied a rightful voice in school policy. Community activists, Afrocentric scholars from across the nation, and parents of poorly educated children pushed the district to "go Afrocentric," while the majority of the city's resident media commentators, university faculty, and politicians pressured district leaders to reject the movement. Adding to the complexity, one faction of Afrocentrism's most vocal opponents lent their support to implementing a more "inclusive" *multicultural* curriculum in the district, while other opponents advised the district to reject all contemporary efforts to "balance" curricular content.

Charged with "race betrayal" by Afrocentrists if they did not incorporate Afrocentric materials into the curriculum, and with "spinelessness" by the opposing side if they did, district administrators faced decisions fraught with peril no matter which way they turned. Ultimately, the administration decided to implement what I call "circumscribed Afrocentric reform" in the district, which was an effort to conciliate both sides that ended up satisfying no one. To this end, the district instituted a school-within-a-school, "African-centered" program that served a miniscule 120 children out of some 80,000 in the district. The administration's solution won it few friends among either allies or opponents of Afrocentric reform, for it neither fully endorsed nor fully denounced the aims of the controversial Afrocentric movement. For this compromise solution, administrators received withering criticism in the district and the nation, with the *Washington Post* leading the charge. Opponents condemned the superintendent and his staff for caving in to the demands of a radical fringe movement, and proponents of Afrocentrism castigated the superintendent for limiting the program to such a small scale, although they simultaneously praised him for even that level of support.

Another controversy over curriculum content that surfaced during this same general time took place in the state of California. Lasting from 1985 to 1989, this curriculum debate featured much of the same antagonistic rhetoric as the conflict over Afrocentrism in Washington, D.C. In a debate that concerned science-teaching statewide, challengers in the state of California argued that science curricula were biased and discriminatory, and that they, the challengers, had been excluded from the process of determining the content of public school instruction. The system, it seemed to them, had come under the control of a monopoly interest, and it was time to wrest power from this oppressive group. New curricula and materials had to replace the old dogmatic mode of instruction.

Although this sounds similar to the Afrocentric demands described above, the curricular content at the heart of the California debate was unlike the one Washington activists were fighting for. In California, Christian conservatives initiated the debate, charging that secular humanism had militated against truth in science classrooms, and that something immediate, and something fundamental, must be done to return schools to their more honest, Christian roots. They argued that alongside the teaching of evolution of human origins in science classes, there should rightfully be taught *creation science*, a "scientifically based" explanation of the biblical account of creation, in which a divine being created the earth, human beings, and all other species.

Over the past several years, I have examined three cases of Afrocentric challenge made to public school curricula, like the Washington case, and have compared them to four cases of creationist challenge, like the California case. All seven of the challenges that I studied occurred between 1980 and 2000. Like many other Afrocentric battles, the challenge in Washington arose in one of the nation's largest and poorest, predominantly African American school systems. Condemning public schools for shortchanging generations of their children, Washington D.C. supporters of Afrocentrism demanded that public schools rewrite their social studies and history curricula to emphasize the contributions made to U.S. and world history by Africans and African Americans. One of its specific solutions was to reorient African American children toward their African past, and also to honor the accomplishments of ancient black Egyptian culture—which is said to have lent so much of its teachings to Greek and Roman civilization. It was a movement that embraced black nationalism, essentialism, and traditionalism—a form of conservatism that has long been one strain of African-American social and political thought.

Likewise, in many respects, the California creationist case was characteristic of other creationist battles being waged in the country during this time period, both in the demography of its supporters and in the claims they made. First, it was a challenge from the politically and socially conservative Right. Its proponents claimed that secular humanism and atheism—both of which, they argued, were based on a flawed evolutionary theory claimed as fact—had become established as a state religion in the public schools. One of the greatest abominations to morality, said creationists, was teaching evolution in science classrooms without also teaching "alternative theories" of life's origins. For creationists, evolution is not only biblically proscribed, but scientifically unproven, as well. Therefore, members of this group sought to loosen evolution's "dogmatic" grip on the imaginations of their children by having "honest" scientific evidence presented in the classroom, which casts doubt on Darwinian theory.

Seemingly incomparable on a number of dimensions—in terms of their sociopolitical ideologies, race, region, religion, and specific pedagogical objectives—these two groups of challengers, I will argue, were actually similar, and thus ideal for comparison, in a number of crucial ways.

First, at the most fundamental level, both Afrocentrism and creationism offered solutions to perceived social and educational problems—they were reform efforts to fix schools.[1] Each of these challenging efforts criticized the public education system for imposing its views on pupils and for placing enormous constraints on parents' ability to transmit their own belief systems to their children. Christian conservatives who supported creation science, for example, complained bitterly about secular humanists' monopoly of the education system, which was so powerful, they argued, that children's most profound beliefs were being trampled by administrators and teachers who held the reins of educational control. Similarly, Afrocentrists charged that an omnipresent Eurocentric curriculum has been forced upon their children, forming an oppressive environment that flagrantly has misrepresented Africans and African Americans and deemphasized historical racism.

Second, both challenges used the emotive force of their children's welfare to stake their claims for curricular change. As authors such as Nicola Beisel, and I, elsewhere, have demonstrated, there may be no more compelling social project than trying to protect children from various sorts of insidious harms.[2] Invoking their children as the prime beneficiaries of their action, Afrocentrists and creationists were remarkably alike.

A third similarity between the two was that both groups of challengers publicly insisted that their corrective to the education establishment's monopoly of the curriculum was to provide pluralism in the classroom, not

censorship. Since the 1960s, creationists have argued that they were fighting not to limit teaching—by ejecting evolution from the classroom—but
rather, to have more content added to the curriculum, by teaching evolution and creation science alongside one another or, in a later version of
their argument, by "exposing the weaknesses" of Darwinian theory. Such
a solution, said the activists, is inclusive of everyone's beliefs, Christian
and humanist. In a similar tone, Afrocentrists claimed that they did not
seek to replace a Eurocentric curriculum with an Afrocentric one, for that
would only repeat the miseducation of students and continue an arrogant
disregard for other cultures.[3] Rather, national figures in the movement
proposed to correct the misrepresentation of Africa in world history by
adding previously slighted materials about the continent and its people
and by ridding the school system of only the materials that are biased and
white-centered.[4] Both groups of challengers represented their demands as
inclusionary, not exclusionary.

Capping off this set of similarities was the fact that these challengers
also faced considerable skepticism among a majority of educators—particularly administrators—in the school systems they battled.[5] Given the
unorthodox tenets of each of these curricular movements, many administrators, dealing with their respective challenges, regarded these efforts to
be politically risky, at best, and academically outrageous, at worst. While
they invoked different cultural and institutional criteria to cast doubt on
the two curriculum agendas, large numbers of education professionals
were generally dismayed at being pressed to reform curricula along "non-
scholarly" avenues: so that ancient black Egyptians could be presented
as teachers to the Greeks, or so that the Bible could be used as the departure point for a scientific theory of origins. Whether these professionals
were primarily motivated by a desire to protect their own positions by
keeping change at bay, or to ensure that students be taught what they
considered to be academically rigorous content, the majority of policymakers and administrators in systems challenged by Afrocentrism or
creationism felt threatened by these challenges and wished that these issues had never arisen.

In sum, although the two campaigns for curricular change were sub-
stantively different in their learning objectives, they also shared many
common features. Afrocentrists and creationists felt disenfranchised from
public schools, and they used remarkably similar rhetoric in their fights
over curricula. Both issued a critique of schools' content, and they demanded similar concessions: they claimed that students were discriminated against when they were forced to accept the teachings of an oppressive educational system, and they proposed their own scholarly
correctives to this crisis. Both challenges, as we shall see in later chapters,
can even be thought of as the same type of "identity movements" in educa-

tion,[6] and their proponents viewed as representatives of "discursive politics,"[7] in that their goals seem to have been aimed more at creating new understandings about educational processes—and at achieving respect and status for their group in educational decision making—and less toward ensuring measurably improved academic achievement on the part of their children. And finally, when each group of challengers presented its goals to education officials, a majority of those professionals was skittish about incorporating revisions into the curriculum.

So, what came to pass in these targeted school systems, given the similarities in challengers' objectives and educators' reactions to those demands? What I have found in comparing these two challenges is that, following from their skepticism, school personnel delivered fundamentally the same *ultimate* fate to Afrocentrists and creationists: they fought to preserve their institution's core curricula in history and science. Aided sometimes by the courts and sometimes by public opinion, school staff eventually rebuffed both sets of challenges, so that little, if any, of either Afrocentrists' or creationists' initial curricular demands had serious lasting or widespread effects on students' classroom learning. Fighting to maintain the essence of their "technical core," school personnel ultimately staved off these demands for curricular reforms.

But there is more to the story. What I have found so interesting about the two similar ultimate outcomes in these cases is that professional educators figured out ways to rebuke each challenge using a *different* repertoire of strategies, which resulted in short-term outcomes that varied on multiple dimensions. When confronted with Afrocentrists' demands, school officials generally treated their challengers more respectfully than they did creationists; they appeared to consider Afrocentric demands as legitimate matters to be deliberated; and they allowed Afrocentric proposals for revised curricula onto their official agendas (if not always into their official curricula). In two of my three cases, Afrocentrists were even able to make real headway into school-district educational practices and to change the official history and social studies curricula taught there—at least temporarily. But I soon discovered that a school system's initial apparent respectfulness toward Afrocentric challengers should not be confused with its willingness to grant lasting accommodation. In each of the three Afrocentric cases, school systems eventually watered down whatever Afrocentric victory had been gained in the contested school system, delivering considerably less concrete change to Afrocentric activists than they had initially promised. I call this a process of gradual dilution. While Afrocentrists may have won a few battles, they ultimately won no wars. Nor did creationists win any lasting wars, although school system professionals used a different process from "dilution" to thwart their Christian conservative challengers. When confronted by creationists, educators came out with their fists swinging. There was no initial accommodation, which was then blunted by a watering down process. Professional educational leaders were simply unwilling to accommodate their creationist critics. Despite the fact that the Christian conservative reformers, too, were making claims of bias and discrimination, in all four of the creationist cases studied in this book, the education establishment—by which I mean professional educators in positions of authority—lined up far more forcefully against their creationist challengers than their counterparts did against their Afrocentric challengers. With the backing of such organizations as the American Civil Liberties Union and the National Academy of Sciences, school system officials argued that anti-Darwinist, creationist curricula crossed the line that separated church from state, and they fought tooth-and-nail to defeat their creationist foes.

Now, it is true that creationists, in three of the locations I studied, got themselves elected to school boards or legislative bodies with the support of committed voters, and that they sometimes could muster truly impressive political power to impose temporary creationism-friendly law in their school systems (we will see evidence of these advances in chapters 5 and 6). But when creationists did this, education professionals—people who were trained in education schools, who held educational credentials, and who felt that they should have the authority to make decisions in the system—bitterly opposed them. These official educators could wield institutional power, and they fought back mightily and publicly against creationists' gains from the very beginning of the contests. They did this even when creationists had gained access to the inside of those systems—such as by being elected to serve on the school board. When they fought back (and they always did), professional educators' institutional power trumped creationists' political power. Creationists were unable to parlay their early elective and political gains into positive ultimate outcomes for their side. In each and every occasion that a public school system temporarily "went creationist," eventually some type of public backlash, whether by voters or by the courts—but always encouraged by education professionals—reversed those gains. Time and again, creationists tasted victory, only to have schools (or voters, on behalf of schools) take it away from them painfully and publicly.

Like the Afrocentrists, then, creationists were unable to attain lasting, concerted change in the school systems they challenged. Afrocentrists gained some concessions, but educators found ways to make their concessions temporary—often by surreptitious or, at least, behind-the-scenes, means. Creationists, meanwhile, also were sometimes able to seize political power in school systems, but they, too, were eventually defeated, although in the creationists' case, the defeat was trumpeted publicly. In both cases, but by different routes, schools were able effectively to minimize their challengers. It is to both the similarity in these challenges and their variance that this book will be addressed.

Consequential Challenges?

What does this matter? Should we care if Afrocentrists and creationists traveled different routes to ultimately similar fates in these seven school systems? Is it important that Afrocentrists were, generally, more effective than creationists in their efforts to claim legitimacy for their ideas and to get those ideas on educators' agenda—at least initially—while creationists' arguments fell on relatively deaf ears? Should our interest also be piqued by the fact that even in Afrocentrists' encounters with educators—where school officials went so far as to praise and even, sometimes, implement policy in their favor—that their efforts ran into eventual obstacles to real change? As subtle as those obstacles to Afrocentric reform may have been, they were still heady, and professional educators were primarily responsible for constructing them. Should we be interested to observe that the obstacles that creationists confronted, on the other hand, were not subtle in the least, and that education bureaucracies, in fact, loudly announced their antipathy toward this set of challengers? The question I am raising is this: even if we grant that studying Afrocentrism and creationism might be interesting in an ethnographic sense, can the outcomes of their challenges teach us anything about social processes that sociologists care about in a more general sense? Can they tell us, in order of ascending institutional magnitude, anything important about feelings of alienation among individuals in challenger movements; about contentious challenges in public schools; about the dynamics of open conflict in large institutions, generally; or even about everyday life in late twentieth-century America? Or were the Afrocentric and creationist challenges just two fringe curricular reform efforts, among many, that occurred on the margins of American pedagogical life and that can tell us nothing newsworthy about our lives in large institutions or about sociological theory?

Not surprisingly, given the book-length attention I devote to these challengers and to the responses they received from school systems, I argue that these challenges did matter, and I will make the case that exploring marginal challenges such as Afrocentrism and creationism, and the outcomes they achieved in schools, can reveal a great deal not only about the racial or religious frustration, respectively, that some groups of citizens experience in public schools in contemporary America, but also about the dynamics surrounding challenge activities in the United States—especially in public schools—and the ways in which organizations like school systems respond to challenges from their different constituencies. The main thrust of the argument is that these school systems managed to absorb protest, to quell institutional change, when either creationists or Afrocentrists were on the frontlines. It was not that Afrocentrists won stunning victory in case after case while creationists suffered humbling defeat; or, conversely, that creationists achieved brilliant success while Afrocentrists were sent away by school systems with no gains. There is no single "success metric" that can account for the outcomes realized in these two different challenges. But by looking at the two challenges in depth—both in comparison to each other, and individually, for each of the seven cases—we can see why and how outcomes developed in the schools as they did. In general, Afrocentrists were better able to get American educators to consider their requests and treat their complaints as valid, which illustrates that some cultural discourses about bias have greater power to resonate with American understandings (at least American *educators'* understandings), while others are not so endowed. Creationists, meanwhile, often took advantage of voter disinterest in their communities, and collected enough ballots on election day to win majorities on school boards. These events indicate that a structure of political opportunities in any given institution may be beneficial to some challenging groups but not to others. Finally, in the case of both Afrocentrists and creationist challenges, we will see that the presence of organizational routines in large institutions like public schools are sometimes helpful, but often injurious, to challengers. At a more abstract level, studying events such as these seven challenges might prepare us to make better predictions of when challengers will be able to push embattled institutions to change their ways of doing things and, alternately, when these institutions will be able to stay their course, dispensing, one way or another, with their adversaries. These are issues that occupy the highest order of theorizing in the sociological discipline, and they emerge visibly in this comparison of little respected, much vilified education challenges.

Understanding Outcomes

The Meanings of these Challenges: Cultural Analysis of Afrocentric and Creationist Efforts

As I began investigating these seven Afrocentric and creationist challenges, seeking clues to what they might be about, their ground-level activities seemed important from many theoretical angles.

From my home branch of cultural sociology, I sought to make sense of the two fascinating challenges using a sort of *cultural analysis*, in which

the meanings of the challenges would emerge front-and-center as provoc-
ative aspects of the conflicts to be studied. How were Afrocentrists, as
challengers to schools, different from creationists? How were they similar
in surprising ways? Some of the most absorbing issues arising from a
culturally sensitive look at these challenges include questions about the
way these groups defined themselves as people with legitimate claims, and
then presented their demands for change to multiple audiences; how they
constructed identities for themselves vis à vis others in the challenging
field (such as Afrocentrists against multiculturalists, and creationists
against advocates for prayer in the schools); and how they used particular
forms of language in their claims making. I decided to look at the identities that both camps forged for themselves, that they applied to their foes,
and that they reserved for their supporters. I tracked the values, practices,
and norms that prevailed in each challenge, that bound members to one
another, and that kept other groups, with other practices and values, defined as the "enemy."[8] I investigated the lines of distinction that separated
these groups' members from others in schools; I explored their academic
experiences and credentials, their occupational locations in the academic
world, and their presence on the country's historical stage. Chief among
this line of questioning is an analysis of each group's written and spoken
discourses: how they presented their ideas about children, justice, and
America to themselves and to other audiences. In the words of cultural
sociology, I studied the ideational and symbolic elements of Afrocentrists'
and creationists' claims about schools, and schools' ideational and symbolic responses to their critics. Central to this area of study were questions
surrounding the challengers' use of rhetoric, and the degree to which their
"framing" of the issues resonated with and, perhaps, even changed the
wider cultural discourses of the day.

Because a study of these challenges would be desiccated without an
understanding of the groups' cultural foundations, I launch the book with
an examination of this type. The exploration focuses particularly on the
claims each group of challengers made about its position in American
educational and social life, and the counterclaims that other institutional
sectors (such as the media and political actors) issued in response.

But although a cultural analysis of these challengers leads to important
insights into what it was like to be a marginal curricular movement in the
United States in the last years of the millennium, it cannot capture the
entirety of these groups' experiences in the schools. There is more to Afrocentrism and creationism than the meanings they sought to alter in
schools, the identities they crafted, and the rhetoric they used to state their
demands. As David Tyack and Larry Cuban indicate in *Tinkering toward
Utopia*, challengers' claims do not fall into a black hole where no one
hears them. In the examples studied here, Afrocentrists and creationists

advanced their arguments in organizational and political settings, where people in positions of power had the authority to do something about those claims. I found it necessary to examine the various ways that education professionals approached these two sets of challengers, and to look at the consequences that resulted from that varying reception.

Challenges as Social Movements

My study of the seven Afrocentric and creationist efforts continues, then, with intellectual wrestling of a different kind, when I turn to a *social movements* approach for exploring the dynamics and outcomes of these challenges. The area of social movements and collective action is the long-time home of sociological research into protest activism and other "weapons of the weak." Social movements researchers have developed a useful tool kit of concepts that can be applied to Afrocentrists' and creationists' organization of their resources, their mobilization of adherents to their causes, their strategies of culturally "framing" their issues, and their attempts to exploit the political opportunities that resided in their school systems, while also skirting the political constraints that lurked there.

Given the explicit rhetoric of injustice that each set of challengers used, social movements research beckoned for a role in the examination of these school battles. In their sense of having been excluded from the public school system, in their claims of inequity, in their collective identity as people struggling for the rights of their children, and in their sense of efficacy in being able to correct these multiple wrongs, Afrocentrists and creationists sounded very much like "social movements" that struggle against entrenched institutions. Although Afrocentrists and creationists were equipped with only a smattering of material assets and organizational know-how (instead benefiting mostly from cultural resources), and despite the fact that they targeted only the more limited organization of school systems (and not the state, at large), and even though they took their causes directly to school authorities (rather than to a mobilizable public), on a variety of other dimensions, Afrocentrists and creationists looked a great deal like other groups that traditionally have been studied as social movements. The lessons learned from the study of a host of other movements—from prohibition to civil rights—I thought, could be applied to the project of understanding the two groups' experiences in schools.

Applying a social movements analysis to these challenges, however, required some adaptation of movements theory—an adaptation that, I believe, will contribute to an emerging synthesis in the area of political sociology, which is exemplified in the theoretical work of Doug McAdam, Sidney Tarrow, and Charles Tilly.[9] For one, it has been argued that we now live in a world where movement-like contention has become far more frequent than it was just thirty years ago, and that the kinds of struggles that Afrocentrists and creationists were waging from 1980 to 2000 have become the modal form of contentious politics in Western democracies.[10] Unlike the social movements that have inspired mainstream social movements theory—large, political, and disruptive challenges such as the civil rights, pro-life, or environmental movements—the kinds of struggles that have become far more common in Western societies in the past few decades are generally local rather than national movements; they take place within institutions rather than "in the streets"; and they target institutional power rather than what is ordinarily considered to be "political" power. Analyzing creationism and Afrocentrism using a social movements lens acknowledges a willingness to think more broadly about what we mean by the term "movements."

Second, tapping the social movements literature for insights into what, exactly, Afrocentrists and creationists were able to accomplish in the schools—that is, their outcomes—yielded surprisingly mixed results. Until recently, movements researchers have spent relatively little energy trying to understand challenger outcomes. As much as the study of movement origins and trajectories has become something of a growth industry in the field, according to some scholars, the *effectiveness* and the *outcomes* of those challenges have remained more obscure, due to researchers' comparative inattentiveness in this area. Because so much research effort has flowed toward questions of movement formation and emergence, some scholars argue,[11] we have few keys for understanding the conditions and circumstances that led to the eventual rebuke of both Afrocentionists and creationists, the processes leading to their temporary success and failure, or the actual effects gained by either movement. We are even less prepared to know why subject bureaucracies (the organizations being challenged) respond positively or negatively to their challengers' demands, how they deliver certain kinds of victories and defeats, or about their very ability to accommodate Afrocentrists' and creationists' claims.[12] While education scholars such as Larry Cuban and David Tyack have studied this question of reform outcomes from the perspective of education policy,[13] few movements researchers have studied the subject organization as a possible source of outcome variation. This is a wide gap in knowledge, which, though beginning to attract important and interesting study for other types of institutional challenges, leaves a fairly open path for understanding what happened in the Afrocentric and creationist challenges.

Following this path, I have found three prominent concepts already developed in movements research to be useful for studying the two challenges' outcomes in school systems, even if these concepts to this point have been marshaled only rarely to study the results of institutional struggles. The first of these three ideas is *framing,* the rhetorical activity that movement leaders use to try to connect their arguments about a set of issues to audiences' common-sense understandings about those same issues. When successful, movements' framing activities result in "frame resonance," whereby an audience "buys into" the logic of the movement. The second social movements concept that has guided my thinking about Afrocentrists' and creationists' outcomes is the concept of *insider / outsider* location in the challenged field, a measure of different actors' access to the routine structures of power in a system. The third concept is the traditionally structural factor of *political opportunities and constraints,* or the economic, political, and social variables that exist at the time of a challenge and that characterize the windows of opportunity for challenger emergence and formation in an embattled institution.[14] These three ideas—laid out in their most abstract form here—cover the cultural and structural terrain usually described in movement studies: specifically, the cultural ties that challengers forge with audiences using rhetorical strategies, and the structural opportunities that arise in the field (negative and positive) affecting challenger activity. And yet, as currently understood, the three concepts have not been put to full use to theorize outcomes and, so, cannot capture the varied results that Afrocentrists and creationists realized in these seven cases. In later chapters I will trace in greater detail the intellectual foundations of these ideas, but for now, I will highlight only the extensions to these movements concepts that the study of Afrocentric and creationist challenges can make.

FRAMING. According to scholars who study framing, movement leaders produce and employ frames that will legitimate their goals and tactics, maximize the public's attention to and support for the movement, and defuse and preempt counterframing by the movement's opponents. Applied to these two challenges, framing raises the central question, How did the leaders of the creationist and Afrocentric challenges try to marry their arguments about oppression in the schools with their audiences' understandings and values about education, justice, and other related issues? As many movements researchers have described, challenging movements use framing techniques in a number of ways: to *diagnose* some problem that they believe needs attention (that is, to indicate events or conditions as problematic); to give a *prognosis* of what should be done about the problem (to indicate the solution to these unjust conditions); and finally, to solidify the *identities* of the various sides in a challenge, defining who rightly belongs on the side of justice and who does not (to draw boundaries between "us" and "them").[15]

In most studies that discuss framing, movements researchers have looked at challenge leaders' efforts to link their preferred frames with the frames of a mobilizable public, and to study whether the movement is able to "resonate" with that public's values and beliefs to spur citizens to action. But, far fewer movements scholars have studied the direct effect of challengers' frames on the very organizational members they are trying to sway—*establishment insiders*—and to ask why it is that some challenger frames have the power to compel actors who seem ideally situated to reject challenger arguments. Framing's direct persuasive connection with organizational decision makers has received little consideration largely because so little movements research has focused on smaller institutional challenges in a particular organization (like schools) where public mobilization may not be so effective, and also partially because researchers assume that challengers have little influence on power holders. Movements scholars have paid only scant attention to the ways that challengers may frame issues to persuade institutional incumbents, in addition to movement participants and bystanders, of the justice of their cause.[16]

And yet, as I will be demonstrate throughout the book, it is costly to overlook this realm of framing activity and potential resonance if we are to understand the outcomes in the seven Afrocentric and creationist cases. Professional educators' vulnerability to framing techniques varied significantly across these two challenges, with Afrocentrists' claims leading to greater frame resonance with educators' cultural understandings than creationists' frames were able to achieve. When Afrocentrists diagnosed a problem in American education pertaining to young African Americans' historical and present poor performance in substandard schools, they were pitching their arguments directly to school power-brokers, and their arguments resonated with some. When they recommended a solution that involved the incorporation of Afrocentric concepts, the "fix" they proposed was directed to those in decision-making positions. The solution may have seemed extreme to many professionals in the schools, but to others (even those with enormous amounts of authority in these systems), the solution seemed not too far a cry from multiculturalism—a form of curriculum that had grown familiar and expected in schools. When Afrocentrists warned that those who turned their backs on the challenge were "racist," the frame was meant to raise pronounced fear in educational quarters, and it was often successful. These appeals to professional personnel, as we will see, resulted in some resonance with educators, and ultimately assured Afrocentric challengers at least some voice in the curriculum discussions in the three school systems. In contrast, a lack of resonance with professional educators handicapped the creationist challenge.

INSIDERS AND OUTSIDERS. Acknowledging that there may be additional targets of challengers' framing activities, besides just a mobilizable public, brings forth another prominent issue in movements research that is useful for the study of Afrocentrists' and creationists' varying outcomes in the systems they challenged. This issue concerns the "inside" and "outside" locations of various actors on the challenging field. As suggested above, if we direct our attention to the right spots, we can see that Afrocentric and creationist frames may appeal to the latent—and sometimes even to the explicit—values of decision makers located *within* school systems. When this happens, we should recognize that education professionals— like policymakers, administrators, and teachers—may go along with challengers' goals in ways totally unanticipated by scholars. Theorized by most movement researchers to be always oppositional to challenge efforts, "insiders," on occasion, may believe in the frames that their challengers advance, and they may not always act to defend their organizations from external pressure. They may even, sometimes, act directly on behalf of those challengers, as they did in two of my cases. Or, at the very least, they may choose not to throw roadblocks in challengers' way.

Although some in the social movements literature, like Sidney Tarrow, have cautioned us to expect that insiders will act in the interest of challengers only when it is politically expedient or helpful to the insiders' own careers,[17] data from these seven cases will suggest that there are exceptions to this rule. Sometimes challenger arguments actually persuade professional insiders; sometimes, in fact, insiders work alongside challengers to move their organizations toward change. The relationship between challenger frames and the persuadability of insiders, I believe, has thus far been undertheorized in the social movements literature, and the subject will have to take a more pronounced spot on the research agenda if we are to understand how many challenge events actually unfold—particularly, perhaps, in institutional arenas.[18]

Related to this question of insider persuadability is the question of who constitutes an "insider" in challenges like these, in the first place. "Insiders" have long been considered to be those members of the polity, or institution, who have regular access to decision-making resources. "Outsiders," on the other hand, are those who lack such access. Using these terms, we would assume that both Afrocentrists and creationists were outsiders placing demands on insiders since, by common definition, contentious politics occur only when some faction lacks access to decision-making authority in the first place. But events in this study suggest that we should reconsider the rigid line that has been drawn to separate so-called "organizational insiders" from "challenging outsiders." Two of many examples from my data can be used to recommend a reexamination of this type. In one of the locations I studied where Afrocentrists demanded changes in school curricula, I discovered the following unexpected scenario (unexpected from a social movements perspective, anyway): it was the *superintendent of schools*—and not "outside" constituents—who led the charge for Afrocentric reform in his district, having been convinced by a prominent Afrocentric scholar at a nearby university, among others, that such change was necessary for the benefit of children. Fighting *against* the superintendent in this case, were members of his own administration, members of the board of education, and many teachers—particularly white teachers—in the district. Fighting *alongside* the superintendent were parents from a small community group called the Shrine of the Black Madonna. According to rigid definitions, does the superintendent fit the role of an "insider" or an "outsider" in this challenge? If we have only these two options to choose from, we would miss much of the cultural resonance, structural alliances, and important nuance that occurred in the Atlanta case—and many other challenges, I suspect. In a second example involving two of the creationist cases described in this book, movement leaders (routinely known as outsiders because they were marginalized as legitimate voices in school decision-making) were elected to official seats on state and local school boards, putting them in position to enact creationism-friendly policies in their districts. But in both of these cases, members of the professional education staff in these school systems, administrators and teachers who had been hired or appointed to their positions years earlier, worked tirelessly to oust the pro-creationist school board members and reverse their conservative impact on the curriculum. Were the creationism-friendly, duly-elected school board members insiders or outsiders? If we considered them simply to be outsiders, how could we account for their power to implement policy as members of the elected board? If we counted them as insiders, conversely, how would we explain, first, their inability to convince professional education staff of the legitimacy of their policies and, second, their ultimate failure to institutionalize "anti-Darwin" instruction in the systems where they held power?

I will argue that research has suffered when the field of contention is divided like this into two hermetically isolated, dichotomous categories— "inside" vs. "outside"—when data often do not warrant such a sharp division. And our understanding of Afrocentrists and creationists is jeopardized, too, if we cling to this strict division of movement actors. The tendency to divide has attenuated our understanding of the links that may exist between "insiders" and "challengers" in any given site, whether those links are built on shared cultural assumptions (as was the case in the first example, where the superintendent in Atlanta believed in the Afrocentric movement's goals), or divergent structural locations in a school system (as was the case in the second example, where school board members in two of my cases aligned with creationist groups to challenge science teaching). The sharp divisions between "challengers," on the one hand, and "elites," on the other—to use different terms for the same concepts—is an oversimplification of the real world of contentious politics.

So, one of the goals of this book is to flesh out the kinds of relationships that exist between "insiders" and "outsiders" in contentious struggles and to go beyond the line that has been drawn to divide the two sides so neatly. This one particular task of the book has been made lighter by the heavy lifting that has come before in this area, as a few other writers in sociology and political science have also problematized this division. In *Faithful and Fearless*, for example, political scientist Mary Katzenstein has demonstrated that "insiders" have often aided and abetted "outside" challengers in two American institutions—the military and the Catholic Church; and in a forthcoming manuscript, Doug McAdam, Sidney Tarrow, and Charles Tilly reconsider the roles that the once-labeled "polity members" and "challengers" play in challenger outcomes.[19] Although the points of entry into this terrain may differ from my own, I have found it very fruitful to situate my arguments in this new area of political and sociological theory on movements and to try to add back to its insights.

Afrocentrism and Creationism: Contentious Challenges

What can be discovered by extending a social movements analysis to these two groups of challengers? Here were two highly marginalized contests in schools—hardly the typical site of protest that we are accustomed to conjuring up when we hear the term "social movement," as noted earlier in this chapter. Neither Afrocentric nor creationist struggles were highly disruptive. They did not involve mass mobilization, and they were not aimed against narrowly defined state power.[20] But they can tell us a great deal about how challengers often wage battles against authority in today's world and, in so doing, they can contribute to a body of work that is now emerging on contention. The study of social movements is broadening these days to become a more inclusive study of contentious politics in a wide variety of social fields—whether the conflict is occurring traditionally at the level of the state, in smaller subunits of the state (in public school systems, for instance, as in challenges like these two), within private organizations (in the fight for domestic partners policy in corporations, for instance),[21] or against large public institutions (such as gay rights activism in the military). Scholars are realizing that in today's Western society, contention has become more common, particularly at the local level.

Not only that, but the old duality between "interest groups" (those groups working within the pluralist system) vs. "social movements" (those working on the political margins, or at the extremes of conventional political structures) is collapsing, according to several leading movements scholars.[22] The understanding of contentious politics, in other words, is being expanded to include any occurrences where (1) there is a system of institutionalized power in place, (2) there are power holders within that system who wish to maintain power, and (3) there are other actors in the field who are relatively powerless, and who contest the power of seated authorities.

While adding to this literature on contentious politics, I have also found that studying challenges to an institution beneath the level of the state (and not to the state itself) can sensitize us to an arena of factors that is seldom commented on in the broader social movements literature, but which, I argue, should be analyzed in depth. Because states—the de rigueur locus of social movements research into challenges—are normally seen to revolve around issues of *political* power, scholars in the social movements field traditionally have trained their sights mostly on the political aspects of challenge dynamics. While this may make sense epistemologically, the consistent emphasis on the political power of state regimes has led movements researchers to neglect other sites of power, such as the organizational power of established institutions to fend off challengers. Or, so I will argue. Institutions rely not only on their political bases of control, I hope to show, but also on the organizational routines that give them authority. Recentering the analysis around targeted institutions other than those with political authority—like around schools, a subunit of the state—allows organizational features to emerge as important factors in outcomes. These are factors that I think should be studied more closely and that can contribute enormously to the field of contentious politics, an argument that I will introduce in the next section of this chapter and revisit throughout the next several chapters.

Finally, looking more locally at challenge, rather than at just national protest activity, also gives us insight into processes that otherwise get overlooked in our studies of the cultural zeitgeist. If one were concentrating on national protests surrounding public school curricula from 1980 to 2000, for example, one would probably be led to believe that conservative issues received a much warmer reception during this time. After all, twelve of these years occurred during the conservative Reagan-Bush era, and the other eight were subsumed by a reconstructed Democratic leadership that also touted many conservative values. Organized school prayer, the posting of the Ten Commandments in school rooms, back to basics, the "protection" of marriage as a symbol for our children, and the return of family values, generally—these and other traditional ideas enjoyed a good deal of support from leaders at or near the top of the nation's political structure during these decades. Should creationism not have been greeted with at least some tolerance by educators, given this political environment, and should Afrocentrism not have suffered much more of a pariah status, given its far distance from these national political hot-button issues? We might conclude so if we chose to restrict the study of contentious politics to only those challenges that reached the national stage. But what I have found in studying these seven school systems in the East, West, North, and South is that more locally based political and social movements often diverge from national trends, and that if we want to know about protest, we have to look at local settings, as well.

What all of this means is that there is much to be gained from analyzing Afrocentrism and creationism—and the responses each received from school systems—using the concepts developed by scholars in the social movements area. And the study of marginal curriculum challenges can also add back to the subfield.

Schools as Organizations

As the study of these challenges has been laid out thus far, I will look, first, at the Afrocentric and creationist movements from a cultural perspective, and I will map the ideational and symbolic aspects as they existed in the two intellectual movements. Second, I will examine the challenges using a social movements, or contentious politics, approach, aimed at describing both the rhetorical resources the challenges were able to muster in their respective struggles with school systems and the political opportunities they encountered there. Along the way, I will describe how the targets of Afrocentrists' and creationists' framing activities were broad enough to include organizational "insiders" like superintendents, teachers, and school board members, not just members of the public. I also will give evidence suggesting that the challengers themselves may hold positions inside the school system. This means that the line between "insiders" and "outsiders" is fuzzier than scholars have previously assumed.

Having now suggested that institutional insiders may be an additional set of challenger targets (as well as challenge initiators), it becomes important to examine more closely the *organizational dynamics* that these challengers confronted when they staked their claims in schools. What cultural expectations did professional educators hold concerning challengers' rights to make demands? Which conditions caused some school districts to be vulnerable to challenge while others were not? How did schools seek to handle their challengers under various circumstances? What we should gather from the posing of these questions is that no matter what kinds of resources and opportunities the Afrocentric and creationist challengers could assemble on their own behalf, they were never in complete control of their resources' performance in the organizational field where they battled. As one researcher, Kelly Moore, has written, the actions of protesters are only one determinant of social movement outcomes. Equally important are the characteristics of targets.[23] Another way of putting this is to say that challengers' actions do not get made in an organizational vacuum, where all school systems, say, are equivalently structured, and respond to all challenging acts in like manner or by like means. On the contrary, school systems are home to myriad organizational structures and cultures of their own, and these practices, routines, and beliefs, too—in addition to challengers' own resources—contribute to the success of challengers. As much as we can ever say about the influence that discursive and political environments might have on Afrocentric and creationist outcomes, it won't be enough until we also analyze the organizational practices that exist in the school systems they are challenging—especially the daily routines governing administrators' actions that challengers confront. Having analyzed the movements qua movements, that is to say, we should then turn the question around and analyze how schools, as long-standing organizations, responded to these challenges—a method that provides a complement to an emphasis on challengers.

ORGANIZATIONAL CONFLICT. How should we "turn the question around" and consider these challenges from an organizational perspective? To make sense of Afrocentric and creationist outcomes, I will draw on two areas of recent theory that help highlight the effects of organizational routines and practices on challenging movements, generally, and on these African American and Christian conservative challenges, particularly.

The first area I will tap directs our attention to the fact that organizations, such as the school systems where Afrocentrists and creationists made demands for change (or the military, the Church, corporations, the federal government, or any other organizational entity, for that matter), can be chaotic places, where supporters of one goal may be in conflict with supporters of another goal and both, meanwhile, may be aligned against the goals of a third faction. Organizations are not the unitary, purposive, rational entities that so much of the social movements literature depicts them to be. Typically imagined by social movements researchers to be a wall of unified opposition against which challengers constantly butt their heads, organizations can be viewed differently. Organizations are frequently messy decision makers, typified by contentiousness in "group relations, departmental conflicts, and career frustrations," as Walter Powell has written.[24] In other words, the seemingly stable organizations with which challengers are so often depicted to be doing battle are much more likely to be conflict-ridden entities, to some greater or lesser extent. Contentiousness is a hallmark of organizational experience, in

fact, and many scholars who study organizations have begun documenting not only contention, but even challenger-like activities inside these
once-perceived bastions of calm.[25]

In a similar vein, education policy researchers have documented internal conflict as a permanent fixture among school system insiders. In fact,
school systems are organized around the very fact of countervailing interests and goals. David Tyack and Larry Cuban differentiate between three
levels of education insiders: lay policymakers, who are elected and sometimes appointed to school boards; administrators, who have professional
degrees and work in the bureaucratic offices of school systems; and practitioners, particularly teachers, who instruct in the classroom.[26] Distinguishing among these three different levels, and bearing in mind that each
of them often has its own distinct interests, values, and practices that
potentially conflict with each other, is a strong corrective to assuming
singular goals and consensus within targeted organizational ranks.

Why is the reality of conflict important, and why have movements studies largely neglected its presence? Answering the first question is easier
than accounting for the second. I will argue that organizations research
and education policy studies—both of which describe routine conflictual
relations among organization insiders—capture much more fully the reality of school life that these Afrocentric and creationist challengers encountered than the picture of assumed stability that is usually drawn in studies
of social movement activity. Conflict is the stuff of organizations, even
before any external challengers come on the scene to "mess things up."
If we foreground this fact about school systems—that schools (and all
organizations, by extension) are chaotic, politically divided, and rarely
unified in their intents and purposes—then we may be able to spot more
accurately the "weak links" in organizational personnel and governance
structures that make certain organizations vulnerable at different times
to different challenger claims. Afrocentrists, for example, appealed to education officials using rhetoric about the "injustice" done to African
American children and the "progressive" nature of their proposed solution. Where there was conflict among school system members over the
veracity of this proposed problem, or over schools' goals for solving it,
some administrators, teachers, and policymakers nudged closer to challenger positions, saw clearer connections between Afrocentric goals and
their own objectives in the district, and facilitated the incorporation of
Afrocentric materials into current, legitimate curricula (again, at least
temporarily so). Creationists, meanwhile, had a different experience with
the school systems they encountered, but no less built on organizational
conflict. Since nearly all education professionals on record in each one of
these school systems adamantly opposed the creationist position, challengers had little chance of convincing these permanent staff members of

the legitimacy of their claims, as the Afrocentric challengers were able to do with some key educators. Creationists, therefore, tried to exploit schools' conflicts with their *constituents*, instead. Appealing to voters' sense of "fairness" and "balance," creationists actually expropriated power from long-term school professionals by getting themselves elected to policy-making bodies, like school boards and legislatures. Once voted into these positions, these newly elected policymakers encountered serious conflict with the professional staff in their departments of education. Department staff and faculty were deeply skeptical of Christian conservative programs, but they were mandated to follow the public will, which was the will of the elected board.

Such areas of conflict have not been ignored by social movements researchers, as anyone who has read studies of political processes will note. But while movements scholars have not shied away from describing such occurrences of contention within organizations as occasions for challengers' "political opportunities," few have conceived of the challenged institution as almost always tending toward the "messy," and fewer still have acknowledged that these opportunities are, therefore, always potentially in place. Movement theorists, instead, have preferred to understand the challenged institution as generally stable, with only occasional (if exploitable) conditions of elite cleavage, changes in economic conditions, or decreases in repressive tactics. We will not be able to see a central dynamic in the Afrocentric and creationist challenges if we overlook the influence of mundane organizational conflict on their temporary and ultimate outcomes.

NEW INSTITUTIONALISM, PART I: THE HOMOGENIZATION OF EXPECTATIONS. A second area of organizations research that I will use to analyze these curricular challenge outcomes is what is known as new institutionalist theory, which can help us grasp the decisions made by education professionals concerning what they thought were appropriate and legitimate responses to their marginal Afrocentric or creationist challengers.

Old institutional theory, exemplified by Phillip Selznick's famous Tennessee Valley Authority research, studied organizational administrators' attentiveness to community demands and their willingness to concede programs to their constituents—even if constituents' demands often contradicted the stated mission of the organization. Organization leaders did this, according to Selznick, for political reasons—to curry community support and to maintain their positions in their agencies. Approaching Afrocentric and creationist challenges from an old institutionalist perspective, we might ask what portion of the population of a school system was African American or Christian conservative, respectively, and we would study whether and how administrators sought to accommodate those constituents' concerns (depending on their numbers and political power in the system).[27] We can see clear links between old institutionalist organizational theory and the political opportunities strand of social movements theory: both concentrate, in some sense, on decision makers' vulnerability to constituent demands.

New institutional theory, on the other hand, emphasizes the influence of a completely different set of actors on educators' decision making. New institutionalists speak not of decision makers' mindfulness of the community's demands but, instead, of decision makers' conformity to the expectations of members of their *own organizational sector.*[28] Researchers working in this area explain organizational behavior as action that comes from following routines within the organizational field, which embody widely shared beliefs about social reality. In this study, the organizational field home to these widely shared beliefs is the larger school system: state and national.

Thinking about these challenges from a new institutionalist perspective suggests a couple of routes of study. The first route is to realize that the seven different school systems under challenge in these cases should be viewed as something more than just seven discrete organizations with locally idiosyncratic ways of responding to demands for change. These seven school systems, instead, should be understood to be members embedded in a larger institutional network of American education, in which particular forms of shared culture influenced professional educators' decision making at home, including decisions about response to challengers. Institutional norms and values, picked up in such venues as education schools and at education conferences over the course of school members' careers, ended up exerting great influence over how educators viewed Afrocentric and creationist challengers, as well as shaping their decisions over whether or not challengers' demands should be accommodated. More abstractly, these "institutional scripts" guided the local school systems, shaped how reality was constructed there, and influenced the "way things are done" in multiple realms of the systems' operations. The presence of these scripts constituted the everyday organizational lives of school personnel and, even more than that, gave value to their activities and shaped their senses of self.[29] Applied to these seven challenges, new institutional theory can help chart the kinds of expectations for change that school officials across the seven systems held, the practices they used to ensure a given level of certainty in running their systems, and the kinds of power possessed by people differently situated within the school systems themselves.

An example of how institutional insights affect our analysis of Afrocentric and creationist outcomes might be helpful. As we all know from the debates that have attended it, the curricular reform known as multiculturalism has become something of a nationally institutionalized "given" in new-millennium school curricula—at least in its most moderate form as cultural appreciation. No longer can a credible history of the United States be taught solely, or even predominantly, as the salutary vanquishing of indigenous peoples by Europeans. Now, in schools across the nation, history must incorporate the experiences and contributions made by native and oppressed peoples to the wider culture. Although multicultural curricula vary extensively from one school district to another and, indeed, from one classroom to another, it is simply no longer legitimate for schools to neglect Africans, Asians, women, Native Americans, Latinos, and other previously oppressed groups in history classes. Multicultur-alism may range from weak to strong forms of inclusion,[30] but cultural sensitivity has become both an institutional norm and an institutional practice, insofar as it is taught as normative to would-be teachers in their education classes, and as it is incorporated into the everyday activities and visual aids of classroom materials, posters, songs, standardized tests, after-school plays, and so forth. The norms and practices of multicultur-alism pervade school district curricula across the country. Teachers from Kentucky talking to teachers from California would understand the basic outline of a tenth-grade history course, say, in their colleagues' West Coast school system.

Given this established culture of at least minimal multiculturalism across U.S. school systems, and a general acceptance of its logic, it is increasingly rare for challenging movements like Afrocentrism or crea-tionism to advance their claims without appealing to educators' commit-ment to pluralism, to their recognition of difference and value in all peo-ple's backgrounds, beliefs, and ideas; in short, to some resemblance to multiculturalism. Certainly, the three occasions of Afrocentric challenge that are included in this study—intellectual distant cousins to multicultur-alism already, in their emphases on the problems of racism and the alter-native positive identities that can be crafted for African American children through an altered curriculum—cannot be understood unless they are sit-uated in the national conversation that has taken place in schools about multiculturalism.

Is this true of creationism, as well? Can we see the effects of institution-alized multiculturalism on the creationist campaign? Actually, yes: cre-ationists, too, realized that their arguments would have a better chance of influencing action in school systems across the country if they were framed as commensurate with the goals and practices of multiculturalism, rather than of scripture. Creationists piggybacked their claims onto the multiculturalism infusion project, also seeking to have God represented—and, they said, world religions, in general—in textbook content, in stan-dardized tests, in teacher lectures.[31] Aware of multiculturalism's institutional credibility, creationists did not speak of *replacing* evolution in the classroom, but of *supplementing* it with new scientific studies of genetic change, of the irreducible complexity of certain biological functions, of questionable Darwinian theory. They attempted to align their practices with the practices already accepted in the wider institution of public school teaching—an important component of which is now multiculturalism and its emphasis on inclusion. That creationists failed to convince education insiders of the correctness of their practices does not indicate that they did not attempt to tap into the common-sense logics and practices with which educators were familiar. Educators simply used more potent means to rebuff them.

I will argue that only when we understand these everyday, organizational routines that characterize school personnel's "ways of doing things"—such as the now common-sense incorporation of multicultural materials into the school curriculum—will we be able to contemplate more completely their reactions to the two different cases of challenge, Afrocentrism and creationism.

NEW INSTITUTIONALISM, PART II: THE EFFECTS OF LOCAL EXPECTATIONS. I stated above that there were two avenues of study suggested by new institutionalist theory, and for the last couple of pages I have described the first—the consensus that has built up around certain ways of doing things, like teaching subjects from a multicultural perspective—in virtually all U.S. schools from coast to coast. This homogenization around preferences and activities has been shaped by schools of education, textbook publishers, and the like.

The second avenue suggested by new institutionalist theory is to take seriously the observation that organizational routines are also established at the local level in each school system, not just at the level of the larger field, and that these local practices also constrain or enable challenger efforts. Because public education in this nation is a system that is run more locally than nationally, state departments of education and local school boards have a great deal of say in how their curricula will actually be structured and how their outputs (e.g., students' learning) will be measured. Although tied together ideologically by a national normative structure, this nation's state and local school systems are home to a huge variety of unique structures. Systems of testing vary from state to state and across districts, for example, as do protocols for developing curricula, teacher rewards, and extracurricular activities. Even if challengers' demands may make some wider cultural sense to educators because of their family resemblance to multiculturalism, for example, or because they have parallels with extant instruction, each system's *local* practices surrounding teaching and curriculum allow for varying amounts of revision to be concretely integrated into its system. Because these local organizational imperatives heavily, and variably, influence how schools decide to incorporate or deflect reforms into the system, they must also be added to this study of Afrocentric and creationist challenges and outcomes. Recognizing that local organizational variation may exist simultaneously with institutional practices provides the only path for sketching the full profile of these challenge events.

Taking these multiple facts into account, I have designed the study to account for differences in the outcomes of these cases, both *between* types of cases (comparing the three Afrocentric challenges to the four creationist challenges), and *within* types of cases (comparing each of the three Afrocentric cases to one another; and comparing the four creationist cases to one another).

So, when all is said and done, a comparative study of Afrocentric and creationist challenges in seven U.S. school systems from 1980–2000 is not only intrinsically interesting, but also places us squarely at the intersection of three different sociological subfields—cultural sociology, social movements, and organizational sociology—not to mention theories of race, religion, and education. Looking through each of these lenses, separately, clarifies different dimensions of these challenges. Looking through them all at once, however, will yield an even better understanding of who Afrocentrists and creationists were, what they were fighting for, and how schools responded to each of them. Until recently, I would argue, sociologists have done too little work at the intersections of these approaches. Cultural sociologists often have studied discourse without demonstrating how discursive acts "matter" in concrete political and organizational contexts. Organizational researchers frequently have explored the reproductive capacities of stable institutions but have neglected to discuss the disruption of such duplicative processes by groups like challengers. And social movements researchers have focused on questions of when and why collective action events (like challenging movements) emerge to alter institutional control, but they have not considered as carefully the institutional processes constraining and enabling those challenges. In the current state of the sociological enterprise, too rarely have the three analytical paths had occasion to meet.

I intend for the analysis of these cases to braid these strands together. The study of culture, for instance, can be made more substantial by looking historically and comparatively at ground-level, institutional challenges like these, which use language forms and images to advance their causes. A comparison of Afrocentric and creationist efforts can demonstrate how discourse operates in real time and in concrete practice, and how very similar rhetoric—about bias and educational neglect—"works" differently, depending on the identity of the claimants, the cultural and historical period in which the rhetoric is used, and the organizational context in which the arguments are received.[32]

Meanwhile, in seeking to explain Afrocentric and creationist outcomes in the schools, we will see how the social movements literature benefits from an infusion of organizational insights. While recent work in the study of movements has encouraged examining the interrelationships between cultural processes, organizational mobilization, and the structure of political opportunities in social movements' emergence and success,[33] a crucial factor that I believe this work has generally overlooked is the everyday logics that operate in organizations, and the ways that these practices contribute or detract from challengers' success. It is not just the extraordinary circumstances, resulting from volatile change, that generate political opportunities; rather, commonplace, routinized practices, or institutional cultures at both the national and local levels also shape challenger outcomes.[34] What is more, if we do not consider institutional factors that influence challenger processes and outcomes, we will miss noticing a crucial distinction between *political power* and *institutional power.* Creationists, for example, seem to have been unable to convert raw political power into institutional power (transforming their votes on school boards into lasting curricular revisions), while Afrocentrists seem to have been unable to sustain any real institutional power once their revisions had been incorporated into the curriculum (converting curricular change into universal teaching processes).

Finally, organizational theory is hungry for insights that can come only from exploring significant instances of institutional change, such as from occasions of social movement activity. Having spent many of the last twenty years documenting the "structuration," or the establishment and maintenance, of durable routines in organizational worlds, many organizations scholars are now trying to figure out how and why change is possible in these apparently hardened institutions. "Stickiness" was the dominant metaphor used to describe institutions in the early days of institutional theory: once a cultural script and a set of practices had consolidated in a field, so went the theory, then it was very hard to break the mold of those routines in that institution. For years, in fact, the whole idea of "institutional change" seemed to many institutionalists to be an oxymoron; change and institutionalization were often theorized to exist at opposite ends of the sociological enterprise.[35] The analysis of challenges like Afrocentrism and creationism can be helpful in revising the assumption of this opposition. Both challenges did frequently make headway in their respective districts, but then they also got thwarted by schools. Acknowledging and investigating the competing presence of conflict, institutionalized scripts, and local organizational structures in the public school system adds to new institutional theory.[36]

What Is to Come

Having discussed the abstract features of these challenges, I want next to present a brief but, I hope, instructive sketch of late-twentieth-century Afrocentric and creationist movements. In chapter 2, I will introduce the intellectual roots of both movements and the work that actors have been doing within each to define what constitutes "Afrocentrism" and "creationism." Both of these movements took place in the context of larger historical movements. Many Afrocentric ideological concepts, for example, had their origins in Black Nationalist thought,[37] while the creationist movement in the 1980s and 1990s had roots in several important episodes in American history, including repeated conflicts between orthodox and progressive Protestants, seventy-five years of legal debate in this country concerning the teaching of evolution and creationism in the public schools, and the rise of the New Religious Right in the late 1970s.[38]

As for the rest of the book, beginning in chapter 3, I will provide in-depth analyses of the three Afrocentric and four creationist cases, in turn, describing the various actors involved in each location, the rhetoric used there, and the outcomes that resulted in each of the cases. We will see the pattern emerge of early inroads made by the Afrocentrists, followed by significantly diminished later results; and we will note the temporary political coups that creationists sometimes won, followed by publicly heralded defeat.

In chapter 4, I investigate the strengths that Afrocentrists possessed as rhetorical entrepreneurs and as exploiters / casualties of political and organizational opportunities. I demonstrate why, in the 1980s and 1990s, Afrocentrists had an easier time getting professional educators to consider their demands, while creationists faced more hardened opposition among professionals. In that chapter, I will look in depth at the three discursive resources Afrocentrists had access to and that creationists generally lacked. Afrocentrists had a compelling problem that educators could not deny (the poor education that generations of African American students had received in American public schools); they could use an effective charge of discrimination against reluctant school officials (they called educators "racist" if they were white and opposed to Afrocentrism, "race traitors" if they were black and opposed); and they were contesting a discipline that was seen to be more or less negotiable (history, in contrast to creationists' target of science teaching). Upon describing these rhetorical resources, I then turn to the politics and organizational practices influencing Afrocentric outcomes.

In chapters 5 and 6, I compare creationists' rhetorical assets to Afrocentrists' assets, and find that on all three of the cultural dimensions, creationists were less advantaged than the Afrocentrists. Additionally, creationists were encumbered by a fourth cultural burden that Afrocentrists were completely unhindered by: legal precedent, which could automatically thwart their campaign's progress. I will illustrate how their adversaries always condemned creationists for abridging First Amendment guarantees of separation of church and state. Then, I turn to the question of politics and the organizational routines that the four school systems used in the creationist cases, and I will look at their distinctive contributions to creationists' ultimate defeat. In this discussion, I will describe the relationship between the political power that creationists sometimes were able to garner and compare that kind of power to educators' institutional, or professional, power. I find that political power to make decisions does not easily convert to bureaucratic professional power to implement them.

In chapter 7, I revisit the theoretical arguments I have introduced in this chapter and analyze the differences in Afrocentric and creationist outcomes in terms of culture, politics, and organization. This discussion will set up a final consideration of how an examination of Afrocentrism and creationism matters for social scientific theory.

Two

The Challengers

BEFORE DESCRIBING the specifics of how Afrocentrists and creationists made out in their challenges in the seven public school systems, we should know more about the history of these two groups. In this chapter, I describe the social, cultural, and political characteristics of those who made up Afrocentrism's and creationism's constituencies; the kinds of identities that adherents crafted in these efforts; and the kinds of claims activists drew upon from the cultural landscape and from past struggles in schools. I set out to describe, through this context, what Afrocentrists' and creationists' goals were for their children's education and for society's betterment. For roughly the first half of this chapter, I will refrain from describing the seven actual conflicts from 1980 to 2000 that I studied and will delve, instead, into a description of each of the challengers as a type (Afrocentric and creationist). Although this general picture of Afrocentrists and creationists gloss over the particulars in each case of local struggle, the overall portraits will provide a context for the challenges that occurred from coast to coast.

Following this historical overview of the two challenges, I will describe my reasons for selecting the seven cases and the ways in which I chose to collect and analyze data for them.

Afrocentrism: An Essentialist Formulation of Race

People who identify as Afrocentric—and about 25 percent of the African-American population sees itself in common cause with Afrocentrism's descriptions of a problem and its solutions—perceive the world as filled with racism, injustice, and dishonesty surrounding matters of race and equality.[1] Where many citizens of the United States take pride in their nation's stated ideals and see a clear connection between the country's principles of democracy and their own everyday lives, Afrocentrists see only hypocrisy in the nation's position on race and the actions it has taken in its name. Afrocentrists fault the United States for making empty promises about equal opportunity for all people, and they have sickened over what they understand as America's propensity always to resist the path to greater freedom, equality, and opportunity for its African American citizenry.

Afrocentrists, of course, are not alone in making this critique and, like activists on the Left of the political spectrum, they point to a number of glaring examples of inequality in the economic, social, and political spheres of the United States. But Afrocentrists depart from many other "justice" movements by training the focus of their critique on the cultural sphere of African Americans' continued bondage and on nationalist and essentialist understandings of what it means to be descended from Africa. The main claim Afrocentrists advance is that Africans' and African Americans' intellectual history has been disregarded, at best, and systematically omitted, at worst, by this nation's major institutions of learning and culture, particularly its schools and universities. Identifying the realm of institutionalized meaning-making and identity-construction as the one in most need of immediate overhaul (that is: schools), this group has "gone cultural" in its demands for reform. According to one scholar who has written extensively about Afrocentrism, but who, himself, aligns more with the multicultural camp, Afrocentrists are tired of waiting for political solutions like civil rights laws to improve poor African Americans' sociopolitical situation, or for economic fixes like Affirmative Action to ensure occupational and educational equality. Instead, Afrocentrists have focused on the cultural domain of knowledge production as the most productive site for improvement.[2] To eradicate the extraordinary disaffection experienced by African Americans in this country, Afrocentrists press for changes in their own and the majority population's acknowledgment of their contributions to world and national history. They call on schools as the first among many American institutions that must undergo radical change.

Introduced in the early 1980s by Molefi Kete Asante of Temple University,[3] Afrocentrism has grown in black studies programs at universities around the nation as Maulana Karenga, Tsheloane Keto, Asa Hilliard III, John Henrik Clarke, Leonard Jeffries, and others have pursued both the intellectual bases of the project as well as its infusion into college, high school, and elementary school curricula. The intellectual project of Afrocentrism is to "study African peoples from an Africa-centered prism" by placing the continent "at the center of any analysis of African history and culture, including the African American experience."[4] The humanities scholar Ali Mazrui labels this perspective a constructive response to the Eurocentric bias that has pervaded intellectual thought, and that has established European civilization as the standard by which all other civilizations are judged.[5] Afrocentrism, according to another scholar, "seeks to liberate African studies from this Eurocentric monopoly on scholarship and thus assert a valid worldview through which Africa can be studied objectively."[6]

The Afrocentric methodology rests on two primary assumptions. The first principle is that analysis of any subject with roots in Africa must begin with "the primacy of the classical African civilizations, namely

Kemet (Egypt), Nubia, Axum, and Meroe. . . . Adequate understanding of African phenomena," according to Asante, "cannot occur without a reference point in the classic and most documented African culture."[7] Studies of *African American* phenomena are no less tied to this methodology than are studies of *African* phenomena, since Afrocentric scholars view African American experience as, first and foremost, a dimension of African history and culture. Afrocentrism recognizes no division between the African past and African American history, and regards as ahistorical and mythical any social science that does not trace these continuous African roots.[8] So if, for example, a scholar sets out to study "Africans in the inner cities of the Northeast United States, it must be done with the idea in the back of the mind that one is studying African people, not 'made-in-America Negroes' without historical depth."[9]

The second major premise upon which Afrocentrism is based is that all people of African descent possess essential cognitive, cultural, and aesthetic characteristics in common. The wife of Molefi Asante, an Afrocentric scholar in her own right, Kariamu Welsh-Asante, for example, argues that there is an African Aesthetic, which is "based on seven 'senses' shared by all Africa-descended people around the globe: polyrhythm, polycentrism, dimensional, repetition, curvilinear, epic memory, and wholism."[10] At its most controversial (and many Afrocentric scholars, themselves, reject such notions), this conception of race has included suggestions about personality based on melanin content and other genetic hardwiring. Whether at the extremes or not, however, defining the characteristics that are inherent in all African American people is seen as "emphasiz[ing] the uniqueness of black folks' cultural truth" and creating cultural solidarity.[11] In addition, by hailing to a pure African tradition that is said to preexist white civilization and contamination, "blacks become dominant by virtue of either biology or culture, [and] whites are allocated a subordinate role."[12]

Combined, these two premises—that all African American social phenomena can be traced to some degree or other back to Africa, and that all people of African descent share essential race characteristics—provide the foundations for Afrocentric curricula at the grade-school to high-school levels. In addition to these foundational concepts in the curriculum, Afrocentrists have presented new, and often disputed, claims about African history and its influence on Western thought, as well as an emphasis on the contributions of African Americans to the progress of this nation. Afrocentrists correct world and American history books for their neglect or oversights of African experience in one of two ways: by asserting the preeminence of Africa and its descendants in the course of world historical events, or by underscoring the presence of subjugated African peoples throughout time and the remarkable triumphs of those oppressed over systems of oppression.

In "Afrocentricity versus Multiculturalism?: A Dialectic in Search of a Synthesis," Ali Mazrui refers to the first of these methodologies as the "celebratory" stream of scholarship in the Afrocentric literature, or as "Gloriana Afrocentricity," which is to say that it emphasizes kings and queens in ancient Egypt, and others who sat at the top of the cultural hierarchy. This stream he contrasts with "Proletariana Afrocentricity," which calls attention to the contributions of enslaved Africans to modern culture. Some of the most hotly disputed historical claims advanced by Gloriana Afrocentric scholars are that much of Western civilization—including theories attributed to Aristotle and other Greek philosophers—was actually learned at the feet of ancient black Egyptians and stolen from them; that ancient black Egyptians discovered the fundamentals of species evolution, astronomy, and human flight; and that Napoleon's army used the Sphinx's nose as target practice to eradicate evidence of its Negroid features and origins—a European effort to conceal blacks' contributions to world art and history.[13]

African essentialism and new historical scholarship—the bases of Afrocentric thought—are, then, designed to reverse the Eurocentric bias of traditional teaching and to generate interest and success among African American students. How this agenda got carried out across the school districts and in the individual classrooms discussed in this book was variable, as we will see in chapter 3. In the few Washington, D.C., classrooms where Afrocentric curricula had been adopted, for example, each day began with an "opening ritual," in which "children say affirmation, they hug each other, they sing, they dance." This practice had been implemented, said the director of the program in one school, because "our people understood that we are spirits that have a body, not bodies that have spirits."[14] Other programs emphasized modified curriculum content, rather than what were considered to be African-derived practices. In the Atlanta school district, for example, "African-ness" does not get expressed so much through ritual in the classroom. Instead, primary emphasis is placed on using supplementary materials (such as the controversial *African-American Baseline Essays* written for the Portland, Oregon school district) to add information about African and African American contributions to world history.

Historical Roots of Afrocentrism and Its Relationship to Other African American Curricular Movements

As the description above lays out, Afrocentrism is a philosophy based on an essentialist conception of race that posits the cultural, behavioral, and lifestyle unity of all descendants of Africa, no matter where they have ended up following the black Diaspora. Academics at the university level have been primarily responsible for developing Afrocentric principles and concepts, and then they and others have subsequently adapted the intellectual program for use as a reform in local school systems, mostly those in predominantly black urban centers. In its practical application in public school curricula, Afrocentrism calls for an overhaul in the scholarly foundations of social studies and history instruction. In the sociologist Howard Winant's terms, Afrocentrism might be thought of as a "racial project," insofar as it is an interpretation, representation, or explanation of racial dynamics and, at the same time, an effort to change the organization and distribution of resources along racial lines—in this case, educational resources.[15] It has been waged by African Americans who have been disappointed by the failures of their country to live up to its promise of inclusion and equal opportunity, who have become enraged by the closed access to their children of the American dream of social justice and mobility, and who have lost their faith in black and white political leadership to address their grievances.[16]

There are many historical roots for this movement. For decades, African American social scientists have explored the class and cultural politics that have divided and continue to divide the black community ideologically. Perhaps most famously, these divisions were implicated in the conflict between W.E.B. Du Bois and Booker T. Washington over the appropriate stance of African Americans toward white society and their own racial identity: as to whether aggressive protest for full legal rights and equality should be the primary fight, or whether economic improvement without an explicit political and racialized edge should be the path to peaceful coexistence. According to contemporary researchers, such conflicts always play out at least partially along class lines.

One lens for viewing the modern-day dimensions of this enduring conflict about racial ideology within the American black community is provided by the authors Manning Marable and Leith Mullings.[17] They argue that twentieth-century black intellectual thought has responded to issues of racial identity in three distinct ways: by using an *integrationist / inclusionist* rhetoric, a *separatist* rhetoric, or a *transformationist* discourse. The first of these, the *inclusionist* vision, incorporates the "traditional integrationist perspective of the earlier twentieth century, but also neoliberal and pragmatic currents" of the modern era.[18] It disdains racial particularity and isolation, asserts that African Americans should be considered "Americans who happen to be black," and opts to work within established institutions to affect public policy. It finds support among the black middle class, the professional and cultural elite, and public sector employees, who denounce "identity politics" as both demagogic and painfully divisive.

The *separatist* orientation encompasses black nationalism of years past as well as contemporary Afrocentrism. Its advocates include Marcus Garvey and his Universal Negro Improvement Association of the 1920s and Elijah Muhammad and the Nation of Islam in the 1960s. In its emphasis on race as a fixed category around which blacks must primarily define themselves, and in its deep skepticism about the willingness of the white power structure ever to relinquish its hegemonic position, it represents the opposite formulation to integrationism. It encourages retrenchment of identity into race alone, where race "remains the fundamental axis around which blacks need to be mobilized for liberation."[19] Its primary support derives from the marginalized African American working class, and it is most likely to gather force under several conditions, such as when African Americans lag far behind others in society in economic gains, when both major political parties reject calls to address racial inequality, when the traditional black leadership is either unwilling or unable to articulate the grievances of the disaffected, or when there is an acceptance by middle-class black leadership of the dominant cultural discourse within the social order.[20]

Marable and Mullings map out a third intellectual movement they call *transformative,* which centers on the eradication of all forms of inequality, not just racial inequality. It challenges the "institutions of power, privilege, and ownership patterns of the dominant society."[21] Here, racism is understood to be an unequal relationship between social groups, based on power and violence, rather than as any sort of fixed reality of life. Support for the transformationist perspective, though relatively weak, is found most heavily in the "radicalized elements of the black intelligentsia, the more progressive elements of the black working class and middle class and also, to some degree, among marginalized youth."[22] As we will see in the case studies describing the Afrocentric challenge, sometimes educators presented this form of identity as an alternative to Afrocentrism, hailing it as "multicultural" and "inclusionary," rather than Afrocentric and exclusionary.

It is clear that the central concerns addressed by Afrocentrism—a sense of disappointment and pessimism surrounding issues of mobility and respect—have been commonplace among many African Americans in the past decade and in decades prior.[23] Yet Afrocentrism is a movement that has *not* attracted overwhelming support among the majority of African Americans in this country and, in fact, has proved divisive within the African American community wherever its tenets have been advocated.[24] Much like the Black Nationalist movement of the 1960s to which it is related, Afrocentrism erects substantial boundaries around factions of the black community, particularly along class and cultural lines. These boundaries appeal to some and repel many others. These divisions also cause discord in school systems.

As an example of the boundary-making that Afrocentric advocates have frequently engaged in, *The Black Scholar*, in 1993, published a collection of essays debating issues familiar to those I have just reviewed: African American identity, generally, and intellectual movements like Afrocentrism and multiculturalism, specifically. In his contribution to the forum, Molefi Asante, the foundational Afrocentric theorist from Temple University, encapsulates many of these debates. He argues that many black intellectuals seem interested in "leaving the race," by which he means seeking to suppress their identities "as blacks." Why do they do this? He claims that upper-middle-class African Americans fear strong racial identity—and Afrocentrism, in particular—because they are frightened of African agency, solidarity, and self-determination, and are unconnected to a black identity felt on the streets of the inner cities. Motivating this fear, he says, are middle-class blacks' careerist ambitions and, ultimately, their need for approval from whites. He ends his essay with a "Ten Commandments-esque" list that he claims is the "accommodationist's" guide to behavior. Because it states so clearly many of the criticisms that some Afrocentrists make of other African Americans, particularly of those in positions of power (as we shall see in the cases that lie ahead), and because it infuriates so thoroughly (and sometimes strikes fear in) those accused by it, I reproduce it here in full. In its content is found much of the discourse that underlies debates about Afrocentric curricula in school districts:

- Thou shalt not accept an African origin.
- Thou shalt not mock the white man.
- Thou shalt not threaten the cultural imperialist.
- Thou shalt not identify with Africans.
- Thou shalt not despise the legacy of the white slave-owners.
- Thou shalt not speak evil of Thomas Jefferson and George Washington.
- Thou shalt not praise other African men and women.
- Thou shalt not seek to create values for African survival.
- Thou shalt not work to develop an African identity.
- Thou shalt not allow anyone to call you African.[25]

Afrocentrism versus Multiculturalism

In the 1980s and 1990s, Afrocentrism was not the only attempt among black scholars and educators to deal with the problems of black children's education and the obstructed mobility of much of black America. There were other African American voices that also argued that a cultural corrective must be put in place to reverse racist historical wrongs. But these other voices supported a distinctly *multicultural* form of instruction instead of an Afrocentric curriculum. Like proponents of Afrocentrism, multiculturalists fought textbook and curriculum content deemed Eurocentric and racist; unlike Afrocentrism, black multiculturalists made communion with other racial and ethnic groups (including whites) and demanded the inclusion of other minority groups' contributions in the classroom. The two agendas—Afrocentrism and multiculturalism—often were at odds in school districts across the country and created fissures among African Americans fighting for reforms. But the presence in school systems of dedicated supporters of multiculturalism also presented opportunities for Afrocentric activists, for the latter could sometimes bridge the rhetoric of the two camps and make their appeals for Afrocentrism seem familiar to those in positions of power.

In contrast to Afrocentrism, whose definition may be multidimensional but is more or less cohesive, multiculturalism is a movement whose exact definition is impossible to specify. As many have pointed out, people mean a great many things when they speak of multiculturalism, for its prescriptions range from "minor changes in English and history curricula to the restructuring of entire schools."[26] At its most basic level, however, multiculturalism's philosophical claim is that there should be a "parity of esteem of all cultures";[27] that "members of the different groups should appreciate and respect the other cultures in their society";[28] that while the world's cultures and societies may not be empirically equal (e.g., one society may be more democratic, richer, or more troubled than the next), they are all *morally* equal.[29] Thus, proponents of multiculturalism advocate a broadened curriculum that includes the contributions of all cultures to the making of the nation and the world. Such a curriculum is said to benefit society in a number of ways: it introduces facts about America and the rest of the world hitherto neglected in textbooks, it promotes understanding among people of different ethnicities, it emphasizes the cultural interdependence of all people, and it prepares young people to navigate more successfully the global culture and economy that we now inhabit.

Proponents of multiculturalism also come from a larger range of institutional and political positions than do Afrocentrists and are apt to have a variety of opinions concerning their more "radical" colleagues. Academic and policy notables commonly known as neoconservatives—like Diane Ravitch and Arthur Schlesinger—identify themselves with the moderate wing of multiculturalism, and they have little patience for either the more identity-driven factions in the multiculturalism movement or the entire

Afrocentric perspective. Their most plaintive protest against Afrocentrism concerns the "trashing" of a common culture and the attending loss of solidarity that occurs when each of society's racial and ethnic groups takes on a "tribal mentality."[30] Meanwhile, educators—including many African American educators (school board members, mid-level administrators, superintendents, and members of teachers' unions)—generally distance themselves from the multiculturalism that Ravitch et al. represent, but happily assume the "multicultural" mantle while also eschewing the goals and scholarship of Afrocentrism,[31] which seems to them dangerous, politically and academically. Others in the multicultural camp are sympathetic to the claims of Afrocentrism and, despite the fact that they may have practical or philosophical reasons to withhold their support, end up advocating for the Afrocentric challenge in their home districts. These last are the key group of supportive "insiders" mentioned in the previous chapter: trained professionals who serve in the education establishment, who have institutional authority to implement reforms, and who are willing to extend their influence to the Afrocentric challenge.

Not surprisingly, Afrocentrists consider the ideology and reforms advocated by the more moderate side of multiculturalism to be both woefully inadequate for solving the problem of African American inequality, as well as ideologically suspect—even "integrationist," according to Marable's and Mullings' typology. Rather than placing a few sporadic and disconnected items about African Americans or Hispanics, say, in the fundamentally biased curriculum, Afrocentrists argue that public school curricula must "undergo a thoroughgoing transformation."[32] The hallmarks of this prescribed transformation consist of new scholarship to be infused into the curriculum: scholarship that talks entirely differently about the role of Africa and African Americans in world culture. As the "antithesis" of Eurocentrism, Afrocentrism replaces multiculturalists' emphasis on pluralism and all cultures' interdependence. It stresses instead the uniqueness of African peoples and the impact of African people on world civilization, and proposes that the ultimate "other" to white hegemony is Africanity.[33] Afrocentric scholars believe that their mission is revolutionary and, as such, irreconcilable with the conventionally pluralist claims of multiculturalism.[34]

We see from these descriptions that there are a variety of approaches to identifying as "African American" in the United States, and that there are deep historical roots of cleavage in the black community concerning racial self-definition and the means for promoting those definitions in the nation's institutions. Any conversation about curricular challenges that use race as a primary site of contention must be situated in this historical conversation. When we turn our attention back to the Afrocentric challenges—when we come to the descriptions of Atlanta, Washington, D.C., and New York state in the next chapter, that is—we should bear in mind the historical divisions discussed here.[35]

Creationism: A Brief History of a Moral Crusade

Creationism as a Moral System

In the previous section, and in very broad relief, I described the terms of the historical and contemporary debates in the Afrocentric challenge. Now, I will turn to the creationist struggle to change science curricula in the public schools. What are creationists fighting for, and by what means are they waging their battles—rhetorically and historically? Educators and creationists have long locked horns over the teaching of science in public school classrooms, creating a context of animosity that blanketed the conflicts in the 1980s and 1990s. Mapping out this context is a necessary first step for understanding what happened in Louisiana, Kansas, California state, and Vista, California, in the 1980s and 1990s.

Ever since Charles Darwin published *The Origin of Species* in 1859 there have been religious people, mostly Christian, who have been deeply offended by the theory of natural selection. Over the decades, believers in the biblical account of origins have predicted many insidious consequences of evolutionary thought, including Nazism as the logical outcome of survival-of-the-fittest ideology and, in the Progressive era, the exploitation of labor by justifying competition and discouraging reform.[36] Germane to all of these predictions is the ultimate consequence of evolutionary theory: that people who believe in naturalism will choose to take the path away from God. Losing one's faith in a preordained world ordered by a creator leads to the moral decay of individual and social life. The outcome of this last threat—when people lose their faith in an ordered world—is severe: people feel free to indulge in selfish, immoral behavior, which is good neither for themselves as individuals with souls nor for society as a whole. Evolution is seen to contribute to moral decay in the United States because it "provides a theory of man's origin independent of the God that the atheist believes does not exist. "According to creationists, the atheist's next conclusion is very dangerous to society. If man is an animal, then, like other animals, he is amoral."[37]

While there are some basic beliefs that all creationists share (that there is a superior force known as God that created the universe, that all people become degraded when they don't believe in Godly creation), there is a great deal of variation in what being "a creationist" means. Unlike most popular conceptions of believers in divine creation, those offended by evolution do not compose a homogeneous group. Nor should they necessarily be characterized as a scientifically ignorant group, say several scholars who have studied the movement, for there are many figures among creationists who seek the *scientific* basis for their creationist beliefs in the disciplines of biology, geology, etc.[38]

Nevertheless, according to these studies and the work of the National Center for Science Education—an organization located near Berkeley, California, that is much despised by creationists in its commitment to ensuring evolutionary teaching in schools—those falling under the umbrella term "anti-evolutionist" have long been divided in some fundamental beliefs over how creation occurred, as well as in their latter-day efforts to find a decidedly scientific basis for their rejection of Darwinian theory. There have been a variety of strands of creationism, from those adhering to a literal interpretation of the Genesis account, on one end of the spectrum, to those allowing for a considerable degree of evolution in their conceptualizations, on the other.

The Literalists: "Young-Earth" and "Old-Earth" Scientific Creationists

The most conservative readers of the biblical account of creation are known as *literalists*. Literalists include "young-earth" creationists, who are so called because of their strict, unmetaphorical belief in the six-day creation between 6,000 and 10,000 years ago. Adherents of young-earth creationism generally follow the work of Henry Morris, until recently the president of the Institute of Creation Research, the preeminent research center for young-earth creationism in the United States, located in El Cajon, California. Morris and his followers "accept Genesis literally, including not only the special, separate creation of humans and all other species, but also the historicity of Noah's Flood," which they believe was responsible for all of the earth's fossil record.[39] The Institute's members—particularly Morris and his *Genesis Flood* co-author John Whitcomb—represented a milestone in the effort to present a scientific rationale for special creationism.[40]

Before one can understand the passion behind many creationist challenges in the schools, it is necessary to understand why the age of the earth is so crucial to young-earthers' conceptualization of creation. It involves the concept of biblical inerrancy. If one were to grant that the "days" written about in Genesis actually were millions or billions of years, as contemporary science tells us, then it would ineluctably lead to the conclusion that dinosaurs, for example, would have lived and died long before humans. If this were so, that would mean that death and dying—the experience illustrated so painfully in the Judeo-Christian story of the Fall of Man—came long before Adam and Eve were ever cast out of the Garden of Eden. And that is in direct conflict with a literal reading of the Bible, which suggests that the Fall took place some thousands of years ago.[41] If one is to hold onto belief, say the literalists, then scientific hypotheses must conform to and, indeed, support, biblical data.[42]

"Old-earth" creationism is a less literal wing than young-earth creationism, but it still seeks to reconcile a biblical description of creation with contemporary scientific methods and knowledge. Old-earthers are divided in their approach to biblical interpretation surrounding creation. Some old-earthers believe that God created the earth epochs ago and that each of the "six days" of creation written in the Bible represents thousands of years. These creationists are known as "day-agers" because of their metaphorical, though still closely attentive, reading of the Bible. Another faction of old-earthers argue that there were two periods of creation, not one: one ancient, one more recent, separated by two floods, Lucifer's and Noah's. This faction adheres to what is known as "gap" theory, not "day-age," since its members hypothesize that a gap existed between a more ancient period of creation and the special creation of human beings during Adamic time, separated by a natural catastrophe.[43] Allowing for either of these two looser interpretations about the age of the earth unshackles the old earth faction from insisting that God's world is only thousands of years old, and brings it into closer alignment with contemporary scientific knowledge.

Although there are some important differences between the old-earthers (of either camp) and the young earthers, both groups are known as literalists, who support *scientific creationism, or creation science,* since their theories of origins are firmly rooted in how the Bible describes creation to have taken place, with relatively small digressions from scriptural text.

Progressive Creationism and Theistic Evolutionism

Next on the continuum, according to the National Center for Science Education (NCSE) categorization, are *progressive* creationists, among whom there is also considerable variation.[44] The basic idea of this broad group, though, is that a powerful God created the earth and its inhabitants, but that God's work can be understood through modern scientific means, without recourse to a literal reading of the Bible. The most conservative form of progressive creationism, according to the NCSE creation / evolution continuum, purports that God created "kinds" of animals, which share no common ancestors (and which are therefore not affected by "macroevolutionary" processes, though they may be affected by "microevolutionary" change—about which, more shortly). This faction of progressives generally believes that God created the natural world, and then set evolution in motion as the means by which life would take hold and continue. A group calling its project "intelligent design" also ranks among the progressives. Like *theistic evolutionists*, who represent the last rung on the creationist continuum, advocates of intelligent design also find it possible for Christians to believe that evolution is part of God's plan. But the intelligent-design camp rests the bulk of its argument on what members see as the "scientific problems" with evolution: that so much of life is simply too sophisticated to have arisen due to pure coincidence. In their words, life on earth is far too "irreducibly complex" to have been formed through random processes like undirected natural selection. If undirected natural processes could not have produced such complex systems as the eye, or the bacterial flagellum, for example, then they must have required a designer.[45]

Members of the progressive creationism and theistic evolution wings—aware of the scorn heaped on their more literalist colleagues, the scientific creationists—are unlikely even to call themselves "creationists," although some progressives are currently fighting to reclaim the term to represent their views, as well, as we will see later in the case of Phillip Johnson, a professor of law at the University of California, Berkeley, and a leading proponent of the intelligent-design movement. This contingent adheres only to the credo that "the earth, life, and humanity owe their existence to a purposeful, intelligent Creator."[46] Others who reside on this part of the continuum—such as many modern Catholic church leaders—are also likely to talk about "compatibilism," the view that God works through natural processes like evolution.[47] All together, I call this section of the National Center for Science Education's continuum (from the progressive creationists to the theistic evolutionists), the "elite," or "intellectuals," of the movement, for they often view their own ideas and scientific knowledge as more sophisticated than those of the literalists. They also have organized together in groups separate from the literal creationists, in organizations such as the American Scientific Affiliation, located in Buellton, California, a group that is open only to those with science degrees and who generally disdain what they consider to be the less scientifically sophisticated young-earth, day-age, and gap theorists.

This intellectual, or elite, end of the creationist spectrum (the progressives, the intelligent-design advocates, and the theistic evolutionists) is reconciled with some aspects of evolution. But members of this group are also quick to point out the limitations of naturalistic evolution, making a clear distinction between "microevolution," with which they are comfortable (because this process provides only for variation within species, such as moths developing darker wings for camouflage in response to pollution) and "macroevolution," which is anathema to their beliefs because such a process requires "major innovations" in speciation that occurs naturalistically, without the guidance of a creator.[48]

As we shall see in the case studies, it mostly has been the literalists (old-earth and young-earth), and *not* the elites, who have been out on the frontlines of curriculum battles in the United States, and involved in the grassroots movements to change the way science is taught in their school districts. Partially, this is a matter of historical progression: intelligent design is a more recent later-day rhetorical and intellectual adaptation to the legal obstacles scientific creationists have encountered in their challenges (as we will see in the next section), and intelligent-design proponents simply have not been around as long, and so have not mounted as many challenges in the schools. In addition, the relative dearth of intelligent-design challenges has been a matter of priorities: elites of the movement have focused their efforts on other parts of the educational universe besides primary and secondary school instruction, namely, on convincing scientists in the academy of the validity of their scientific claims. But this pattern has been altered in the late 1990s, most notably in Kansas—the most recent case included in this study—where members of the school board who supported "anti-evolutionist" content used a partial intelligent-design strategy to stake their claims for curricular changes. Arguing that lab studies and direct observation cannot prove either that God created us or that we have evolved from a common ancestor, creationists in Kansas cited scientific weaknesses in the Darwinian account of evolutionary processes. Creationists didn't try to bring creationism *into* the classroom; they simply gave school districts license to keep evolution *out*.

History of Creationism in U.S. Public Schools

Just as there is a significant intellectual backdrop to the Afrocentric movement and the challenges in its name in the 1980s and 1990s, so there is a political and legal history that provides the background for the four creationist cases included in this book. The true dawn of the creationist movement broke with the publication of Charles Darwin's manuscript, of course, but it wasn't until nearly seventy years later in the United States that creationism found itself in the public spotlight. Then began the "trial of the century": *Tennessee v. John Scopes.*

From the vantage point of seventy-five years hence, the "Scopes Monkey Trial" of 1925 lives on in the collective consciousness as the case that was supposed to have put to rest the "outmoded" claims of anti-evolutionists. Although the court's final ruling in that case reasserted the state of Tennessee's right to ban the teaching of evolution (thereby declaring the anti-evolution side the winner), the humiliation that defense attorney Clarence Darrow heaped on William Jennings Bryan during that trial resonated across the nation. Darrow's defense of Scopes in the name of civil liberties, and his excoriation of the anti-scientism written into the Tennessee law, seemed to ring the death knell for the teaching of unfettered Godly creation in the nation's public-school science classes.

But what really occurred subsequent to the Scopes trial was a kind of mollification of creationists. During the years following the Scopes trial, American school districts and textbook publishers played it safe with the entire topic of origins, and generally hedged references to evolution, when they didn't entirely excise them. Absent from textbook discussions of biology and geology were explicit evolutionary terms. Using words like "changing forms" and "development" rather than "evolution," educators avoided controversy with their constituents.[49] During this period when the language in textbooks and curricula remained vague, from about the 1920s to the 1960s, believers in Godly design were satisfied with scientific instruction in the schools and, for the most part, remained quiet. For all intents and purposes, their interests were being served: evolution in no way was being clearly and exclusively taught to their children. There was nothing harmful from which to protect their Christian progeny, no sacrilegious content to be concerned about.

This changed in the 1950s when American educators and scientists, with the government's support, decided to strengthen the science training that American children received. The Soviets' successful launch of Sputnik in 1957 put American policy makers on alert to the lethargy of American scientific instruction, and the federal government sought to reinvigorate young minds with scientific findings and the scientific method. Scientists at the time, who had been unaware of the dearth of evolutionary instruction in the public schools, warned that much more concise language about evolution would have to be included in any such reinvigorated curriculum.[50] Government leaders agreed, evolution became more clearly discussed in the classroom and in textbooks, and, for the first time since 1925, creationists were spurred to renew their public challenges to evolution in the schools.[51]

Adaptation of Rhetoric

In the past forty years of creationist rejuvenation, challengers have developed four main lines of argument over how to teach evolution and creationism in public-school science curricula. Each one of these arguments was designed to overcome a First Amendment claim made against creationism by evolution's advocates. Three of these arguments have been

Diff kind of Creationism

described in detail elsewhere, by such writers as Christopher Toumey in *God's Own Scientists* and Edward Larson in *The Creationists*, while the fourth has only recently advanced and been recognized and analyzed by outside organizations, such as the National Center for Science Education. I will call the framings of these projects, respectively, (1) exclusive creationism, where creationism was to be exclusively taught in science classrooms, and evolution was to have no place; (2) creationism-alongside-evolution for *scientific* reasons, where creationism was to be taught in science courses because it was claimed to be just as empirically demonstrable as evolutionary theory was, if not more so; (3) creationism-alongside-evolution for *First Amendment reasons*, where creationism was to be taught alongside evolution in the schools to ensure that evolutionary teaching did not abridge students'—especially Christian students'—freedom of religion rights; and finally (4) the most recent intelligent-design arguments, where the term "creation" has been dropped completely from curriculum demands, but where evolution is to be deemphasized in classrooms in order to give space to "alternative theories" of origins.[52] I will describe each of these briefly in this chapter. I will add more detail in chapter 5.

The first of these arguments—exclusive creationism—faced its demise thirty years ago. Following a series of U.S. Supreme Court rulings in the 1960s clarifying the separation of church and state, in 1968, the Supreme Court ruled unanimously in the case of *Epperson v. Arkansas* that a state prohibition of evolutionary instruction in schools was clearly unconstitutional under the First Amendment. In this case, the court "invalidated an Arkansas statute that prohibited the teaching of evolution. The Court held the statute unconstitutional on grounds that the First Amendment to the U.S. Constitution does not permit a state to require that teaching and learning must be tailored to the principles or prohibitions of any particular religious sect or doctrine."[53] As a result of this court ruling, few proponents of creationism ever again attempted to outright ban the teaching of evolution from public school classrooms.

But although movement activists recognized that efforts explicitly to ban evolution would no longer be viable, creationists' concerns about evolution did not dissipate. They learned to adapt to the new legal environment, and, in the 1970s, scientific creationism became the central tool in creationists' arsenal. Shocking many Americans who thought such issues had already been settled, believers in Godly design revealed this second strategy for arguing that information about creation ought to be provided in the public school classroom. Rather than seeking completely to jettison evolution from the curriculum, this new breed of creationist reformers posited that their own theories were also supported by scientific evidence and so should be presented in science classes. Just as evolution draws on empirical data, they argued, so too does scientific creationism. Adhering to the Baconian scientific method in its reliance on hard, observable facts, creation science, in fact, was claimed by its supporters to be even *more* tied to data than evolutionary theory was, because evolutionary theory arrogantly fills in all the empirical gaps with *theory*,[54] or *prior hypotheses*,[55] while creationism only describes what is actually seen, and it "sticks to the facts." For science to be taught fairly, according to scientific creationists, using this second strand of reasoning, public schools should not be allowed to privilege evolution when creationist theories offer just as solid scientific evidence as the alternative. At the very least, according to this second strategy, *doubts* about Darwinian evolution had to be taught in the schools to adhere to scientific method.

The third line of argumentation—which emerged around the same time as the scientific discourse did—held that the creationist account of origins must be taught alongside evolution in the public schools because evolutionary concepts had given rise to secular humanism—*which was itself a religion*—and that the teaching of evolution, then, represented an establishment of religion that infringed on Christians' free exercise of their faith. The solution: to teach the two scientific theories (evolution and creationism) side-by-side, eliminating, according to the creationist argument, any de facto infringements. Through the late 1980s and 1990s, the creationist effort relied on both the science and civil rights arguments to present a two-pronged attack on evolution. As such, it was aimed at (1) diluting the theory of evolution to the level of hypothesis or speculation, and (2) winning equal time for the doctrine of special creation.[56]

How did schools and textbook publishers respond to creationists' two-dimensional effort? We will see these strategies very clearly in three of the four creationist cases presented in this book: in Louisiana, in Vista, California, and in the battle over the California state science framework. But for now, suffice it to say that creationists won no lasting official victories in the 1980s and 1990s. However, they did succeed, in many respects, in hemming in the forthright instruction of evolutionary concepts. With the advent of "balanced treatment" arguments and creationists' continued success in having evolution viewed as controversial, many individual instructors and even whole school systems have shied away from clear presentations of evolutionary concepts. Instead of the "two theories" that creationists say they support, the default in American classrooms through the early 1990s has been to teach no theory about origins.

In response to this trend, organizations such as the National Center for Science Education have mobilized academic scientists, in particular, through the late 1980s and into the 1990s, to contest this state of affairs, and scientists have become increasingly involved in drafting evolution-heavy science frameworks in their states (as we will see in Kansas and

California) and for national organizations, such as the National Academy of Sciences. Not surprisingly, creationists have adapted to these activities. Reacting to states' and local school districts' incorporation of ever more explicit evolutionary content into the curriculum, creationists have developed the fourth strand of anti-evolution rhetoric. As will be seen most prominently in the Kansas case, intelligent-design arguments have recently replaced the "equal-time" strategy for deemphasizing evolution. Absent in this fourth strand of recent creationist challenge is any actual reference to God or to divine creation; instead there is an openness to teaching "alternative theories" and to considering the "weaknesses" of current prevailing theories of origins—particularly, the random processes of natural selection. While the fourth branch of creationist argumentation still emphasizes both the *scientific* and *constitutional* necessity of deemphasizing evolution in the curriculum, as did its two earlier predecessors, it is much less explicit in proposing a godly creator than the creationist challenges that preceded it.

So, what we have in creationist battles with schools is an ongoing pattern of action and reaction, with school boards facing mobilized constituencies on both sides of the issue. When states or local school systems incorporate stronger presentations of evolutionary concepts into the classroom, creationists protest. They argue that "honest science" is not being taught, and that their constitutional rights are being stifled. When creationists stage these protestations, educators mobilize to fight back, invoking both the constitutional mandate to separate church from state and the intellectual necessity of teaching bona fide science. Creationists, in the face of these counterclaims, try to don the mantle of scientific neutrality and legitimacy, and they make appeals to fair treatment under the law. But evolutionary science is well defended, and schools have been able to shun creationist activities. We will see this scenario played out again and again in the cases described in this book, despite important variation in the particular politics and organizational contours of each case.

Case Selection and Methods

Selecting from a Universe of Cases

Having just spun two separate narratives of these challenges and their histories, the task now is to lay the basis of a comparison of the one to the other. Clearly, these are very different challenges, as acknowledged earlier—they concern different constituencies and they are home to different complaints about public schooling. But therein lies the logic of comparing them. Despite their many differences, their similarities also are impressive, not the least of which is the fact that both challenges battled for the sake of children in their state or local public schools—the same institution, in sociological terms—and that schools considered both sets of challengers to be marginal interest groups, whose curricular demands were hardly the stuff of standard pedagogy. Seeing what happened to challengers of each type motivates the study.

What was the basis for selecting these particular seven battles as the best occasions for study? Over the past twenty years, Afrocentrists and creationists have mounted a large number of fairly serious challenges to public school systems from coast to coast. Afrocentrists, for the most part, have been active in urban areas with large African American populations, ranging from capital cities to smaller ones, such as Atlanta, Baltimore, Chicago, Detroit, Oakland, Washington, D.C., Camden, New Jersey, and Prince George's County, Maryland. We have also witnessed demands for Afrocentric inclusion in locations without African American majorities, as distantly located as Portland, Oregon, and New York state. When creationists have challenged school systems, meanwhile, they have made their most noticeable appearances in southern locales, such as Arkansas, Oklahoma, Florida, Louisiana, and Mississippi, although they also have been found to have political appeal in such far-flung locales as New Hampshire, New Mexico, and areas of California.

Of the many locations across the country where Afrocentric and creationist curricula have been proposed, the seven cases that I chose to study were what I considered to be among the richest and most diverse occurrences of these two campaigns during the twenty-year period of the study, involving whole school districts or state school systems. I was interested in including cases that involved public debate over an effort to institutionalize curricular change, and rejected those cases where students may be taught either of these two types of curricula surreptitiously. While it is surely true that both Afrocentric and creationist materials were then, and are still being, taught by individual teachers at their discretion (without it becoming public record), I have limited my interest to challenges that took their efforts public, presenting outright contest to schools' routine practices. I did this because I am interested in studying not only the challengers' campaigns to change curricula, but also the institutional responses those challengers received from school systems.

In the preceding chapter, I briefly described the Afrocentric challenge that occurred in Washington, D.C., in the early 1990s and the creationist challenge that took place at the state level in California in the late 1980s and 1990s. These two were part of the larger seven-case study I examined for this book. In addition to these, the two other Afrocentric challenges that I selected for study were (1) the Afrocentric-inspired district-wide reform that occurred in Atlanta from 1988 to 1996, and (2) the statewide

debate surrounding Afrocentrism and multiculturalism in New York between 1987 and 1995. By including Atlanta and Washington, D.C., in the
set of cases, I made the decision to study locations that were more typical
of the universe of Afrocentric challenges: they were urban and predominantly African American districts. By electing to add New York state to
the study (a school system at the state level that is not majority black), I
decided to study one location that was less standard among other cases.
I did this to see the degree to which context mattered for these challengers,
in terms of both race and system level.

The three creationist challenges in this study besides the state challenge
in California were (1) legislation that was passed by the state of Louisiana
in 1981 to mandate creationist content whenever evolution was taught in
science classrooms (a law that ultimately was rejected by the U.S. Supreme
Court in 1987); (2) a series of events in Vista, California, from 1992 to
1994, where the local school board attempted to "balance out" evolutionary teaching; and (3) the more recent case (1999–2000) in Kansas, where
a majority of state school-board members voted to eliminate evolution as
a topic on statewide assessment tests, thereby allowing school districts
and/or teachers around the state to delete evolutionary concepts from the
science curriculum if they so chose. Just as I included more and less typical
cases for the Afrocentric challenge, I did so, too, for the creationist challenge, by the same rationale: to be able to study context comparatively.

I should note that when I began this research in 1995, events in Kansas
were a long way off from occurring: anti-evolution activities did not
begin at the statewide level there until 1999. Until that point in time, this
study included only the six earlier comparative cases. But because events
in Kansas seemed both intriguingly similar and intriguingly different
from other cases in this study, and because the Kansas creationism events
captured the national media's attention so thoroughly (becoming a sort
of poster child for supporters of both evolution and anti-evolution teaching), I have chosen to include it in the project. Over the course of the
twenty-year period, these seven cases generated a great deal of attention
in their local communities and in the nation at large and, in so doing, I
would argue, they came to represent in many aspects the two issues for
a national audience.

Besides selecting these cases because they were among the national flash
points for Afrocentric and creationist issues during this time period, I also
chose this set of seven because they displayed considerable variation in
the process of contention. Among the three locations where Afrocentrists
launched their challenges, Afrocentric challengers achieved "symbolic"
success in one of these (Atlanta); they achieved "circumscribed" success
in another (Washington, D.C.); and they had to settle for near outright
rejection in the third, after a brief period of accommodation (New York

state). While they differed in the process of getting to their endpoints, however, the three Afrocentric challenges bore a strong family resemblance in ultimate outcomes: eventually, their respective school systems diminished them. Among the creationist cases, there was also little variation in ultimate outcomes—eventually all four school systems repealed creationist inroads, in one way or another. But, as in the case with the local Afrocentric challenges, there was a great deal of variety among the processes used by creationist challengers to push against established educational routines and gain at least temporary victories in the systems they battled. In two of these cases (Kansas and Louisiana), statewide bodies actually adopted creationist curricular demands; in another (Vista, California), Christian conservatives gained enough power to impose minor creationist-friendly reforms in their school district; while in the fourth case (California), no gains were made at any point in the process, save the most superficial compromise language at the very end of the science framework revision cycle.

In other words, what I have attempted to do is select challenge events that, together, present us with both positive and negative events in each of the challenges. While it will become clear when I go through each case that such tidy terms as "positive" and "negative" underestimate the dynamics and outcomes of challenger events in these locations—it is difficult to classify many of these processes and outcomes as one *or* the other (e.g., victorious *or* failing)—the effort to select cases with as much variation as possible was crucial for understanding the contours of Afrocentric and creationist outcomes and schools' responses.

I also selected these seven cases because they occurred at different levels in the educational structure: at the local level in some cases (Atlanta, Washington, D.C., and Vista—two Afrocentric and one creationist) and at the state level in others (Louisiana, California, Kansas, and New York—three creationist and one Afrocentric). I elected to include these different levels for two reasons: first, because this selection reflects the real world of education contentiousness, in that both Afrocentrists and creationists mounted challenges at these two levels. While it probably would have been simpler for comparison's sake to select cases at the same level of the school organization (such as only at the local school-district level or only at the state level), such comparison would have lost substantial claims for representing the field of actual challenge. It would have been cheating, in a way, to have excluded one or the other purely to make the analysis of cases easier. Second, it makes sense to have diversified this variable, since I am concerned in this study with the impact of organizational and political practices on challenger outcomes. Because schools' organizational and political practices vary so significantly in state and local school systems, I found it necessary to examine both levels.

Methods

Because these seven sites of challenge were among the most widely noticed
Afrocentric and creationist struggles of their era, these cases produced a
great paper trail through the pages of local and national media. Taking
advantage of this paper trail, I collected and analyzed anywhere from 100
to 200 news stories and editorials from the premiere newspaper in each
location, which I determined to be the *Atlanta Journal-Constitution*,
Washington Post, *New York Times*, *New Orleans Times-Picayune*, *Los
Angeles Times*, *San Diego Union Tribune*, and *Kansas City Star*. I collected the majority of the articles using the Lexis-Nexis database, in which
I began searches using keywords such as "creationism" or "creationist"
or "evolution," and then used names, terms, and text as they arose in
those initial documents to complete a search. I would continue using
this method until I generated no new stories for a case with the different
combinations of keyword searches. While I cannot be certain that I ex-
hausted the universe of articles in each location for each challenge using
this search method, I am confident that I unearthed the vast majority of
articles written about the challenge in each locale, and that these news
accounts can very adequately form the backbone of an historical narrative
for each case.

A note: none of the *New Orleans Times-Picayune* articles for this time
period were available on the Lexis-Nexis service, nor were the early years
of the *Atlanta Journal-Constitution*. To collect articles in these publications, I used the *Reader's Guide to Periodicals* and microfiche archives.
All together, I read and coded approximately 1,000 media articles for the
seven locations.

I put the articles to use in two ways: to analyze the media discourse
that surrounded each challenge event and to construct a chronology of
events for each case. For the discourse analysis, I constructed a simple
coding scheme to determine when news articles were neutral, supportive,
or opposed to the challenge in question, and I kept a record of the precise
frames used to build that support or opposition. I used this coding scheme
to analyze how and when the major media outlet in each location reported
on the challenge (I will discuss media reaction to these challenges in chapters 3 through 6). For the chronology, I used the media pieces to recon-
struct the major events in each challenge—at least those "major" events
that were covered in the newspaper—and created a timeline for each case.

I supplemented my media-derived chronologies with two other sources
of data: primary documents (such as state curriculum frameworks, school
board minutes, department of education policy statements, etc.), and
through selective interviewing. Hard copy documents were useful for dis-

covering background information and history in the cases, filling in gaps in chronologies, and for corroborating evidence from other sources, such as by providing verbatim policy language that had been referred to in the media or in interviews.

As for the interviews: in Fall 1995 and Fall 1996, I met with thirty-six people across the country who had been central to Afrocentric and creationist debates in five of the seven cases. For each of the cases except Louisiana and Kansas, I interviewed such participants is challenge leaders, system administrators, education consultants, and media commentators, among others, using semi-structured interviews. The group of interviews for each case was designed to present a cross-section of professional policymakers and administrators representing the school systems, as well as people acting on behalf of the two challenges and those in professional organizations opposed to the challenge.[57] The interviews took between ninety minutes and about two hours to complete, and were tape-recorded and then transcribed. Among my interviewees in the Afrocentric cases were Leonard Jeffries, professor of Black Studies at City College of New York and a leading proponent of Afrocentrism; Thomas Sobol, former commissioner of education for the state of New York; Nathan Glazer, a Harvard University sociologist who served on a New York task force appointed by Sobol; Diane Ravitch, former U.S. assistant secretary of education in the Bush administration and a professor in the School of Education at New York University; and Ali Mazrui, a humanities professor who also served on a New York task force. Among the interviewees for the creationist cases were Bill Honig, former superintendent of public instruction for California public schools; Henry Morris, founder and president emeritus of the Institute for Creation Research; Phillip Johnson, professor of law at the University of California, Berkeley, and a leader of the intelligent-design wing of creationism; John Wiester, chairman of the Science Education Commission of the American Scientific Affiliation, an organization of theistic evolutionists and intelligent-design proponents; and Eugenie Scott, director of the National Center for Science Education, an organization based in Berkeley, California, committed to defeating creationist challenges to public schools. A full listing of my interviewees appears in the appendix.[58]

It would be folly to claim that any of these seven cases, or all of them put together, are representative of the many other Afrocentric and creationist challenges that have occurred in the United States during this time period. Nor would I want to make such a claim, since empirically, we see a great deal of variation in the details of each challenge. What I argue, instead, is that looking at these seven cases, which have been selected to vary on both their dependent and independent variables—to borrow language from another community of discourse in the sociological field—

yields insights into the distinctive patterns of action that occurred in Afro-centric cases, as compared to creationist efforts. These differences can be explained using a sophisticated set of theoretical tools, and their analysis produces insights that we could never divine using quantitative methods.

Theoretically, I chose to study these challenges comparatively for many reasons. Unlike many other comparative studies of contentious politics, this one is not across countries or societies (as is increasingly being done in the social movements literature), nor just across structural conditions, such as political conditions, for the same challenge.[59] This study of Afro-centrists and creationists, instead, compares across types of challenge in the same nation under generally the same structural / political conditions. It is an examination of two different sets of challengers using similarly motivated rhetoric at the same point in history battling the same institution, but whose experiences in schools exhibited both remarkable differences and similarities. This study does not locate general causes or invariant models for Afrocentric and creationist challenges; as Marco Giugni points out in one essay, "there are no such invariant patterns in social life."[60] Rather, following Giugni's lead, by looking at such comparative cases, we can say more about the historically contingent combinations of factors that shaped the possibilities for challengers to effect institutional change. In this comparison of Afrocentric and creationist demands made in public school systems, we will see the interplay of cultural beliefs, political opportunities, and organizational arrangements as they influenced ultimate challenge outcomes.

Three

History of the Three Afrocentric Cases: Atlanta, Washington, D.C., and New York State

HAVING LAID out the historical context for the Afrocentric and creationist challenges in the previous chapter, I now embark on the first of four chapters in which I look in detail at the seven cases that make up the comparative study. In this chapter, I will describe events and outcomes in Atlanta, Washington, D.C., and New York state, and will draw attention to the *cultural frames* that the challengers used in each of these cases to mobilize support for their cause. A frame is a set of images, symbols, or narrative tropes used by social movement leaders to tap into the cultural beliefs held by their target audience. Leaders articulate their problems and solutions using these culturally resonant "signifying agents" in an effort to have their goals make sense to their potential adherents. One way to think about framing is to understand these activities as efforts to condense wide-ranging suggestions about some problem and its solution into a coherent and compelling package.[1]

As we move from one site to the next, we will see that Afrocentrists used three powerful rhetorical frames to set out their position: (1) that the *problem* they addressed was undeniable, yet fixable; (2) that those who opposed them were either *racists* or *race disloyalists* in their challenges; and (3) that history and social studies should be "real" for the students who learn them, requiring that these disciplines be sufficiently *flexible* to accommodate the new scholarship that Afrocentrists were developing. These three relatively successful frames by no means guaranteed that Afrocentrists could transform whole school districts in their image; in fact, critics internal and external to the school systems challenged the Afrocentric effort with a set of concerned questions (or what researchers call *counterframes*) to dispute Afrocentric concepts: Will Afrocentrism teach untruths? Will it threaten national unity? Will it do anything to improve the achievement of the very groups it is intended to help?[2] Despite the burden of these counterframes, however, Afrocentrists' framing resources were powerful enough to convince members of the school systems in Atlanta, Washington, D.C., and New York state that they at least would have to deal with their challengers as if they were real players in the game of curriculum development. I will introduce these three cultural frames in this chap-

ter and study them more carefully, along with the political and organizational resources that formed their backdrop, in the next chapter.

The First Link in the Chain: Portland, Oregon, Launches Afrocentric Reform

Before taking on the three Afrocentric cases included in this book, it is
necessary to back up a few years and set the context for these challenges.
To appreciate fully Afrocentrism's adaptation in public elementary
and secondary schools in the United States, we must travel west from the
East Coast environs where my three cases occurred. We have to go to
Portland, Oregon.

Much to the surprise of most observers, the first school system to consider an Afrocentric curriculum was far from Detroit, Chicago, Oakland,
or any other school district with similar population demographics—that
is, with a majority-black student body. Before either Atlanta or Washington, D.C., even considered implementing their official Afrocentric curricula, Portland, Oregon, had initiated the first public school program that
rightfully could be called a bona fide commitment to Afrocentrism. While
small-scale Afrocentric projects had dotted the country up to that point,
housed in privately funded academies, no Afrocentric program to date had
become as widespread or influential as the one that originated in Portland.[3]

The Portland program had its public debut in 1987 when the school
district released a set of curriculum guides called *The African-American
Baseline Essays*, which, upon their release, were both hailed and berated
by educators and scholars across the nation. With a 74 percent white, 14
percent black, 7 percent Asian, and 2 percent Hispanic population,[4] this
Pacific Northwest city was a highly unlikely first site in the Afrocentric
reform movement. But it had, in the form of its then superintendent, Mat-
thew Prophet, a hearty supporter of Afrocentric curricula. It was Prophet,
along with his staff, responding to African American parents' anger over
busing in his district, who decided that the school system should be proactive in its stance toward race relations. Rather than busing children long
distances to desegregate schools, hoping that such action would shift racial attitudes, the superintendent and his supporters decided to change
attitudes about race by quintessentially *cultural* means. The district's
teachers would teach children of all racial and ethnic backgrounds about
their ancient heritages and the contributions that "their people" had made
to world history, starting with the African people. In this mode, Prophet
commissioned the Afrocentric scholar Asa Hilliard to begin work on the
first of six proposed reference volumes of essays to document different
"geocultural groups" to be infused into the curriculum from that day

forward.[5] Called the Multicultural / Multiethnic Education Baseline Essay Project, Portland's venture in this area was understood around the country to be Afrocentric because of its foundations with Hilliard and its beginnings in the area of African American culture.

Having begun life as an academic response to putative omissions in the scholarly record, the Afrocentric project had not immediately found its way from the universities, home of its origins, to the public schools. Instead, the issues had been percolating at the academic level for several years before being adapted for use by school teachers. Asa Hilliard, a professor of urban education at Georgia State University and a foundational scholar of African-centered education, had a great interest in seeing these more theoretical intellectual shifts become useful in grade schools and high schools across the nation, and he became one of the early pioneers of such adaptation to the lower levels of schooling. Almost without exception, if a school system anywhere in the country were considering the idea of infusing Afrocentrism into the curriculum, Hilliard's name would have showed up on the list as one of several possible architects of the incipient program, as we shall see in all three cases included in this study.

The *African-American Baseline Essays*, for which Hilliard is primarily responsible, is a reference volume made up of six individual essays in the areas of language arts, math, science / technology, social studies, world music, and art.[6] Six Afrocentric scholars, presented as "individuals knowledgeable about the specific discipline and recognized as an expert on African and African American history" wrote one essay, apiece;[7] Asa Hilliard edited them; and the Multicultural / Multiethnic Education program in Portland, under the direction of Carolyn Leonard, coordinated the effort. The essays were designed to serve as a resource guide for teachers who wanted to teach about African and African American contributions to world history, but who were thwarted in their interest by the dearth of such information in any available textbooks and curriculum guides. According to editor Hilliard in the opening pages of the document, "The *Baseline Essay* is intended to be a short story of the experience of a particular geocultural group within a particular academic area from earliest times to the present. . . . It provides a sense of coherence, continuity, and comprehensiveness to the experience of a particular group within a given academic area. Taken all together, the *Baseline Essays* are the story of a people."[8] They are designed to be "informative and uplifting" and to document the "contributions of a geocultural group."[9] They were also designed to be used by the district's teachers, who would then draw on the information contained within to supplement their classroom materials.

The collection of African American essays was the first to be published by the Portland district, but even as the district released this publication in 1987, it stated that additional essays were to follow. The remaining essays would reflect the contributions of the other five "geocultural groups" identified by the Portland School District: Asian Americans, European Americans, Hispanic Americans, American Indians, and Pacific Island Americans. In 1993, the American Indian essays were released; the Hispanic and Asian essays, as of early 2001, are in draft form, according to the Portland school district website.[10]

The African American essays were not official policy for long before critics around the country began assailing their creators' motives, methods, and output. The scholarship of the "knowledgeable experts" was questioned most vigorously, particularly when it asserted that ancient black Egyptians built human gliders, that Pythagoras and other famed Greeks studied under the Egyptians (who, it was said, had what we know of today as "black" skin), and that modern medicine stems from black Egyptian tradition, not Greek knowledge. Critiques of the essays written by educators and academics were published in the media; and the criticisms grew increasingly obstreperous as more commentators and scholars across the country became aware of them.[11]

Although controversial, once the Afrocentric materials had been infused into the Portland curriculum, the essays wielded great influence on interested school systems across the country. School systems including those in Washington and Atlanta looked to the essays as a model of teacher instruction and classroom pedagogy. The content of the *African-American Baseline Essays* proved important beyond the boundaries of Portland when other school districts began borrowing heavily from them in developing their own programs. Atlanta was one of the first sites to import the essays whole-cloth into its African American Infusion program; a curriculum administrator in Washington, D.C., regarded them as "excellent" and as possible foundational materials for the district; and districts from Detroit to Fort Lauderdale drew on them for historical information to be taught to children in the classroom.

While many school districts were choosing to rely on the *Baseline Essays* for enhanced information on African and African American history, others found that doing so put their districts at risk of intense scrutiny and condemnation. Once a number of districts across the country went public with their use of the essays, the chorus of critics increased sharply, as skeptical journalists, parents, and educators investigated the essays' content more thoroughly and found them lacking. It comes as little surprise, then, that school systems that had not yet adopted the essays but that were thinking of incorporating some form of Afrocentrism into their curriculum sometimes used the essays as a negative reference point for what that school system was decidedly *not* implementing. For instance, when education leaders in New York attempted to bring credibility to their district's unique efforts in multiculturalism, some in the school system pointed to the *African-American Baseline Essays* to say that their own program resembled little of those. The *Baseline Essays* found both advocates and adversaries in the rest of the education world—not to mention the wider public—and ended up playing a role in all three of my cases.

While Portland is not one of the cases that I studied for this book, I introduce it here because it represented the first district-wide experiment in drafting and infusing Afrocentric curricula into public school class-rooms. It is also important because it presages many of the dynamics that we will see in the three Afrocentric cases that I do study. First, like the other cases, particularly that in Atlanta, Portland's Afrocentric project found support among some number of powerful education professionals in the district—in this case, from the superintendent, no less. This was clearly a case in which an education "insider" leant his voice to Afrocen-trism, and even led the charge for its incorporation. Second, Portland got the ball rolling by developing the *Baseline Essays*, a key event in the sur-vival of Afrocentrism in the future, since these materials made it possible for other districts to engage in the campaign without generating their own curricular materials—a costly enterprise requiring a number of resources, including financial, political, and teacher training. Finally, it was Portland that first widely introduced the idea that Afrocentrism, and not a more "moderate" solution, was needed to address the problems of race in cities. Portland's lead would be an important turning point in schools systems' spreading willingness to entertain Afrocentric claims.

"Big Bang" in the Black Mecca: The Relatively Smooth, Though Not Peril-Free, Process of Instituting African American Infusion in Atlanta, 1989–92

If any school district in the nation seemed to have been eminently poised in the 1980s to implement a system-wide Afrocentric curriculum, Atlanta surely was it. Known for decades as the "Black Mecca" for the African American middle class because of its professional, social, and academic opportunities (the city is home to two of the country's most historically elite black colleges, Spelman and Morehouse), Atlanta has long attracted a populace of blacks and whites that believes strongly in its own image of peaceful race relations and in its system of mutual respect. A sense of mission pervades Atlanta, a kind of "If we can't do it, then nobody can" attitude toward solving social problems, particularly those disproportion-ately affecting African Americans. Not only that, but the district has one of the highest percentages of black students and staff in the country. With approximately 85 percent of its school teachers, and more than 90 percent of its students African American, this urban school district is conscious of itself as a place where black children should be educated well.

And yet, until 1988, when a new superintendent was brought in from outside the system to get the schools back on track, the district had long been headed by what is now thought of as a lackluster leadership, one that did little to make progressive strides in education. Despite the city's reputation as a progressive black-run city, the school district had not even entertained the idea of multicultural curricula by this late date. With a member of the old-guard, Alonzo Crim, occupying the superintendent's office until 1988, and another, Benjamin E. Mays, heading the school board for many years, the city's schools had stayed the course of mainstream, American inner-city public school education. Which is to say that it was not doing a very good job of educating children. Despite being the home to great African American political and social leaders, the city's school district had a failure rate rivaling any other urban district. The schools stood out as a public embarrassment to the city's reputation as a can-do political system run by prominent African American leaders.

By most accounts, including interviews with personnel that I conducted and from articles published in the local newspaper, the *Atlanta Journal-Constitution*, under Crim's and Mays's leadership there also developed a system of entrenched nepotism, favoritism, and mutual back-scratching among the largely African American, middle-class personnel employed by the Atlanta school district. With tentacles reaching up to top administrative positions and down to the hiring and firing of custodians who were relatives of school board members, the Atlanta school district administration of that era is now remembered as rife with routinized conflicts of interests and "status quo" politics. One of my interviewees, Murdell McFarlin, former public information officer for the superintendent's office in the late 1980s and early 1990s, had this to say about the political and social atmosphere in the district under the Crim administration:

> There were administrators, . . . principals, . . . directors—curriculum directors—who had held those positions for many years. Really, they had done nothing. . . . I don't want to say that they had done *nothing*, but their levels of achievement were minimal in terms of outcomes, of what had been produced: low test scores, high drop-out rates. That kind of thing. It was all a self-fulfilling. . . . I'm in this to see (a) how many Mercedes I can buy, (b) how many. . . . And I am serious! When I came to the system, 90 percent of the focus was on what you looked like. What you wore. What car you drove. Now, when I say 90 percent, I mean from your kindergarten teacher on up. . . . It's not good. It's a very sad commentary. And I feel very, very bad about it. Because (a)

I'm black, (b) I work for the system, (c) I have children that finished this system, (d) my husband works for the system, (e) it's run by blacks.[12]

If significant change was of interest to any constituency of the school district—inside or outside the boundaries of authorized decision making—it seemed unlikely to have come about under the pre–1988 administration.

Despite this lethargy on the part of many system leaders and staff, there were some members of the community and even some administrators and teachers in the district ranks who were not completely quiescent to the leadership style of their superiors. Citizens sometimes did try to push the district into taking innovative action on their children's behalf, as did proactive administrators. In 1987 during the Crim administration, for example, a Black Muslim church group called the Shrine of the Black Madonna began pressuring the Atlanta school board for more and better representation of African and African American contributions to world history in the public school curriculum. A typical "outsider" group, in that it was composed of people far from the levers of power within the school district, the Shrine was made up of students' parents and their religious leaders, who demanded that the district begin representing the history of Africa and African Americans differently in the curriculum. They sought to help district administrators recognize the glorious past of African kings and queens, making graphics of the African dynasties for use in Atlanta classrooms. Yet, despite their vociferousness and fierce support of the Afrocentric cause,[13] the groups' demands went unheeded for several months.

But not forever. As the demands became louder and the tenure of his position was winding down, Superintendent Crim finally acknowledged the demands of the Shrine of the Black Madonna and other community groups. In what can only be seen as a concession to parental concerns, the superintendent appointed a committee called the Black Studies Planning Group to work with the department of program planning and development to "expand what existed"—what *little* already existed concerning African roots, according to sources—in the district curriculum.[14] After long months of lobbying for their cause, the Shrine and its fellow activists finally gained a voice in school affairs around this issue: along with faculty from local universities, local business people, and school district staff, members of the Shrine served on the Black Studies Planning Group.

And yet, while Crim was in office, the planning committee's status was low, and the committee never progressed to the level of issuing any recommendations, despite staying in place for years. It might have made progress, given the commitment of several of its members, including officials from the district administration. But the administration under Crim did not support it strongly, according to one district administrator with whom

I spoke, curriculum specialist Mae Kendall, and according to *The Atlanta Journal-Constitution*. And so whatever gains the committee might have made were obviated by the leadership's lack of care.[15]

A New Administration, A Set of New Possibilities

In 1988, the ground shifted in Atlanta. Despite a contentious vote on the school board—a body long known for its fractiousness along the lines of race, the section of the city from which members hailed, and just plain personality clashes—members split the vote 5–4 to hire J. Jerome Harris as the next superintendent of the Atlanta public schools. The consequences of the board's selection for Afrocentric reform were to be considerable, although this was not immediately visible to those who had elected Harris to the helm.

Having served as the community superintendent for the New York Board of Education in Brooklyn, New York, Harris had a reputation as an aggressive, take-no-prisoners administrator. While being recruited for the Atlanta position, Harris had pledged to the school board that he would take a "get-tough" attitude with the district's schools, so that it could become "the first successful predominantly black inner-city school system in the country."[16] Describing Atlanta's failure to teach its children well, Harris was quoted just a few months into his new position, saying, "Because we're governed by black folks, run by black folks and taught by black folks, the message sent out [by low test scores in the district] is too strong, and it must be stopped."[17] His plans to correct this problem struck fear in the hearts of many in the district, and included a number of policies with which several members of the board, his administrative staff, and, foremost, teachers, strongly disagreed. He promised to close unsuccessful schools in the district, reconfigure administrative ranks, move teachers around to other schools following closings, enforce what he called "stand-up teaching," and lay off bad teachers. His start date in the district of August 1, 1988, was greeted with much apprehension throughout the system, from the members of the board down to the teaching corps.

Others in the district, however, were excited by his arrival, regarding it as a needed corrective to years of neglect that black children had received in the Atlanta schools. Staff who had grown weary of the stagnation among their colleagues looked to Harris as their leader, the superintendent who could usher them out of the morass of the status quo. Board members who had voted him in believed that his aggressive stances toward incompetent teaching, low test scores, and under-performance throughout the district would result in programs that could effectively root out the problem. The *Atlanta Journal-Constitution* editorialized that his readiness to do combat with the entrenched system was precisely what the schools needed. Teachers who had been frustrated by the implacability of previous administrations trusted Harris to reward their efforts. So, among the ranks of many of the school district's closest observers, there existed great anticipation about the energy and the programs Harris would introduce into the system. But whether Afrocentrism would be part of Harris' get-tough plan remained to be seen.

Proposing African American Infusion: Confusion Surrounding Its Origins

As we will see in the chronology of the African American Infusion Program, one of the most fascinating aspects of the Atlanta public schools' ultimate decision to introduce an Afrocentric curriculum into the district is that several parties have taken credit for it, and in the city of Atlanta, many accounts coexist, to this day, over who actually proposed the program, and how it was acted on. Having consulted with several actors who were involved in some way with its development, I now have collected a number of versions of its origins. Seeking triangulation of data through newspaper accounts, interviews with participants (ranging from school board members to the district's archivist), and school board minutes, I have tried to clear up the ambiguity that surrounds the sources of the program's founding. I have been only partially successful.

Frustrating though ambiguity is, I have decided to make a benefit out of a situation that otherwise could be considered a research conundrum. I have concluded that I should consider it important data that there are nearly as many "origin myths" surrounding African American Infusion in Atlanta as there are people to tell it. Whether one trusts administrators, board members, or journalists to give the most accurate account depends both on one's own predilections and institutional location and the parsimony of their account. I, as an outside investigator with no vested interests, find myself with a troubling *Rashomon* sensibility on this: like the filmmaker Akira Kurosawa's filmed fable, I suspect that the true story lies somewhere at the crossroads of the following narratives, and that the divergent accounts say much about the interests and placement of people who are telling each version. Nevertheless, I lean heavily toward the second narrative account listed below, given the frequency with which I heard it and the administrative positions of those who told it.

STORY 1 OF THE PROGRAM'S CONCEPTION AND INCEPTION: HARRIS DID IT, BUT ONLY UNDER DURESS. One story that has made the rounds among school staff and the Atlanta community is that while Superintendent Har-

ris may have entered the Atlanta system with myriad, take-charge programs for raising the performance of Atlanta schoolchildren, the infusion
of African American materials into the curriculum was *not* among them.
The *Atlanta Journal-Constitution* published an article in early 1989 reporting that Harris had brushed off parent demands (predominantly from
Shrine of the Black Madonna members) that the schools infuse African
American content into the curriculum to raise children's self-esteem. Having introduced the argument that children's sense of self and academic
performance were being irreparably harmed by schools that neglected to
teach them about the past eminence of Africa, the newspaper reported
that Harris told Shrine members that he did not agree with these requests.
His position: that the district had to concentrate on children's *academic
performance* in the basic disciplines, not on their self-esteem. He also was
quoted as saying that teaching children about their heritage was parents'
responsibility, and was unrelated to the job of public education, according
to one member of his staff, Gladys Twyman, who herself had heard this
story second-hand.[18]

In this narrataive of the superintendent-as-reluctant-Afrocentric-sup-
porter, Harris held fast to his stated priorities until, one day, he had an
epiphany about the Afrocentric cause. His change of heart was due, it is
said, to a series of conversations he had begun holding with other members of an organization called the National Alliance of Black School Educators (NABSE—of which Harris was president), an organization that
counted among its members many advocates of Afrocentrism, or African
American Infusion, including Asa Hilliard of Georgia State University.
According to this account, it was out of this series of meetings that Harris
decided that black children in his school district must, indeed, learn that
theirs is a heritage filled with past glories, and that Afrocentrism was the
correct route for gaining that knowledge. The arguments that had
sounded thin when the Shrine members made them now rang true to Superintendent Harris: there *was* a problem with black children's performance that *could* be corrected by Afrocentric materials. Where once he
had responded that no academic performance in the district was so low
that it should be corrected by Afrocentrism, Harris was now arguing that
African American children could not afford another year in school without learning of their ancestors' contributions to world history. In December 1988, just five months after his start date as superintendent, Harris
was presenting his ideas about Afrocentrism at the Atlanta Conference
on Educating Black Children, where he argued that "black educators
must do more to instill pride in inner-city students. For young blacks, the
key to self-esteem is knowing about the history of black people and their
achievements." Jawanza Kunjufu, a prominent Afrocentric scholar (who

wrote *Countering the Conspiracy to Destroy Black Boys*, also presided at the conference.[19]

In this version of events, Harris' conversion to the wisdom of Afrocentrism gave infusion the jumpstart it needed in the district: When Dr. Harris took that stance for the first time in public, "that's when the big push came to mobilize more quickly," said Asa Hilliard, the Georgia State University professor, in retrospect.[20] As Harris conceived of it now, the goal of the infusion program was to "put emphasis on the contributions of blacks in every subject area at every grade level."[21] His idea was to tap into this new area of scholarship, educate the thousands of teachers in Atlanta schools in the new knowledge that Afrocentrism represented, and have children learn about their distinguished pasts, thereby improving their academic performance.

Let's take a moment to pick up on the critical points in this version of events, which was advanced by one of my eight Atlanta interviewees. Until his "conversion," J. Jerome Harris, superintendent of the school district, had stalwartly rejected outsiders' efforts to convince him of the logic of Afrocentric curriculum. He counterargued, in fact, that community support for the "self-esteem" benefits of Afrocentrism was misguided. Like many others in the education world whom we will see in Washington, D.C., and New York, Harris was not swayed by the argument that self-esteem derives from Afrocentric scholarship. However, the argument for Afrocentrism became far more convincing to Harris—again, who like the Portland superintendent, might be considered to hold a consummate "insider" position in the school system—when it was advanced by differently positioned "outsiders": a group of academics and other high-status black educators from across the country. Hearing the support for Afrocentrism from these figures triggered Harris' own support for an Afrocentric program—support that he intended to be contagious among his staff and on the school board.

STORY 2 OF THE PROGRAM'S CONCEPTION AND INCEPTION: HARRIS HAD THE IDEA FROM THE BEGINNING OF HIS TENURE. A second version of events surrounding the program's lineage—the version advanced by three other of Harris's deputies with whom I spoke, Murdell McFarlin, his public information officer at the time; Mae Kendall, his curriculum director; and Cathy Loving, the school district's archivist—follows many of the same lines as advanced in story 1, except for one major difference. McFarlin, Kendall, and Loving recount that Harris joined the Atlanta school system with an Afrocentric program *already* conceived, and that he even used it as a selling point with the board to be selected as superintendent. According to Mae Kendall, the germ of the Infusion program was contained in Harris' philosophy that "All children can learn," and that black children's education will be "more profound and lasting if it is based on subsequent truths of their personal heritage."[22]

In this version of events, Harris entered the school district committed even then to the Afrocentric cause, but proceeded cautiously with his agenda so as not to incur the suspicion of school board members. Remember that this was a district with a legacy of conflict and political posturing—both of which were reportedly widespread at every level of the system. Harris, a strategic and shrewd actor according to all observers (both detractors and fans), put his plan, his "baby," into action, according to Cathy Loving,[23] by organizing key professionals inside the district to work on the theory and practical implementation of African American infusion before even mentioning the issue to the school board. Knowing that the board was a fractious body, marked by extreme sensitivity to his renegade swagger and ideas, Harris considered it wiser to present a well-researched and complete Afrocentric proposal to the board at a later date, rather than an abstract vision at an earlier one. Among the key people Harris brought together for the project, according to McFarlin, Kendall, and Loving, was the hometown scholar Asa Hilliard and the district's curriculum personnel, which included curriculum director Mae Kendall and members of her staff from each discipline. These three interviewees reported that during this time Hilliard worked with the curriculum coordinators on infusion materials and arranged for other Afrocentric scholars from across the country to provide in-service training to all staff coordinators. With Harris's approval, the Portland *Baseline Essays* were used at this stage to introduce Afrocentric concepts to high-level curriculum staff, according to a project coordinator, Gladys Twyman.[24]

In April 1989, after several months of work, Harris's group of consultants and administrators finished their preliminary work on the Infusion proposal, according to Mae Kendall, and the superintendent presented his case for Afrocentrism to the school board. Expressing the Afrocentric argument that children will learn better when they see people like themselves represented in the curriculum, the board adopted Harris's vision and voted to allocate $1 million to initiate and support the project. It happened as smoothly as that: unanimous support for the African American Infusion Program. While we must bear in mind that there is some disagreement over whether this sequence of events accurately depicts the origins of the Infusion program, there is one thing we do know without qualification: that board members—each one of them, in whatever sequence of events given—cast their ballots for the infusion project.

Whether or not this was a unanimously *enthusiastic* vote is up for debate. Interviews with several members of Harris's former staff, including Gladys Twyman and Murdell McFarlin, indicate that some white members of the board cast their affirmative votes with reservations, expressing a reluctance to spend so much money on a program that they believed was "not really needed" and which, they feared, would "turn the whole system black."[25] Cathy Loving, the district's archivist, says that Harris had to push for the program "against all odds" because many in the district did not want it, and because some board members and administrators "threw a hissy fit" over the financial resources that were to be devoted to it. Meanwhile, others in the district and at the *Atlanta Journal-Constitution* maintained that both black and white members enthusiastically embraced the proposal.[26]

So, there is some confusion here. The role of outside challengers in story 2 (the Harris-leads-Afrocentric-curriculum narrative) is even smaller than their role in story 1 (in which the Shrine of the Black Madonna and university scholars had to work to impress their vision on the superintendent). But although stories 1 and 2 diverge in some details, in other ways, the stories are sufficiently consistent to lead us to the same endpoint. In both of these chronicles of events, we have a form of contention that took place largely on the professional inside of the district, with a superintendent who sought to convince his board of the benefits of Afrocentrism. In the next account we will see a continued small presence for "outside" challengers, while those who are said to have championed the program switch identities.

STORY 3 OF THE PROGRAM'S CONCEPTION AND INCEPTION: THE MEDIA'S CHRONOLOGY OF EVENTS AND THE ACCOUNT OF HOW YET ANOTHER MEMBER OF THE BOARD PROPOSED THE PROGRAM. Providing a third version of how the African American Infusion Program found its way into the Atlanta school system was the *Atlanta Journal-Constitution* and its editorial writers and education reporters, including Betsy White (now Betsy Hammond), a reporter with whom I first spoke in 1995 and then again in 2000.

For two years prior to Harris' arrival in Atlanta, the city's major newspaper had been playing an interesting role in bringing the issue of infusion to the public's attention. It had been doing this by shaming the city, in effect, for not having already implemented a program like Portland's. In January 1989, for instance, The *Atlanta Journal-Constitution* ran several articles that detailed the neglect of black history in the Atlanta board-approved textbook on Georgia history. "While Atlanta school officials have spoken for several years about the need to 'infuse' information about Africans and black Americans into the entire curriculum," stated the article, referring to Superintendent Crim's administration, "their rhetoric, so far, has done little to change the typical course of study for Atlanta students." The writer noted that even the preponderance of black teachers in the school district had had surprisingly little effect on better teaching about African and African American contributions to society. The article also indicted the Black Studies Planning Group (the group that had been appointed in 1987) for having made no concrete recommendations for how to infuse materials about Africans and African Americans into the curriculum.[27] Another article published on the same day praised white Portland's leading role in drafting an African American infused curriculum, and it discussed the role that Atlanta's own Asa Hilliard played in guiding school officials in drafting the *Baseline Essays*, noting the cruel irony of Atlanta's local hero being better supported by a distant city.[28]

As for the history of the program's actual formulation in the district, the *Atlanta Journal-Constitution* named a third person as initiator: Robert Waymer, an African American member of the school board who had become committed to the Afrocentric concept before Harris had ever even arrived on the scene as superintendent. According to the newspaper's account, Waymer moved to commit $1 million to the project in April 1989 (at the same meeting that was said to have entertained Harris's proposal, according to the first two accounts), and the proposal was unanimously approved.[29] In an interview several years after the fact, the reporter, Betsy White, reiterated the paper's chronology of events, even though that chronology differs from the other accounts I have outlined above. She said that it was "definitely" Waymer who suggested the African American Infusion Program, and that he did so because he wanted to show that he had some power in the face of a strong superintendent and a powerful district comptroller.[30] Whatever his reasons for proposing the funding, however, Waymer's plan "raised [the project's] profile and potentially accelerated the timetable," according to a later interview with the same reporter.[31]

When asked about this account of the infusion program's inception, both Murdell McFarlin, the spokeswoman who once worked for Superintendent Harris, and Cathy Loving, the archivist, maintained again that Harris was the genius behind the program, and that if Robert Waymer or any other board member claimed credit for infusion, it could only be for *supporting* the superintendent in his plan, not for *proposing* the program.[32]

Whatever the Original Source, the Program Is Instituted

As we can see by the accounts given above, there is a good deal of confusion over where the African American Infusion Program came from and who in the various ranks of the district organization were full-fledged supporters of the reform.[33] Despite the different claims of credit, however, a couple of things are certain. First, the "framing" of the project differed little from version to version. Whoever was making arguments for African American infusion using familiar symbols and images, those supporters argued that the *problem* of African American children's failure in the district would be much aided by the *solution* of Afrocentrism. A critical path for aiding children's ability to learn, according to this framing of the argument, was to teach them Afrocentric concepts. These concepts would give them self-esteem and would correct the current Eurocentric account of world history, and from this, children's performance would improve. Second, with support from various actors inside the district, African American infusion was implemented in kindergarten through fifth grade beginning in 1989 and, in subsequent years, it has expanded to the higher grades and has received several million dollars of funding, according to the project's coordinator Gladys Twyman.

And, no matter which of these versions of the facts is most accurate, Atlanta represents a case in which district personnel, at a variety of levels and locations in the hierarchy, supported Afrocentric materials—both in word and deed, where "word" signified public rhetorical support for the claims of Afrocentrism's benefits, and "deed" signified financial support. Yes, there were some signs that not everyone supported the idea in its entirety, but for all intents and purposes, consensus ruled the day for Afrocentric reform in Atlanta: among professional education insiders (like the superintendent and some of his staff), political education insiders (such as school board members who had been elected to represent their constituency), and media writers and community activists. To that end, the district has now funded the program to the tune of several millions of dollars, with moneys divided among three main areas: (1) purchasing the *Baseline Essays* from Portland and other curriculum materials in later years, (2) buying supplemental materials like posters and maps to be used in the classroom, and (3) developing and providing in-service training for teachers and administrators. The movement had originated and mobilized support. But what of the outcomes in the district: would they continue on the path of success?

Obstacles to Complete Infusion

Once the argument for infusion had been agreed upon, the big decisions were yet to come in the district. For, after the large sum of money had been committed to the program, it was up to district administrators to further develop infusion materials, train teachers in the basics of Afrocentric scholarship, and try to convince those same teachers actually to incorporate the new materials into their curricula so that it would reach the students who were said to need it. The district's task was huge, despite the enthusiasm that surrounded the idea of infusion in corners of the system.

The first step in infusing the new program throughout the district was to pilot the program. A year after the board had voted to support African

American infusion, the district hired outside scholars, like Asa Hilliard and Ivan Van Sertima, to train administrative staff in the new knowledge and techniques constituting Afrocentric learning. The district also purchased tens of thousands of dollars worth of materials to include in the training sessions for teachers. Having taken these preliminary steps to educate a corps of district leaders in the knowledge base of Afrocentric thought, the school system began taking applications from area schools to serve as pilot schools. In each pilot school, a contact person went through at least eighty hours of training, receiving the same materials and access to experts that the central administrators had received.[34]

Once the pilot program was underway, then began the system-wide teacher-training program, in which virtually all teachers in the district attended sessions where they learned about the new curriculum. These teacher "in-services" constituted the bulk of program funding, with each teacher receiving $300 for his or her efforts, and with substitutes hired for each teacher out each day.[35] The Portland *Baseline Essays* were used as the primary text in this training, with supplementary materials coming from identifiably Afrocentric works such as Van Sertima's *They Came Before Columbus* and non-Afrocentric authors as well, such as John Hope Franklin's *From Slavery to Freedom: A History of Negro Americans*.[36] The scholars—which again included some of Afrocentrism's best-known advocates, like Hilliard—were also on hand to deliver lectures to the corps of teacher trainees. The in-services trained teachers in both "content" that could be used in a revamped, infused curriculum, including information on ancient Egypt, blacks' influence on mathematical theory, aviation, medicine, etc., as well as "applications" in the classroom. The district gave all teachers their own copy of the *Baseline Essays* in the training sessions.

By 1995, six years after the program's initial funding, the Atlanta school district had trained nearly every teacher in its ranks in African American infusion. Curriculum personnel whom I interviewed in 1995 insisted that teachers were overwhelmingly receptive to the training and new materials. Yet when asked if there had been any resistance among teachers to the infusion project, these same personnel were not shy about reporting the occasional presence of stubborn personnel. There were, in fact, two major types of resistance that recalcitrant teachers engaged in, said my interviewees. One type involved teachers who simply did not want to take the time to be trained in new methods or new lessons and, so, held off on training for as long as possible, sometimes years. These teachers were as likely to be black as they were to be white. The second type of resistance, however, came from white teachers who thought infusion was inappropriate for their classrooms. Resistance, said my interviewees, would be expressed through crocheting, knitting, or reading during training, or it would come in the form of disparaging evaluation comments turned in at the end of a session. Also during teacher training, school district administrators received phone calls from "rednecks" and "white professionals," who complained bitterly about the forced "indoctrination" of Afrocentrism, one trainer told me.[37] Also during this period, according to the journalist Betsy White, the *Atlanta Journal-Constitution* began receiving outraged phone calls from whom she guessed were the "husbands [of] white teachers" going through African American infusion training, complaining of brainwashing and lies.[38] In other words, it was when teacher training began that a faction of education insiders—this time practitioners, or teachers—began resisting the change.

Whither District Politics Post-1990 and the Infusion Program along with Them?

For a variety of reasons related to the history of Afrocentrism in Atlanta, but that are not germane to it, within two years of selecting J. Jerome Harris for the position of superintendent, the Atlanta school board decided to fire him; the school board, itself, underwent radical personnel changes amidst highly charged elections; and several staff who had been allied with the superintendent and his reforms resigned from the school district expressing dissatisfaction. In the rubble of all of these changes, twelve years later, the African American Infusion Program still stands.

But it is a reduced program. While African American infusion lives and breathes to this day, its main proponents have left the district, either by force or by will of their own. Without the strong support of these committed administrators and board members, fervor in the district for the program has greatly diminished.[39] In other words, the infusion program started with a big bang, but its firepower dimmed noticeably over the years.

Betsy White, then of the *Atlanta Journal-Constitution*, has several theories about how the infusion program is faring to date, and why it has not resulted in the kinds of district-wide classroom reforms it promised in the beginning, even with the continued expressions of support it receives in the district. She suggests that a variety of factors have limited the program's impact, despite its symbolic prominence: an old teaching staff that already has a tough job of educating kids and doesn't want to incorporate new information into its lesson plans; the lack of serious commitment within the administration (because many of Harris's allies among administrators left the district after he was fired); the difficulty of using the *Baseline Essays*—even for teachers who would like to—since they are not grade-specific. Perhaps White's most interesting theory, however, is that many teachers in the district (perhaps, especially, white teachers) have chosen to opt out of teaching the materials in the African American Infusion Program because there is no clear incentive for them actually to teach the program. Because district-wide standardized tests do not cover Afrocentric materials, teachers who don't want to teach the materials simply ignore them. Betsy White believes that district administrators understood all along that teachers would be able to opt out of teaching the revised curriculum, and that those same administrators did not close off such a possibility. In effect, according to White, administrators—both in Harris's time and thereafter—manufactured a "token victory" for their Afrocentric challengers, such that the constituents who demanded Afrocentric reform believed that they had won real concessions from their adversaries, while teachers opposed to the change did not feel pressure to partake of the new curriculum materials. I will describe this result as an *organizational* feature of the district in more detail in chapter 4.

While Gladys Twyman, the director of the infusion program, does not buy into White's description of the failure of the program to make substantive change, she does acknowledge the journalist's point that some in the district have been less committed to the African-centered curriculum than others. A formal evaluation of the program in 1990 showed that Afrocentric instruction in the schools was uneven, with some teachers incorporating more Afrocentric materials into their lesson plans than others—further evidence that teachers have autonomy in their approach to the program.[40] Twyman uses even more precision to pinpoint this variation: she concedes that schools in the northern area of Atlanta—which is home to a larger population of white teachers and students—use the African-related materials less than teachers and students in other parts of town.

While White describes the possible conditions that allowed African American infusion to falter, and Twyman provides details on the gaps in the program's delivery in the schools, others internal to the district offer more sanguine assessments of the program's longevity and efficacy. Midge Sweet, a white member of the school board fairly new to the governing body when I interviewed her in 1995, for example, argues that she has been nothing but completely satisfied with the direction that the African American Infusion Program has taken over the years. At one time, she thought, some of the training in the district—which was based on the *Baseline Essays*—had been "demagogic." Now, said Sweet, the district has swung around to a more "multicultural" education instead of just African American.[41] Children are learning less from the *Baseline Essays* than they once did, and are receiving more of their education from sanctioned multicultural materials than from Afrocentric sources. From Sweet's vantage point, this is a positive outcome.

As of 2001, the African American Infusion Program is still in place in Atlanta, offering the only year-round African-centered curriculum in art, history, math, music, science, and literature classes in the Southeast region.[42] If Afrocentrism has chalked up a "win" in any major school system, it is in Atlanta's. This success was borne of insider support for what began as outside pressure on the district to do things differently for African American children. And yet, for all its promise, I would argue that Afrocentrism did not penetrate to the core of the curriculum in the Atlanta school district. It is in many ways more of a paper victory than a practical one. Typified by what I am calling a "big bang" process of reform, Afrocentrism started strong out of the gate in Atlanta, but experienced a more qualified finish than we might have predicted, given its promising beginnings. Some teachers enthusiastically have used the new materials, while others have not; content has become more "multicultural," rather than "Afrocentric" over time; and administrative support for the program has visibly slackened. In Chapter 4, I'll provide the analytical tools for understanding this outcome. But for now, let us proceed to the challenge in Washington, DC.

"Circumscribed Reform" in the Nation's Capital: The Effort to Please All the People All the Time with a Program of Limited Scope in Washington D.C., 1989–94

If great expectations marked the atmosphere surrounding Atlanta's implementation of an African-American infusion program, did the same hold true for Washington, a school district whose racial profile closely resembled Atlanta's? Would rhetoric about schools' failure to educate African American children push Washington educators toward an Afrocentric curriculum, as it had in the Black Mecca of Atlanta? Or would the unique arrangement of political figures and organizational policies in the nation's capital lead to a different set of outcomes for Afrocentric claims?

Gamblers might have a hard time deciding where to place their bets on this one. On the one hand, Washington D.C.'s public school district is home to the highest percentage of minority students in the nation[43] (92 percent of them African American[44])—and it also exhibits indications of astronomical failure. The dropout rate in the district has hovered around 42 percent for years, and 98 percent of those dropouts are black.[45] Also like Atlanta, Washington has long been criticized for its inept and bloated school bureaucracy, unsuccessful in providing even a modicum of quality education to its 80,000 students.

On the other hand, Washington, D.C., during this time period struck a different pose in the public eye than did Atlanta. Unlike the Georgia city, there was nothing "can do" about any part of Washington's political image—neither in its schools nor in other parts of its governance. While, like Atlanta, it may have had one of the largest African-American middle-class populations in the nation, its city government in the 1980s and 1990s was hardly renowned for progressive policies improving the lives of its poorer denizens. And let us not forget, due to its proximity to the seat of federal power, this "deficient" city government finds itself not in-frequently at the center of a national discourse about the failure of urban areas to manage resources and control their problems. The governance of Washington, D.C., is often pointed to as a national disgrace.

So, did these realities create a venue for successful Afrocentric claims, or were challenger demands thwarted in the district? As I will describe below, a system of "circumscribed reform" came to typify Washington's experiences with the Afrocentric agenda—an outcome considerably dif-ferent in its details from either Atlanta's "big bang" compromise or the results we will see in New York. Nevertheless, Washington Afrocentrists' *ultimate* results will resemble the outcomes obtained in all six of the other cases in this book: schools found ways to minimize their inroads.

Historical Roots

Long before the late 1980s, when the District of Columbia had its first encounter with demands that its schools consider Afrocentric re-forms, a number of individual educators in the D.C. area had begun work on their own projects for incorporating greater African American content into their classrooms. Some of these teachers were located in the public school district, but most of them were part of a broader national movement of independent schools that had begun in the late 1960s. Dur-ing this time, for example, two educators named Abena and Kwaku Walker, a husband-and-wife team, were members of a national black in-dependent school movement, and laid the foundations for what they would later call the African Learning Center in Washington. Established in 1982 outside of the public schools, the Walkers' program emphasized both new scholarly content about Africa to be added to the curricula (as we have seen in Portland and Atlanta), as well as an ideology and methodology that, the Walkers said, diverged from traditional methods used in American public schools. These methods, which stressed "cooper-ative" and "more loving" learning, were said to be based on African concepts that posited different models of interaction between children and their teachers. In years to come, the Walkers would play a large role in D.C. Afrocentrism.

By the late 1970s, personnel employed by the district and working near the heart of all this independent activity, also began thinking about how to create a curriculum that would focus more attention on the contribu-

tions of African Americans. Under the superintendence of Floretta Mc-
Kenzie, teachers began developing coursework that would help district
children "know who they are" and that would stop them from "devaluing
themselves," according to one informant, Betty Topps, an aide in the superintendent's office.[46] But it was only later, in the late 1980s and early
1990s, that the Afrocentric movement, per se, actually took off in Washington. Its propulsion would be aided by three developments: first, the
emergence of an Afrocentric community action group, which pressed its
claims on the district; second, the hiring of a superintendent who, for
political reasons, would align himself with the Afrocentric cause; and
third, the headway that Afrocentric knowledge was beginning to make as
"legitimate scholarship" in the academy—particularly at Temple University (home of Molefi Asante) and Georgia State University (home of Asa
Hilliard). With these three developments, many actors in the district were
becoming more amenable to the possibility of a serious relationship with
Afrocentrism.

Let's look, first, at support for Afrocentrism that came from *inside* the
district. In 1988, contrary to what board members publicly said they were
looking for in a superintendent, the D.C. public school board selected a
long-term district staffer to succeed McKenzie as superintendent of the
system. They hired Andrew Jenkins, a thirty-year veteran of the district,
who had at one time or another over those years served as a teacher,
principal, administrator, and chief deputy to the former superintendent
of the D.C. schools. Jenkins' selection as superintendent was a surprise,
given that the school board had publicly announced its interest in "revi-
talizing" the administration by hiring from outside the district. But "buck-
l[ing] to community pressure"—particularly administrative pressure,
which was interested in seeing one of its colleagues selected for the position—on a vote of 6–5, the board chose Jenkins.[47] If board members
weren't expecting a revitalizer in this selection, its members at least
thought Jenkins would bring stability to the district, given his long-term
contact with personnel.[48] They were wrong.

Which is where the *outside* community activist group comes into the
picture. At just around the time that Jenkins was selected to hold the
superintendent's seat, an upstart community group called Operation
Know Thyself was organized in the district. Founded by Valencia Mohammed, a mother of six children in the D.C. schools, and by Hodari Ali,
the owner of an Afrocentric-oriented book store, Operation Know Thyself formed with the express purpose of petitioning the D.C. Board of
Education to develop and adopt an Afrocentric curriculum for its schools.
Betty Topps, assistant to the superintendent, recalls that Operation Know
Thyself's tactics were quite confrontational and "almost had a religious
fervor" to them. Their goal: to get the school system to address their

children's needs, particularly their need to "understand who they are."[49] Mohammed's and Ali's selling points for their program focused on its ability to increase esteem among black children by letting them know that Africans did "great, positive things," and to implement a curriculum that didn't just show the "Eurocentric" world, with Eurocentric values. Operation Know Thyself's primary interest in the program was to restore what they saw as the truth in the schools about blacks' contributions to world history.[50] Using this rhetoric, the group sounded very much like the Afrocentric challenge in Atlanta, or like anywhere else, for that matter.

Although it was an outside movement, Operation Know Thyself's framing of the problem struck a chord of recognition with district officials. In Spring 1989, Jenkins—new to the board and interested in charting a path for his superintendency—ordered school district staff to begin examining how black culture and history were taught in the city's schools. Taking up the charge, staff studied district social studies textbooks, teacher training materials, and lessons used during Black History Month. They compared these to other school districts' progress in this area— districts like Atlanta and Portland. Superintendent Jenkins went on record at the time saying that the district needed to "improve in this area." He pledged his commitment to an Afrocentric curriculum,[51] and to demonstrate that commitment, he appointed the African Centered Education Task Force.[52]

Involving personnel from inside the district as well as university faculty and community members from outside, the task force was asked to define what an African-centered education might mean for the district, both "ideologically and cognitively."[53] Although the committee was divided into those who leaned multicultural versus those who leaned more Afrocentric, its members agreed that the district should fund revised curricula emphasizing the contributions made to history by Africans and African Americans. When the superintendent approved of the committee's recommendation and sent it to the board, that body unanimously voted for the proposal, agreeing to spend $750,000 to incorporate African-centered learning in every subject area, in every grade in the district's 175 schools.[54] Afrocentrism seemed unstoppable.

But although it had just committed three-quarters of a million dollars to the development of a curriculum, no one in the district was clear about how the money should be spent. Specifically, there was no program in development at that point. School officials *did* support the program as a way to boost students' self-worth—which was, by extension, seen to be a means of stemming student violence, dropout rates, and poor test scores—they simply had no unified agenda for how that self-worth ought to be taught in their district. They sought proposals from both within the district and without for how to spend the allotted money.

The Walkers and the African-Centered School-within-a-School Model

Abena and Kwaku Walker comprised one party that welcomed the school system's newfound dedication to Afrocentric education. Responding to a district charter that requested outside proposals for innovative curricular programs, the Walkers submitted a forty-page document to Superintendent Jenkins, detailing their desire to develop an African-centered curriculum for a model school in the D.C. system.[55] Basing their proposal on their independently run African Learning Center, they proposed two main activities to the district: to implement African-centered education across the city, but first to pilot a model program at Webb Elementary School, a school in one of the poorest sections of the city. Their funding request targeted a portion of the $750,000 that had recently been committed to Afrocentric reform.

Echoing the main strands of Afrocentric pedagogy heard elsewhere in the country, the Walkers' proposal promised that the "African-centered method" would improve students' attendance, academic performance, character, and self-esteem. The proposal also proposed to use new techniques of African-centered teaching, including the training of teachers and parents in methodologies said to have emerged from Africa (such as "cooperative learning" and "dependence on love").[56] School board members found the ideas interesting, and in June 1990, Superintendent Jenkins agreed to a contract with the Walkers to train a group of ten teachers and several parents in Afrocentric content and techniques.[57] If the training were successful, the district, on Jenkins's word, promised Walker that she could open a small school-within-a-school program to educate a limited number of children. And so began one of the most controversial Afrocentric programs to arise in the nation, despite its relatively quiet and consensual beginnings.[58]

Entanglement in Politics

The year 1990 was a tumultuous one in the D.C. public school system, as the school board quickly grew tired of its compromised selection of Andrew Jenkins as superintendent. Not unlike the contention surrounding Atlanta's choice of superintendents, the governing board in the nation's capital also regretted the appointment it had made, although for different reasons. Critical of Jenkins's inability to handle problems and make visible reforms in the district (including such basic activities as getting an accurate count of the number of children enrolled in the district and hiring sufficient numbers of teachers to educate them), several board members were eager to get rid of their relatively new leader. To this end, the board held a series of private sessions to discuss firing the district superintendent.[59] The school board took its first formal action against Superintendent Jenkins in the summer of 1990, when members discussed buying out the final year of Jenkins's contract.[60] Board members went so far as to offer the superintendent $250,000 to step down a year before his contract was up.

When Jenkins heard about the board's plans to fire him, he shed his reputation for passivity and energized himself and his supporters to resist board action. And resist, he did, with the assistance of the parents who had recently rallied to his side in appreciation of his advocacy of Afrocentric education. He called on these advocates of Afrocentrism to protest the board action, and they showed up in large numbers upon his request. At the board meeting that was to have decided his fate, the presence of "100 cursing, jeering protesters" pressured the board to decide against firing him.[61] As the *Washington Post* reported on the meeting in a scolding tone, "the board reversed its commitment to firing Jenkins not because high-powered members of the city council had urged it, or because any other of the city's power-brokers had weighed in on the issue. The board reversed itself because of a group of demonstrators, which was composed of parents, teachers, and community activists."[62] Among these activists were members of Operation Know Thyself.

Perhaps in gratitude to the support of Afrocentric activists, shortly thereafter, Jenkins told a radio interviewer that Afrocentric education had become the centerpiece of his administration's reform program.[63] According to a Howard University professor, Russell Adams, Jenkins recognized that his continued tenure in the district depended on the support he could get from Afrocentric supporters. Without this constituency's support, he could not withstand the onslaught of the board's disgruntlement over his ineffectiveness in other areas. His newfound zealous commitment to Afrocentrism was a political bow to active community support.

Having made grudging temporary peace with Jenkins following the July decision to allow him to stay, members of the board could not suspend their frustration with Jenkins for long, and in Fall 1990, board members again focused their attention on his ouster.[64] With the support of the *Washington Post* editorial pages, which advised that members be resolute in their convictions for firing this time around, in December 1990, the school board voted 8–3 to dismiss Jenkins. Without mentioning the state of the Afrocentric curriculum in its decision, the board fired Jenkins for his laxity on a number of district issues.[65]

As in the earlier go-around during the summer, Jenkins strenuously attempted to keep his job. He had encouraged teachers and principals to leave their students during the day to protest at the board meeting, and he also had relied on his allies—among whom Operation Know Thyself members were the most active—to drop leaflets at schools encouraging students to skip classes so that they and their parents could attend.[66] The leafleting worked: approximately 400 protesters showed up at the meeting, and their presence created a melee. Immediately before the decision was announced to dismiss Jenkins, students, parents, and community activists threw debris at the board, and one board member was hit in the head with a glass pitcher. During the fracas, Jenkins made no effort to quell the disturbances, according to the *Post*, and, in fact, encouraged the protesters even more when he launched an "attack on the board, calling it an unethical, racist, power-hungry pawn of the *Washington Post*."[67] Among other accusations, Jenkins claimed that the board was undermining his plan to have schools put more emphasis on African heritage.

It is in this rhetoric that we are introduced to the second of three cultural resources that were invaluable to Afrocentric challengers. In addition to the articulation of a "problem" concerning children's educational performance and their self esteem, which we have already seen expressed in Portland, Atlanta, and Washington, Jenkins now also lobbed the charge of "racism" at his adversaries. Suddenly fearful that he was losing his position, this friend of Afrocentrism attempted to reverse fortunes by condemning his adversaries—the board of education—as hostile to black improvement. For a period following his immediate dismissal, Jenkins went on record repeatedly stating that he was fired predominantly because of his desire to introduce an Afrocentric curriculum to District schools, a curriculum that would benefit black children. Jenkins was heard on a radio talk show saying that it was not a coincidence that he was fired at precisely the time that he had initiated an interview process for a vice superintendent for Afrocentrism. He also charged that the board had no intention of going forward with the program, were he to be dismissed.[68] In short, Jenkins cast himself as a sacrificial lamb on the altar of racist antipathy toward the Afrocentric cause, leaving the system tense over the issue. Board members, meanwhile, insisted that they continued to support a revised curriculum.

The Arrival of a New Superintendent

The next two years in the D.C. public school system were marked by two significant personnel changes, as well as continued ambivalence surrounding Afrocentric education. In Spring 1991, the system became home to a new superintendent whose commitment to Afrocentrism was unclear and, presumably, weak. Five months after Jenkins's dismissal, the board announced that it had found the outsider it long had been seeking to take over as superintendent. The board appointed Franklin Smith—former head of Dayton, Ohio, schools—to be superintendent, hoping that he would somehow be able to improve their financially strapped, drop-out-ridden, bureaucratically top-heavy, and now politically riven school district.

Upon arriving in the district, Smith wasted little time registering his position on the Afrocentric curriculum that his predecessor had so strongly championed. Smith issued a statement saying that he was uninterested in backing away from a revised curriculum in the district, but that he was professionally committed to a *multicultural* curriculum instead of an Afrocentric one. In an interview with the *Washington Post* he clarified his views on the issue: "Quite obviously, with a population of 90 percent African . . . , you can't ignore the fact that an African-centered curriculum will be a major portion of that 'multiculture.' But I'm not going to be part of doing a *disservice* to our young people by just indoctrinating them with one culture when we live in a global society" (emphasis added).[69] Not surprisingly, such statements led to distress among advocates of Afrocentrism, especially when Smith seemed to "ghettoize" the Afrocentric / multicultural project by placing responsibility for its development in a less prominent part of the administration—the relatively low-status Values Education unit—than it had been in previously.[70] Nevertheless, even with this statement, the district continued to commit funds to African-centered pedagogy in the district, including the Walkers' school-within-a-school program at Webb.

In 1993, Things Fall Apart: Washington Erupts over African-Centered Education

If patience and good will had been noticeably frayed over the three years of planning an Afrocentric curriculum, from 1989–92, then 1993 was the year when the very last thread of diplomacy came undone in the District of Columbia Public Schools surrounding this issue. The racially antagonistic rhetoric of 1990 that surrounded the now ejected Superintendent Jenkins and his supporters was but a whisper of distrust compared to what was to come.

Recall that in 1990, Abena and Kwaku Walker applied for and received part of the $750,000 that the district had budgeted for incipient Afrocentric education programs; over the next two years, the Walkers had developed and begun testing their program outside of the school district with teachers and parents. In March 1993, now under the leadership of Superintendent Franklin Smith, the district's Office of Research and Evaluation issued a positive report of the proposed Walker curriculum and its teacher training at the Webb school, and in August of that year, after three years of development at a cost of some $260,000, the Walker program at Webb Elementary School was scheduled to begin as the district's first African-centered program, with kindergarten through sixth grades.[71]

But there was one hitch. As the school year approached, district administration—at the urging of the *Washington Post*—became unnerved that it had yet to see what it had paid for in the form of a curriculum for the African-centered school-within-a-school. A month prior to the first day of class, in fact, Abena Walker had yet to submit her teaching plan to the school board and administration. In a *Washington Post* report, Superintendent Smith and Thomasina Portis, then director of D.C.'s Values Education branch and Abena Walker's supervisor, admitted that they were still not sure over what would be taught to students in Walker's program, though they had been reassured by Walker that the curriculum was sound.[72]

It was at this point that a second issue also emerged to envelop the Walker curriculum in controversy. Beside the fact that a D.C. school was about to house her at-that-time unknown curriculum (a point that seemed scandalous enough to area journalists), the *Washington Post* discovered that Abena Walker's educational credentials were unconventional, and *inappropriate* by their own standards of legitimate credentials. The newspaper revealed that Abena Walker had granted herself a master's degree from her own nonaccredited Pan-African University, and that Pan-African University was also the site of teacher training for the Webb program. The *Washington Post*, hot on a story that its editors seemed to think illustrated so well the pathologies of the school district, was not about to let go. For the next several months, its writers turned absolutely vigilant in their excoriation of Walker, her curriculum, and the district's expenditures to both.

Reaction to the *Post's* revelations about the Webb program and Abena Walker were mixed and sometimes came from unlikely places. Once an ally of Abena Walker's in Operation Know Thyself, Valencia Mohammed had since been elected to the school board, in 1992. Given that Afrocentric education had been the issue that won her a place on the school board, one might have expected Mohammed to have defended Walker to the press. But instead, Mohammed expressed deep concern that Walker's lack of credentials would delegitimate the broader concept of Afrocentrism throughout the district and, for that reason, she withheld her official support for the Webb program.[73] She said this while also mentioning that she, herself, was developing a separate Afrocentric curriculum in the district. Meanwhile, David Hall, the school board president who had helped engineer Superintendent Jenkins's forced departure, won few admirers at the

Post when he went on record supporting Walker, saying that he was not concerned about her credentials. Said Hall, "Certification is not the most important thing. There are plenty of people with Ph.D.'s who can't teach. Do I want people with certification, or do I want children to learn?"[74]

One week later, in the midst of the controversy over her credentials, and now even closer to the district's school year start date, Abena Walker submitted for the first time a five-page curriculum plan (two pages on her classroom plan, three pages on teacher training) to Constance Clark, deputy superintendent for educational programs and operations in the district. The plan outlined how the African-centered classes would use the curriculum already in place in the district for those grades along with "the infusion of the history, culture, and contributions of Africans and African Americans and other races and ethnic groups" and "special programs in the arts, the martial arts, and African languages." Its "instructional methodology" would include "showing genuine love, concern for, and identification with students."[75]

But this seemed inadequate to Clark. Complaining that it lacked substance and details about pedagogy, supplies, and materials, the deputy superintendent of educational programs returned the five-page curriculum proposal to Walker two weeks before the school year began.[76] It should be noted that Deputy Superintendent Clark was no opponent of Afrocentrism, generally speaking. In fact, Clark was something of a fan of Afrocentric curricula, as those curricula had been put into practice elsewhere. She had seen "wonderful" model Afrocentric programs in her past travels to other school districts in the country: for example, in a Detroit academy for black boys (where she was "very impressed") and in Portland, Oregon, where she attended a conference on Afrocentric education (where the "excellent curriculum" based on Asa Hilliard's *Baseline Essays* left her "thoroughly impressed").[77] It was *this particular* Afrocentric curriculum proposal that Clark found deficient, the five-page outline that had been submitted by a now controversial outside proponent.

At the same time that Clark, a member of Smith's staff, deemed Walker's curriculum plan insufficient, however, the superintendent himself decided that the curriculum would be implemented in the school-within-a-school program. Having read enough of a subsequent "inch-thick" document submitted by Walker, he continued to support her work and planned for the African-centered classes to begin two weeks later at Webb. To a *Washington Post* reporter, Smith explained, "I'm not alarmed. I'm not uncomfortable. We don't have to have the whole year's curriculum in place. You can always revise it in part."[78] Regarding his faith in the director of the program, Smith reiterated, "Here's a person who has been working with the program in our system and been training our teachers and has the respect of the parents of the children in the program. Why should I be, all of a sudden, concerned?"[79] It probably didn't hurt the program's chances, to put it mildly, that during this time, Smith had also met with nearly fifty parents whose children were slated to attend Webb and who themselves had gone through Walker's parents' training. In this meeting, Smith witnessed first-hand parents' die-hard support for Walker and the school.[80] These parents were outraged that Smith had consulted with other Afrocentric experts during this time (he had brought in both Asa Hilliard and Molefi Asante during the tensest days of controversy), and the parents no doubt impressed Smith with their willingness to oppose the superintendent in the next appointment cycle if he turned his back on them.

The dominant local media seemed unimpressed by the political pressure Superintendent Smith undoubtedly was under, however, and the *Washington Post* targeted Abena Walker's lack of conventional credentials and the Webb program's purported lack of curriculum for intense critique for several months in Fall 1993. In addition to the near-daily news accounts published about the district's decision making over whether or not to proceed with the Webb program (from August–October, 1993), the *Post* printed more than a dozen editorials and opinion-editorials about the local program in that same time frame. Of these editorials, only two were favorable toward Abena Walker, her program, and the sponsoring district. The rest were critical, when not overtly hostile. While the *Washington Post* was not the only media outlet in town—some of the district's black-owned newspapers and radio stations threw their support behind the African-centered program—the prominent newspaper did carry the most weight in the nation's capital, and propagated negative information about the program to a national audience.

Weighing Criticisms and Support for the Program: The Superintendent's Call to Expand

Obviously, 1993 was neither a fantasy public relations year for the Washington, D.C., school district nor a banner year for the concept of Afrocentric education. Day after day the media presented more incriminating data in an effort to discredit Walker's program at Webb, and the most the district could do, it seemed, was try to duck the barrage. By the end of the year, neither Abena Walker nor Superintendent Smith had released a detailed curriculum outlining the content of the current Webb classes, and the *Post* seemed to have been vindicated in its attacks on the superintendent and his underlings.[81]

And yet, in July 1994, before an official evaluation had been made of the program and released to the public, and in the epicenter of what could have become another seismic reaction to news of the Webb program, Superintendent Smith announced his decision to expand the Webb program from its current six classrooms to seven classrooms, so that it now included a seventh-grade class. Smith said that he had decided (without the board's input) to expand the program, based on his own observations of its success, comments from parents, and the feeling that the classes needed another year before they could be fairly evaluated. In making his announcement, Smith—tellingly—said that the program met the demands of parents and appeared to have had no negative effect on children's education. It may not have "made as much progress academically or developmentally as I had hoped, but I don't think we did any harm," said Smith.[82]

Smith's decision to expand the program by this very small increment was motivated, in all likelihood, by twin desires: to satisfy Walker's supporters by giving them what they wanted, while also keeping the rest of the district off-limits to the Walker approach. In subsequent years (until he was released in 1996), Smith kept the school-within-a-school program open, albeit highly contained. Lacking the will either to expand it significantly or cut it out entirely, the school district allowed Abena Walker's curriculum to stay in place, and even to increase by a classroom here and there. Even after a six-month study comparing Webb to a comparable school revealed that the Walker curriculum led to more parental involvement, better self-esteem among students, higher test scores on the Comprehensive Tests of Basic Skills, and less disruptive behavior in the classroom, the district continued to keep the program tightly bounded, particularly in contrast to the flagship African-American Multicultural High School that the district had opened in another part of town.[83]

Nevertheless, by 1998, Walker's school was in its sixth year with some 150 students, and yet another grade was added to the school-within-a-school program (now kindergarten through eighth grade).[84] Undaunted by the institutional hoops that they had always been forced to jump through, Walker and her teachers and parents geared up to fight several more times for more space, first, so that they could add a preschool and a ninth grade, and then ultimately to expand the program to twelfth grade and to get out of the Webb location and into their own building.[85] Abena Walker and her supporters were steeled to hang in and fight.

So, Afrocentrists' outcomes in Washington had a different tenor, compared to the outcomes achieved by challengers in Atlanta. In response to community demands, the Washington school administration conceded only what I am calling "circumscribed reform": pure Afrocentric content and methods, yes, but for just one small program, and for only a limited number of teachers and students, and only in the poorest section of the district—but where parents were demanding it most ardently. Washington's African-Centered Program at the Webb School has remained a small school-within-a-school program without serious possibilities for expansion, and it has constantly battled a skeptical, critical, and vocal *Washington Post* throughout its short history.

Nevertheless, it would be a mistake to say that Atlanta's challengers "succeeded" where D.C.'s "failed." Clearly, it would be a difficult—and probably untenable—task to try to measure outcomes using the same metric from case to case. We should see, instead, that there are different kinds of success and different kinds of failure experienced by Afrocentric challengers. To the degree that the Washington school district did accommodate an Afrocentric proposal for reform, we can say that Walker and her colleagues enjoyed some success. Success was limited, of course, to just one part of one school, but the intensity of those reforms was high. Atlanta, in contrast, promised that all classrooms across the district would have access to Afrocentric materials. But there, the incorporation of these materials into actual teaching was highly variable and, in fact, not really knowable. Intensity in Atlanta, we should say, was weak, while its scope was far-reaching. Such are the lessons gained from an examination of two of the three Afrocentric cases.

"Outright Rejection" in the Empire State: The Wrenching and Publicly Vilified Process of Revising the New York State Social Studies Curriculum Framework, 1987–95

Compared to either Atlanta or Washington, D.C., New York state presents a rather different sort of case in which challengers attempted to introduce Afrocentric reforms. It is different in terms of the location of the school system in the educational structure, the outcomes that resulted there, and even whether it can be labeled a case of "Afrocentric" effort, in the first place. It was only at the beginning of the battle that the New York case might rightfully be said to have been at least partially about "Afrocentrism"—as opposed to "multiculturalism" in ensuing years— but I include it in this comparison of three Afrocentric challenges because it speaks loudly to the issue of how efforts that were *perceived* to be, or *constructed* to be, Afrocentric-inspired were handled in school systems where there was little insider or outside support for the challenge. In the pages that follow, I will demonstrate that the demands for revisions in New York were dubbed "Afrocentric," and that this negative labeling affected the chances of acceptance of even subsequent *multicultural* revisions in the state. While education decision makers leached out, from very early on, all specifically Afrocentric components of the challenge, leaving only a brand of multiculturalism to be dealt with, their critics continually labeled their actions as Afrocentric-initiated. Because of the state education department's determination to separate itself from any Afrocentric content, I call New York state schools' response to Afrocentrism "outright rejection."

Despite the outright rejection they faced, however, Afrocentric challengers in New York still had their moment in the spotlight. As one component of a larger challenge, supporters of Afrocentrism pushed the state commissioner at least to take seriously their claims about the problematic education of African American children. The polite reception of their ideas, followed by hostile rejection may not fit anyone's definition of "success," but it is a powerful demonstration of Afrocentrists' ability at least to get their ideas on the educational agenda.

The Complaints

This case begins in March 1987, when the New York State Board of Regents selected Thomas Sobol to become the State Commissioner of Education, a position serving 2.5 million children throughout the state. Until that time, Sobol had served as superintendent of the Scarsdale school district in Westchester County, New York, where most of his charges were not only white, but middle class to upper-middle class as well. The selection of Sobol did not please all of the state's constituencies, particularly black and Hispanic state legislators, who believed that they had been promised a black commissioner.[86] In fact, Sobol was not even the Regents' first choice, an honor that belonged to a black former deputy chancellor of the New York City school system, who rejected the job offer.[87]

Stepping into this fray, Sobol moved quickly to extend a peace offering to his most vocal critics.[88] In the first months of his tenure as commissioner, Sobol appointed several advisory groups to deal with minority issues, among them, the Task Force on the Education of Children and Youth at Risk, which later issued a report criticizing the state for having a two-tiered education system, "one largely suburban, white, affluent, and successful; the other, largely urban, of color, poor, and failing."[89] The most famous, or infamous, of his appointed commissions, however, and the one that ended up casting a pall over Sobol's entire tenure as commissioner, was the seventeen-member Task Force on Minorities: Equity and Excellence. By November of his first year as commissioner (just four months into his post), Sobol had asked this group to determine whether the state's curriculum guides "adequately reflect[ed] the pluralistic nature of our society."[90]

To Sobol's chagrin, most public accounts of the commissioner's decision to appoint the task force (including all articles published in the *New York Times* around this time) argued that this was purely a political move.

They proposed that this white commissioner, who had just come from one of the wealthiest and whitest districts in the state, wanted to prove that he had African Americans' interests in mind, and that he was responsive to their concerns.[91] But not only was the appointment of this committee political, according to many of these critics, it was also absurd and a waste of resources. This was an outrageous time to be empanelling a new group to examine the curriculum, his critics argued, since the state's ninth- and tenth-grade social studies sequence *only that year* had been completely overhauled to reflect global cultures. Led by a team of Department of Education staff and appointed consultants (including the historian Eric Foner), the state had just put into place an unprecedented diverse course of study: a two-year world history sequence divided equally among Western Europe, Latin America, Africa, and other areas.[92]

Advocates of the new task force, however, were unmoved by these recent changes to the history curriculum. Many critics in the state—including those who identified more as "multiculturalists" than as "Afrocentrists"—complained that the 1987 revisions were merely "mentioning," or "contribution," history. In "contribution history," said critics, other groups besides white males are added to history books not as central actors contributing to the historical narrative but as incidentals to the plot, trivialized in side bars and "special interest" pages, marginalized as "curiosities."[93] Making claims not unlike those previously heard in Atlanta and Washington, D.C., champions of the first task force cited biased curricula as problems that could be solved by a history curriculum that went further than any previous revisions to represent hitherto neglected peoples. Commissioner Sobol said that he himself found the intentions of the 1987 revisions to be "honorable," but agreed with his political critics that the revisions contained "too many gaps," and required further critique and development. To provide this critique, Sobol appointed to the task force some of his own harshest critics to represent different racial and ethnic groups.[94] As future media writers would frequently point out, only one member of the new seventeen-person advisory group was white.

The "Curriculum of Inclusion" Report

By appointing the Task Force on Minorities, Commissioner Sobol explicitly acknowledged the legitimacy of his critics' two strong claims, which we have seen before: that there very well may have been a "problem" of European overemphasis in the school system that the 1987 revisions had not corrected, and that angry African American and Hispanic groups across the state had a right to investigate school curricula for biases in their children's education. But I would like to suggest that Sobol's appointment of this group also indicated the power of a third kind of cultural resource that Afrocentrists had in their arsenal, but which I have not yet addressed. By recognizing as reasonable the claim that history and social studies classes across the state should incorporate the experiences of greater numbers and groups of peoples than ever before represented, Sobol was, in effect, lending credence to the claim that the social sciences and humanities are *flexible enough* to accommodate a range of social goals besides educational ones. The teaching of history—or English courses, for that matter—cannot remain as they are, according to this claim, as long as certain societal groups believe themselves to be underrepresented by their content. And the social studies and language courses are ideal places to be making these changes because these disciplines are *negotiable*.

I write about this cultural resource for the first time as if it emerged out of the blue in New York, although, of course, this is not the case. In fact, it is no surprise that the challengers in New York advanced this claim of negotiability, nor is it a surprise that Sobol gave it his assent. After all, that is precisely what Afrocentrists implicitly were claiming in Atlanta and Washington, too. This is the intellectual undergirding of multiculturalism, as well: that these two disciplines—history and social studies—must be made to reflect the realities of the students in the classroom, and that they lose no credibility by doing so. This idea has become matter-of-fact, I would argue, among most educators: the humanities and social science subjects are more negotiable and less insulated from shifting social concerns than they have ever been considered before.[95] Asserting itself less forcefully in the other cases, this concept came to full light in New York.

An example from the early stages of the New York struggle will help clarify the point. When asked why her task force had focused on history and social studies as the main disciplines in need of change, Hazel Dukes, director of the New York chapter of the NAACP and former chair of the Task Force on Minorities, reflected on the malleability of disciplinary truths, citing the greater negotiability of the humanities and social sciences compared to the hard sciences or math disciplines:

> We wanted our education system to be one where children would be excited to learn. And how do you excite people to learn? You excite people to learn by letting them share or participate in discussions in a real sense: that it's "real" to what they are participating in. Some subject matters such as physics and biology, it can't be "real." But literature can be "real." English can be "real." History most certainly can be "real," you know. So, finding curriculum and fitting in that which can help motivate people to understand that there is some greatness in his-

tory, and can be from them. And they succeed from those who have gone before them.[96]

The challenge in New York gives us significant insight into how this resource of disciplinary negotiability could work for the Afrocentric challenge, and later, the multicultural effort in the state.

Appointing Consultants: The Achilles' Heel of New York's Experience with Afrocentrism

After a year of work but no consensus, in 1988, the task force's seventeen members approached Commissioner Sobol and asked if they could hire four consultants to help them complete their work. Agreeing to the proposal, the commissioner granted funding to the group for the nominal fees required to hire the following four experts: Leonard Jeffries, chair of the Black Studies Department at City College of New York; Shirley Hume, professor at Hunter College; Carlos Rodriguez Fraticelli, professor at Hunter College; and Lincoln White, whose affiliation was not listed in subsequent reports.[97] The four were to look at the curriculum from the perspective of African American, Asian, Latino, and Native American interests, respectively, and to assist task force members in making their recommendations.[98]

According to Leonard Jeffries—an increasingly visible advocate of the Afrocentric movement in the late 1980s, if also a controversial figure even within Afrocentric movement circles—he, at least, was nothing but blunt with task force members, warning them at the outset that he would be unwilling to "sugarcoat" whatever findings might emerge from his study. He knew and warned members that he "would have to deal with the truth":

> And if I dealt with the truth, it would produce flak. . . . And if they [the task force members] were prepared to deal with that, and the reactions that will come, then, good, we should proceed. If not, then don't bother to even start the process with me. And after a time they came back and said, "Okay, we understand the implications, and let's go."[99]

The decision to hire Jeffries and the three other consultants would pave the way for a media assault on the task force and the rest of the state education department for the next several years.

For the report that the task force ended up producing would ultimately be interpreted in many quarters as a "flat-out screaming attack on Western Culture," as the *U.S. News and World Report* journalist, John Leo, put it.[100] The "Curriculum of Inclusion" report, the group's final product, stated that elementary and secondary education across the state—even after revisions had been made in 1987—was highly flawed and would have to be restructured to represent the history and achievements of people of all cultures.[101] According to the report, New York's curriculum materials did not "individually or collectively, adequately and accurately reflect the pluralistic nature of society in the United States" (p. 12). Among the report's most contested statements was its charge that the curriculum contained "systematic bias," and its indictment of the "stereotyping and misinformation" contained in school texts (p. iii). Both of these, it said, have "had a terribly damaging effect on the psyche of young people of African, Asian, Latino, and Native American descent," leading to their disappointing performance (p. 6). "African Americans, Asian-Americans, Puerto Ricans / Latinos, and Native Americans have all been the victims of an intellectual and educational oppression that has characterized the culture and institutions of the United States (p. iii). Furthermore, said the report, the contributions of people of non-European heritage have been "systematically distorted, marginalized, or omitted" in the "Eurocentric" curriculum (p. 12); which must be rewritten so that minority students "will have higher self-esteem and self-respect, while children from European cultures will have a less arrogant perspective" (p. iv).[102]

For several months, the "Inclusion" report more or less saw only the inside of Commissioner Sobol's office, while the commissioner and his staff discussed a strategy for dealing with what they knew to be incendiary content. With words from the report like "pathology," "racial hatred," and "misinformation" ringing in their ears, the commissioner and his deputies predicted that critics in the media and other sectors of the establishment would vilify the report loudly and publicly, if the education department did not somehow qualify the report's content. But rather than punting on the whole project, given the animus that was sure to be expressed upon its public unveiling, Sobol sought to gather more advice and counsel on what exactly to do about the report. To this end, before presenting the report to the Board of Regents and the media, in November 1989, Sobol brought in four new outside consultants of his choosing to talk with him about the report. The consultants invited this time to advise Sobol on the report ranged from the identifiably Afrocentric to the identifiably anti-Afrocentric: Asa Hilliard, the well-known Afrocentric scholar and editor of the *African-American Baseline Essays*; Diane Ravitch, former assistant secretary of education in the Bush administration, historian of education, and primary author of California's recently updated history and social studies curricula; Edmund Gordon, professor of psychology at Yale University, a known moderate on issues such as multiculturalism; and Virginia Sanchez Korrol, professor of Puerto Rican Studies at Brooklyn College, and former committee member on a New York Department of Education project called "Latinos in the Making of the USA: Past, Present and Future."

At the meeting, according to interviews with both Sanchez Korrol and Ravitch, Asa Hilliard was the first to present, and he agreed with the recommendations being made by the "Curriculum of Inclusion" task force, although the report, to his mind, did not go far enough. He talked at some length about the curriculum's neglect of the accomplishments of ancient Africans, but the exclusion of such content was generally so great in the current New York framework, he said, that whatever the state did to rectify the situation would be a step in the right direction.

Ed Gordon was the next to speak, and his message was "gentlemanly" and "moderate," according to Sanchez Korrol, and "judicious and wise," according to Ravitch.[103] His presentation primarily concerned the state's responsibility to prepare all children to live in a variety of environments: whether they ended up in the affluent sections of New York City, rural Mississippi, or the ghettoes of New Haven.

Sanchez Korrol was next, and she argued that the report was not so terribly radical, and that it echoed current thought in the university, such as "bottom-up" social history and the burgeoning body of work concerning scholarship on minorities. She did find fault with several gaps in the report—primarily, the absence of gender or class in the analysis, as well as the report's emphasis on discrete ethnic groups, rather than the interrelationship between them. But since she regarded the report as just advisory, and not binding, she looked at "A Curriculum of Inclusion" as a first step in the right direction toward revision.[104]

Recalling her turn at the podium as "a very unpleasant experience," Ravitch found that her first public statement on the report was a far more extensive critique than those of the others who had preceded her.[105] The bulk of her comments concerned the report's "failure to be multicultural," and "its affirmation of 'multiple ethnocentricities', and 'multiple ethnocentrisms,'" as she called them. By her recollection, she went on to criticize the report's failure to talk about "the importance of being sensitive to all kinds of different groups, and being able to feel as a human being, and being able to put yourself in somebody else's shoes, regardless of their color or regardless of whatever differences there were amongst you." Her presentation was not greeted kindly, leading, she says, "to all kinds of screaming and shrieking, . . . a horrible ordeal."[106] The event for Ravitch hit its nadir when Regent Adelaide Sanford, a former Queens principal, accused Ravitch of having "grandparents [who] owned the slave ships that we came on," to which Ravitch responded that that was very unlikely since her grandparents lived in a "shtettl in Eastern Europe and didn't own slaves."[107]

After receiving these four sets of comments, Sobol sat on the report for three more months before finally publicly presenting it to the Board of Regents in February 1990. At the Regents' meeting, the commissioner tried to temper reaction to the report. While Sobol said that he accepted *sections* of the task force report—particularly the central thrust of the argument that the curriculum continued to be unbalanced—he also sought to distance himself from it on several fronts. He rejected the task force recommendation to appoint a special assistant for cultural equity, and he argued that the rhetoric of the report was offensive to many. He insisted that this document was purely advisory, that he had never formally endorsed it. Finally, he stated that for any real work to be done on the curriculum, a more reasonable, "racially balanced," and "reputable" committee would have to be pulled together to look into the subject. Sobol recommended that the board allow him to convene such a committee—one that was fully separate from the current task force, but which would bear the task force's insights in mind as it began its work.

According to one Regent, Walter Cooper of the Rochester region, once Sobol had presented the report to the board, the regents discussed both "A Curriculum of Inclusion" and Sobol's recommendation that the Department of Education appoint a second, more "reputable," committee. With various members condemning the report alternately as "more of a statement of ideology, than as having educational content," or as an "instrument for trashing the traditions of the West," or as separatism, or as a distortion of history, or as an agenda for self-esteem, the Board of Regents summarily rejected the report, according to Cooper, just as Sobol had suggested they do. Members reached consensus that "A Curriculum of Inclusion" was not a valid instrument for changing the syllabi in the social studies in the state of New York, and they instructed the commissioner "to go back to the drawing board, reconstitute [a second] task force, and come back with a different report."[108]

The board took this action in the face of racial rhetoric that must have caused them some discomfort—just as it had caused Sobol discomfort at the beginning of his term. This time, however, the rhetoric was aimed at both white and black officials. For example, Walter Cooper, who is African American, was treated to complaints about his *inauthenticity as a black man* when he joined others on the board to vote down the recommendations of "A Curriculum of Inclusion." Here, as in Washington, D.C., Afrocentric advocates used the argument of "race betrayal" to push education officials to act on their behalf. Cooper, however, indicated that such rhetoric had been ineffectual in New York; he was undaunted by racial coercion. The "resource" (when used against blacks) that had moved the D.C. conflict toward a more Afrocentric outcome appears to have not made a large impact in New York.

Media Response to "Curriculum of Inclusion"

Despite the board's and Sobol's rejection of both the tenor and the specific demands of the "Inclusion" report, the media pounced on the education department as if it had been a most avid supporter of the task force's work. Once the report had been made public, that is, the media response was loud and furious and, seemingly uninformed that the report had been all but denounced by the commission and the board. Columnists in the *New York Post* and the *New York Times*, as well as in national magazines like *U.S. News and World Report*, *The National Review*, *The New Republic*, and *Time* took after it eagerly. In these negative media accounts, detractors often indicated that the "known Afrocentric scholar Leonard Jeffries" had been brought in to consult to the task force, and they often averred that "A Curriculum of Inclusion" was, thus, informed by Afrocentric goals, even if they didn't always actually call it "Afrocentric."

The columnists were not alone in their disdain for the document: they were able to find numerous educational experts and historians who were willing to provide a critique of it. Diane Ravitch, California Superintendent of Public Instruction Bill Honig, renowned education specialist James Comer of Yale, and many others criticized the report, calling it hyperbolic and unsubstantiated in its accusations of racism and miseducation.[109] In June 1990, Diane Ravitch, along with Arthur Schlesinger and other leading historians, issued a public statement condemning the "Inclusion" report, saying that the paper was "a polemical document, [and] viewed division into racial groups as the basic analytical framework for an understanding of American history. . . . It saw history as a form of social and psychological therapy whose function is to raise the self-esteem of children from minority groups."[110] Critics also divined the fingerprints of Leonard Jeffries to be all over the document—a connection that immediately discredited its content in education and political circles. While Jeffries, at that time, had yet to deliver his Albany speech (in July 1990) in which he made multiple comments disparaging Jews for their role in the slave trade and in which he accused Diane Ravitch of being a racist, he was already suspected of harboring prejudices. This reputation did much to detract from "A Curriculum of Inclusion" and from subsequent reports that were to be issued later from the department of education, as we shall see.

It wasn't as if the uproar surrounding "A Curriculum of Inclusion" surprised Sobol, he said in a 1995 interview. After all, during the months before the report became public, he had discussed with his deputies its potential impact on the administration. Even though he says that he and his staff knew that it would be inflammatory and, very possibly, jeopardize their agenda of "school reform, *writ* large," Sobol decided to keep the report as it was and present it to the board. He explains that this was an attempt to do the right thing by "giving voice" to previously unheard constituents. But even if he and his deputies had anticipated some negative media response, he still couldn't fathom the newspapers' "willful" misrepresentation of the report as having received his blessing, when it most emphatically had not, he says.[111] He was "creamed" for that report, he later complained.

The Second Committee

Media response notwithstanding, Sobol empanelled a second committee in April 1990, as he had requested and as the Board of Regents had instructed him to do. With angry columnists skeptical now of his every move, Commissioner Sobol began looking for those "scholarly" voices to place on this second, "more balanced" committee. From the outset, the second panel was to be made up of a mix of educational experts, including teachers, administrators, and university-level scholars from departments of history, geography, anthropology, sociology, political science, and / or economics.[112] Sobol also chose members who, together, represented greater racial and ethnic diversity.[113] Also significant from symbolic, political, and practical perspectives was that no one from the first advisory group, the Task Force on Minorities, received an invitation to participate on the second committee, although Asa Hilliard, who had advised Sobol in November 1989, was invited to join it. Sobol decided to exclude all prior task force members in order to differentiate the mandate and any future findings of the second committee from the fallout surrounding the first group's report.

    Once in place, Sobol characterized the newly formed committee as having a more specific goal than the previous task force:

> It was no longer, "Here's a bunch of angry people, what's on their mind?" but now it was, "We've had this recommendation that something be done with the social studies curriculum. Let's put together a group of people who know a little bit about that. And ask them to tell us what they think needs to be done: review the curriculum and tell us what needs to be done along these lines."

Asked to what extent the findings of the first task force were to be the mandate of the second committee, Sobol reported.

> It wasn't that the findings were the charge, but that the *issues* [that the task force had brought up] were the charge. It was this way: "This

first group has said to us that the curricula that exist right now deal inadequately with the story of the major minority groups in this society. What is your more informed view? Are they right? Are they not right? If they are right, to what extent are they right? Where are the gaps? What should we be doing?"[114]

With this mandate, the second committee, officially known as the Social Studies Syllabus Review and Development Committee (later to be widely known as the "Diversity Committee"), was composed predominantly of leaders of state school organizations and of academics from a variety of disciplines and institutions. Its task was to "go the next step" with the recommendation that the state curriculum needed to diversify.[115] From here forward, multicultural, not Afrocentric, content was to be at the center of the debate. Except in very small bits and pieces, Afrocentrism was cooled out in the New York revision process, not to be heard from officially again.

Yet, while the Diversity Committee was widely recognized as being made up of acknowledged leaders in educational issues, its critics in the media and in education and political circles still found it tainted by its predecessor, the Task Force on Minorities. Despite members' own and Sobol's many protestations from the beginning of the process to the end, the Diversity Committee was unable to convince its critics that it was a wholly different entity with a wholly different approach to the issue of diversity. Said critic Diane Ravitch, for example:

I thought . . . that the people involved were responsible educators. . . . It was clearly a much more mixed group in terms of race. And it had some representation of people who, in advance, didn't approve of the "Curriculum of Inclusion," Arthur Schlesinger being the best example. But, most of the people on that second panel were chosen because their views were predisposed to be sympathetic to what the commissioner wanted.

They had been chosen, according to Ravitch and other critics, partially not to disappoint the first task force.[116]

Although such criticisms lingered over the selection of committee members, during the course of the next year, most appointees to the Diversity Committee (with a few exceptions like Arthur Schlesinger and Nathan Glazer) felt that the state department of education had anointed them with an important role in developing a new form of multiculturalism. There was a sense of "specialness" that emerged on the committee, according to two of my interviewees and other reports—the view that their charge would result in innovative models of history and social studies pedagogy.[117] The product would not be anything like Afrocentrism: it would push beyond the narrow confines of concern about one race and one historical experience; it would span all experience: racial, educational, American.

"One Nation, Many Peoples": Deliverance through the Second Committee Report?

What emerged from the second committee's work was the report "One Nation, Many Peoples: A Declaration of Cultural Interdependence," which the members submitted to Commissioner Sobol in June 1991. The committee's first general point was that the state department of education needed to revise history and social studies curricula across the state to give more attention to the contributions and roles of nonwhite cultures in American life. They concluded this even after the state had so recently undertaken revisions. According to one of my interviewees, a member of the second committee, Virginia Sanchez Korrol, a number of the practitioners and academics who wrote the report wondered why, if the social studies framework had just been rehauled, there were still so many gaps in the knowledge base? "Why was there still a sense of 'them' and 'us'? Why had the new scholarship in social history and ethnic studies not been included?"[118] On issues like these, the report sounded similar to "A Curriculum of Inclusion"—if not in its details, then insofar as it posited both the "problem" of European-centered content in the schools and the "flexibility" of history and social studies to reflect changing scholarship.

But in a distinctive turn away from the central message of "A Curriculum of Inclusion," the "One Nations" document placed philosophical and pedagogical emphasis on the concept of "multiple perspectives." This constructionist concept advocated that schools are responsible for helping students understand that *all* events should be viewed from multiple angles, that each person should be able to step outside his or her own interests and point of view for perceiving events, and to understand that a person's position in the world affects the way he or she views world events. Such understanding, according to the authors of the report, leads ultimately to children's appreciation of the nation's diversity of experience, opinions, and power.

Most members of the committee I spoke with were pleased with the content of the report and the intellectual space it opened up for the concept of multiple perspectives. But a few other committee members—like Nathan Glazer, who nonetheless voted for the multiple perspectives changes—were less convinced of the report's importance as either an intellectual or a practical document. Glazer, the Harvard sociologist, recalls that the mission of the committee often seemed ethereal to him, resistant to being pinned down and made concrete through real policy initiatives. He speaks of the committee's work with profound ambivalence:

[I had] a certain amount of skepticism as to whether anything at all was necessary. . . . I didn't see some burning problem that had to be dealt with. . . . But I thought, "Well, what are documents like these?" They are not scientific or social scientific documents. They are consensus documents of the sort of things one *should* do. I think that they can be criticized endlessly, and properly. And maybe certain documents shouldn't exist. But you need some overarching thing which leads to a kind of consensus when you are dealing with elementary and high school curricula. . . .

So, my point of view . . . was that there's no great problem, except a problem *politically*, and that we ought to be responsive to the political problem. What's the point of the committee otherwise? It's inconceivable that we would have made a report that said, "We don't think that multiculturalism is a problem," or "We think we're multicultural enough, so let's drop the whole thing" [laughs]. We were not going to do that! So, we did something that indicated some degree of consideration of these pressures, without the militancy or the extreme formulations of the first report.[119]

Glazer also interprets the multiple perspectives approach of the report as a strategic innovation: something to differentiate the first and the second reports.[120]

Despite the near-consensus that was struck on the committee—even among ambivalent members, like Glazer[121]—two of the historians, Arthur Schlesinger and Kenneth Jackson of Columbia University, were unwilling to sign the document. Their shared point of contention concerned what they considered to be the report's emphasis on "ethnicity" and "separate groups," which put "common culture" in jeopardy.[122]

Sobol, who had been initiated into disputatiousness with the release of "A Curriculum of Inclusion" knew that these two dissents would likely invite further finger-pointing and aggressive attacks from outside quarters. So, even though Sobol praised the report as "thoughtful, scholarly, constructive," and reported that he would use it as the basis for recommending revisions to the Board of Regents, he chose not to submit the report to the Board unfettered.[123] Instead, before it was publicly released to the Board, Sobol wrote his own twenty-seven-page statement concerning curriculum revisions (called "Understanding Diversity") and submitted that document to the Board along with the fifty-page "One Nation" report. In the memo "Understanding Diversity," Sobol borrowed from various parts of the report, incorporating many phrases from Schlesinger's dissent and Glazer's cautionary addendum, as well as from the main body of the document.

Sobol's primary goal in writing "Understanding Diversity" was to point out what he labeled the sharp differences between the recommendations found in the "One Nation" report and those contained in "A Curriculum of Inclusion." The commissioner provided a list of the specific actions this report was specifically *not* undertaking (implying that "Inclusion" might have been guilty of the same), such as "trashing the traditions of the West," implementing an "Afrocentric curriculum," "ethnic cheerleading and separatism," "distorting history," implementing a "curriculum of self-esteem," or developing a "study of American history based on ethnicity or culture alone."[124] His point was also to take from "One Nation" what could be used in the next step of the process: actual social studies curriculum revision. But if this effort at distinction was a strategic inclination, it also was a futile one. For, in expressly endorsing each of the second committee's basic guidelines alongside his own document, Sobol was only setting up himself (and the effort at curriculum reform) for more disappointment.

The media spilled more contemptuous ink. Journalists' response to "One Nation, Many Peoples" took the state department of education, the commissioner, and committee members by surprise. Given the more "reasonable" tone of the second report, the committee members' belief in the "specialness" of their work, the report's purported advances in the intellectual direction of "multiple perspectives," and Sobol's strategy of issuing the more palatable "Understanding Diversity" document along with the report to the board, education department staff, Commissioner Sobol, and certainly members of the Diversity Committee themselves expected the media and other outside observers to greet the report warmly. After all, the report offered significant intellectual advances over the first task-force report, they believed, and it had been touted as a "blue ribbon" commission. Nothing in it would set off alarms the way the first one had, so they imagined.

But skeptical journalists and other critics on the political and educational landscape did not buy into what they saw as the commissioner's marketing efforts to differentiate between the goals of the task force and the second committee. With their radar on high, they detected in the second committee's activities what they believed to be the political *traces* of "A Curriculum of Inclusion," and they were unwilling to be convinced that the first report's "separatist" and "political" agenda really had been loosened totally by shifting members and by the passage of two years' time. In other words, "A Curriculum of Inclusion" continued to elicit a great deal of suspicion, even though Sobol and the state had for all intents and purposes roundly rejected the rhetoric of that report. Sobol, himself, reflecting later on this reigning suspicion found in the media and in his critics' statements, said,

> In most of the press treatment of this whole episode, subsequently...In the *New York Post*, for example, I was always paired with Leonard Jeffries. This was the "Sobol-Jeffries report." People criticized me for choosing the wrong friends and so on and so on.
>
> They knew—because I told them again and again—how it happened. . . . And nobody ever reported it, much less commented on it. They never reported it.
>
> So, you see, that's what I fault people for. It's not the *discomfort* and the *unease* and the *wanting to safeguard cherished values*. That's perfectly acceptable! But to be so angry and so threatened by what was going on that they would just distort the facts and criticize unfairly just seems to be beyond the pale.[125]

Due to the committee's inauspicious dealings with Leonard Jeffries, and the "strident" tone of the first report, *future* committee work that critics might otherwise have regarded merely as efforts to incorporate multiculturalism and, then, "multiple perspectives" into New York's curricula, was, instead, tinged throughout for many observers as *Afrocentric-inspired* challenge. Critics duly treated this work with suspicion and hostility.

Even then, the final blow had not yet been delivered. Before the noise could die down after the board's vote, and the committee's report had a chance to distinguish itself from "A Curriculum of Inclusion," Leonard Jeffries, the most controversial of the four consultants to the first task force, delivered a now infamous speech on July 20, 1991 in Albany, New York. In this speech, addressed to the Empire State Black Arts and Cultural Festival, Jeffries lambasted several of those involved in the curriculum controversy, and made it thereafter impossible for the press to treat the work of these committees at all objectively. For, in his speech in Albany, Jeffries unleashed a torrent of epithets on Schlesinger and Ravitch, accused Jews of having financed the slave trade, charged that whites are "ice people," not sun people, and that Jews and Italians are responsible for denigrating blacks in Hollywood. Whether it was true or not, as Jeffries later charged, that the media response to this speech was *designed* to "derail and chase away the change that Sobol's reports had called for,"[126] clearly this was the effect media coverage had. The revision process begun by Sobol's appointment of the first task force was thereafter doomed to produce reports that would never seem credible to its wary critics.[127]

Conclusion of New York Activities

And there were other reports to be produced. It would just be a frustrating process to get them out. Over the next several years, and even following Sobol's departure from the office of commissioner, the state department of education called on a number of new committees and subcommittees to continue the process of rewriting the social studies curriculum. But by now, after so much negative publicity and so much angst had been expressed in and about the school system, this was a low-energy, low-excitement exercise. The social studies project was further hindered by multiple other bureaucratic exigencies. First, the newly convened committee, called the Social Studies Curriculum Committee, was plagued by internal difficulties. There was infighting, bred not only by the large number of members on the committee, but by the turf wars that some of these members were involved in. Some members of these subsequent committees had worked on previous revision groups, and they wanted their old work to remain in place. Some members were from the teaching ranks, and they did not want teaching routines to change (although other teachers on the committee championed the multiple perspectives idea); and some members of these subsequent committees were administrators who worried about asking teachers to alter curricula. There was a combination of old and new faces (several of the third committee's members had served on the second committee, more had not), and these were just some of the conflicts that proved onerous. According to multiple reports, this was a difficult committee to work on, and two prominent members, Nathan Glazer and Catherine Cornbleth (both of whom had served on the "Diversity Committee"), ended up resigning, rather than enduring the stalled process and its diminishing returns.

Second, Sobol's legacy learning-and-assessment guide, the "Compact for Learning," was also at this time being drawn up and released for comment, under the supervision of a body called the Curriculum Assessment Council. The council by this time had oversight over the social studies revision effort and, needless to say, council members were uninterested in facing the vitriol that previous incarnations of the committee had bred. The message coming from the council: Do nothing that will draw attention to these activities. Said Virginia Sanchez Korrol, in a long vent over the stultifying impact of the Compact mission on the social studies curriculum, "It was doomed, it was just doomed."[128] She was not the only person among my interviewees who felt this way: Ali Mazrui, Linda Biemer, and even Nathan Glazer lamented the imposition of more political and bureaucratic weight on the revisions.

Third, at the same time that this new committee was trying to represent some of the "multiple perspectives" lineage in its work, a national policy

called Goals 2000 had recently cropped up as a national standards movement, and its concerns, too, had to be included in any curriculum
makeover. Finally, over the course of all this time, there was a general
shift to the Right in New York politics, such that Democratic Governor
Mario Cuomo lost his seat to conservative Republican George Pataki,
and within the state education department, there was a retrenchment into
conservatism, largely due to the bashing it had taken for several years
over issues of multiculturalism. Historically, then, it was a trying time to
be working on changes in the social studies and history curricula, particularly on anything that had the mark of noncanonical content.

The long and short of this process—emphasis on "long," not "short,"
since it took another three years for the curriculum committee to come
up with a recommendation—was that there resulted very little change in
the state social studies and history curriculum, despite years of lightening-
hot rhetoric and high-profile appointments to committees. Not only did
Afrocentrism not see the light of day by the end of this process—having
been drained out years before—but neither did anything new in the *multicultural* direction, given its purported connection to the first report.

Responses to the Outcome

Not many actors involved in the New York process were pleased with the
changes that ultimately resulted in the frameworks. From participants on
the second and third committees, to columnists in the media, to outraged
critics like Leonard Jeffries, came forth varied, but unanimously scathing,
criticisms of the time and effort that went into appointing these committees, all for naught. Advocates of multiple-perspectives multiculturalism
decried the hype that diverted attention away from their own intellectually sophisticated project; Afrocentric scholars bemoaned the lack of
courage demonstrated by white administrators; more conservative self-
titled multiculturalists complained that after all the damaging uproar, little of substance actually had been developed; and traditionalists criticized
the education department and its commissioner for subjecting our country's cultural principles to political maneuverings in the first place.

Linda Biemer, an advocate of multiple-perspectives multiculturalism,
expressed deep dissatisfaction over the outcome of the process, a process
that more or less ran aground irreversibly by the time it arrived at her
committee (the third committee in the chain). Asked whether the framework fulfilled the promise of the "One Nation, Many Peoples" report (a
report she considered "wonderful"), she said, "[No], I think it's pretty
late-1950s, early 1960s," meaning that the framework seemed to hearken
back to an earlier, more conservative era in representing the nation's di-

versity rather than presenting a forward-looking vision. When asked how much the framework reflects the "One Nation" report in specific multicultural content, she responded, "I don't think very much, unfortunately. I mean, there is the word 'diversity' in there, and the words 'multiple perspectives' and all those things are in there. But I just think they are not strongly in there."[129] The greatest loss of it all, she says, is that New York did not grasp the opportunity to come out with something innovative, as it has had an historical reputation for doing.

Ali Mazrui of SUNY, Binghamton, also held a low opinion of the final product developed during this seven-year period, arguing that this is what happens when administrators are cautious not to offend the public. "This recommendation [the framework] is in danger of being so wishy-washy that it will not have much of an impact."[130] Similarly, Virginia Sanchez Korrol remembered that "the bureaucracy that bogged down the committee's work was so burdensome, that 'One Nation' was literally forgotten."[131]

On even less forgiving notes, Diane Ravitch and Leonard Jeffries provided point-counterpoint readings of the New York social studies debate. Ravitch first criticized the framework for offering very little that was new, and then disparaged the process that gave rise to so much animus:

> I don't think it's very different from the 1987 curriculum. I mean, we went through all of this angst. For what? It became a kind of platform for a lot of people who made a lot of noise. . . . Why did we go through all that? What was all the ranting and raving about "Eurocentrism?" I don't know. . . . Leonard Jeffries, finally because of the things he was saying, finally discredited his views. Because it became clear that his anti-Semitism and his racism were so virulent. And at a certain point, he just wasn't taken seriously anymore. So, I don't know if that's good or bad. I don't like great expressions of anti-Semitism and racism. I don't think they are healthy in society.
>
> I think you can take any curriculum, whether it's the 1987 New York curriculum or the 1987 California curriculum and you can say, "It should have said something else, it should have said something stronger, it should have said something weaker." I mean, you can never get a document like this and have it be perfect. And sometimes the critics are right. Maybe it should be stronger or weaker or say more about something and less about something else. And that's fine. But to turn it into a kind of culture war? I don't think that's a good idea."[132]

Finally, Ravitch's greatest ideological nemesis, Leonard Jeffries, had this to say about the social studies and history revision process in New York:

What [the process] has revealed to us is that you cannot trust white folks—even good ones. And I've said that over and over again. And I'm saying it again. They don't have the strength to fight for what is right. Sobol is not strong enough to lead a fight of this nature. Because he's up against a system that Arthur Schlesinger and them represent. It's much more sophisticated than anybody realizes. When you have a three-point system of Arthur Schlesinger representing the Anglo elite, you have Diane Ravitch representing the conservative establishment, and you have [Albert] Shanker [former head of the American Federation of Teachers] representing the progressive Marxist, labor establishment . . . all of them opposed to blacks. So, with system analysis, I see clearly what's up.[133]

After seven years and four committees' worth of work, New York got a social studies curriculum that, by all accounts, represented only the most negligible change, if any, over previous revisions. It certainly produced untold amounts of animosity in the state, but it did little to make Afrocentrists, multiculturalists, or devotees of a more traditional canon happy. It should be considered to have been an "outright rejection" of Afrocentric aims.

And yet . . . before writing off the process as a total loss for the Afrocentric component of this struggle, we should ask whether or not Afrocentrism's advocates had cause to consider any part of the process a victory. And to this question, a careful, qualified "yes" is in order. At a minimum, the process brought to the Afrocentric challenge a sense of legitimacy— at least for a short while, from 1987 to 1989. Commissioner Tom Sobol seemed to be earnest in his attention to his critics, and he allowed identifiable advocates of Afrocentrism like Leonard Jeffries and Asa Hilliard to serve as his own or committees' consultants. Although they may not have been invited to stay long at the decision-making table, Sobol did issue the initial invitation to Afrocentrists, among others, and this should be counted as at least some form of symbolic success. It is less than what was gained in either Atlanta or Washington, D.C., but as we will see in the creationist cases, it gained more credibility than creationists were ever able to manufacture among education professionals in the school systems they fought.

Conclusion: Afrocentrism's Cultural Resonance

What is obvious in the preceding sections is that the three Afrocentric challenges studied in this book both resembled and diverged from each other significantly. *Differentiating* each from the other was the specific curricula content that challenge proponents hoped to incorporate into their respective district classrooms, the political messages that were built into those curricula, the particular amount of attention that was to be paid to black Egypt, the teaching methods that were to be used in the classroom, the experts on whom the revisions relied, and the ways in which they were successful and unsuccessful. *Similar* across all three cases was that challengers sought to amend the teaching of history and social studies with new, heretofore neglected, scholarship about Africa and African Americans; to promote the self-esteem of black students by depicting Africans and African Americans as central historical actors; and even to decrease the arrogance that white children are said to naturally assume when they are exposed to Eurocentrism.

Also similar were education professionals' reception of those arguments. In all three of these cases—even in the system with the least amount of positive change, New York state—school system bureaucrats acknowledged that the claims of their Afrocentric challengers held some validity. School officials knew that they had to work with their challengers, at least through some parts of the process, and even if this was sometimes only to quiet Afrocentrists' critique of their system. In Atlanta, many educators in administrative positions worked willingly with challengers. In Washington, they did so under duress. In New York, most education professionals were actually frightened by the challengers' politically costly demands. But in all three, at various points in the process, high-placed staff responded to the Afrocentric constituency as if its members had legitimate demands to make or, at least, the right to have their demands heard.

Nevertheless, the three school systems also ended up delivering to all three sets of challengers less than what challengers had originally called for. While we witnessed the "big bang" that started Atlanta's African American Infusion Program, we also saw that its effects were diminished as time wore on and as the program wound its way through the realities of the school district. We know that in Washington, the superintendent who inherited the commitment to Afrocentric reform, Franklin Smith, was willing to grant Abena Walker's Afrocentric program several hundreds of thousands of dollars, but only under "circumscribed" conditions: one school, in the poorest section of town, which Smith allowed to grow only minimally over the years. And we know that New York state's encounter with the Afrocentric challenge (to the extent that pieces of it can be called Afrocentric at all) resulted in an outcome that can only be called "ultimate rejection."

In the next chapter, I will use historical data from the three cases to think more theoretically about the rhetorical power that Afrocentrists possessed and the political and organizational obstacles and opportunities that they ran into. What was it about Afrocentric claims that won them at least a modicum of respect from education professionals, and sometimes much more than that? To begin this more comparative process, I will discuss in greater detail the three successful framing strategies that Afrocentrists were able to employ in their challenges, as we have glimpsed here in the historical record. Upon attending to these cultural resources, I will then look at the political and organizational structures they encountered, which sometimes facilitated, but more often minimized, Afrocentrists' inroads into the schools.

Four

Cultural, Political, and Organizational Factors Influencing Afrocentric Outcomes

ALTHOUGH INTERESTING from a historical standpoint, the foregoing chronology of the three Afrocentric cases leaves us with a deluge of data that will remain a mind-boggling puzzle unless treated to some form of systematic analysis. With analysis in mind, I have two goals for this chapter which, at first glance, may seem to be at cross purposes. The first is to demonstrate the *similarities* of cultural resources available to all Afrocentric advocates in their struggles with schools. Despite their locations in three separate school systems, Afrocentric challengers laid claim to remarkably similar arguments for why they had a right to make demands of schools, and why schools should respond favorably to those demands. Having established these cultural similarities, my second goal is to demonstrate the *differences* that also marked the three cases, particularly when it came to the political and organizational factors in place in each school system. What I hope to demonstrate convincingly in this second part of the chapter is that while Afrocentrists in all three cases may have been similarly culturally endowed, their access to political and organizational opportunities varied in their own systems, and these differences led to the disparate outcomes we have witnessed.

Once I have tackled these two tasks, and we understand the Afrocentric cases more thoroughly, it will be possible to take the next step—the central point of this book—and compare these three cases to the cases involving creationists. I will begin this "between-challenge" comparative work in chapter 5.

Resonant Cultural Resources

Cultural Resource 1: Resonance of Afrocentrists' "Problem" and "Solution"

As evidenced in Atlanta, Washington, D.C., and New York State, Afrocentrists had access to an extremely powerful weapon in pressing their claims against the educational system: they argued that they were addressing a problem that was undeniable to all but the most conservative members of the education establishment, and they said that they were providing a solution to that problem which fit well with the aims of a progressive education.[1] According to its advocates, Afrocentrism addressed a seemingly intransigent problem in American education: the educational and social plight of black children, who for decades had been trailing whites, and now Hispanics, in school achievement. Even if many educators found the solution of Afrocentrism to be dubious—with its questionable scholarly claims and its promises to increase black children's self-esteem—those same educators regarded the *problem* of black children's lower achievement to be real. It was impossible for educators to disavow the argument that *something* must be done about black children's failure rates. Even in New York, where multicultural revisions had only just been incorporated into the social studies curriculum, Commissioner Thomas Sobol and his staff reacted supportively to the criticism that the education of African American and Hispanic children was problematic.

In sociological terms, Afrocentrists were using a frame—or a set of compelling images, statements, and symbols—that resonated with the education officials whom they were challenging. As defined in chapter 1, resonance between challengers and audiences occurs when a movement's frames strike a deep responsive chord among members of an audience and potentially influence their actions.[2] Challenge leaders explicitly strategize which frames to use in their mobilization efforts and, judging by the actions that Afrocentrists and their supporters were able to generate among administrators on their behalf, one wonders if they could have selected a more effective set of symbols and metaphors on behalf of their agenda. For, in choosing the image of poorly educated, unjustly failing African American children at the hands of the public schools, Afrocentrists used a frame that was highly compelling to school decision makers.

Giving further heft to their cause, Afrocentrists argued that their solution to this problem was based on the quintessentially American ideals of equality and liberty.[3] Equality for black children could not be achieved in this country if their ancestors were marginalized in the sidebars of textbooks, argued Afrocentrists; liberty would never belong to African Americans, as a people, if they could not compete academically. Because of the strength of this frame, with its roots in the historical battles that African Americans have fought against systematic racism in this country, Afrocentrists were able to present themselves as *people who had the right to protest discrimination*, a construction that drew upon the experiences of their forebears in the antislavery and civil rights movements.[4]

We saw this framing of schools' historical bias arise in every one of the three cases. Outside of these three school systems, Afrocentrism's advocates also used this frame widely, as in this opinion-editorial written in

*There is consensus
there's a problem among
Afr. Am*

1989 for the *New York Times* by Kris Parker, aka KRS-One, a rap song-writer and producer. Parker wrote the editorial in the midst of the turmoil in New York surrounding the release of the "Curriculum of Inclusion" report, and it was meant to explain the cause of Afrocentrism to a skeptical public:

> Young black kids experience a more subtle form of racism when their heritage and culture are stripped from them early on in their schooling. While no single cause accounts for the problems of inner-city kids, much of what black youth is missing—self-esteem, creative opportunity, outlook, goals—can be traced to what we're not learning in schools.[5]

This frame was contained, as well, in Atlanta's Mae Kendall's description of the problem: "In the case of minorities, particularly a lot of blacks, our history has *never* been presented with the essence of truth that there should be, in terms of historical data." Kendall, the former director of program planning and curriculum development, continued by saying that she has seen what happens when people finally do learn something positive about their ancestors:

> We have tapes of little children just blossoming as a result of finding out things about themselves that they did not previously know. And about their families and their background, and the true history. I've seen students' eyes just take a whole new turn in a more positive manner when they realize that, for example, in Georgia history that there were other things that presented a more positive picture than people in cotton fields.[6]

How could mainstream educators ignore such claims, even if those claims were accompanied by the more "radical" program of Afrocentrism rather than by the program of multiculturalism? For many of the education officials I interviewed and otherwise researched, Afrocentrists' rhetoric about the problem of black children's education made proponents' demands tough to ignore. While there were critics in the press and universities who cried foul when front-line education officials treated Afrocentric challengers with magnanimity and respect, it was difficult for school authorities themselves to refute these claims about the failure of black children and the role that a biased curriculum had played in this outcome. The level of enthusiasm among educators for a particularly *Afrocentric* reform may have varied—as we have seen good evidence for—but even those most critical of the Afrocentric solution had to acknowledge that Afrocentrists were addressing a problem that they, too, found pressing.

Some educators in these three cases agreed with both the premise that there was a profound problem in the schools that needed attention, and that a key part of the solution to that problem rested with Afrocentric education. According to Gladys Twyman, the project coordinator in Atlanta, administrators decided that they ought to implement an Afrocentric modification in the district at that time, not a multicultural one:

> We are concentrating on African Americans at this time. And trying to incorporate, or to teach, to provide instruction from an African-centered perspective, rather than from the perspective of the European, which is what we've got.
>
> In a *multicultural* program you emphasize multi cultures, many cultures. And our thinking in the Atlanta Public Schools was that before you can know about other cultures, you should first know about yourself. "Know thyself" kind of thing. Know who you are and where you are coming from and what your place in the world is, and then you can start studying and appreciating other cultures. But first you've got to know who you are and appreciate yourself.[7]

With support like this found among administrators in Atlanta, the African-American Infusion Program could take off at full throttle, even if it would eventually end up idling at a lower speed.

Other establishment insiders, however, similarly bemoaned the problem of underachievement among African Americans and other minorities, but parted paths with Afrocentrists over solutions. As we might recall from Washington, D.C., Superintendent Smith (the second superintendent in the district during the Afrocentrists' challenge) was reported early in his tenure to have rejected the Afrocentric claims made by Abena Walker and others that Afrocentrism was the appropriate correction in his district to poor performance and low self-esteem. He argued that a decidedly *Multicultural* multicultural curriculum should be incorporated in his school district instead. His stance was reiterated by one of his aides, who stated her own support for the *problem* Afrocentrists discussed, but not for the solution. Describing the environment of low achievement in the Washington school system, Betty Topps, executive assistant to the superintendent, explained that many education insiders in D.C., like the superintendent, would have liked to have gone the multicultural route. But it was political pressure that forced the district in the direction of Afrocentrism:

> In this school system we want to have a curriculum that, from beginning to end, and content to content, infuses the contributions of our students' cultures into everything they learn: math, science, first grade, third grade, fourth grade, whatever, and throughout. If you looked at our curriculum documents, you would eventually not get to see an *Africa-centered* curriculum, an *Hispanic* curriculum, but you would get to see a curriculum that has all these elements built—fully integrated—

into all of its components. And that's the thrust of our curriculum renewal.

But, at the same time having said that, the politics of the situation is that there is a significant and verbal enough component of our population to have us try and look at small situations—school-within-school situations—where we are going to focus on African-centered.[8]

It was this kind of community pressure—armed with the rhetoric of an age-old educational problem—that convinced D.C.'s Superintendent Smith to continue lending support to Abena Walker's African-Centered Learning Program.

Nathan Glazer, the sociologist at Harvard University and a member of the second curriculum task force in New York, also referred to "the problem" that Afrocentrists were addressing. School systems across the country, he argued, had to respond to the Afrocentric challenge because the problem it addressed was serious, even if, to many, the Afrocentric solution, per se, was unattractive. In these cases, educators retreated to symbolic reform:

Basically, the issue that arose was the sense of a black community that was upset, needing to, in some way, be mollified or reassured, something of that sort. . . . There is a demand, a vague demand, that there should be change. [There is] a general responsiveness among the professionals in the educational community of "Yes, you are right, there should be." And an inability to figure out what that change should be. . . .

Because in the problem of social studies education—it's true, you can talk about other cultures and Asians and American Indians and Hispanics, but the issue is blacks. I mean, it always comes down to it. It's not only size [of the group], it's history. It's the whole complicated relationship. So, there is a reality there. If blacks were performing in schools, let's say, between the way Hispanics perform and the way whites perform, rather than below Hispanics, I doubt we'd have the same issue. It's just that on all tests and so on, there is this very difficult problem of very low levels of performance. So, something must be done. And that drives reform.

So, you have it there. A problem that drives the whole thing, with a response which is hardly adequate for dealing with it in one way or another, but one you can at least get your teeth into.[9]

In his book *We Are All Multiculturalists Now*, Glazer has made the further point—a very good one, I would say, given my findings in this study—that many parents have become willing to try anything to solve the problem of their children's poor performance, and that this willing-

ness influences the actions of educators. "We should also bear in mind,"
Glazer has written about more moderate multiculturalism, "that although
parents are not usually enthusiasts of multicultural education, they are
ready to try almost anything—uniforms, schools for black boys, Afrocentric curricula, schools of choice—to improve the achievement of their children in school." This is less ideological, it seems, than it is practical: as
parts of the American citizenry have become more desperate to improve
their children's academic achievement, their enthusiasm for alternative
paths has grown.[10]

While many educators would not render their dilemma exactly as Glazer
has done here, and most would deny that they engaged in "mollification,"
this description is apt. Sometimes educators genuinely wanted to implement change in the Afrocentric direction (as we saw with the superintendent in Atlanta, and in the case of the first superintendent in Washington);
sometimes they were forced to (as in the case of the second Superintendent
in Washington). Sometimes they turned their backs on the challenge, but
not without having to come up with some kind of adequate response addressing those original concerns (as in New York, where years of committee work followed the rejection of Afrocentrism). But in all of these cases,
public school personnel regarded Afrocentric challengers' description of
the problem as a reasonably accurate assessment of African American children's poor performance. Educators sometimes then gave strong support
and sometimes only superficial support to the Afrocentric solution. But
they offered some level of understanding of this Afrocentric claim.

Cultural Resource 2: Racial Discrimination

Whether given expression in Washington by Abena Walker, in New York
by Leonard Jeffries, or by Asa Hilliard's trainees in Atlanta, the problem
that Afrocentrists described—African American students' disadvantages
in the public schools—had a very real perpetrator. The first-line enemy
responsible for the historical poor performance of black children was
white racism. First, historically (in terms of de facto and official laws)
and, now, pedagogically (in terms of what children learn in school), white
bias and prejudice were the root causes of African American failure in
this country's schools. From the founding of the nation, racist attitudes
about Africans' and African Americans' contributions to world and
American history shaped the content of textbooks and daily classroom
lessons, and were fed as a steady diet to all children. Afrocentrists denounced whites for now being, and for always having been, biased against
blacks, as well as resistant to change. As Abena Walker, the head of the

Webb school in Washington, put it, "the whole white power structure is against this kind of movement."[11]

As we have seen, this charge often caused white education officials to be apprehensive: the potential for being accused of racism was palpable, and something to be countered with action. Thomas Sobol, the commissioner of schools in New York, clearly confronted this accusation; indeed, it was this allegation that led him to appoint the Task Force on Minorities, according to many accounts. Sobol described the racial antipathy he confronted when he was appointed to the post, an antipathy he expected would continue to grow throughout his term if he did not respond immediately to the concerns of his angry constituency:

> I was appointed commissioner, and a lot of people in the black and Hispanic caucus in the legislature went off the wall because they thought they had been promised a black commissioner. And I clearly wasn't that. And furthermore, not only was I a white guy and middle-aged, but I was from Scarsdale yet, which was an upper-middle-class suburb. So what the hell did I know about educating their kids and what was going on?
>
> Now, if you've got a bunch of people yelling at you and not knowing you and not understanding you, what do you want to do? You want to sit down and talk to them, right? And you want them to tell you what's on their minds, and what's bothering them, and what the story is, and then you want to respond to them, and so on. And so I formed a task force for that purpose.[12]

The promise of being perceived as racist by a vocal constituency was at least one factor in New York that compelled this top white administrator to action, resulting in the release of a report that was widely read as Afrocentric.

But the charge of racial bias was not leveled at whites alone, as we saw in both Washington, D.C., and New York. Afrocentrists also aimed that rhetoric at black educators, though altered, in the form of "race betrayal" rather than "racism." When African American administrators or teachers threatened to resist Afrocentrists' demands, they ran the risk of being labeled as "sell-outs," "assimilationists," or members of the middle class attached to the status quo. They were sometimes even accused of not being "black enough." In other words, added to the baseline enemy of white racism—which was a kind of first-order system to be battled against—Afrocentrists also held accountable all African Americans whom they perceived to be beholden to that system. Several of my interviewees offered clear examples of this sentiment, including Murdell McFarlin, the former public information officer in the Atlanta superintendent's office, who lambasted those African Americans formerly in the district who were interested only in fancy cars and fancy clothes:

> [African-centered education] shifted the social peer structure. Because people who had heretofore not been in the "in" clique—like Asa Hilliard—they were now being recognized and considered as educators and experts in their field. That had not happened before. And it put those who *had* been in charge of the educational system here on the back burner. *That* was the fight, *that* was the problem. And a lot of it was black on black.[13]

Some proponents of Afrocentrism went much further in criticizing "status quo" African American bureaucrats, intimating that they were "less black" than Afrocentrists. Abena Walker, founder and principal of the African Centered School in Washington, said,

> I diplomatically say that part of the opposition to us was that people fear change. People just fear change. It's human nature, I guess. [Asked which people]: People, period. I would say the people that were fighting against us. . . . Some of the professors at Howard, Russell Adams, the "house Negro" at the *Post*, and he's never even been here to visit our program. . . . I'm talking about those people that publicly denounced us. I say that, first of all, people fear change. Second of all, I'd say those people in the system that denounced us have bought into the system, so anything that threatens their position, their salary, their status quo, is a threat.[14]

Added to the charge that comfortable black professionals opposed Afrocentric education as a means of protecting their own positions in a change-averse system was the even more damning suggestion made by some of Afrocentrism's supporters that African Americans who opposed Afrocentrism were not as racially or ideologically pure as supporters were. Although I did not directly hear supporters of Afrocentrism make this charge—aside from Abena Walker's "house Negro" comment earlier—I did hear reports of such name-calling from those on the receiving end of this labeling. Recall the New York State Regent, Walter Cooper, who is African American and who voted against the recommendations of "A Curriculum of Inclusion." He remembered,

> One of the things that happened when ["A Curriculum of Inclusion"] was delivered to the Board of Regents, and we determined that it was unacceptable for approval, one of the black members of the task force, Dr. Don Smith of Baruch College, made some rather impolite comments that he directed at me. He accused me of having betrayed my race for not having given assent to this document and being part of some una-

nimity of opinion. As if agreement over issues such as these were to be based on pigmentation, and not on rational processes of determining one's own position on such questions![15]

As these three quotes demonstrate, when African American school officials failed to back Afrocentric solutions, supporters of Afrocentrism sometimes expressed skepticism about those officials' commitment to the education of African American children and to the race, more generally. Judging the actions of unsupportive African American superintendents, administrators, and school board members to be traitorous, Afrocentrism's advocates used the bludgeon of inauthentic race identity and commitment to try to persuade educators to act with them. No African American official with whom I talked acknowledged the power of this rhetoric to have moved them toward an Afrocentric program. Nonetheless, it was a charge that Afrocentric challengers made in all three challenged schools systems, and it may have influenced the actions of some high-placed administrators.

Cultural Resource 3: The Negotiability of the Social Sciences

Afrocentrists benefited from a third cultural resource that they may have used less strategically than the other two resources I describe here, but which was no less helpful to their cause. In these disputes over the content taught to children in the public schools, we should recognize that Afrocentric challengers were taking issue with a discipline, or set of disciplines, that had become vulnerable to contestation in American education circles. Since the 1960s, social studies and history—the primary curricular subjects that Afrocentrists deemed Eurocentric—had attracted a great deal of attention from groups that considered themselves to be oppressed (African Americans, women, Native Americans, for example), and that pushed for substantial change in their representation in textbooks and other pedagogical materials. Following these battles, history and social studies have emerged as *the* subjects in the school curriculum whose content can be altered in the face of constituent demands, if and when social conditions require. Their "truths" have become more flexible, more negotiable than those of other disciplines, such as math or science. For both political and intellectual reasons, educators and their representatives have embraced this greater contestability among the social sciences, and pedagogy in these disciplines has become more elastic. Think of the sentiments expressed by Hazel Dukes, of the NAACP and the "Curriculum of Inclusion" committee from the last chapter, who talked about "making history more real" for students by changing curricula in that subject area.[16] Now, whether the study of history is made more real through altering the "facts" or by altering the mix of topics in the curriculum to achieve more balance is a matter of debate among different advocates of change, and I cannot be sure which of these Dukes was championing. I would argue that both of these routes, though, have been facilitated by the growing tolerance among educators for alteration in history and social science subjects.

When asked to give his thoughts on whether the social sciences could allow "multiple perspectives" as part of their instruction, as his committees had crafted, Thomas Sobol, ex-commissioner of education in New York, referred to the greater flexibility of history and social studies as an "unimpeachable" truth. In fact, this understanding of historical negotiability lays the groundwork for academic honesty and growth in the curriculum, as well as in students' intellectual advancement, Sobol said. In his interview with me, the ex-commissioner argued,

> Hey, look, life is complex. And it is possible to view almost any experience from more than one point of view. And part of educating kids is to get them to understand that there are different perspectives to be brought to bear on experience. And you know, to discriminate among them and synthesize and whatever. And I take that to be an unimpeachable truth. I mean, you know, if somebody doesn't think that, well then, I can't really talk to them very much because they are in some different universe from me.[17]

History is contestable. Children should know this. Among more progressive thinkers like Sobol, the intellectually and socially honest goal is not to protect the canon, but to open up these fields to more and greater knowledge, which can be gained through understanding different groups' perspectives on society and the world.

ROOTS OF HISTORY'S "NEGOTIABILITY." Perhaps the impetus for this movement of multiple perspectives began in the academy, but like so many academic movements, its tendrils have now reached primary and secondary education. Elite campuses across the country have generally taken steps to modify to some degree the traditional Western canon, and public schools at the lower levels of education have followed suit. The possible trickle-down process (from university to primary / secondary) is one that cannot be discussed at length here, but two facets of that process might at least be introduced. Intellectual movements like Afrocentrism or multiculturalism may be particularly compelling to public school educators because it is at their level—rather than at the university level—where those "oppressed voices" discussed in academic publications are most likely to reside. The unprivileged classes who want to have their voices heard are not abstractions at the primary and secondary levels of education, educators might argue; they are the very *real constituencies* who vote and send their children to school in poor minority districts. Changing the history curriculum to include this constituency is not just an intellectual exercise with epistemological implications. Rather, it is a matter of political survival for those in decision-making positions; they must respond in some fashion to voters' demands.

An additional reason why changes like these may ultimately sift down to the public schools from the university is that staff in the primary and secondary levels may attach themselves to the latest academic trends because the academy's discourse bestows on them prestige and status. To follow the academy's lead is to be cloaked in intellectual legitimacy. Since the academy has made historical truth seem less certain, it is easier for public school officials to loosen their own grip on social studies and history curricula. Whereas members of the "hard sciences" achieve greater consensus than do social scientists, and use more sophisticated language—such as Greek letters and formulas—to express that agreement, there is little that now seems "proven" in the social sciences. Lower-level educators adapt to these realities in their own teaching. In short, we should not be surprised if the scholarly movement that started as questions of epistemology in the academy has eventually seeped down into history and social studies classes in elementary and high schools. This seepage would make the social science disciplines vulnerable to movements like Afrocentrism.

Or, perhaps, the answer is even less complicated than this university-prestige model: many educators—from college professors to high school teachers—know that history can be seen from multiple angles, as Thomas Sobol has claimed. History can and should be allowed to be more elastic to accommodate community demands.

Whatever the concept's foundations, it is not surprising to find that a cottage industry has grown of authors and thinkers who find this position repugnant and who decry the decades-long subjection of the social sciences to "relativism."[18] While the *hard sciences*, these writers lament, have been unable to escape completely unscathed from the influence of phenomenology, ethnomethodology, radical feminism, and post-modernism, the traditional search for truth in the *social sciences* has been affected even more by these movements. Whether motivated more by practical, intellectual, or political interests (and conservatives argue the last), these "radical" research streams have opened up the social sciences and humanities to criticism that they have long privileged the work of dead, white, European males over the contributions of other voices. To those who mourn the loss of a canon, these challenges must be rooted out of the education system from whatever level they emerge, to the extent possible.

When college professors teach courses with feminist or other "radical" content, they should be audited, exposed, and compiled on lists of the "politically correct" by attentive conservatives. And when school system constituents fight for greater representation in the public schools, they should face tough scrutiny. Whether it is multiculturalism or Afrocentrism seems only a matter of degree to these writers.

The existence of this cadre of conservative writers, seeking to protect the "Western Culture" tradition, is perhaps the greatest evidence for the argument that the social sciences have been opened up to debate over the past thirty years or so. While it is dangerous to interpret the presence of opponents as proof for a successful intellectual movement, the data suggest that the disciplines Afrocentrists struggled against were more negotiable than perhaps any other subject in elementary and secondary curricula. Together with the two other tools in their cultural repertoire, the argument that history can be presented to meet constituents' needs was compelling. We should bear this point in mind as we think about the other challengers described in this book: the creationists and their struggle against mainstream science education.

So, I find that Afrocentric challengers in Atlanta, Washington, D.C., and New York could craft their arguments for greater African American inclusion in the curriculum using these three cultural resources: a "problem," a "threat," and the fact that the disciplines they challenged had long been considered to be "negotiable." In all three Afrocentric cases, these claims resonated, to some greater or lesser degree, with educators' understandings about race, pedagogy, and social reality in American life.

And yet we have something of a puzzle on our hands. If Afrocentric challengers in all three cases had access to the same resonant frames, then why did the outcomes of their struggles vary in intensity and depth, as we saw in the preceding chapter? Why did the Afrocentric challenge in Atlanta make different advances into public school curricula than the challenge in Washington, D.C., and why did both of these make greater inroads than the challenge in New York state? If Afrocentrists based their demands on the same general set of claims, why didn't they "work" similarly to promote the cause in the three locations? How and why did different school systems treat their Afrocentric challengers differently?

Fortunately, we can solve this puzzle by considering other types of resources and constraints present in the three school systems (besides cultural frames), which also influenced challenger outcomes. As we saw in chapter 3, sometimes the political and organizational structures of a school system—with their cleavages and / or alliances among staff, their political supporters and / or detractors in the community, their routines for establishing curricula and measuring performance—enabled challengers, and sometimes they obstructed them from winning a victory in these systems. It is to these factors that I now turn my attention.

The Influence of Six Political and Organizational Variables on Afrocentric Outcomes

Of the many differences present in the three Afrocentric cases that deserve close observation, I will argue that six central political and organizational factors varied across these cases, and that these factors influenced the amount and kind of curricular change that could occur in each of these school systems.[19] Given that I have only three cases, but six factors leading to variation, the best I can do below is argue for plausibility, rather than causality—a project I hope to carry out judiciously. The following is a synopsis of the variables that I found to be most important from case to case:

(1) *Local versus State School Systems*. Of these three cases, two, obviously, are *local* school systems (Atlanta and Washington, D.C.) and one was a *state* school system (New York). Because local districts and state systems are different in a number of respects (for instance, in the selection of their boards of education and in their implementation policies), there are a number of ways that school systems may handle the demand for reforms. Furthermore, there are obvious differences in states' and local school districts' responsibilities in determining curricula: states set the guidelines for what is to be learned in local school districts, as we saw in New York. Partially because of this broader responsibility for curriculum content, the New York education department faced a greater number of both organizational and political hurdles in the challenge / curriculum revision process than did either of the two local systems.

(2) *Heterogeneity versus Homogeneity of the Challenged System*. The two local systems, Atlanta and Washington, are racially homogeneous to an extent that few states in this country are, let alone New York is (as we know, both Atlanta and Washington have student populations that exceed 90 percent African American; as of 1995, New York state's student population in public schools is 57 percent white, 20 percent African American, 17 percent Latino, 5 percent Asian, and less than 1 percent Native American).[20] The pressures that system administrators faced either to adapt to or ward off a *single constituency's* demands were strongly related

to the presence or absence of other key constituencies in that environment. Where an African American community, imagined to be supportive of Afrocentrism, represented a large share of the constituency (as in Atlanta and Washington), Afrocentrism had a better chance of advancing. Where a black community was judged to represent just one faction among many (as in New York), Afrocentrism had a greater likelihood of being stalled. The presence of these constituencies strongly influenced the political possibilities for responding to challengers.

(3) *The Degree to which Multicultural Revisions Had Already Been Made in the School System.* By the time the Afrocentric challenges were being made in all of these locations, the concept of *multiculturalism* had already become familiar in American schools, and it was widely accepted as a reasonable and integral part of a legitimate education. But the extent to which multicultural revisions had been incorporated into the routine practices of the three school systems varied dramatically at the time that the different Afrocentric challengers began their efforts. One might hazard a guess that where multicultural content had already been incorporated significantly into a system, Afrocentrism would have been able to move in more smoothly, since the arguments made for both of these types of curricula overlapped to a considerable degree. But as we saw in the case studies, the reverse seems to be true. In the one case where extensive multicultural revisions already had been made in the system (New York), educators and other decision makers were *more* averse to additional change than were those in the two systems where very little multiculturalism had yet been introduced (in Atlanta and Washington). On the basis of this surprising finding, I speculate that where there was an ideology that there *ought* to be a more diverse curriculum, but where there was an absence of any change to date (as in Atlanta and Washington), an organizational vacuum appeared that could be filled more easily by Afrocentrism.

(4) *Means of Student Testing.* As was mentioned briefly in the case histories, the means of testing across the three school systems varied, and these, too, influenced the nature of change that administrators and teachers were willing to make in the curriculum. One of the only ways that school systems measure teachers' performance (and ultimately school and district performance) is by how well students score on standardized tests. (Whether this is a reasonable means of gauging teacher effectiveness is controversial but, as it stands, this is the primary way that teachers are evaluated, to the extent that they are formally evaluated at all.) Given

this system, teachers in all three systems would have been motivated to include instruction in any subject matter that was likely
to be covered on standardized tests. If the tests covered Afrocentric materials, then teachers would have an incentive to teach Afrocentric content; if the tests did not cover Afrocentric materials,
and teachers *knew* that the tests would not cover Afrocentric content, then teachers would be free *not* to teach Afrocentrism, if that
were their inclination (as we saw in Atlanta). This, too, was an
organizational feature of the school systems that profoundly influenced administrators' responses to challenge.

(5) *Advocacy by the Media.* It is clear that the media influenced the
progress of challengers' efforts in these three cases. It is not surprising to observe that when the media supported revisions (as
they generally did in Atlanta), it was easier for challengers to secure some success in the school system; when the media were un-
abashedly critical of proposed revisions, administrators' ability to
accommodate challengers was constrained, even if administrators
otherwise might have been willing to compromise further with
those challengers (as in Washington and perhaps in New York).

Contributing to media reaction, I argue, was the reputation of
the particular school system being challenged: its visibility on the
national stage as a successful or failing system, and the symbolism
it carried for the issue of educating black children. Journalists'
seemed to be swayed by whether the system seemed to be part of
a larger inner city problem (as in Washington); if it were embedded in a city that is the symbol of the African American middle
class (as in Atlanta); or if it were a smaller part of a majority white
establishment (as in New York state). Media coverage, including
discussion of each system's reputation, placed political pressure
on administrators to respond to challengers either negatively or
positively.

(6) *Insider Support for the Challenge.* A sixth organizational variable
contributing to outcomes was the presence or absence of insiders
in the school system who were willing to champion the cause of
Afrocentrism for their schools. Whether by responding positively
to the challenge once it had begun, or by jump starting the struggle by initiating and developing demands for change, insider support—when present—facilitated greater success for challengers.
Insider support for Afrocentrism was most prominent in Atlanta,
where the district's superintendent and many of his administrators were committed to the cause and helped generate enthusiasm
for the program. The total absence of such initiation was evident
in New York, while in Washington, D.C., a sprinkling of insider

support could be found, helping to put into place the "circum-scribed reform" that occurred there.

In the following sections, I will demonstrate that these political and orga-nizational factors mattered significantly to the outcomes of the three Afro-centric challenges, even though the challengers' cultural claims remained more or less constant from case to case. I will describe how each factor allowed some Afrocentric challengers to have relatively deep or intense levels of success in some school systems (albeit temporarily, in most in-stances), and how the absence of certain factors in other locations frus-trated challengers' ability to make serious inroads in the curriculum.

Institutional Influence 1: State versus Local Systems

The first and most obvious feature that differentiated two of these cases from the other was their location in the public education system. The Atlanta and Washington, D.C., cases involved *local* school districts, while the New York case involved a *state* system. The three systems' different locations in the educational world placed different constraints on admin-istrators for handling the Afrocentric challenge.

Because state education departments have primary responsibility for developing the parameters of curricular content in the American public school system,[21] it follows that state education departments also have to observe more rigid guidelines when responding to curricular challenges than do local school districts. The long and arduous course of trying to revise the curriculum in New York state was testament to this fact. In New York, the process for handling the proposed revisions included the appointment of various task forces and committees (including, but not exclusively, The Task Force on Minorities and the "Diversity Commit-tee"); the publication of committee reports ("A Curriculum of Inclusion," "One Nation, Many Peoples," among others); the multiple submissions of Commissioner Sobol's recommendations to the Board of Regents; the creation of curricular frameworks; the distribution of those frameworks for public comment; and the integration of national standards and other semi-related school system goals into those frameworks and reports, such as the state's "Compact for Learning," New York's overarching approach to pedagogy.[22] Although the reforms in Atlanta and Washington, D.C., had to be approved by their respective boards of education and internal administrators, they were not required to meet a similar array of stan-dards and criteria as New York state demanded.

State systems are *not* the same thing as local school systems *"writ large."*[23] Because of its procedures for curriculum decision-making, the state system in New York seems to have been more constrained in its ability to adopt challenger demands, whereas the two local systems seem to have had more degrees of freedom in handling curricular challenges. Whether the challenge was Afrocentrism or some other, we should not be surprised that the local school districts were able to adopt new curricula more smoothly than could the state school system, all things being equal, primarily because they were not as "multi-tiered."[24]

Institutional Influence 2: Homogeneity versus Heterogeneity of the Challenged System

Another factor, which is strongly related to location in the education structure, is the racial and ethnic composition of the school system, and who its constituents are, or at least, who decision makers *perceive* them to be. Constituent composition can be seen to be a type of "charter" for individual systems, insofar as administrators act on behalf of, or in response to, their *imagined communities*.[25] Atlanta and Washington are racially homogeneous (both above 90 percent black), while New York state is racially and ethnically more diverse, as was noted earlier. One can imagine that it was easier for administrators to cater to an educational "racial project" of their constituents if the *rest* of the community was the same race, rather than racially diverse.[26] Even if the concession actually contradicted other school system goals, the political currency gained from satisfying constituents was expected to be high, as many have pointed out, including those in the institutional school of organizations theory.

Although I do not have direct evidence for this claim about constituencies, we have witnessed action in these cases that lend it support. In both Atlanta and Washington, there were vocal activists in the districts—the most vocal in both places being groups affiliated with the Black Muslim community—pressuring school administrators to support Afrocentrism. Certainly the main impetus in Washington to allow the African-centered school-within-a-school program to move forward in the face of harsh public criticism was parents' support for the program, as Howard University's Russell Adams indicated to me.[27] Parents had expressed their support forcefully, dating back several years, through protests at board meetings, campaigns of petition-signing, and angry press conferences, all of which were covered heavily in the *Washington Post*. I would argue that the two sitting superintendents in D.C. during the period of conflict over Afrocentrism, Andrew Jenkins and Franklin Smith, simply found it impossible to look these parents in the face and say no to their demands, especially when those demands could be served in a highly contained manner (as Smith treated them). According to the superintendents' calculations—especially Smith's—real political fallout would have been endured from a number of angry black parents if the district rejected the proposals for the African-centered program.[28] The school board in Atlanta felt that it faced similar demands for Afrocentric change, given the complaints that black parents and even media writers had been registering for years.

New York was a fundamentally different story, for neither parents nor community activists were involved in the challenge—and if they had been, no *one* challenging group would have represented a racial majority. This was a challenge that was fought among academics and practitioners, not constituents, and after the first round of debate was over, with the release of "A Curriculum of Inclusion," the political context dictated that the commissioner and his staff address *academics'* concerns about the proposed revisions, not those of African American and Latino constituents.

The three cases were clearly affected by their location in the educational system (local vs. state) and the racial-ethnic composition of that system (homogeneous vs. heterogeneous).

Institutional Influence 3: The Degree to which Multicultural Revisions Had Already Been Made in the School System

Let me now turn to the presence or absence of multicultural curricular content in each system. Recall that I have been arguing that one of the greatest cultural advantages that Afrocentrists had at their disposal was the forceful resonance of their arguments about the "problem" of African Americans' poor performance in U.S. public schools with public school educators' beliefs. Even if district administrators were reluctant to incorporate Afrocentrists' solutions whole-cloth into their curriculum, officials did see genuine wisdom in their demands to add content that accentuated African Americans' contributions to U.S. and world history. This had been one of the central tenets of multiculturalism, after all. And although multiculturalism was still not *universally* accepted as a public good—see, for example, the writings of Robert Bork—public school systems, by the time these Afrocentric challenges came along in the 1980s and 1990s, had generally endorsed the pluralist impulse behind multiculturalism.[29] The fact that multiculturalism had already become standard in pedagogical circles made Afrocentrism's stated problem more comprehensible. When multiculturalism began to be more widely accepted during the 1980s— with its criticism that the traditional history curriculum was biased and unusable—a path was being laid for potentially even more radical identity-oriented curricula to seem acceptable in the future.

Although all forms of multiculturalism have their roots in movements from previous decades, such as the community control movement of the

1960s, multiculturalism as legitimate, official, universal curricula has entered school systems across the nation neither simultaneously nor similarly.[30] In some school systems, multiculturalism has emphasized the contributions of all peoples to world history; in others, it has highlighted not only the contributions made by certain ethnic groups, but the pain, suffering, and resistance also experienced by them. And there have been other forms besides, as Michael Olneck has described in his review of curricular frameworks, reports, and guidelines. Given the absence of a national standard for what "pluralistic" history instruction should be and how it should be incorporated into a school system, multiculturalism has followed no automatic track into school classrooms.

Let's review the causal relationship between multiculturalism and the adoption of an Afrocentric curriculum offered in point 3 of the previous synopsis. I suggested that the presence of an accepted multicultural ideology in school districts would lead to multicultural content in classrooms, which would then lead to tolerance for Afrocentric content, since the arguments made by Afrocentrists appeared similar to multiculturalism, at least on the surface. This expectation coincides with movements literature on "early risers" and "latecomers," in which it is proposed that movement initiators pave the way for many different forms of later challengers, having already weakened the challenged institution. If this guess were correct, then Afrocentrism would have had the greatest chance of infiltrating systems that had already implemented significant multicultural curricula, and it would have had the slimmest chance of success in systems where real multicultural change had not yet taken place.

Applying this prediction to my three cases, one would guess that the school system in New York state—which had implemented widespread multicultural changes in the curriculum in 1987 (before Sobol's appointment to office)—would have been the most likely to be friendly to the Afrocentric challenge, while Atlanta and Washington, D.C.—both of which had long *discussed* setting up an official multicultural curriculum but had yet to act concretely on any of these discussions—would have been less likely to do so. New York's revisions should have provided the most helpful blueprint; Atlanta's and Washington's previous inaction should have posed the greatest obstacles to the new Afrocentric challenge.

But, as we know, this is not what came to pass. New York was the least successful of the three cases, not the most successful. Although there were myriad other reasons why the state did not "go Afrocentric" (cultural, political, and organizational), one predominant part of the official rhetoric used against further modification was that the state had only recently spent an enormous amount of time, money, and energy revising curricula to be less Eurocentric in their presentation of history.

According to Nathan Glazer's written analysis of the New York case, it was school teachers and administrators on the second committee (the "Diversity Committee," on which Glazer served) who were the most circumspect about changing the curriculum again, given the recent revisions that had been made in the state and with which they were satisfied. Although several of the academics on the committee were open to debating the substance of multiculturalism in the curriculum, public school staff (those who actually worked in the schools and who were now serving on the committee) were far more reluctant to revise the content further. According to Glazer,

> Those . . . who worked in the schools seemed less concerned about the degree of multicultural tilt in the report than about what it meant for the *practical work* of teachers and administrators. New curricular guidelines would mean that school teachers, who had been teaching a curriculum that itself had just recently been adopted after a long process of consultation, would now have to learn a new one, and prepare their students for new tests. The issue of just what was in the curriculum or in the tests, seemed to concern them less than the fact that the curriculum and the tests would be *new*, and would therefore pose a threat to teachers.[31]

The previous efforts at and, indeed, the incorporation of, multicultural content in the schools thwarted the advance of more revisions in New York. Drawing on Glazer's insights, we should see that educators had less stomach for changes—especially for those they saw as having Afrocentric origins—than they might have had if recent multicultural changes had not been made. This finding is similar to those in Doug McAdam's preliminary work on temporality in movement cycles, in which he has written: "[T]here is good reason to suspect that those movements which arise fairly late in a reform protest cycle are disadvantaged by the necessity of having to confront a state that is already preoccupied with the substantive demands and political pressures generated by the early risers."[32]

Meanwhile, in the majority-black districts of Atlanta and Washington—where administrators had for years vocally supported multiculturalism without making any substantive district-wide changes in its direction—multiculturalism was like a disembodied idea whose time had come. This view could be seen clearly in the pages of the *Atlanta Journal-Constitution*, which early on chided the Atlanta school district for lagging behind other school districts—particularly the *white* school district in Portland—which were making use of Atlanta's resident scholars' concepts in their revised African-centered curricula. By comparison, the school district in Atlanta was seen to be only making noises about its loyalty to African American concepts.[33] It was in the two cases where tangible multicultural change of any sort had yet to arrive that Afrocentrism entered into the school systems more easily.

Generalizing from the New York case on this dimension, one might say that previous revisions in the multicultural direction, combined with other political and organizational constraints in the system, helped inoculate the state's public schools against future efforts at more controversial revisions like Afrocentrism. Generalizing from the Atlanta and Washington cases, one might say that in districts where there was an ideology that supported the aims of multiculturalism, but where no actual multicultural program had been implemented (much to the chagrin of the community), the districts were vulnerable to the more disputed program of Afrocentrism. In these systems, an organizational space had been made for a non-Eurocentric curriculum, but nothing had yet come to fill it.

Institutional Influence 4: Means of Student Testing

Just as the level of multiculturalism already instituted in a system played an influential role in the system's capacity to incorporate Afrocentrism, so, too, did the system's means of testing: another organizational variable. Testing in school systems is the central means for ensuring teacher accountability, particularly in an environment where there is "loose coupling" between what is officially required by the district and what actually goes on behind the closed doors of the classroom—that is, where there is very little direct measurement or oversight.[34] Even when teachers are disinclined to alter their syllabi for any number of reasons (an aversion to changing their routines, say, or disagreement with a new set of materials), teachers are more likely to be persuaded to conform to official curriculum standards if their own performance is evaluated by their conformity.[35]

Teacher evaluation occurs through the indirect means of student testing, which is designed to work as follows: All states have a set of standards delineating what students in their classrooms should learn in the different disciplines at every grade level, as we saw in detail in New York. These standards are set out in documents like the state's social studies framework or its science framework. From these standards, syllabi are then developed, either by a committee appointed in the state (as in New York) or through adoption of other states' documents. The syllabus for each discipline at each grade level includes particular curricular exercises to be used in the classroom. At the end of the year, students in the districts take some form of standardized test to measure how well they have learned the material set out in the syllabus. Not only students' performance but also teachers' and schools' performance are measured by these student tests. When students have learned the materials poorly (as measured by test scores), their schools and teachers are held responsible for not having taught the material well. Because principals are held accountable, to some extent, for the scores, they put pressure on teachers to cover whatever materials are included on the standardized tests.

Compared to most industrialized nations in the world, education in the United States is a remarkably decentralized institution. With this general decentralization comes decentralized testing procedures, which vary from state to state and even from district to district, particularly in the different tests that can be used to measure student performance. In the Atlanta and Washington, D.C., public school districts, for example, nationally available tests (the Iowa Test of Basic Skills and the Stanford Achievement Test, respectively), are used to measure students' performance, while in New York State, the schools rely on the state's Regents Examinations to measure students' performance.

ATLANTA. To explain how a particular testing protocol could influence the outcomes in these three cases, I will first discuss the case of the Atlanta school district and its experience with the African American Infusion Program.

With major financial and personnel resources behind it, this program seemed to have been singularly primed to have changed the way history and social studies were taught in every schoolroom in the district. As we know, the district spent millions of dollars on materials and teacher training, and administrators in the district devoted countless hours to incorporating the new materials into the existing curriculum. Personnel in the district's curriculum division cross-referenced established educational goals and outcomes with the new program, and they developed curriculum learning objectives (CLOs)—the sine qua non of "legitimate" education—for the new content.[36] With all of this activity devoted to making the new curriculum thoroughly legitimate and incorporating it into the routines of the district, one would have expected the entire system—meaning all teachers in all classrooms—to have infused these materials into instruction. And, as we saw in the case history, many teachers did enthusiastically embrace the new materials, and they began teaching them to their students.

But teachers who were unhappy with the new materials—because they would be forced to change their methods or because they disagreed with the content of the revisions or because they knew that teaching Afrocentric materials would not increase students' test scores (a recent pressure in the district)—found a loophole for avoiding African American infusion if they wanted. This loophole came in the form of testing in the district which, before and after the African American Infusion Program was in place, was based on the Iowa Test of Basic Skills, a national achievement test. The Iowa test included no items that were tailored to individual districts—Atlanta's or elsewhere. Rather, it measured students' achievement only in the most generic skills in language, mathematics, and reading, not in any specifically African-oriented content that the children were learning in their Atlanta classrooms.[37]

What the Iowa test meant for teachers who were averse to teaching African-centered materials was that they did not *have* to teach the revised curriculum if they did not *want* to because the Iowa test would not reflect mastery of any locally distinctive curriculum. According to one of my respondents, the journalist Betsy White, teachers in Atlanta did not feel overwhelming pressure to teach the new materials:

> There wasn't a lot of a sense that "We really *had* to do it, and that the bigwigs were really, really, *really* behind us." I mean, of course they were: they were calling in everybody [teachers] to go through the training. But, was it going to show up on the standardized tests? *No.* [But], were test scores the thing that were going to determine whether you got transferred all over the schools? *Yes.*[38]

According to White's analysis, with the arrival of Superintendent J. Jerome Harris in the district, the Iowa test scores had become centrally important to teachers' sense of job security; thus, they were intent on having their students score well on them. But these test scores were not going to be affected by whether teachers taught African American infusion in the classroom, and teachers knew it. Far more important to their survival in the system, they understood, with this new, demanding superintendent, was to teach only those materials that would allow their students to score higher on the standardized tests.

In an evocative illustration of her point, Betsy White described a hypothetical encounter between Superintendent Harris and a school teacher in his district named Amy:

> Harris made improving standardized test scores *all important*. Teachers' job were on the line if they didn't boost ITBS [Iowa Test of Basic Skills] scores. And you certainly know that Afrocentric teaching will take away from, rather than enhance, the sort of panic-driven, teach-to-the-test, short-term gains in test scores that Harris's stance prompted among most Atlanta teachers. "Amy, I want you to attend a training session on the ignored history of Africans in all the major disciplines, and I want you to figure out how to incorporate that new knowledge into everything you teach (even though it is left out of all the textbooks you'll continue to use), and we all know how important that is to our students. And I also want you to raise reading and math skills of our

kids, as measured by standardized test scores. Both of these are very, very important to me and the district.

We won't check on your lesson plans, or in any way verify whether you add the role of Egyptians in math or anything else into your teaching. But if you and your fellow faculty members don't raise test scores this year, you'll all be transferred to other schools (and get no say in which school) and will be publicly exposed as unworthy teachers whose school had to be reconstituted." What am I *really* saying to you about my priorities?[39]

Because students were not going to be tested on this content, and because Harris had made their scores on the Iowa tests the focus of attention in the district, Atlanta's school children did not need to learn infused materials. And since the teachers' and schools' performances were being evaluated only on material that was standard throughout the country, standard material was all that many teachers were going to teach to their students. They simply did not have to change their classroom routines. All this meant that the district could make a big deal out of devoting millions of dollars to African American infusion, but it did not have to risk alienating its teaching staff. Teachers could easily, and without the risk of sanctions, decline to teach anything new, if they so desired. I believe this teacher choice—a consequence of the form of testing in Atlanta— limited African American infusion in the district.

WASHINGTON, D.C. The District of Columbia Public Schools also use a nationally developed test to evaluate students' performance (in this case, the Stanford Achievement Test). But testing played a smaller role in constraining Afrocentric curriculum in Washington than in Atlanta because the Afrocentric revisions were in a set-aside program, separate from the rest of the district. Reluctant teachers outside Abena Walker's African-centered school-within-a-school were not asked to incorporate these revisions; only enthusiastic teachers, who had volunteered to be part of the program, were expected to teach African-centered material. Because all the teachers in the separate African-centered school *wanted* to participate in it, no back-door efforts were required to circumvent the content, as some teachers in Atlanta engaged in. In Washington, as long as the students in the African-Centered Program performed as well on the Stanford Test as did students in the rest of the district's schools, the Afrocentric program could continue to teach Afrocentric materials.

NEW YORK. New York, as we have seen, uses a different kind of standardized test at the high-school level to assess students' performance, and I argue that the state's distinctive system of evaluation contributed to that school system's response to the challenge. Because the New York case provides the greatest contrast with the Atlanta case, I will describe it in some detail.

New York is a self-proclaimed "top-down" education state, which develops its own standardized tests—called Regents Exams—to measure students' learning and performance.[40] These tests are based on the state's curricula and syllabi, which are also developed in-state, and the tests are taken by every public high-school student to graduate. This is a far different scenario from the examination protocols in Atlanta and Washington, D.C., where knowledge of classroom content is evaluated using national, and therefore much more generic, tests. Unlike these two districts, where unique district content goes unevaluated on students' final achievement examinations, New York's specially tailored tests gauge whether students have learned the educational content explicitly set out in its statewide curriculum guides. This means that *any* content that appears on the syllabus has some likelihood of showing up on the Regents Exams, and teachers may be held accountable for any change that is made in the curriculum. Unlike the teachers in Atlanta, who could find a loophole and not teach revised materials if they so chose, teachers in New York need to teach revised content if their students are to perform well on the statewide tests. Because these scores directly reflect back on teachers' instruction, they make high-school teachers, anyway, accountable to curriculum revisions. The Regents Exams ensure that any new content—or, at least some parts of it—will be tested. Even if the use of Regents Exams cannot *guarantee* that teachers and schools will teach such testable content, it surely encourages instruction in those areas.

We should expect that this difference in testing practices in New York would have elicited a different sort of boundary protection from the type we saw emerge in Atlanta. Atlanta's testing program, which did not measure Afrocentric infusion, allowed the district's unenthusiastic leaders to concede to their community constituents, even while they had no means of evaluating whether teachers successfully incorporated the infused materials. On the basis of journalist White's close observations and other accounts of the Atlanta program, I suspect that a number of Atlanta's board members and administrators could take comfort in pleasing their multiple constituencies—the community and their pro-Infusion staff—with the African American program. Many members of the African American community would cheer the changes, but personnel would not feel alienated by new teaching requirements, since reluctant teachers could simply ignore the new curricular changes.

In New York, this situation was not possible. Pleasing a small constituency by including revisions in the curriculum would have angered personnel because teachers actually would have been held responsible for teaching the new material, which would have been included in the Regents Examinations. Insights into these concerns were described by Linda Biemer, the dean of the education school at SUNY, Binghamton, and a member of the third New York committee:

> Some of the administrators were there [at committee meetings], and they kept saying, "Well, you've got to think about . . . you know, I'm an administrator, what will I tell my teachers?" You had teachers there, a couple of them who didn't want to change things. They felt they were really representing teachers. One person was there representing teachers, but he also represented the union. He was the leader in one of the state teachers' unions. And I think he was engaged in a bit of "Don't change things" protectionism. Especially because his union had been critical of one or the other of the earlier reports.
>
> And it was very difficult for people not to go back to: "Well, now, will these questions be on the Regents [Exams]?"[41]

If the New York school system wanted to protect against revisions of any kind, it had to keep the curriculum buffered from those revisions from start to finish. It could not afford to allow change anywhere in the process because tailored standardized tests were used to measure potentially every item in the curriculum. There would be no pleasing factions of the African American constituency (or other constituencies represented on the first task force) via any symbolic means; it was just too risky for the system to do. The project that was perceived to have its roots in an Afrocentric vision had to be "cooled out" much earlier in the New York process (e.g., at the time of curriculum development) than in the Atlanta or D.C. project. As we know, the state dealt with the challenge with outright rejection.

Institutional Influence 5: Media Effects

Thus far I have discussed several similarities in political and organizational influences in Atlanta and Washington: the level of the system they occupy (local school districts), the high degree of racial-ethnic homogeneity (predominantly African American), the extent of multicultural revisions implemented previously in the district (little to none), and the districts' means of student testing (outside standardized examinations). On these dimensions, the New York case has provided all of the important variation. On the dimension to be discussed in this section—the influence of the media, a generally neglected site of study in the social movements literature—we will see greater similarities between Washington and New York, with Atlanta providing the important variation. In both Washington and New York, the dominant media, the *Washington Post* and the

New York Times, respectively, were highly critical of the school system's engagement in what they considered to be Afrocentric terrain—calling it by turns "hostile," "separatist," and simply "inaccurate."

In Atlanta, media commentators proceeded differently, by expressing early and sustained support for local Afrocentric revisions. For years before the African American Infusion program even got off the ground, the *Atlanta Journal-Constitution* had been complaining pointedly about the glaring absence of multicultural content in Atlanta schools and had been calling on the school district to correct the situation. The paper had even sought to shame the district for its neglect of African American students when it covered Portland's decision to hire Asa Hilliard of Georgia State to develop the *Baseline Essays*. Why, asked the *Journal-Constitution*, should the predominantly white Portland school district get to procure the talents of the Atlanta hometown scholar, Dr. Hilliard, when Atlanta could not do the same?[42] Because the *Atlanta Journal-Constitution's* coverage differed so much from the *Times* and the *Post*, it requires more commentary.

According to Betsy White, once the school board and superintendent promoted the idea of African American infusion with the newspaper's support, the *Journal-Constitution* was interested in tracking the progress of the program because (1) it had devoted space in the past to the absence of African and African American contributions in the curriculum, (2) its audience would be interested in the program's existence and effects, and (3) it wanted to monitor the program and track whether it was succeeding in its mission.[43]

Although supporters of African American infusion might heartily disagree with White that the newspaper was largely "uncritical" of the program, it is certainly true that the *Atlanta Journal-Constitution's* coverage of the local program was far less antagonistic than the articles that appeared in the *Washington Post* or the *New York Times* about the efforts in their respective locales. With the exception of one editorial in 1990, virtually all other stories in the *Atlanta Journal-Constitution* about the African American Infusion Program were generally positive. With headlines such as "Black History: Filling in the Blanks," "Taking Pride in Their Heritage: New Curriculum 'Infuses' African History into Other Subjects," "It's Time to Teach Ancient Egypt's Heritage," "Black History Month Praised, but Year-Round Program Urged," and "Is Black History an Ornament that Adorns February?" the newspaper created a supportive atmosphere in which the African American Infusion Program could take hold.[44]

It is interesting to note that although the newspaper looked kindly upon the *local* infusion program, it published far more skeptical, if not hostile, commentary about other experiments with Afrocentrism across the country, many of which were similar to Atlanta's program. One might surmise that such a response would be possible if the newspaper differentiated between Atlanta's infusion program and all other Afrocentric initiatives, which had become the targets of pundits nationwide, and / or if it wanted to give its school system a break and let it work out the kinks locally. Both alternatives are supported by the data, and both allowed the Atlanta school district to progress further with training and funding for the program without the harsh scrutiny given the proposals in the Washington and the New York press.

The overall pattern that emerges in this differential media coverage between Atlanta, Washington, and New York seems to have been built, at least partially, on how local journalists viewed their system's symbolic weight in the nation: how central, visible, and important this district was for representing the education of African American children. The media discussion concerned whether the school district was seen as a microcosm of the nation's problem with inner-city, African American school districts (Washington, D.C.); as the symbol of what a progressive African American school district ought to be able to accomplish (Atlanta); or as a resource-rich, forward-thinking, progressive educational institution (as New York state had been seen for so long). The images of previous success or failure that the media drew for each of these school systems seemed to constrain the actions that administrators could then take in the face of challenging rhetoric.

Institutional Influence 6: Insider Support for the Challenge

The final organizational factor to be addressed in this chapter is the extent to which insiders in each of the school systems supported and sometimes even initiated the fight for revised curriculum in their home district. For the present discussion, when I describe establishment insiders' role in curricular change, I will use the definition of "insider" traditionally outlined by social movements scholars: insiders are those vested with authority to make decisions, and who have routine access to resources of all sorts in the system. Although I will turn a more critical eye to this terminology in chapter 7—where I tease out the "political" power from the "institutional" power that different establishment insiders possess—for now, I will treat "insiderness" as a quality that we can locate unproblematically. In the next paragraphs, I recap below how insiders, like administrators and district heads, responded to Afrocentrists in Atlanta, Washington, and New York.

Obviously, the Afrocentric challenge enjoyed the most sustained support from establishment insiders in Atlanta, where not only top curriculum administrators, but also the superintendent, took up the cause of Afrocentric revisions. Even though outsiders, like the Shrine of the Black Madonna, also lobbied for change, as did parties like the local newspaper, the heart and soul of the Afrocentric success in Atlanta was the powerful Superintendent J. Jerome Harris and his group of devoted administrators. Together, the superintendent and his hand-picked staff persuaded the school board to commit millions of dollars to materials and teacher in-services for the African American Infusion Program. With their power to revise curriculum guidelines and their access to school district funds, these insiders proved essential to Afrocentrism's grand debut in Atlanta.

Abena Walker's African-centered learning curriculum in Washington, D.C., also enjoyed the support of insiders—at least in the form of the eventual lame-duck superintendency of Andrew Jenkins, the first sittting head of schools during this time period. As we will recall from chapter 3, the controversial Superintendent Jenkins took on the Afrocentric mantle late in the middle of his short-lived tenure, and he was able to work with the school board to commit $750,000 for eligible Afrocentric pilot pro-grams. Due to several leadership flaws, however, the school board soon dispensed with Jenkins, and his replacement, Superintendent Franklin Smith, was not so dedicated to the Afrocentric cause. Although Smith ended up conceding ground to Abena Walker and her African-centered curriculum, this superintendent consistently advocated multiculturalism, foremost, as an appropriate curriculum in Washington, and he subse-quently kept tight boundaries on how far Afrocentrism could spread in his district, once Walker's program was launched. Meanwhile, other district insiders who might have supported the African-centered school-within-a-school, such as Valencia Mohammed (Walker's former collaborator and later a school-board member), declined to support Walker's program, cit-ing its director's infamy as a mark against Afrocentric curricula. In short, without the clear commitment of insiders in the District of Columbia, alongside harsh criticism from the *Washington Post*, Walker's Afrocentric curriculum—despite its popularity among devoted parents—was left to survive as a small program, but never receiving the resources to grow.

The Afrocentric struggle in New York, as we know, suffered the most irreparable harm from insiders who backed away from the Afrocentric agenda quickly, vocally, and publicly, without ever adopting the solutions that it proposed. While Leonard Jeffries's critique of the New York curric-ulum did elicit sympathy among select insiders for its general findings of European overemphasis in the state's social studies and history curricula, the report "A Curriculum of Inclusion" caused education insiders (such as the superintendent and Board of Regents) to retreat from its tone and specific findings. At no time did explicit Afrocentrism win the approval of establishment insiders. For this, it sustained permanent injury.

Conclusion *or read all*

Different processes of debate and varying degrees of Afrocentric revision took place in Atlanta, Washington, and the state of New York. Although Afrocentric challengers and their supporters had similar cultural resources in their repertoires, the political and organizational structures they encountered in these different school systems sometimes lessened, sometimes increased the power of these rhetorical frames.

Atlanta

Atlanta's Afrocentric reform can be called a process of "big bang" reform, wherein there was a large outlay of funds and system-wide training in new curricula, but content changes were not reflected in tests at the end, which meant that teachers in the district who did not want to change their syllabus did not have to. Atlanta teachers knew that they would not be held accountable for their students' knowledge of the African American curriculum because their students were evaluated through nationally standardized tests. These tests did not reflect local variations in curriculum (like Afrocentric content), and it was the scores on these tests by which Atlanta teachers would be evaluated. This process curtailed the extensiveness of Afrocentric revisions in Atlanta.

Yet, at the same time, the Atlanta challenge ended up achieving more visibility than either of the other two cases because its supporters' arguments and actions resonated culturally and organizationally with the beliefs of leaders in the district. It also helped that the superintendent was one of the prime challengers fighting for Afrocentric reform in his district, although he did have to convince a school board with covert political ill will that his was a program worth supporting—despite some teachers' aversion to it. Nevertheless, the media left the program largely unscrutinized, the board funded an expensive program to overhaul the curriculum, and the district used decidedly Afrocentric materials to do so—the *Baseline Essays* among them.

Washington DC

Washington, D.C., achieved marginal success of a different sort, typified by what I am calling "circumscribed reform." This challenge was contained, or circumscribed, when the superintendent set aside only one part of the school system for Afrocentric revision (in this case, the poorest part of the district with the most actively vocal community supporters), but nowhere else, and he did not allow the program to expand to any other schools outside the original setting. According to one of my respondents, Russell Adams, a most skeptical critic of Afrocentrism, the superintendent of the D.C. schools was willing to gamble with the poorest segments of the black population, but not with other sections of the city. Whether Superintendent Franklin Smith was willfully "gambling" or "experimenting" with those students' lives is something only he could say.

But we do know that being introduced in a nearly all-African American school district in the shadow of the Capitol, a district that had systematically incorporated almost *no* multicultural content to date, but that was home to parents and other community members pressuring for change, greatly facilitated Afrocentrism's progress. Despite an extremely oppositional press bearing down on the district's "experiments" with Afrocentrism, the other organizational and cultural factors present in the district allowed the one African-centered school to open, and then sustain itself, in the school system through the last years of the 1990s.

Meanwhile, we can label New York's encounter with Afrocentrism as "outright rejection." Although Afrocentric advocates found their way on to Sobol's early committee and advanced the cultural claims that have become so familiar (and sometimes powerful) in Afrocentric challenges, the state education department, its board, and its several commissions made clear that the committee's mandate for curriculum change would not be tolerated. Some reforms ultimately did make it into the curriculum via the subsequent series of committees. These came in the form of multiculturalism and multiple perspectives, and were verifiably measured by the state's Regents Exams. But even these reforms were attenuated because their architects were presumed to be associated with the first committee. In New York, the few elements of "multiple perspectives" from the second committee that found their way into the new curriculum were the result of tooth-and-nail battles to overcome suspicion and to differentiate its work from "A Curriculum of Inclusion."

All of this is to say that the Afrocentric challenges (just like the creationist challenges, as we will see next) were shaped by myriad forces— some at the level of resonance with *cultural* belief systems, some at the level of *politics*, and some in the details of local *organizational* policies, like testing or the recency and tenor of previous curricular revisions. While it is difficult to generalize from these three cases which of the factors will be present and influential in future Afrocentric challenges— there are simply too many confounding variables to be found in each case to presume such universality—one of the central aims of the chapter has been to identify the conditions that were favorable or unfavorable to outcomes in this type of curricular challenge.

A second byproduct of the chapter has been to uncover the relationship between structure and culture in these challenges. While culturalists in the social movements field decry movement theory (especially political process models) for its structural biases, we can see clearly in these cases that structural context shaped how similar cultural arguments across three different political structures would be interpreted. Meanwhile, structuralists in the social movements cadre who criticize cultural accounts of movement activity for ignoring structural influence, must recognize that it is often cultural arguments (as seen in the first part of the chapter) that actually *produce* occasions of political opportunity, and not the other way around.[45] Activist education officials in Atlanta, for example, were eager to thwart their "status quo" colleagues in their district, but it was not until Afrocentric challengers presented them with a perfect cultural argument did these activist officials have the discursive power to launch their fight.

In the next chapter I finally turn to the creationist challenge in the public schools to see whether educators treated these challenges with the same level of attention and, sometimes, solicitousness as they did the Afrocentrists. Are all challengers to public school systems greeted with a modicum of respect from education professionals (at least as they are first presented), or are educators' responses tailored to the challengers' particular claims and resources? Comparing the history of the four creationist cases to the Afrocentric cases will bring us closer to an answer.

Five _____

History of the Four Creationist Cases: Louisiana State, California State, Vista, California, and Kansas State

IN CHAPTERS 3 and 4, we saw the role that culture, politics, and organization played in the Afrocentric cases. We found that school systems proved resistant to lasting reforms in all three cases, with insurgent achievements ranging on a scale of practically zero (New York) to modest and largely symbolic (Atlanta and Washington, D.C.). Sensitized to these processes, we should now wonder if the same sort of factors figured into the creationist battles with school systems. If Afrocentrists used similar rhetoric across their three battles, but achieved varying rates of at least temporary success along the way, would the same be true of those fighting for creationism? How similar were the claims that each set of creationists advanced in these different school systems? How similar were their outcomes? In this chapter, I describe the four creationist challenges in detail, chronicling the process of struggle that took place in Louisiana state, California state, Vista, California, and Kansas state. As I did in chapter 3 for the Afrocentric cases, I will give a chronological history of these events and also draw attention to the major claims that the challengers made in them, as well as to the counter claims made by their adversaries.

What I have discovered in these cases is fascinating. First, studying the cases chronologically, I found that, over just the past twenty years, creationists have shifted their rhetoric to adapt to an educational and social environment that clearly perceives their central claims to be illegitimate. We know from chapter 2 that creationism has changed significantly from the 1920s to the 1980s. But the degree of change that has occurred in its rhetoric over the past two decades is equally astonishing. The three challenges that I studied which took place earlier in this twenty-year time period—those in Louisiana, Vista, and the state of California—all fit within the "literalist" tradition of the creationist movement, meaning that, at some level (although by different means), challengers in these locations sought to "balance" science curricula by adding the theory of divine creation to them. And in each of these cases, though by quite different processes, education professionals meted out to their creationist challengers ultimately similar fates. Although professional educators, as we will see, were forced to surrender political power at times in those districts (for instance, more politically moderate candidates sometimes lost elections to Christian conservatives in school board races, allowing those conservatives into the "inside" rungs of decision making), professional educational leaders in each of these school systems eventually were able to come back and discredit their creationist challengers in a public and celebrated fashion. Somewhat differently from the Afrocentric cases—where education professionals in Atlanta and Washington effectively minimized challenger gains through more covert mechanisms like testing, and in New York where education officials granted at least a modicum of official "voice" to the Afrocentric cause—school system professionals in Louisiana, Vista, and California consistently and aggressively repudiated the creationist case.

The fourth creationist case I studied, in Kansas, proceeded somewhat differently. While education professionals ultimately defeated the challenge there, too, in a most public manner—a product of intense campaigning on the part of the education, science, and media communities—it looked, at least for a while, that outcomes in Kansas might chart a new path for the creationist movement. By 1999, the year their challenge went public in Kansas, advocates for creationism had realized that U.S. courts would always ultimately rule against their movement if their goals were regarded as religiously motivated, or as an establishment of religion. With Vista, Louisiana, California state, and other failed challenges to guide them, creationist challengers in Kansas understood that they would serve their project ill to mention a creator at all in their proposals. Having realized this, challengers in Kansas did not advocate the addition of *divine creation* to the curriculum; rather, challengers argued that they sought merely to deemphasize naturalistic evolution and to introduce new ideas—*pluralistic* ideas—into the science classroom. By removing the obviously religious from the challenging rhetoric, while also adopting the language of pluralism (even multiculturalism), creationists in Kansas made it more difficult for school systems to fight back against this challenge with the might that they once had.

And yet, just a year later, in August 2000, creationists in Kansas met a fate similar to that of their predecessors: the majority of the board members who had voted for the "deemphasis of evolution" were, themselves, voted out of office. Despite continued rhetorical adaptation, the challenge had been tossed out. Again.

So, let me begin this description of creationist cases with Louisiana, the first of the four cases in the chronology. I will then work my way through the two California cases and end up in Kansas, as of the year 2000. While I describe these events, I will draw attention to the fact that creationists, like Afrocentrists, were able to achieve some victory along the way to their ultimate defeats, and that these gains were often multidimensional—different in intensity and depth in each location. But the major difference between the two challenges, Afrocentrism and creationism, will also begin to emerge. While Afrocentrists were able to garner the public support of some members of the professional leadership of school systems (superintendents, commissioners, administrators)—even if this was often qualified support—creationists got only on the wrong side of professional educators in public discussions. Despite the fact that creationists were able, in three of the cases, to make their way to the inside of their school systems via *politics* (such as by being elected to school boards), this set of challengers was unable to convert its political positions of power into any kind of *professional* recognition of legitimacy. I will clarify the theoretical importance of this difference in chapter 7.

The New Creationist Front: Scientific Creationism in Louisiana, late-1970s to late-1980s

Having been beaten back by numerous federal court rulings in the 1960s, creationism's advocates laid low in the public sphere for nearly two decades. In the late 1970s and early 1980s, however, creationist activity had a renaissance, as new organizations were formed to promote scientific creationism and as leaders innovated novel strategies to respond to constitutional prohibitions.

One sign of this resurgence was seen in the early 1980s, when two Southern states passed laws requiring that creation science be taught alongside evolutionary theory in science classes, and a dozen other states had similar legislation pending, according to the American Civil Liberties Union (ACLU).[1] But this was not the same creationism as in earlier days, which had sought to include creationist theory in science classes simply because it was the word of God. This newer form of creationism, instead, was said to be founded on scientific evidence, not biblical faith; and its stated goal was designed to provide a counter balance to evolution in the classroom, not to replace it entirely.

We can now look back at the 1970s and early 1980s and see several key events that laid the groundwork for the reemergence of the creationist challenge in U.S. schools and courts. The first was the establishment of the Institute for Creation Research (ICR) within the Reverend Timothy LaHaye's Christian Heritage College in 1970. Founded by Dr. Henry Morris, a geologist with a doctorate from the University of Minnesota, the institute was formed so that creation scientists and staff could conduct research aimed at providing evidence for young-earth creationism, particularly the branch concerning catastrophism following the flood in Noah's time.

A second major event contributing to scientific creationists' increased activity during this period was the 1978 publication of an article in the *Yale Law Journal* by Wendell Bird, then a law student at Yale University and, later, a member of the staff at ICR. The article was a sort of legal blueprint for the creationist arguments that would be presented to multiple courts throughout the 1980s. The crux of Bird's argument was that neither evolution nor creation had been witnessed first hand and that this, therefore, was "one of those areas where the inferences from the scientific evidence can legitimately differ."[2] Since knowable truth about origins was up for grabs, according to this argument, children should be taught both accounts in their science classes.

In 1980, another supporter of the cause made headlines when he went on record in support of creationism. During his bid for president, Republican candidate Ronald Reagan revealed that he had "a great many questions" about evolution, adding that "recent discoveries down through the years pointed out great flaws in it."[3] Although he never again publicly mentioned creationism, this popular candidate and later president gave great comfort to creationism's champions during this time.

But the events that drew the most attention to creationism in the early 1980s were the two previously mentioned states' decisions to legislate for scientific creationism. Both were in the South, and both would see court battle because of their actions. The first to act was the state legislature in Arkansas. In 1980, both houses and the governor in Arkansas signed off on Act 590, which required that if evolution were to be taught in the state's public schools, then creation science must be taught there also. Schools could choose not to teach evolution at all, stated the law, but if evolution were taught, then teachers would also have to present the theory and evidence for sudden creation. Lawmakers presented the law as "fair to both theories" and scientifically rigorous.

The Arkansas legislator who introduced the bill went to great lengths to define his terms, spelling out "creation science" in detail. In part, the law read,

> Creation-science includes the scientific evidences and related inferences that indicate: (1) *Sudden creation* of the universe, energy, and life from nothing; (2) The *insufficiency of mutation and natural selection* in bringing about development of all living kinds from a single organism; (3) Changes only *within fixed limits of originally created kinds* of plants and animals; (4) *Separate ancestry* for man and apes; (5) Explanation of the earth's geology by *catastrophism*, including the occurrence of a

worldwide flood; and (6) A *relatively recent inception* of the earth and living kinds [emphasis added].[4]

Upon hearing that the law had passed in Arkansas, the ACLU immediately filed suit against it, calling it a clear abridgement of First Amendment guarantees. Little did the legislators know that the very precision of their terms would be the downfall of their legislation.

In June 1980, just as the Arkansas law was making its way to federal court, the issue of creationism began heating up in nearby Louisiana. Using language very similar to the Arkansas Balanced Treatment Act, the Louisiana bill also was modeled on a sample bill created for the ICR by Wendell Bird, now a leading national theorist for scientific creationism.[5] Louisiana State Senator Bill Keith, Democrat of Shreveport, introduced his bill to give equal time to creationism and evolution, but this time, he and the law's drafters were careful to shield themselves from what were quickly coming to be viewed as the vulnerabilities of the Arkansas bill. Whereas the Arkansas bill was crystal-clear in its definition of creation science, the Louisiana bill was designed to keep creation science vague. Not only was the ICR's mission statement kept out of the bill (that the Institute is a "Christ-focused creation ministry where science and the Bible live in harmony"),[6] but the Louisiana bill no longer listed the six defining characteristics of creation science that were contained in the Arkansas bill.[7] What's more, Keith argued that the act's purpose was to protect the "academic freedom" of teachers and students and to ensure "neutrality" toward diverse religious convictions. Just as with the Arkansas bill, however, Louisiana mandated that if the subject of origins were to be taught at all, then teachers would be required to give "balanced treatment" to theories of creation and evolution, and neither theory could be presented as proven scientific fact.[8]

Despite a local media barrage leveled against the bill and a minority effort within both chambers at least to amend it, the Louisiana House voted to pass it, by a vote of 71-19, as did the Senate, by a 26–12.[9] The decision then was sent up to an ambivalent Governor David Treen, who announced that he had decided to resolve his doubts about the constitutionality of the bill in favor of the legislature's overwhelming support for it.[10] Treen signed the bill into law on July 20, 1981, despite the protestations of local newspaper editorial writers, scientists, and education officials. Explaining his decision to sign despite personal qualms, the governor stated that it was his "legal opinion that the bill, contrary to its author's intention, does not make the teaching of 'creationism' mandatory, but only *permits* it." Admitting that it was a "very difficult decision," Treen decided that the will of the legislature should prevail.

In a move that came as a shock to no one, five months after the bill was signed into law, the ACLU filed suit in federal court in New Orleans, arguing that "balanced treatment" was religious teaching, and therefore unconstitutional. It accused lawmakers of violating First Amendment guarantees of separation of church and state, and it also challenged the law as being too vague and broad, and of hampering academic freedom.

But the ACLU's lawyers were not the only ones doing research in the law library to draw up their legal strategy for a fight in the courts. Much to their surprise, the Louisiana attorney general's office, headed by William Guste, brought its own case to federal court on behalf of the state and its legislature, suing the department of education, among others, for not having begun the process of implementing "balanced treatment" in the state's schools. Guste sued to have the Balanced Treatment Act declared *constitutional* and to force the state's education system to implement the new law, which, to date, it had not done. Since the time of the law's passage, Louisiana Superintendent Kelly Nix, along with his department of education, had not executed the law's creationist reforms, pending any and all future court action. Arguing that it would be far too expensive for the state to fund training and the purchase of books when it seemed likely that the courts inevitably would rule against the law, educators had been dragging their feet on implementing the change. Nix's wait-and-see strategy infuriated the creationism law's sponsor, Sen. Bill Keith, who, with other lawmakers, had requested that the attorney general bring suit.

Meanwhile, Back in Arkansas . . .

Not many weeks after the two Louisiana suits were filed, a district court judge in Little Rock, Arkansas, ruled against the Arkansas Balanced Treatment Act, calling it an abridgment to the Establishment Clause of the U.S Constitution and stating that its sole purpose was to advance religion. Regarding its religious content and nonsecular purpose, Judge William Overton noted that the "statute used language peculiar to creationist literature in emphasizing origins of life as an aspect of the theory of evolution. While the subject of life's origins is within the province of biology, the scientific community does not consider the subject as part of evolutionary theory."[11] He also gave a detailed description of "science" and declared that "creation science" was not a member of that community.

Despite their disappointment that a fellow bill had gone down to defeat, proponents of the Louisiana law were optimistic about their own bill's chances in court, and they directed attention to what they heralded as crucial distinctions between the two states' bills, particularly the Louisiana law's silence on its religious origins. Given the host of compelling differences that they believed distinguished the two states' laws, supporters of scientific creationism did not mourn their defeat in Arkansas but instead prepared for victory in Louisiana.

Because the Louisiana law was the basket into which creation scientists had decided to place their eggs, and because this was thought to be the case that would pave the way legally for other states' future balanced treatment laws, all of the movement's resources were amassed behind it, and many of the biggest names in creationist legal circles came to the aid of the embattled bill. Joining Guste as legal counsel on the case were Wendell Bird, creationism's top legal mind, and John Whitehead of the Rutherford Institute, a conservative think tank in Manassas, Virginia.[12] Bird's and Whitehead's fees—a sensitive topic following the Arkansas case—were to be paid not by the state, but by private donations collected by the newly created Creation Science Legal Defense Fund.[13]

Intent on benefiting from his position as plaintiff in the Baton Rouge case (which had been filed first), rather than as defendant in the New Orleans venue, Attorney General Guste and the rest of his pro-Balanced Treatment team appealed to the New Orleans Federal District Court to dismiss the ACLU suit, pending a decision in their own case. Meanwhile, the ACLU made a similar move, asking that Guste's suit be dismissed, pending its court action. Because Guste's team had been strategic and had filed the day before the ACLU did, however, Guste won this battle, and it was his case that was to be decided first. The New Orleans judge, Adrian Duplantier, postponed action on the ACLU lawsuit, pending the outcome of Guste's claim against the department of education.

Unfortunately for the creationist cause, winning the role of plaintiff rather than defendant did not have the positive effect that Guste had hoped for. Instead, the Baton Rouge judge dismissed the case on summary judgment.[14] This was the first loss the Balanced Treatment Act was to suffer at the hands of the courts, and it cleared the way for the U.S. District Court in New Orleans to take jurisdiction in the ACLU's case. A court date was set for 1983, and the Civil Liberties organization—representing some thirty plaintiffs including the Board of Elementary and Secondary Education (BESE), a local school district, teachers, parents, and clergy—was set to square off against Attorney General Guste and his team.[15]

In Judge Duplantier's New Orleans courtroom, the ACLU recommended that the court decide this case, too, in summary judgment. On behalf of its plaintiffs, the ACLU lawyers argued that the state legislature had no authority to legislate curriculum, since the state constitution, under Article 8, Section 3, vests authority in the state Board of Elementary and Secondary Education to determine policy and curriculum for the public schools.[16] Rather than trying to win on substantive grounds—that is, on the content of the law, and whether the law's terms were constitutional—the ACLU sought to have the case decided on technical grounds. Yes, argued the ACLU on behalf of the claimants, these officials had been elected to the state legislature; but, no, they were not granted educational decision making that could affect local school districts throughout the state. Arguing that the Balanced Treatment Act was a mandate to local school boards and, therefore, represented an unconstitutional takeover of the education department's authority, the plaintiffs complained that legislators had illegitimately crossed the boundary from their jurisdiction to professional educators' authority.[17] Arguing against this position, the legislative sponsor of the law, Sen. Keith, no doubt used sarcasm when he complained how odd it was for the board to be making this claim of unconstitutionality now, when the schools had only recently accepted as legitimate the legislative action recently taken on sex education and the teaching of free enterprise in the schools. He attributed to the school board a "bias" against scientific creationism.[18]

In response to this set of arguments, for the second time in five months, the federal courts decided against the scientific creationism position. In November 1982, in a ruling on a pretrial motion submitted by the ACLU team, Judge Duplantier declared the Balanced Treatment Act unconstitutional, by terms set out in the Louisiana state constitution. He ruled that the legislature, indeed, had exceeded its constitutional bounds when it ordered creation science to be taught whenever evolution was taught in the science classroom. Such power, Judge Duplantier ruled, was reserved for the education department. Just as in the case that had come before his colleague in Baton Rouge, Judge Duplantier did not deal with the federal issues of the case (e.g., constitutional issues regarding church / state) or with any of the components of creationism in this ruling. Instead, he focused on the methods by which the law had been enacted.

Disappointed again, creationism's advocates tried a new tack—still in the realm of the legal world, but at a different level of the institution. Following the federal court ruling, Attorney General Guste and Governor Treen appealed to the 5th U.S. Circuit Court of Appeals and asked it to permit the *Louisiana* Supreme Court—a state court, not a federal court—to review Duplantier's ruling on the constitutionality of the legislature's action. Their strategy was to get a review from the state Supreme Court, which might decide in favor of the legislature's authority to determine curriculum. If this were to happen, went the plan, then the federal appeals court might return the case to Duplantier's federal court to consider the First Amendment issues involved in the Balanced Treatment Act.

And this is precisely what was to happen. The 5th U.S. Circuit Court of Appeals did grant the motion, and it sent the law to the state's Supreme

Court for study. In October 1983, in a 4–3 decision, Guste and his team received their first victory: the Louisiana State Supreme Court reversed Duplantier's ruling on the unconstitutionality of the legislature's action, and upheld the right of the state's elected representatives to require balanced treatment of evolution and creation science, saying that it was a "question of a Legislature's authority to establish and maintain education within the state."[19] Again, the state Supreme Court ruling dealt only with the narrow question of whether the legislature *could* pass such a law, not with issues pertaining to the First Amendment. But it had voted yes, eventually sending the case back to Duplantier's court for trial. This time, the court would have to judge the merits of teaching creationism, per se, not just the technical issue of whether the legislature had acted within state constitutional bounds.[20]

Once the case returned to New Orleans, however, Judge Duplantier again ruled quickly against the defense in January 1985. In a summary judgment requested by the ACLU-represented plaintiffs, the judge ruled that the Louisiana Balanced Treatment Act's purpose was so clearly religious that no trial was necessary, and there was no need to put "the people of Louisiana through the very considerable, needless expense of a protracted trial."[21] This time the decision was based on the content of the law (e.g., creationism), not on its methods of enactment. This was the third in a series of federal court defeats for the Louisiana law, and Duplantier's decision was upheld later that year by a three-person subpanel of the 5th U.S. Circuit Court of Appeals, to which Guste and co-counsel Bird had appealed.

Creationists had been wise to put their faith in the Louisiana Attorney General as a committed ally to the Bird and Whitehead team. Not to be dissuaded by a series of defeats, Guste sought a rehearing of the case before all fifteen judges of the appellate court, rather than just the subpanel of three. His central argument for a hearing before the full court rested on the claim that the three-judge subpanel, to which his side had previously presented, had virtually ignored his central argument that the law had been passed to *safeguard academic freedom*, not to advance religion. His strategy in appealing to the appeals court again: if he were to win the rehearing before the appellate court (this time, the full court), then the case would be returned to Duplantier's courtroom for a trial; if he were to lose in the appellate court, he would appeal directly to the U.S. Supreme Court.

In a close 8–7 decision delivered in December 1985, the appellate court refused to let all fifteen of its members reconsider the subpanel's decision. Just as Duplantier had decided in his summary judgment, and the three appellate judges had concluded in August, the full appeals court rejected the defense claim that the purpose of the Balanced Treatment Act was not religious.[22] Nevertheless, the strongly worded dissent written by the seven-judge minority seemed to the creationist team an irresistible invitation to appeal their case once more.[23]

Despite the ACLU's and the media's incredulity at the attorney general's ability to survive, survive he and his case did. Upon barely losing the full-court appeal, Guste took his case directly to the U.S. Supreme Court. In a letter to the editor in the *New Orleans Times-Picayune* in August 1985, Guste explained his decision to appeal the ruling to the nation's highest court. He argued that, first, he had a duty to defend Louisiana's laws against court challenges, and that this law had been passed by large majorities in the legislature (by 79 percent in the House and by 68 percent in the Senate). Second, four years after the bill first passed, the House had just voted to commit more funds to his appeals process. Third, Guste argued that no outside lawyer fees were being incurred by the state, since the Creation Science Legal Defense Fund was collecting private donations for fees. Fourth, he stated that the Louisiana Balanced Treatment Act was significantly different from the Arkansas law, and so argumentation that was successful in striking down the Arkansas law would be irrelevant in this case. Fifth, again, unlike the Arkansas law, claimed Guste, the purpose of the Louisiana law was to ensure "academic freedom," explicitly written into the act. Finally, explained the attorney general, the expert witnesses prepared by the Louisiana team were far better prepared than in the Arkansas trial and would come equipped with heady scientific knowledge. In order for their expertise to be known, the case required a trial, or at least the reading of affidavits. Because of its sophistication, the case had to be heard in court, and not dismissed prematurely.

Creationism Reaches the High Court

To many people's surprise—both creationists' and evolutionists'—this logic caught the attention of the nation's highest court. In May 1986, having received Attorney General Guste's request to overrule the 8–7 decision by the 5th U.S. Circuit Court of Appeals in *Edwards v. Aguillard*, the U.S. Supreme Court agreed to hear the case. Creationists considered this a major victory and even regarded the Court as potentially friendly, with the conservative William Rehnquist in place as Chief Justice, Antonin Scalia as intellectual leader of the conservative justices, and an unknowable quantity in other Reagan-appointed justices.

This was no obscure case going before the Supreme Court. Advocates for creation science clearly regarded the case as their single greatest hope in gaining public legitimacy and the legal right to present scientific evidence for their project in classrooms. They had arrayed on their side the most sophisticated legal thinker on creationism, Wendell Bird; they had won a technical decision in the Louisiana Supreme Court; and now they had reached the U.S. Supreme Court, where at least a couple of the justices could be counted on to be sympathetic to their cause.

On the other side of the courtroom, however, would sit the ACLU and its advocates for evolutionary science, who regarded this case to be no less important. Where scientific creationists saw an opportunity for a new day to begin, when secularism might be forced out of the schools, legal scholars, academic scientists, some parents, and many public school personnel perceived this as a threat to return to the days before reason had set in. Testament to the defendants' feeling of threat to science was an unprecedented twenty-seven-page amici curiae brief submitted to the high court by seventy-two American Nobel science prizewinners. The brief's central message, not surprisingly, was that creation science assuredly did constitute religion, not science, and it had no place in classrooms where instruction in science occurs. As the brief was delivered, a news conference was also held by three of the signatories, including Stephen Jay Gould, paleontologist at Harvard University, an avid creationism detractor. In some of the most scathing critique to be aimed at creationism, Gould argued at the press conference that creation science was "just a phony new legal strategy to circumvent legal precedent banning religion from the public schools. . . . It is a whitewash for a specific, particular, and minority religious view in America, Bible literalism."[24]

On December 10, 1986, Wendell Bird presented the state's case to the U.S. Supreme Court, with Louisiana Attorney General William Guste at his side. Bird's team was supported financially and philosophically by a wide range of national groups, including the Concerned Women for America (a group headed by Beverly LaHaye, wife of Timothy LaHaye, a longtime leader in Christian conservative circles), the National Association of Evangelicals, the Rabbinical Alliance of America (an organization of Orthodox rabbis), the Catholic Center, and the Free Methodist Church of North America.[25] Bird's greatest hope was that the U.S. Supreme Court would order a full trial for the Louisiana law in Judge Duplantier's federal district court. Were a full trial to be held, he would be able to show to the court the mountains of depositions, scientific evidence for creation science, hypotheses, and filmstrips that his team had gathered. Having "assembled a thousand pages of depositions and affidavits for the case," the team wanted these testimonials to see the full light of day.[26]

Representing the plaintiffs before the Supreme Court was Jay Topkis, partner with the New York law firm Paul, Weiss, Rifkind, Wharton and Garrison, whose firm agreed to handle the case pro bono for the ACLU.[27] Topkis's hope was that the justices would draw on legal precedent simply discard the law, and not order it back to Duplantier's courtroom. He particularly pointed to *Lemon v. Kurtzman* (1970) as precedent of choice, a case which had established a standard for judicial review involving the establishment clause of the First Amendment. The Lemon Test, as it has come to be known, is used to determine whether a law has a secular purpose or if, instead, its primary purpose is to advance or prohibit religion, or in any way encourage an "excessive government entanglement with religion."[28]

The primary argument advanced by the state's team, led by Bird, contended that the goals of the Balanced Treatment Act were to present the scientific evidence for creation, not to present religious content. It was certainly possible and even probable, Wendell Bird acknowledged, that some Louisiana legislators who had voted for the bill had done so out of a desire to have religious doctrine taught in the classroom. But these votes were in the minority, he argued, and they should not be held up as evidence that the *primary purpose* of the law was to advance religion. In fact, the primary purpose of the act was fairness, argued Bird, and in the bill's absence, there was a constraint on academic freedom and fairness in public schools.[29] Arguing that there was no conflict with the Court's prior rulings against religious teaching in public schools, Bird argued that the Louisiana law did not require religious teaching, or even any reference to the Bible's statements that God created the world and man. Creationism, he argued, was a scientific fact, separate from religion, and was supported by affidavits from scientists submitted to the court.[30] Bird also denied Topkis's charge that the law was an attempt to thwart the teaching of evolution.

The Ruling

Seven months after the hearing was held, on June 19, 1987, the Supreme Court ruled 7–2 against Bird's arguments that creation science should be taught alongside evolution, upholding the 1985 appeals court decision. In a seventeen-page decision that evoked First Amendment guarantees, Justice William Brennan wrote that the act advanced religious doctrine and that states were not permitted to require the teaching of creation alongside evolution if such requirements were intended to promote religious beliefs.[31]

First, Brennan argued that the purpose of the law was to restructure science curriculum so that it conformed to a particular religious viewpoint. On this basis alone the law was illegal since it failed the first prong of the three-prong Lemon Test. According to this first prong, all laws must have a *secular primary purpose*, and because the Balanced Treatment Act was judged to have religion as its primary purpose, there was no need even to investigate the second and third prongs of the test. But the court did assess Louisiana's law by these criteria as well, and the majority of justices found that the Balanced Treatment Act's *effect* was to advance religious doctrine by either banishing evolutionary theory or presenting a religious viewpoint that rejected evolution in its entirety. The Court also found that the law violated the First Amendment's clause against government entanglement in religious affairs, insofar as it sought "to employ the symbolic and financial support of government to achieve a religious purpose."[32]

Although the loss was a serious blow to creationists in Louisiana and across the land, there was a silver lining to the dark cloud. In a dissent that ran almost double the length of the court's decision, Justice Antonin Scalia wrote (and Rehnquist signed) a scathing review of the court's ruling. Scalia argued that the court's decision was repressive and illiberal and that it prohibited Louisiana's citizens from having "whatever scientific evidence there may be against evolution presented in their schools."[33] He also argued that the Court had willfully interpreted the actions of the Louisiana lawmakers at their most negative. He dissented on the grounds that the Balanced Treatment Act was not established solely for a religious purpose (the first part of the Lemon Test), and he used the dissent as an occasion to call for the dismantling of the Lemon Test in judging First Amendment cases, suggesting that "courts abandon their practice of investigating the 'purpose' of laws that are challenged as violating the establishment clause."[34]

The End of an Old Friend?

In general, the local media responded warmly to the Supreme Court ruling, and there were none more pleased than the long-critical editors and columnists at the *New Orleans Times-Picayune* who, for years now, had been decrying what they saw as the legislature's destructive plan of action. Since the very beginning of the legislature's action, the New Orleans local paper had criticized the law as a sham, and as political cowardice on the part of the House and Senate members, and most especially, of the governor, who should have known better than to sign off on an unconstitutional bill.

National media writers also generally expressed relief. By and large, journalists were quick to give a eulogy for scientific creationism, interpreting the rejection of the law in court after court as its justified death knell. Most observers of the case's journey through the courts assumed that once scientific creationism had been vilified by a large majority of Supreme Court justices, advocates for creationism would give up the cause of inserting creationist theory in the public schools.

Yet there could be heard a few voices here and there, in both the local and the national press, warning that public education must not let down its guard. True, wrote Harvard law professor Lawrence Tribe, following the *Aguillard* Supreme Court decision, creationists had suffered in the courts. But wouldn't there be other terrain on which they would fight their battles?[35] And in another *New York Times* essay, Stephen Jay Gould warned that scientific America should not too optimistically write off the creationists' ability to come back with yet another campaign against evolution, following its ingenious repertoire of strategies over the past six decades. Creationists might now try lobbying textbook publishers or persuade local school boards to adopt their own publications, Gould predicted.[36]

Indeed, Gould was correct, as we shall see in the next two cases. But the question is, could scientific creationists make more headway in these other domains—in the more contained institutional realm of school systems, rather than in a state legislature? We should read the Louisiana challenge as a test case for the power of political actors to impose a legislated creationist act onto a school system that was on record as oppositional—at least at the level of its top administrators. When education leaders, saddled with the responsibility for carrying out a program that was anathema to them, refused to do the bidding of the legislators and governor of their state, both sides sought relief from the courts. The creationists lost.

By the mid-1980s to early 1990s, then, creationists began shifting their efforts to other domains. Creationist forces mounted one of their most visible efforts in California state, where the public schools' science framework was slated for revision. Rather than focusing on legislation enacted by politicians, in this case, scientific creationists focused on policymakers in the department of education and on the state board of education. Having tried their hand in the political arena and having lost there, scientific creationists would now seek greater success in the very den of their adversaries—among education decision makers, themselves. Let me now turn to the next chronological case in the creationist lineup: the events that took place statewide in California from 1985 to 1989.

Creationism in the Golden State: California State Science Framework Debates, 1985–89

Since the time that creationists had turned their thoughts away from trying to *omit* evolution completely from science teaching (in the 1960s, when *Epperson v. Arkansas* invalidated that effort, see chapter 2) and toward the "balanced treatment" of creation and evolution in the teaching of origins, California has been the site of varied creationist activity, both at the state level and at the local level. Over this time, much of creationists' attention has been focused on the state's science framework, a document that outlines the principles and objectives of science teaching in the public schools.

All states have documents like California's framework that guide curriculum in a variety of disciplines (as we saw in the New York case). What makes California's science framework so important, though, is the effect this document has on the adoption of textbooks not only in *California's* local school districts but, subsequently, in adoption of books across the country. This is because California has a state-run textbook adoption process, which gives it enormous influence on other states. Although twenty-one other states are also adoption states (Texas, among them), none of these other adopter systems is as big as California's, which in the mid-1980s represented about 12 percent of the nation's textbook purchases, or more than $100 million per year across all disciplines.[37] Historically, textbook publishers have catered to the demands of the large adoption states, like California and Texas, and then have made no changes in their books thereafter. Through the 1970s and 1980s, for example, book publishers followed Texas's adoption standards after that state criticized science texts for portraying evolution as fact. As a result, the teaching of evolution was qualified and abridged in books across the nation.[38]

Prior to 1985, the year that marks the beginning of the California creationist struggle I study in this book, creationists had been clinging to a fifteen-year-old foothold that they had won in the state to tone down evolutionary content in textbooks, much like in Texas. In 1969, the California framework had been in the process of revision as part of its regular seven-year cycle. The conservative board of education—many of its members appointed by then-governor Ronald Reagan—surprised and enraged teachers, scientists, and education officials across the state when it endorsed a request made by Christian conservatives to include a statement that evolution was much less than certain, and that creationism was no less valid than evolution as a theory of origins.[39] In its endorsement, the board engaged in three years' worth of conflict with its own appointed advisory panel of scientists and science educators, as well as its own textbook commission. The compromise that was finally struck between these forces in 1972 held that (1) evolution was a theory, not a fact; (2) dogmatic statements about evolution and other matters were to be removed from the science curriculum and replaced by conditional statements; (3) speculations about ultimate causes were to be considered nonscientific; (4) and, finally, creationism, as a philosophy of origins, could be taught in social science courses.[40] These qualifications about evolution and science stayed on the books uncontested for more than a decade.

Once they had succeeded in getting these modifications written into the state science framework, Christian conservatives who believed that their children's rights to learn about creationism had long been violated in California schools sought to have the state enforce the new ruling. Education department officials, as one might imagine, had been loath to enforce what they considered to be illegitimate science teaching, just as administrators also had been in the state of Louisiana after the Balanced Treatment Act was passed. In one suit brought against the California Department of Education and the Board of Education, plaintiffs demanded that the state "direct science teachers to tell students that there were other theories of how life came into being, besides the theory of evolution."[41] The plaintiffs charged that evolution was still being taught "as fact" and as the source of all living forms, even after the 1972 policy had been enacted. The court ultimately ruled against the plaintiffs, when the judge decided that the education policy on teaching evolution did not violate creationists' rights. At the same time, though, creationists were elated with a caveat attached to the ruling—a caveat that ordered the board and the department of education to circulate the policy statement to all California schools and to textbook publishers. If the various parties involved in the issue were made aware of the policy, said the judge, then the rights of Christian conservatives would be protected.[42]

As creationists celebrated the judge's order to distribute the policy, their opponents criticized the ruling as dangerous. They argued that the decision would lead to great confusion among teachers, who would avoid teaching evolution because they would no longer be sure that their principals and school boards would support them if they were to teach science, categorically. Conservatives also would get the idea from the ruling, said worried educators, that evolution must be presented as "only a theory," and parents and students would have no idea what to think.

The anti-dogmatism policy of 1972 and the above court case of 1980 (popularly known as the Segraves case) formed two critical components of the subsequent debate about the science framework in California. A third factor came in the form of new personnel in the state education department. Not long after the Segraves case had been decided and the anti-dogmatism policy had been ordered to be circulated throughout the state, a new era of activist education policy was ushered into the state when Bill Honig was elected superintendent of education. Upon entering office, Honig immediately announced his intentions to improve statewide education, and he threw down the gauntlet to textbook publishers, among others, saying that content must be improved in all subject areas, not the least of which would be science teaching. He also pronounced his intention of bringing to California what he called The Excellence Movement, "an updated version of what used to be called back-to-basics." For these efforts, Honig pressured then Governor George Deukmejian and the state legislature to increase the public schools budget from $11.5 billion a year to $15.5 billion.[43] Political and pedagogical lines were being drawn in the sand.

Textbook Review

With the arrival of a new superintendent committed to reforming instruction in the schools and the anti-dogmatism statement on the books contributing to what many people saw as flabby science instruction across the state, perhaps it should come as no shock that when the routine of reviewing science texts came up in 1985, an uproar was sure to follow. In August 1985, knowing that they had Superintendent Honig's support, a sixteen-member newly appointed science textbook panel concluded that junior high-school science books did not adequately cover evolution, all failing, "to one extent or another, to relate evolution to other biological studies."[44] Due to these omissions, the panel recommended that unless publishers agreed to make changes in the books' content for the following year, California should not use them in the schools.[45] A public hearing was scheduled to be held within the month in Sacramento for publishers' and others' reactions. The board of education would then vote on whether to accept the panel's recommendation.[46]

The public hearing held in the state's capital was attended mostly by Christian conservatives who angrily denounced the panel recommendation, arguing that science textbooks were already too heavy with evolution and were "dogmatic."[47] But despite Christian conservatives' testimony, and even though board members had been lobbied heavily over the past months by the textbook publishers to reject the panel's findings, the Board of Education voted unanimously, in keeping with the panel's and Honig's recommendation, to reject all books currently available for junior high-school classes, particularly seven of those books, which were seen to be particularly egregious in their avoidance of evolution.[48]

Just two months later, eager to stay competitive in the lucrative California market, the publishers whose books had been rejected by the board came back to the science panel with what they called extensive additions to their science textbooks.[49] Upon review, the science panel agreed that these revisions represented marked improvement over the previous batch of books, and they recommended that the board endorse the new books.

But all was not to run so smoothly for, by the time the science panel was making its recommendation, a new set of actors had decided to provide input on the issue of elementary and junior high-school science books. In December 1985, less than a week before the final versions of the publishers' books were due, twenty scientists from San Jose State University, San Diego State University, and the University of California, Berkeley, who had recently decided to monitor the revised school textbooks, reported that the books' coverage of evolution was "still insignificant and wholly inadequate."[50] Upon making this initial report before the board of education in Sacramento, the twenty academic scientists expressed their disdain for the ways in which the books hedged statements about evolution, using phrases like "many scientists believe" that the earth was created billions of years ago, or "most scientists believe" that dinosaurs roamed the earth millions of years ago. Kevin Padian, one of the twenty signatories and a paleontologist at Berkeley, asked sardonically, "What is *that* supposed to mean? If dinosaurs are just a 'belief' that some of us have, what are these bones in the museum?"[51]

The fact that scientists were paying any attention at all to public school textbooks and pedagogy was a novelty, and a bit of a mixed blessing for state department staff. According to several sources, academic scientists had long been uninterested and unaware of textbook content and the school system's selection of personnel to review those books (generally teachers, not academics), and the book-selection process generally didn't show up on their radar screens. This was 1985, after all, two years before the Louisiana Balanced Treatment Act had gone to the U.S. Supreme Court and brought the issue of creationism / evolution to the foreground; and it was California after all, a state known, historically, as progressive in educational matters. Both of these factors had led scientists largely to ignore the degree to which evolution was being elided in public school texts.

But now they were interested. And they were active. And they were about to be disappointed. In the face of criticism voiced at the board meeting from both the scientific community (which argued that the books were weak on evolution) and from a vocal faction of Christian conservatives (which argued that the books were too forceful about evolution), the board acted against both the scientists' recommendation and the creationist pleas, and approved in a 7–2 vote the new set of science committee-approved textbooks.[52] One board member cast his vote saying that if the books pleased neither the adamant evolutionists nor the adamant creationists, then he could feel comfortable voting for the new texts.[53] This "diplomatic" comment aside, neither board members nor Superintendent Honig would say that they were entirely pleased by the content of the books, but they did say that this list of books did represent "probably the best junior-high science books in the country."[54] The books would now be used for the next six years, until the next cycle began. Here was creationist defeat number one in the new era of creationist debate at the statewide level in California.

Science Framework

The next phase of the struggle between creationists and evolutionists was to come in late 1987 and run through 1990, with the appointment of a new panel of educators called the Science Curriculum Framework and Criteria Committee. Having recently put the new textbooks in place for the next several years, the state education department now turned its attention to revising the state science framework, the capstone of all documents guiding science instruction in the state. Given the criticism academic scientists had heaped on state educators during the textbook selection process two years earlier, the board appointed three academics to this round of science curriculum development, including Kevin Padian, the Berkeley paleontologist who had taken exception to the textbooks' hedging phrase, "scientists believe." Notably, unlike Commissioner Sobol's first task force in New York, which gave "voice" to marginal Afrocentric critics, the science committee in California had no representatives with creationist allegiances seated on it, no appointed members who would argue for concessions to the Christian conservatives. Superintendent Honig did not consider these important voices to be heard.

As my interviewees recalled, there were two distinct phases to developing this framework: first, writing an introductory statement about the methods and goals of science and, second, writing the body of the science framework.

DRAFTING THE INTRODUCTION TO THE FRAMEWORK. Drafting the introductory statement, which came to be known as the Policy on the Teaching of Natural Sciences, was intended to lay out the state's commitment to teaching rigorous science, and to clarify once and for all the "anti-dogmatism" statement that had long been on the books. Regarded as "something of a veiled threat about teaching evolution and ideas about the origins of the earth and life,"[55] this policy, committee members determined, had been dominating the teaching of evolution in the state of California ever since it had been passed in 1972. The new committee's intention was to denude the statement of its power to qualify the teaching of evolution. Although the committee knew that altering the anti-dogma statement in the framework would invite intense antagonism from creationist challengers, the committee's first order of business was to change the statement in the document's introductory pages.

The science panel was correct to expect conflict over changes in the anti-dogma statement: as soon as it became public knowledge that the committee was altering the introduction, Christian conservative groups became incensed. Led by the Reverend Lou Sheldon of the Traditional Values Coalition (TVC)—a southern California organization best known for its opposition to gay rights legislation in the state—supporters of creationism began attending public hearings and writing hundreds of letters to board members. They argued that the anti-dogmatism policy "was one of the good things" about state education policy because it "opens a small window" of opportunity for creationists who want to have evolution tempered in the classroom.[56] It should be left alone.

Incurring the wrath of Christian conservatives attending these meetings, Superintendent Honig advised the board to support the committee's new draft statement, arguing that the ambiguity of the old anti-dogmatism statement, first, caused many teachers to all but sidestep teaching evolution, for fear that they might violate the policy; and second, provided a rationale for still others to insert creationist theory into science lessons.[57] It also encouraged textbook publishers, he said, to treat evolution in vague terms, if at all. In January 1989, the state board of education followed Honig's recommendation and supported the new policy, passing the two-page statement on the teaching of natural sciences by a unanimous-voice vote.[58]

Having eaten up nearly a year's worth of work, the introductory statement turned out to be the greatest political hurdle of the framework process, just as the committee had intended it to be. It was in this section of the framework that the panel most explicitly laid out the intentions for the teaching of evolution. Portions of the statement make it abundantly clear that creationist alternatives to evolution would not be tolerated in the classroom:

> The domain of the natural sciences is the natural world. Science is limited by its tools—observable facts and testable hypotheses.

> Discussions of any scientific fact, hypothesis, or theory related to the origins of the universe, the earth, and of life (the how) are appropriate to the science curriculum. Discussions of divine creation, ultimate purposes, or ultimate causes (the why) are appropriate to the history, social science, and English-language arts curricula.

Expanding the anti-dogmatism language to cover the teaching of all science, not just theories of origins, the statement also included the following paragraph:

> Nothing in science or in any other field of knowledge shall be taught dogmatically. A dogma is a system of beliefs that is not subject to scien-

tific test and refutation. Compelling belief is inconsistent with the goal of education; the goal is to encourage understanding.

And the committee added this paragraph on religious beliefs:

> Philosophical and religious beliefs are based, at least in part, on faith and are not subject to scientific test and refutation. Such beliefs should be discussed in the social science and language arts curriculum. . . . If a student should raise a question in a natural science class that the teacher determines is outside the domain of science, the teacher should treat the question with respect. The teacher should explain why the question is outside the domain of natural science and encourage the student to discuss the question further with his or her family and clergy.

This last paragraph clearly removed the possibility of discussing the "scientific" content ostensibly contained in scientific creationism in science classrooms, creationists' central aim in this phase of the creationist movement.

So, while an anti-dogmatism statement did remain in the front piece of the science framework (a bone thrown long ago to creationism's advocates), it had now been expanded to cover *all* of science instruction, and it now existed in tandem with a paragraph differentiating "science" from "religious belief." As such, it guards against the possibility of teaching creationism, rather than for it. Certainly, Lou Sheldon and other creationism supporters recognized the strength of this statement (partially presented as a "compromise" with their interests) and saw that the creationist side had been hurt by its inclusion. Sheldon vowed that the Traditional Values Coalition would carry on the battle as the science panel went the next step in revising the body of the science framework.

DRAFTING THE BODY OF THE SCIENCE FRAMEWORK. The next snag to arise in the process of revising the science framework came several months after the board had approved the document's introduction. In July 1989, the state's science subject-matter committee submitted a 200-page draft of the body of the framework to the California Curriculum Commission. Newly written into the document was the statement that evolution was "accepted fact" among scientists. The framework stated in no uncertain terms that "there is no scientific dispute that evolution has occurred and continues to occur; that is why evolution is regarded as scientific fact." It went on to state that creation science, on the other hand, has been "thoroughly studied and rejected by the leading scientific societies." To further emphasize its point, and in the context of the now two-year-old Supreme Court decision in *Edwards v. Aguillard* of 1987, the committee included a legal opinion from the California education board's lawyer that to give "equal time" to the teaching of creation science in California classrooms was "not appropriate and may be unconstitutional."[59] On top of the introduction, this new language clarified for all that creationism was not going to be tolerated in California's science classrooms.

Although the committee's language was supported by the scientific community and by Superintendent Honig, a number of California school board members—anticipating conservative Christians' protests—had no stomach for such declarative statements, and requested that the science committee tone down its evolution-as-fact language. The science panel, however, maintained its total exclusion of creationism.

Once again, Christian conservatives responded angrily to this new affront and began to pressure the board. Robert Simonds, head of two Christian conservative education organizations, the National Association of Christian Educators (NACE) and Citizens for Excellence in Education (CEE), predicted that "all hell [was] going to break loose" if the board were foolishly to approve the new framework. Likewise, the Traditional Values Coalition leader Lou Sheldon held a press conference preceding the Curriculum Commission's vote to blast the framework for being unfair and to discourage the commission's and the board's approval, stating at that time, "If it's war they want, it's war they're going to get."[60]

Despite the warnings of pitched battle, the Curriculum Commission members voted unanimously to adopt the framework advanced to them by their science committee.[61] Within minutes of the commission's vote, seven of the framework's backers—including the National Education Association, the National Science Teachers Association, the American Federation of Teachers, and the American Association of University Professors—sent a letter to the board of education, urging its members also to approve the recommendations.

A Compromise on Language

Despite the strong encouragement it received from these powerful organizations, the California Board of Education was not prepared to vote as strongly on evolution's behalf as the commission had. Pressured by creationists' lobbying efforts, several conservative, Deukmejian-appointed members of the board ducked for some cover and expressed their unwillingness to approve the framework as it was currently written. A compromise was demanded, and to placate the board, Superintendent Honig worked with board president Francis Laufenberg to alter the wording of the guideline so that it would no longer refer to evolution as "scientific fact."[62] Substituted for this phrase was the statement that evolution is "accepted scientific explanation."[63] The compromise also allowed for the removal of references in the framework to the 1987 decision *Edwards v. Aguillard* and to a National Academy of Sciences booklet, both of which questioned the scientific validity of creationist theory.[64]

Was this a compromise that endangered the teaching of evolution? Although some scientists and others in the state criticized Honig and his department for caving in to creationists' demands, Elizabeth Stage, director of the California Science Project and head of the science panel at that time, was untroubled by having to accommodate the board's demands at this juncture, as long as the document it approved was science-heavy and left no room for creationist content in the classroom. This compromise was purely political, not educational, she said, and geared only toward demonstrating to the conservatives across the state that the board was providing tough oversight on the superintendent—whether it was true or not. But it was not a concession to creationist instruction, she insisted.

> As things went along, basically, people like Kevin [Padian] and Bill Honig, who knew that we were going to have to make compromises and allow the board to show that they had *restrained* us, *put the brakes on*, and all that stuff. . . .
>
> We started out with about 125 percent of what we needed. It's like, sometimes when you are asked for a budget from somebody who you know will feel as if they are controlling the situation only if they *cut* the budget by 20 percent. . . . So, you put in 125 percent of what you need, and wind up with 100 percent. We did the same thing. It wasn't deliberate in the sense of sentence by sentence, but it was deliberate in the sense of saying a lot more strongly and a lot more frequently what we thought needed to be said, so that when it got pared back, it would get pared back to what we thought was necessary and sufficient. Call that 100 percent. And I would have to say that in the end, we got more like 110 percent.[65]

Even after the compromise, the science framework contained 271 instances of the term "evolution" in it, a more than 1:1 per-page ratio. The board had thus approved a strong document on the teaching of evolution in science classrooms across the state, even while its members had also sought to appease creationist lobbyists.

Consequences of the Compromise

Upon hearing of the compromise, Lou Sheldon of the Traditional Values Coalition was quick to call it a "very significant victory," while on the other side of the issue, spokesman Michael Hudson of the People for the

American Way (PAW), the First Amendment rights organization, complained that the Laufenberg-Honig agreement showed the board's vulnerability to "right-wing political pressure."[66] Generally supportive of the Policy on Teaching Natural Science and also of the framework, PAW's leaders were not shy when it came to accusing the panel and Honig of compromising on the issue of evolution, and making dangerous concessions when it was politically expedient. PAW cited the hazards of giving even an inch to the creationists.

The media generally uttered the same kind of critique as did PAW, worrying aloud about publishers' likely interpretations of this sign of "skittishness." If the board blinked when in a showdown with the Christian conservatives, implied at least one columnist in the *Los Angeles Times*, then who was to say that textbook publishers, of all people, would have the fortitude to discuss evolution honestly and forthrightly? Another *Los Angeles Times* columnist argued that the state board of education's action on the guideline should be considered a "symbolic victory" for Sheldon and his TVC, for "making [the phrase about evolution-as-fact] disappear from the guidelines was one small part of Sheldon's larger campaign to erode the standing of evolution science in California schools and elevate the biblical story of creation. Sheldon did not succeed in that larger campaign. Actually he did not come close. But his victory in the key phrase issue was more than had been expected. And in politics, exceeding expectations gives you momentum."[67]

But most educators and scientists voiced sympathy for the political position Honig had found himself in, and they sidestepped the opportunity to criticize him or the compromise, saying that nothing in the new language was scientifically illegitimate.[68] And in response to statements like these from PAW and the media, few of the evolution supporters I talked with had much respect for PAW's critique, in particular, pointing out that the organization had its own constituency to please and resources to raise, and that science teaching would always take a back seat to the freedom-of-speech / separation-of-church-and-state issues that PAW placed at the center of its mission. Kevin Padian, for example, one of the writers of the original framework text, was, like PAW, disappointed at first by the compromise language, arguing that the panel had "been very careful to choose" exactly the words it had wanted for the framework. But in the end, Padian was convinced by Bill Honig's "usual wisdom," which reassured him that the message of evolution had remained loud and clear, and that to compromise on a few small things capitulated nothing to the creationists.[69]

According to Honig, himself, PAW's criticisms were nothing new, if not also unfortunate:

It was interesting, the politics of it. Because the People for the American Way was very active. But those guys are sharks: they're after increasing their own. . . . They're not interested in the issue, they're like everybody else: they want to use the issue to advance their own cause. They want polarization. So, these guys have a stake in saying, "Oh, it's terrible, terrible, terrible.". . . They run to the newspapers and say, "Oh, they've sold out, and they did this, and they did that." And it was over *nothing. . . .*

And they didn't do it for the best reasons. The People for the American Way was doing it because they wanted to build their organization, they wanted to scream. They weren't doing it for kids. It wasn't like, "We want to get the good science out there.". . .

I just wasn't very impressed at the way they handled it. And I was a big friend of theirs: they raised money for me, I talked to them. These guys think that just because they have a point, they can push you around and get their way. You're going to do it their way. . . . See, they hijack your issue, basically. All parties do that. They always hijack the educational issues for their own political purposes.[70]

Despite a series of anxious postmortems from PAW and like-minded journalists and scientists (as we saw earlier), it seems to me that Honig is correct, and that the framework should be considered to be nothing less than a total victory over scientific creationism. Given the board's reputation during the previous two decades for political conservatism and its attention to Christian conservative concerns, the statement approved in 1989 gave far less comfort to creationists in California than even creationism's staunchest opponents might have thought possible. And the books that ended up meeting the criteria of California's textbook review panel— and which include beefed-up sections on evolution to the exclusion of creationist alternatives—are now used throughout the country. Education officials fought back creationism nearly to square one.

A New Breed of Creationist Politics: Targeting Local School Districts, Vista, California, 1991–94

By the time the 1990s rolled around, supporters of scientific creationism had seen their glory days come and go, and it seemed that the old ways of doing business—at the statewide level in Louisiana and California— were doomed to fail. It was at this time that creationists, and the Christian conservative movement, more broadly, began to move away from the idea of making statewide policy and began, instead, targeting local policy boards, such as school districts, as their primary sites of potential power.

Both Christian conservatives as a larger movement and creationists as a subset of that movement began using a new strategy to get themselves elected to these bodies. That strategy became popularly known as running a "stealth" campaign, and it was recommended in Christian Coalition literature of the early 1990s as a viable way for committed Christians to get elected to office and get their policies implemented.[71]

The idea of "stealth" was simple. The goal was to start quietly in 1990 in low-profile government offices; in 1992, the aim was to move up the rung to such offices as county supervisors and assembly members; and by the end of the twentieth century, the goal was to occupy major city, statewide, and congressional offices.[72] Early on, followers of the strategy were to search out open seats on any of a number of boards and councils where elections were usually not contested—water boards, sewage districts, local utilities boards, and school councils. To get elected in these low-turnout contests, candidates were encouraged to campaign heavily at churches, but to avoid public forums where their ideas would be more openly discussed. Voters in those churches were to concentrate their votes only on those candidates who were strongly aligned with Christian conservatism.

When elected to school boards—one of the first links in the "stealth" chain—conservative members generally targeted the same set of issues from district to district. In some combination, they attempted to change the content of sex education programs to teach "abstinence only" curricula, to reject federal or state funding seen to interfere with the rightful role of the family in children's lives (such as free meals for needy students, a program perceived to aid the state in eventually stripping away parental authority), to implement school prayer into board proceedings and in the schools, to renounce "self-esteem" classes that encouraged students to develop their own approaches to moral decision making, and sometimes to include creationism—or at least to temper evolution—in the science classroom.[73]

What critics called "stealth campaigns," advocates, such as Ralph Reed, then director of the Christian Coalition, called "the San Diego model." The approach of starting low and reaching sequentially higher was just grassroots campaigning using church sources and resources, said Reed and his supporters; there was nothing insidious about it. The name "San Diego" came from the fact that Christian activists in 1990 in this part of the country "did more of [this campaigning], they did it better, and they did it longer than many other places," Reed declared.[74]

One of the crown jewels of the San Diego model was Vista, California, where a "pro-family"–majority school board (in the words of a 1995 issue of *Citizen*, the political newsletter published by the Christian conservative organization Focus on the Family) was elected to office, and ended up voting for each of the standard conservative issues listed previously. Over the course of its tenure, the 3–2 majority voted for a moment of prayer before school board meetings, to reform the district's sex education program to conform with the nationally known "Sex Respect" curriculum, and to develop a science teaching protocol that demanded a stance of "anti-dogmatism" in all scientific instruction, but which was designed specifically to allow teachers to present weaknesses of evolutionary theory in science classes. Consistent with the outcome of eventual minimization at the hands of the education community, which we have seen in both the Louisiana and California cases, however, this majority was doomed to have no lasting effects in their creationist efforts. I will turn now to an in-depth look at the case of creationist challenge in Vista, California.

1990–92: Electing Creationism-Friendly Board Members

Vista, California, is a community of about 76,000 people and is located forty-five miles north of San Diego city in North San Diego County, an area that is, by all accounts, on the far conservative end of the political spectrum. Predominantly white and middle class for most of its history, Vista boasted an award-winning school district through much of the 1980s and 1990s. During that time, one of its high schools received national honors for academic excellence, another was recognized as a National Blue Ribbon school, and three schools were named California Distinguished Schools.[75]

But at the same time that the schools were winning these awards, a demographic shift began to rock Vista, when illegal and legal immigrants began settling in North San Diego county in large numbers. This was no slow-growth phenomenon, recalled Pete McHugh, an associate superintendent for instruction in the district: this was explosive expansion that put pressure on all institutions serving the public, not the least of which was the public schools. In 1975, for example, the school system served 10,000 students; ten years later, in 1985, it served 11,000. But in the next decade, from 1986 to 1996, the rate of expansion increased more than ten-fold, and at the end of that period, the district was educating 25,000 children, had built eight schools, and had implemented multitrack, year-round schooling for all its elementary and middle schools. Furthermore, in that same decade (from the mid-1980s to the mid-1990s), the district's minority population had grown from 25 percent to nearly 50 percent, and with the mostly Hispanic composition of these students, so, too, had grown accompanying services for these children, including bilingual education.[76]

With rates of change like these, it doesn't take a clairvoyant (or even a sociologist) to predict that Vista might have been ripe for a conservative backlash. Fed up with monies being spent on "liberal" programs like bilingual education and sex education, Deirdre Holliday, an anti-abortion activist in the community, ran for and won a seat on the school board in Vista in 1990. Hers was a classic stealth campaign, according to several of my interviewees and to the newspapers covering the race: she attended few candidate forums open to the public, and she campaigned, instead, at conservative church congregations, leafleting the cars parked in those parking lots, urging them to vote for the "Christian candidate," remembers Bill Loftus, another associate superintendent in the district.[77] Adhering to the stealth strategy for plurality systems, voters were instructed to "vote for Deirdre only, and [not to spread] votes to the other two candidates that were available. . . . So all [she] need[ed was] 20 to 25 percent of the vote to win," said the district's Pete McHugh.[78]

When she joined the other four members of the school board in 1990, Holliday's was a minority voice. Frequently, at that time, votes on a variety of issues came out 4–1, with Holliday on the losing end. Although a few of her proposals were in keeping with other board members' interests, Holliday was sometimes concerned about programs and policies that the other board members considered odd, such as when she examined the content of the district's kindergarten-to-sixth-grade anti-drug program called "Here's Looking at You, 2000." As one of the other board members at that time, Linda Rhoades, remembered it, Holliday found serious fault with the content of the program:

> She got all the material. And in first or second grade, there is a part in there, there is a little box, and it says "the most important person in the world . . . " and you open it up, and there's a mirror, so the child sees herself or himself. She [Holliday] had a great deal of objection to that. That was one of the things she objected to because *you* are *not* the most important person in the world; *God* is the most important thing in the world.[79]

Concerns such as these struck other board members and administrators as nothing more than peculiar while Holliday was in the board minority. But Holliday's reputation and impact would change from predominantly trivial to consequential following the outcome of the 1992 election, when she was joined on the board by two other identifiably Christian conservative candidates, John Tyndall and Joyce Lee. From that point on, these Christian conservative board members consistently voted 3–2 majorities on issues of importance to them: on science instruction, sex education, prayer, and funding for students with away-from-family needs (such as meals and trips to the doctor). The school district would attract the attention of the *New York Times*, the *Wall Street Journal*, CBS, ABC, NBC, and from England, the BBC, all of which expressed shock and dismay at the conservatism of this governing body. The district would soon be torn asunder by mistrust and animosity for several years to come, and the issue of creationism would help push it there. Challengers who found their way to the political inside of educational policy-making would lead the way.

1992–94: Conservative Actions

Some people in the district who had been watching Holliday during her term in office had read her actions as the danger signs of advancing conservatism, and they had tried to warn the district from also electing Tyndall and Lee to the board in 1992. Months prior to the November 1992 election, members of the leadership ranks in the local teachers' union, known as the Vista Teachers' Association (VTA), had urged the union to reverse its history of apoliticism and to endorse candidates actively—as unions in other school districts did. They had even created a political action committee to put money into the campaign coffers of the three incumbents running on the ballot against Tyndall and Lee in the 1992 race, something that had never been done before in Vista, according to then head of the union, Tom Conry.[80] Other teachers had joined parents, clergy, and community members to create the Community Coalition Network to combat Christian conservative candidates in an assortment of elections, particularly those for school board.[81] In addition, moderate incumbents had endorsed each other over their challengers and warned of the havoc conservatives would wreak if elected to a majority. In general, however, their pronouncements of threat had been treated like that of "Chicken Little," said incumbent board member Linda Rhoades, and were not taken seriously in the community at large.[82]

John Tyndall, in particular, had caught the eye of worried teachers and community members, for as director of accounting at the Institute for Creation Research (ICR)—the center for young earth creationism in nearby El Cajon–he was assumed to be an especially likely candidate to try to get creationism taught in the science curriculum. But even he, at the many candidates' forums he attended, denied vehemently that he or anyone else on the board would be interested in such a course of action, and instead, that he was dedicated to fiscal responsibility and the schools' academic accountability to parents.[83] In an interview two years after his term ended, Tyndall remembered the campaign, saying:

> I was interpreted as [being part of] a "stealth," "extreme right," "trying to take over our schools." I got labeled with being part of a nationwide

conspiracy to take over school boards. I ran fully as independent. I'm not a member of Bob Simonds' group [Citizens for Excellence in Education], or of the Christian Coalition, or of any other groups that they tried to [link to] the stealth underground takeover of our public schools. I ran because I was well qualified and had five children invested in the district.[84]

In November 1992, John Tyndall and Joyce Lee were elected to the school board, and together with Deirdre Holliday, they began crafting policies for the Vista Unified School District.

A Community in Conflict over Creationist Proposals

Clearly, however, Tyndall's stated commitment to secular interests did not ring true for many community members who had voted against him, as evidenced by the intense suspicion with which many Vista citizens greeted their new school board majority. The very first regularly scheduled meeting convened by the new board in December 1992 was attended by a far larger-than-usual audience. At it, a biologist who lived in the community stood up, mollusk shell in hand, demanding to know whether and when the board was going to vote to change the science curriculum, making it impossible for teachers to instruct their students in evolutionary theory— theory that accounts for the ten-million-year-old specimen he was holding.

Addressing the biologist and the rest of the crowd, all three of the Christian conservative board members, in turn, reiterated their disinterest in having creationism taught in the schools. Despite their reassurances, however, one of the board's other two members, Sandee Carter, who was known as a moderate, asked that the topic be added to the next meeting's agenda, given that members of the community had a right to hear the issue discussed at greater length.[85] For procedural reasons, it was impossible to discuss the issue at the present meeting, so it was delayed until the upcoming January board meeting.

The biologist's question and Sandee Carter's action to put the creationism issue on the agenda of the next board meeting served to alert nationwide media to attend the next board meeting. Tom Conry, head of the VTA, in a move designed to thwart creationism's potential advance in the system, sought to get the word out that creationism was to be debated. He remembers that he and his group

started out with not knowing what to do, not knowing who to call, not having this network, not being aware of [any] network[s] . . . out there. So, we made a phone call to Cal State-San Diego, and they put us in

touch with a biology [professor] who kind of monitors this kind of stuff
. . . He, then, called Eugenie Scott [at the National Center for Science
Education] and, at that point, the word just went out. I mean, to every-
where. We had people from the Museum of Man in San Diego, we had
people from the Natural History Museum of San Diego who were here
talking to the board. Eugenie Scott came down and spoke. So, the message got out. And then we just kept talking about it to people."[86]

The effort to stir up interest worked, and between 500 and 800 community members (depending on who provided the count) came to the over-
flow second meeting at a local school gymnasium, joined by members of
the mass media. Streaming into the aisles, crammed into doorways, seated
in front of, to the side of, and behind the board were highly partisan
audience members who came to listen, heckle, and give comments about
evolution and scientific creationism.[87] Once again, however, the three conservative board members pledged that they had no interest in incorporating scientific creationism into the science curriculum, recalled Rene Townsend, then superintendent of the Vista school district, citing legal and financial obstacles.[88] The board then got on with other business, such as
voting to have a voluntary moment of silent prayer before board meetings,
which passed.

Of Pandas and People

The three conservative board members remained quiet on the issue of
science instruction for another couple of months, just as they had promised they would. But in March 1993, John Tyndall tossed a grenade onto
the battlefield. Following district protocol for having new material reviewed by a standing committee of teachers, Tyndall brought in five copies
of a book, *Of Pandas and People: The Central Question of Biological
Origins*, to superintendent Rene Townsend, asking her to have the book
reviewed by the science curriculum review committee. Reportedly "shell-
shocked" at the request, Townsend tried to dissuade Tyndall from submitting the book, telling him that it would just reignite passions around the
subject, and that the standing science committee surely would reject it as
a text.[89] But Tyndall persevered, and as an official to the system, he submitted the book for review for use as a supplemental text to be used in
high-school science classrooms.

While critics, such as the National Center for Science Education's Eugenie Scott, have called the book "thinly veiled creationism," Tyndall maintained that he was submitting the book for review not to *promote creationism*, but because the text posed scientific challenges to the "random

mutation" theory of evolution.[90] In an interview a couple of years after the fact, Tyndall argued that the "book has no theology in it. It *does* operate from an intelligent-design perspective—evolution vs. intelligent design. It *doesn't* talk about whether there's a God or how He did this, or where the intelligence comes from. [The authors] just show . . . that [the evidence] would tend to point more towards intelligent design than it does toward random mutation as a theory of origins."[91] According to its authors, Dean Kenyon of San Francisco State University and Percival Davis of Hillsborough Community College in Tampa, Florida, the book uses current information on biology and biochemistry to argue that there is an alternative to the prevailing theory of evolution, one that points to a "master intellect."[92] The authors, and Tyndall as well, asserted that intelligent-design theory would allow students in the district to form their own conclusions about the origins of life.[93]

After several weeks of review, the committee of teachers came back with an unambiguous recommendation on the proposed supplemental text: *Of Pandas and People* should in no way, shape, or form be used in Vista's high-school science courses. Among the failings of the book cited by the committee was its lack of alignment with the state framework in that it did "not offer data based on testability, objectivity, and consistency"; it did not "present scientific theory"; and the learning was "not experiential." In all, "the committee could find no positive aspects of introducing this book into the science curriculum."[94] At the same time, the *San Diego Union Tribune* ran several editorials and news stories chastising Tyndall for having submitted the text to the review committee in the first place, and pointed out its obvious creationist underpinnings, citing "intelligent design" as "mere euphemism" and "subterfuge" for creationism.[95]

But even while the media, school personnel, and others vented about *Pandas*, these already skeptical factions of the district discovered an additional reason to be suspicious of the Christian conservative board members' creationist intentions. In the midst of the *Pandas* debate, Deirdre Holliday noticed wording that disturbed her in the district's proposed life-science mission statement for the lower grades. The text read, "Living things are diverse, interdependent, and evolving, and students must learn about evolution and interdependence throughout their early education." Holliday moved to have the word "evolving" replaced by "changing," arguing that the word "evolving" presented the statement as fact, that this constituted "dogmatic" teaching, and that the state of California prohibited the teaching of any theory of science as fact.[96] Lee and Tyndall voted with Holliday, while trustees Carter and Rhoades voted against the modification. The science mission statement was duly changed.

Writing a Science Policy for the District

Having conceded defeat on the supplemental textbook issue but having won on the mission statement wording, Tyndall and Holliday took to work again to weaken the dominance of evolution as the prevailing theory of origins in the district. The week following *Panda's* rejection, Deirdre Holliday recommended that a statement of science policy be created for the district. As Tyndall recalls, he and Holliday both had been distressed by the controversy that had "sprung upon us" during both the *Pandas* review and the lower-grades science curriculum standard debate, and they decided that the district "really need[ed] a science policy, [we] really needed to define what our science policy [was]. So, we worked together . . . Deirdre and I got together and hammered out a policy" where, before, the district had had none.[97] Upon hearing of their plans, educators and administrators in the district were concerned that evolution again would come under assault.

The two board members presented their proposed science statement, parts 1 and 3 of which were copied from the California science framework (described in the previous section of this chapter), and part 2 of which was written by John Tyndall, himself.[98] The exact language of the Tyndall-Holliday proposed statement read as follows:

(1) No theory of science shall be taught dogmatically, and no student shall be compelled to believe or accept any theory presented in the curriculum.

(2) To enhance positive scientific exploration and dialogue, weaknesses that substantially challenge theories in *evolution* should be presented [emphasis added].

(3) Discussions of divine creation, ultimate purposes or ultimate causes (the why) shall be included at appropriate times in the history-social sciences and / or English-language arts curricula.

In the face of critics' certain objections, Holliday tried to reassure the public that her proposals would not require the teaching of creationism, but only reveal the weak points of evolution theory. "If it weakens the point [of evolution] to the students, they will be aware that evolution is not an established fact. The purpose is to reaffirm that we are teaching evolution as a theory and that we shouldn't be teaching it dogmatically," she said to the *San Diego Union Tribune*.[99]

Her reassurances did little to lessen anxiety and anger among critics, and many school staff and community members greeted the proposed policy as the threat to evolution that they had been expecting from this Christian conservative majority board. On the night in May 1993 that

Policy 6019 was to be discussed, 500 or so people again packed the school gymnasium to listen, jeer, and present their views to the board on the teaching of science in the district.[100] Once again, national media joined local news outlets to cover the public meeting, and all who were there stayed late into the night as the meeting sailed into increasingly roiling waters. ACLU letters that emphasized issues of constitutionality were read, and forty audience members alternately drew applause and boos when they aired their concerns.[101] No official action was taken on the policy that night.

Seeking to calm teachers' fears following the contentious meeting, John Tyndall drafted a letter to science teachers explaining the purpose of the new policy. Addressed to the Science Review Committee in July 1993, Tyndall wrote,

> There seems to be those who are severely confused about the intent of the proposed Science Policy and [its] implications for science education. . . .
>
> The proposed policy supports good (honest) science in that students should have access to scientific evidence that supports or contradicts theories generally held in evolution or any other science theory being presented. To say that macro evolution is a proven fact is certainly to do a disservice to the development of critical thinking skills. Yes, it is generally accepted by most scientists, but it does have severe flaws that students should be exposed to. To blindly teach unsubstantiated statements that there was no designed order to living matter, but that living matter is purely the random chance offering of billions of years, is to force dogma upon students every bit as much as if you were to force a belief in the Bible.
>
> All I am saying is that weaknesses and strengths in scientific theory should be presented as to allow students to think about how inferences are derived from observations. Is that really too much to ask in a good science classroom?[102]

The answer was yes, it was too much to ask. Teachers and their supporters continued to call the proposal ill advised, harmful to science, and unconstitutional.

Tom Conry, head of the teachers' union, and others in the union's leadership tried mightily at this point to rally his troops to exert pressure on the board, so that the three Christian conservatives would have to back off this most visible challenge to the teaching of evolution. By the next board meeting, Conry's efforts were successful, and teachers and others forced Holliday and Tyndall to change the language in the policy so that it did not question *evolution* per se, but "any theory in science." Section 1 of the policy remained the same, reading:

No theory of science shall be taught dogmatically and no student shall be compelled to believe or accept any theory presented in the curriculum. A dogma is a system of beliefs that is not subject to scientific test and refutation. Compelling belief is inconsistent with the goal of education; the goal is to encourage understanding.

Section 2 was changed to remove singular attention from evolution and to broaden the policy's impact to all areas of scientific inquiry. It now read,

To enhance scientific exploration and dialogue, scientific evidence that challenges *any theory in science* should be presented [emphasis added].

And section 3, under teachers' pressure, was modified to reflect the fact that divine creation already had been incorporated into the social studies curriculum:

Discussions of divine creation, ultimate purposes or ultimate causes (the "why") *are* included at appropriate times in the history-social sciences and / or English-language arts curricula [emphasis added].

Amended as such, the new science policy passed by the now customary 3–2 vote: Christian conservative board members voted for it, the two moderate members voted against it. The vote was accompanied by predictions that the ambiguity written into the policy opened up the door for creationism to be taught in the district, and for the school system to incur huge bills defending its new unconstitutional science teaching protocol. Linda Rhoades, one of the two board members to vote against the policy, explained to the press that the vote unfortunately would be read as giving "the board's blessing" to teachers who wanted to teach creationism in science lesson plans.[103]

Tyndall's perspective on the impact of Policy 6019 diverged from that of Rhoades: the spin he gave it was decidedly more enthusiastic, if he did not exactly acknowledge that it was creation science that he preferred. When asked if the policy actually left room for scientific creationism to be taught in Vista classrooms, Tyndall said,

Not really. What it leaves room for is for evolution to be challenged. To let evolution stand on its own merits. It allows teachers to bring in things like *Of Pandas and People*. . . . What we did was we gave a covering to any teacher, to any science teacher who wants to look at the evidence of evolution. To expose students to weaknesses in evolution, as well as its strengths. They're covered with this policy as far as showing the weaknesses in evolution. They didn't have a license to put in a creation model, but they had the license to *do science* in the science classroom, to present challenges to that which is a theory.[104]

Reactions to the Board, 1993

By the time they passed the science policy, the conservative board members had already raised a host of other issues on the board that further divided the community, such as prayer, sex education, and "parental rights." The board had voted 3–2 to institute an invocation before board meetings; to decline a California state Healthy Start grant that would provide social services for poor families;[105] to drastically decrease bus service and remove free bus service completely to needy students to encourage district integration; to implement Sex Respect, an abstinence-only sex education program for seventh-graders, roundly opposed by parents, the press, and teachers; and even to reject the superintendent's efforts at healing the rift that was driving the board apart.[106]

Among others, teachers and principals were reported to be feeling increasingly embattled within the district. Having been accused by the three Christian conservative board members of harboring secret agendas like secular humanism and socialism, and having been treated to what they perceived as condescension and suspicion, teachers, as a coordinated body, began openly to express their animosity toward the three-person board majority.[107] The Vista Teachers' Association began to get more political and to speak out more against board actions. They also began cooperating with another group of concerned community members calling themselves Community Action for Public Education (CAPE), which was a self-appointed board watchdog group. Armed with tenure, union contracts, and the privilege of academic freedom (at least to the degree that they were not in the direct line of firing by board members, as administrators were), VTA members challenged the three-person board majority on any number of points of disagreement. Equipped with video cameras and the rights of citizens to monitor their elected officials, CAPE members showed up at board meetings ready to observe members' activities and willing to express their disapproval. In fact, the only group clearly missing from this openly adversarial configuration was district administrators— the superintendent and her deputies—who felt both professional and personal pressure to lie low in the political fray surrounding them. Although all of the high-level administrators I interviewed later (in 1996) admitted to having had serious misgivings about carrying out their obligations to this board, none was willing at the time to state publicly her or his opposition to the board majority. Their reticence sprang both from their sense of responsibility to the legitimately elected board and from their calculations of shaky job security in the district.[108]

Recalling the Conservative Board Members, 1994

Increasingly disposed toward activism against the board, VTA and CAPE commenced a highly unusual, laborious undertaking in the district: the effort to recall the three conservative Christian board members before their terms expired. Although some members of CAPE thought that a recall drive would be "too divisive, too much work, . . . possibly polarizing of the community," recalled CAPE leader Barbara Donovan, there was a core group of teachers, parents, and community members who believed that an early recall of Holliday, Tyndall, and Lee was the only reasonable road to pursue for reclaiming the school district from the "Radical Right."[109] Their aim was nothing less than ejecting these conservative members from the board in a special early recall election and to elect in their places a new slate of moderates. The group set up a political action committee separate from CAPE called the Coalition for Mainstream Education (CME), and in January 1994, CME began its effort to recall the three Christian conservatives, including Deirdre Holliday, whose four-year term was up for reelection in the fall of that year.

Although the first attempt at gathering signatures failed by a couple thousand votes, the second attempt started strong and stayed strong with the avid work of CME volunteers. Then, when the second attempt was underway and animosity was at an all-time high in the community following the board's vote on sex education, three decisions were announced in the district soon thereafter that made a successful recall more likely. First, Deirdre Holliday, who had served since 1990, announced that she would not run for reelection in November 1994.[110] This meant that only John Tyndall and Joyce Lee were vulnerable to an attempted recall and that, for procedural reasons, a smaller number of signatures would have to be collected to get the measure on the ballot.

Second, after nearly one and one-half years of difficult machinations with the board, Rene Townsend, Vista's award-winning and highly regarded superintendent, decided to leave the district for a smaller and less well-paid job in a nearby district. She admitted two years later that part of her impetus for resigning from Vista came from not wanting to work for "people like that anymore," and part was from wanting to jump start the recall initiative.[111] As superintendent, Townsend felt professionally obligated to carry out the board's decisions, and she believed that it was not her place to disagree publicly with the board while still in office. In addition, she thought that exiting the district would lead her supporters to become more enraged by the actions of the board majority and recognize the need to get actively involved in the recall.

The third announcement that facilitated the recall was Sandee Carter's decision to step down from the school board. Carter was one of the two moderate board members and, like Townsend, she was widely respected in the district. Citing the discomfort and frustrations that came from working with the conservative board on issues that seemed political and noneducational, Carter decided to not run for reelection.[112] Bureaucratic leaders in the school district were prepared to leave their posts to expel what they thought were illegitimate decision makers.

Together, these three events served to motivate the community's and teachers' opposition to the board, and by June, the campaign had gathered enough signatures to get the recall of Tyndall and Lee on the November ballot.

Despite compelling evidence that they very well might be ousted by the recall, neither Lee nor Tyndall could believe that the end of their terms was nigh. Nevertheless, before the board majority could enact any more potentially divisive policies, the recall campaign succeeded, and all three Christian conservative board members were out of office. Even as Vista citizens voted overwhelmingly for conservative candidates like Pete Wilson for governor and Michael Huffington for senator, and conservative causes like Proposition 187 (the initiative aimed at cutting services to illegal immigrants and their children), these same conservative voters removed conservatism from office at the local level as they recalled Joyce Lee and John Tyndall.[113] Four candidates—none of them Christian conservative—filled the seats left by the conservatives Holliday, Tyndall, and Lee, and the moderate Carter.

Upon winning their seats, the four new board members, plus the winning incumbent Linda Rhoades, announced that their immediate goal was to heal the schism that had divided the community for the past two years. Despite efforts at framing themselves as conciliatory, however, the board failed to convince the district's Christian conservative citizens that their concerns would be represented on the board. The constituency that had voted for Tyndall, Lee, and Holliday in the first place felt, once again, that they had been dealt a very bad hand. The old feelings of disenfranchisement came flooding back, and the bitterness toward public education and its servants returned. John Tyndall, a key spokesman for this constituency, withdrew four of his five children (all but a graduating senior) from the public schools just one month after the recall election.[114] Although he claimed that this was an educational statement, not a political one, it would be hard to miss the bitterness behind it.

Analysis of the Case and Its Outcomes

In the final analysis, most everyone agrees that although much vitriol was expressed in the school district for two years running, no substantive change actually took place inside school classrooms as a result of the majority board's tenure. As Pete McHugh, associate superintendent for instruction told me,

> What has been the ultimate change? . . . Has there been any change in textbooks? The answer is no. Has there been any change in the curriculum? The answer is no. Has there been any change in the staff development for science teachers? The answer is no. Has there been any change in textbooks or procedures in English or Language Arts? The answer is no. So, after it is all said and done, it was business as usual. And the science policy really is an affirmation of what our practice *was*, rather than a change. Although there was some discussion about a *possible* change, it just didn't make it through the political process.[115]

So, the board majority was able to pass a new science teaching policy that explicitly encouraged questioning all scientific theories, and that allowed social studies and language arts teachers to discuss the idea of divine origins. But the California state science framework already contained such guarantees, so this change in Vista policy amounted to only a redundant win, at most. The new Vista policy added that anti-dogmatism in any science teaching was required, but that, too, had been guaranteed previously in statewide school code. A lower-schools science learning statement altered the wording of "the universe continually evolves" to "the universe continually changes," but most people in the district regarded this alteration as merely symbolic. The conservative majority instituted invocation before school board meetings, but prayer is also allowed before each session that the U.S. Congress is convened. The majority did pass the Sex Respect sex education curriculum, but as soon as the new moderate board came to power, its moderate majority rescinded that program. In sum, the board majority's mandate met stiff opposition from professional educators and, by and large, any changes that it had implemented ultimately were undone. True, the board's failure to effect change did not occur before the loss of an honored superintendent and some other cherished members of the district, but as with the other cases where creation science was concerned, Vista board members faced all but absolute defeat. Despite gaining some power for some amount of time, these elected officials were not able to effect lasting change.

Why was it possible for Christian conservatives to win a majority on the Vista school board, but then not be able to shape school policy as they wished? Since the same kind of outcome occurred in Louisiana and, as we will see, in Kansas, too, this question deserves close consideration, and I will address it in greater depth in chapter 6. But for now, I'll report what three of my interviewees told me. John Tyndall reflected,

> Why Vista? I don't know. Unless you bring God into it and say, "Well, God did it. God put me in and God removed me." I'm happy with that. I wouldn't have run if I didn't think God wanted me in there. It wasn't by the prompting of Christian organizations, but by . . . I do believe in God, and I want God to order my steps. Everything I do I hope is ordered by God. He put me in. For why, I don't know. I didn't get to accomplish that which I thought I was running for.[116]

Both Barbara Donovan, the community activist, and Linda Rhoades, the one remaining board member from that time, also puzzled over their roles in Vista incidents. Said Donovan,

> You know, when I think, "How did we ever do that?" it boggles my mind. It was like a moment in time, and you don't even know how you got cast into it, or why you were there. Why did we [my family] move to Vista [just prior to these events]? A place where we had never even driven out to. . . . Why? It's almost like there was a reason for us to have come here. I just view it that way because there is really no rational answer to some of these things.[117]

Rhoades is unclear on how and why Vista became a flash point in the country, but she hopes that there was good reason for all the difficulties she and the district faced:

> If you want to know the truth, I just don't know why Vista. Maybe the time was just right for this. . . . I have never been able to diagnose that, why it happened here. But I will tell you, sometimes I think things happen for a reason. And with us being in the middle of this, I know other districts *did not fall* because they said, "Do you want to be like Vista?" And we were very loud. So, maybe it's a little spiritual on my part, but maybe it was just supposed to happen.[118]

Linda Rhoades knows that Vista had been used as a negative reference point for other districts going through similar strife, and she thinks that Vista's experiences allowed other school systems to avert the same sort of conflict and attendant bitterness.

At the beginning of this section on Vista, I suggested a demographic explanation for the timing of this challenge. This explanation concerns the rapid growth in the district in the numbers of poor, Hispanic children, and the types of social services offered to this new clientele, such as the spending of money on remedial classes, bilingual education, and free meals served in the schools. The overwhelmingly conservative voters of Vista did not look kindly on such government "hand outs" to its poorer constituents, and perhaps they voted in what they thought was an alternative board to correct this trend. Also important to the timing of this board was the growing presence nationwide of a Christian conservative movement that was trying to get members of its political suasion into all levels of office. Once in power, however, the majority found it impossible to stay there, for the attention the board members garnered in going about their business was enough to turn a majority of school system staff and voters in the district against them. Although they were able to obtain "political" power in the district, the conservative majority was unable to achieve "bureaucratic" authority there, and so it suffered a reversal of fate. This is a subject I will investigate more closely in the final two chapters of the book.

So, Vista creationists met a demise that was different in its details but familiar in its overall tenor to the outcomes achieved by their peers in Louisiana and the state of California. But, surely there are school districts in the nation that have gone about drafting anti-evolution policies with less conflict than occurred in the three cases described here, and where at least parts of those policies have been more quietly and effectively implemented without attracting court or voter interference. I will describe two such cases—Alabama and Oklahoma—before moving on to Kansas, the site of the most recent and visible creationist challenge of the last several years.

The Land of Oz, or the Land of "Odds"? Kansas De-emphasizes Evolution in Favor of Intelligent Design

Surprising to most casual observers, who expect challenges to evolution to wane with time, the public losses that creationists have faced over the past two decades in their home locales have done little to dissuade creationists elsewhere to try their hand at crafting policies aimed at deemphasizing evolution in their school systems.[119] On the contrary: although disappointed in outcomes such as those ultimately achieved in Louisiana, California, and Vista, creationists, through their commitment to making the science classroom more hospitable to their children's beliefs, continue to be strongly motivated. As evidence, at approximately the same time that John Tyndall and Joyce Lee were being recalled by voters in Vista, supporters of creationism in several other locations across the United States—in the South, particularly—were waging ever more strategically astute battles to lessen the impact of evolutionary pedagogy in public school classrooms.

Perhaps it was the political victories in Vista that invigorated creationists across the country to attempt change in their districts and states. Or, perhaps it was the ongoing process used by creationists for decades of adapting and updating their social and scientific arguments—in response to their most recent defeat—that spurred conservatives on to action. Probably a combination of the two, challenges in state systems and local school districts continued into the late 1990s and the early years of the new millennium. In one county in Georgia, for example, teachers were required for a short time to tell their students about a variety of theories on the origins of life; in New Hampshire, a bill under consideration in the late 1990s would have made it illegal to teach evolution without parental consent; and in Tennessee, the state legislature debated whether to ban the teaching of evolution as fact, whereby teachers could have been dismissed by the district if they refused to characterize evolution as just "theory."[120]

Creationists actually won a lasting victory in Alabama when, in 1995, that state's board of education approved a plan to place a disclaimer label inside all biology textbooks used in the state's public schools, which would explain that evolution is "just a theory," and that any statements in the book about the origins of life should be considered as merely theoretical.[121] The plan took effect in Fall 1996, when the following insert appeared in biology textbooks:

A Message from the Alabama State Board of Education

This textbook discusses evolution, a controversial theory some scientists present as a scientific explanation for the origin of living things, such as plants, animals and humans.

No one was present when life first appeared on earth. Therefore, any statement about life's origins should be considered as theory, not fact.

The word "evolution" may refer to many types of change. Evolution describes changes that occur within a species. (White moths, for example, may "evolve" into gray moths.) This process is microevolution, which can be observed and described as fact. Evolution may also refer to the change of one living thing to another, such as reptiles into birds. This process, called macroevolution, has never been observed and should be considered a theory. Evolution also refers to the unproven belief that random, undirected forces produced a world of living things.

There are many unanswered questions about the origin of life which are not mentioned in your textbooks, including:
- Why did the major groups of animals suddenly appear in the fossil record (known as the Cambrian Explosion)?

- Why have no new major groups of living things appeared in the fossil record in a long time?
- Why do major groups of plants and animals have no transitional forms in the fossil record?
- How did you and all living things come to possess such a complete and complex set of "instructions" for building a living body?

Study hard and keep an open mind. Someday you may contribute to the theories of how living things appeared on earth.[122]

In 1999, Oklahoma education officials approved the use of virtually this same disclaimer for its state's biology textbooks. To this day, these statements appear in the two states' biology textbooks.

While creationist organizations across the country hailed Alabama's and Oklahoma's textbook inserts as key victories, their celebration was even greater later that year, when another state's school board made headlines in the creation-evolution controversy. In August 1999, in a close vote of 6 to 4, the Kansas State Board of Education voted to excise "macroevolution" from state evaluation tests—the tests used to evaluate students' mastery of various academic concepts—and to remove evolution as one of five unifying concepts in science. Because creationists proclaimed the state's decision as a most important victory—particularly those in the intelligent-design camp—and because advocates of evolutionary teaching framed the vote as an especially chilling example of anti-scientific thinking, I turn to Kansas as the fourth and final in-depth case in my analysis of creationist challenges in the 1980–2000 time period.

In the Beginning

Much like the events that occurred in Vista, by the time the Kansas state school board voted to deemphasize evolution in 1999, that body's members had already established a three-year pattern of conflict surrounding several conservative hot-button issues. In the years 1996 to 1999, issues besides creationism that stirred debate among board members included the math curriculum (whether students should be allowed to use calculators on some parts of the math tests—conservatives viewed this as a "crutch" and preferred a back-to-basics approach); a recently passed Quality Performance Accreditation program (the previous, more centrist board majority had implemented a system for statewide classroom content and student evaluation—conservatives believed that this system robbed communities of local control and injected liberal values like multiculturalism into the curriculum); sex education (conservatives on the board, as in Vista, preferred an abstinence-only program); and the acceptance of federal funding for the school system's operation (some conservatives on the board, including its chairperson, believed that federal funding contributed to communities' loss of local control over the values their children learned).[123] As reported in the *Kansas City Star*, conservatives had also stalled implementation of the Workforce Investment Act, which provided aid to states that develop career programs. Kansas board conservatives disliked this act, arguing that it guided students to jobs that businesses believed were in demand, rather than leaving those decisions to students and their parents. All in all, the issues causing conflict in Kansas were remarkably similar in philosophy, if not in their finer points, to the board debates in Vista. Traditional values, parental control—these were the ideological and rhetorical linchpins of contentiousness in Kansas in the mid to late 1990s.

For the first two years that the 1996 board was in power, a frequent outcome of these conflicts was ballot deadlock, as five conservatives and five moderates on the board cancelled out each others' agendas. On some occasions, however, under increasingly intense media and public pressure to "stop the stalemate" and "get things done," a moderate would join the conservative bloc and vote for issues promoted by his or her conservative colleagues. And just like in Vista, over time, this growing number of conservative victories bred an enormous amount of animosity among board members, the media and, to some extent, the state's voters.

The roots of the math, accreditation, and sex education decisions—as well as of the board's eventual anti-evolution policy—lie in the statewide school board elections of 1996. It was in preparation for these elections that a group of conservative citizens around the state calling themselves the Kansas Education Watch-Network, or KEW-NET, began to think about the board of education as a target for overhaul. Having made little headway during the previous five years (1990–95) lobbying the state *legislature* for its slate of issues concerning parental rights and educational reforms, KEW-NET turned its attention away from the state house and senate and toward the composition of the board of education as a natural place to wrest power away from "liberals," whom KEW-NET members held responsible for inappropriate educational policy in the state. Even though the ten-seat school board with which KEW-NET expressed dissatisfaction was composed of eight Republican members in the early to mid-1990s, the conservative organization gave the board failing marks for being too liberal, and KEW-NET leaders and volunteers committed their time and energy to replacing members whom they considered to be particularly egregious.[124] With a recent sex education and AIDS-information program to spur him on, not to mention the statewide Quality Performance Accreditation program, Jim McDavitt, KEW-NET's president, began recruiting and backing candidates for the five open seats on the board in 1996.

Much like other conservative campaigns of that era, KEW-NET made local control of schools its focal point; found willing candidates to run for office, according to the *Wichita Eagle* and *Topeka Capital Journal* (a charge that McDavitt contests); issued voter guides detailing candidates' positions; and distributed fliers to citizens.[125] Different from the stealth campaign run by Deirdre Holliday in Vista in 1990, these five candidacies were run as public campaigns. But the problem with them, as far as moderates in the state were concerned, was that the conservatives soft-pedaled the depth of their conservatism to the electorate, and that most voting-age adults in the state simply did not seem to care enough to cast their ballots. Despite the *Kansas City Star's* repeated efforts to motivate voters to select "moderate" candidates—running endorsements for the conservatives' opponents, egging on Kansans to be concerned about the "conservative agenda," arguing forcefully that "the state board, which decides important policy questions in education, [was] in danger of being taken over by the religious right"—McDavitt and KEW-NET succeeded, and they helped bring four new conservatives to power, joining a fifth already on the board.[126] It was thus that five conservatives now held half of the ten seats: Linda Holloway, Steve Abrams, Scott Hill, and Mary Douglass Brown joined Kevin Gilmore to form a five-person conservative bloc. In the aftermath of the election, the number of 5-to-5 votes on the board (conservative-to-moderate) became legendary; although not infrequently, as I mentioned earlier, these votes would swing 6–4 when a moderate joined the conservative bloc. Possessing real power, conservatives on the school board were soon preparing to sponsor and vote on their pet projects.

Finally, in laying the groundwork for the controversy that was to come, we should note that there was one more election in 1998, when the other five seats on the board came open (every two years in Kansas, five of the ten seats are up for election; terms last four years). Although several of the personnel on the board changed after that election, what is most significant about the election results was that little changed *ideologically* on the board. The seat vacated by the conservative Kevin Gilmore traded hands to another conservative, John Bacon (a friend of Gilmore's since their days at Mid America Nazarene University), while the other four seats—held by moderates at the time of the election—were again filled by candidates who were thought to be centrist.[127]

It is actually quite remarkable that Gilmore's successor, John Bacon, defeated both his moderate opponent in the Republican primary and his Democratic opponent in the general election, and that the conservative-moderate ratio on the board, thereby, stayed the same. I call this result remarkable because the *Kansas City Star* seemingly had done everything in its power to have the election turn out differently. Probably the most influential paper in the state, the *Star* frequently encouraged readers to consider the conservatives as dangerous to state education. Endorsing Bacon's opponent in the Republican primary, for example, as a "traditional conservative," the *Star* tried mightily to get out the vote for moderates—Democrat or Republican.[128] The newspaper failed, and voting results from the 1996 and 1998 elections, together, paved the way for a contentious couple of years to come. Creationism's advocates had captured half the seats on the inside of the system's decision-making ranks.

Prologue to the 1999 Science Standards

In 1999, following several split votes along ideological lines (as well as a few majority-conservative ones), the Kansas Board of Education turned its attention to the state's science standards, one of several curriculum standards the board was set to review that term. Just as in California and New York, curriculum standards in Kansas contain both a philosophical statement about the discipline under consideration and how it is practiced, as well as more concrete goals for what students should learn in each grade for each subject.[129] Standards provide a blueprint for the content that belongs in classrooms statewide, and local school districts use the state's standards as a basis for developing their own curricula for the district.

While the state board does not control classroom content—insofar as districts are not required to use its standards—the board does have a strong indirect influence on classroom instruction. It exercises this influence by determining the content of *statewide standardized tests*.[130] The logic of standards and testing works similarly in Kansas as it does in New York: (1) the standards outline what is to be known among students in the state for a particular discipline, and (2) they state clearly any and all information that will appear on state assessment tests. If a subject is included in the standards, then it potentially will appear on the statewide assessment tests; conversely, if a subject is not included on the standards, then it will not appear on statewide assessment tests.

As background, it is important to point out that two years before the start of board debate on the science standards, a twenty-seven-member science committee had been convened by the previous board to draft the actual standards for the state's schools. Given the animosity that had developed and become public on the board since the 1996 elections, current board members were well aware that whatever report the science committee produced, it had a high likelihood of earning the now familiar 5 to 5 conservative to moderate split. To try to navigate around this frustrating outcome, the board had decided to give each one of its members the power to appoint one committee member to the science panel, while the state commissioner, Andy Tompkins, had the authority to appoint the remaining members.[131] School board members—or those with *political* power in the system, if not *professional, institutional* power—were given 10/27 of the authority to handpick the architects of this document.

Thus selected—mainly from the state's public schools and universities[132]—the science committee began meeting in June 1998. John Staver, a member of the committee, and director of the Center for Science Education at Kansas State University, recalls that at the first meeting, the committee decided to base whatever new standards it came up with on national guidelines from the National Academy of Sciences (NAS)—a body authorized by the federal government to set science standards in the nation. The NAS had recently completed a set of national guidelines after four years of drafting, revising, and receiving critiques by twenty-two science organizations and 18,000 scientists, giving the guidelines a special kind of "credibility," according to Staver.[133] The standards presented evolution as a major component of science. In addition to drawing on content from the NAS standards (called the National Science Education Standards), the Kansas science committee also tapped into two other national standards that had recently been formulated by national committees of scientists: the National Science Teachers Association's *Pathways to the Science Standards*, and the *Benchmarks for Science Literacy* from the American Association for the Advancement of Science. Having relied so heavily on these national standards in the writing process, the Kansas science committee wrote to all three organizations seeking permission to use their documents, and it had received tentative approval from each.[134]

Using these three standards as their models, the Kansas science committee completed its initial draft of the standards in 1999 and turned the draft over to the board of education. Following the NAS, the Kansas draft called evolution a "unifying concept" in biology that students must understand. This new language effectively overrode the weaker version of the evolution concept written in the previous state science standards, which required only that students in grades 9–12 "develop an understanding" of biological evolution. It is essential to see that, while not perfect from the perspective of creationists, the language contained in the previous state science standards was far more tolerable to their beliefs than this new phrasing about evolution as a "unifying concept."[135]

Understanding the sensitivity surrounding this issue, however, the science committee added language to the standards that were meant to soften the evolution-heavy blow, including the following disclaimer in its initial draft of the new science standards:

> Understands: "Understand" does not mandate "belief." While students may be required to understand some concepts that researchers use to conduct research and solve practical problems, they may accept or reject the scientific concepts presented. This applies particularly where students' and or parents' religion is at odds with science.[136]

One Board Member's Response

Despite the committee's efforts to appease proactively evolution's foes, word of the draft and its strong "advocacy" of evolution spread quickly through both the creationist and mainstream science worlds, and conservative board members expressed their dissatisfaction with the document. Board members Scott Hill and John Bacon stated that they were absolutely unwilling to support the new NAS-modeled standards, with Hill complaining that the standards focused too much attention on evolution, and Bacon indicating that the standards should include other theories.[137] Conservative Steve Abrams also criticized the standards, saying that the science committee's work was unacceptable because of its reliance on faulty, "unobservable," unmeasurable, unfalsifiable evidence.[138]

According to the *Kansas City Star*, not long after they saw that first unsatisfactory draft, another group of Christian conservative citizens assembled an organization called the Creation Science Association of Mid-America to redraft the standards in accordance with their own beliefs about origins.[139] Tom Willis, the organization's president, approached board member Steve Abrams and asked him both to look at the document and submit it to the board of education as a "revised" science standard. Abrams agreed to champion the document before his colleagues on the board.[140]

Among other changes that the Willis / Abrams group made to the original science committee's draft, according to the *Kansas City Star*,[141] were the following:

- Where the science committee's version had listed five unifying concepts of science—(1) systems, order, and organization; (2) evidence, models, and explanation; (3) constancy, change, and measurement; (4) form and function; and (5) evolution and equilibrium—the Willis / Abrams revision removed the unifying concepts and added three areas of science: technology, theoretical science, and historical science.

- Where the science committee's version defined science as "the human activity of seeking natural explanations for what we observe in the world around us," the Willis / Abrams revision stated that science is defined as something that can be *repeated* in the laboratory. (The importance of this emphasis on observability and repeatability will become apparent shortly.)
- Where the glossary of the science committee's version defined evolution, in part, as "a scientific theory that accounts for present-day similarity and diversity among living organisms and changes in non-living entities over time," the glossary of the Willis / Abrams version described evolution as permutations that occur *within* a species, with the caveat that some evolutionary changes can be demonstrated and some cannot (emphasis added).

In addition, according to the Kansas City newspaper, the Willis / Abrams proposal also included language that would leave it to local school boards to decide whether or not to teach evolution, a nod to the "local control" issue that had generally animated the conservative members on the board.[142]

Needless to say, when Abrams presented his ninety-one-page revision to the science committee, calling the changes "slight," John Staver and his committee colleagues found the resulting document unacceptable, and they began lobbying the board not to accept the changes as legitimate science. The scientists went on record saying that if the board asked them to integrate the Willis / Abrams revisions into their standards, they would refuse to do so.[143]

How did the rest of the board—besides Abrams, Hill, and Bacon—respond to the revisions? Two other conservatives on the board, chairperson Linda Holloway and Mary Douglass Brown, leaned toward supporting Abrams's revisions, as well, leaving the board split down the middle, once again, 5 to 5 conservative to moderate.[144] Conservative board members promised that compromise could be reached if the body would leave evolution out of the standards and "allow school districts to settle the debate as they see fit,"[145] a proposal viewed with abhorrence by the original science committee members and, presumably, by the moderate members of the state board, as well. Several of the moderates openly criticized the Abrams proposal as out of line with mainstream voter preferences,[146] but others remained silent on the issue.

It was with particular chagrin that journalists on the *Kansas City Star* began worrying openly that at least one of the moderates on the board might compromise with Abrams and his creationist backers, in order to maintain peace and avoid yet another split vote or delayed approval—trying to dodge the board's statewide reputation for intransigence.[147] Journalists wondered if some moderate board members, sensitive to accusations that they could not get work accomplished because of their philosophical and political differences, were willing to tone down evolution in the science standards to find a compromise position between the original committee's and Abram's revisions.

Media writers also advanced the arguments that creationists misunderstood the scientific use of the term "theory," that creationism does not belong in the curriculum, and that, pragmatically, if the state were to leave to local school districts the decision of whether to teach evolution, then many school districts would simply not teach it—out of laziness or fear.[148]

With the arguments flying fast and furious around their heads, this split board—the board that had suffered much criticism over the past two years for not being able to get work done because of the rifts among its members—made a face-saving move. Knowing that its members were once again evenly divided 5 to 5, board chairperson Linda Holloway decided to delay the vote until a future board meeting.

Crafting a Policy

Working toward a definitive 6 to 4 vote to end the deadlock that had come to tarnish their reputation, during the next two monthly board meetings, in June and July 1999, the members of the state school board staved off a decision on the science standards even while they hosted open forums for public commentary. Although several board votes in the previous three years had been able to break the 5 to 5 impasse, the science issue seemed to many to represent a far more serious matter than previous matters, and compromise was to be hard won. Members on both sides of the issue were using the extra time to craft their own revisions of the standards, each side seeking to write a provision that just one more member could agree with. During this time, the *Kansas City Star* reported that Steve Abrams had teamed up with Harold Voth, a member of the board who had generally voted with the moderates, to use Abrams's first revision as a model on which to base a compromise document.[149]

On the other side, the original committee of scientists—headed again by John Staver—was now in its fifth draft of its version of the science standards.[150] With this draft, journalist Kate Beem of the *Star* reported, the committee sought to calm its critics further by removing the offending "five unifying concepts" language which, hitherto, had included evolution, and which had been included on almost every page of the standards. The committee also modified the name of the concept "Evolution and Equilibrium" to "Patterns of Cumulative Change," clearly an attempt to accommodate religious people who had been offended by the repeated and prominent mention of evolution in the first draft. Finally, the committee included new language in the draft designed to encourage sensitivity among school personnel for students' religious beliefs. This new insert encouraged instructors to teach "with tolerance and respect," and to encourage students to talk with their family or clergy about issues "outside the domain of science."[151]

But while science committee members sought to decrease suspicion by changing some of the language in the document, Staver and his cowriters warned that they had no intention of entirely removing evolution from the standards.[152] This kind of "vigilance" left board member Steve Abrams with little choice, he said, but to proceed with his own version of the framework. In a blow to many observers who had hoped that board members would preserve the original committee's vision for the standards, Abrams responded that no matter how many so-called significant changes Staver and his committee had made in their document "from [his] perspective, no matter what you call it, a rose is still a rose. And so is evolution."[153] The prospects did not look good for evolution's advocates, especially as Abrams and Voth continued to hammer out their compromise standard.[154]

Despite receiving a number of pleas to cast aside the "compromise" language—including a letter written by the presidents of the state's six public universities—the conservative members of the board of education of the state of Kansas finally put the science standards to a vote. At that meeting in August 1999, Steve Abrams and Scott Hill, both conservatives, along with Harold Voth, a member known to be loyal to a certain number of conservative issues but considered a moderate on others, presented their modifications of Abrams' original document to the board. And the ten-person board, long a divided body, voted 6 to 4 in support of the Abrams / Voth compromise. With Harold Voth's yea vote added as the sixth vote to the conservatives' solid five-member bloc (Steve Abrams, Scott Hill, Mary Douglass Brown, John Bacon, and Linda Holloway), the Kansas Board of Education endorsed the Abrams / Voth version of the science standards.[155] By doing so, the board rejected the version of the standards written by its own appointed panel of scientists, it rejected language endorsed by the National Academy of Sciences and reviewed by the Council for Basic Education in Washington, and it removed evolution as a subject that would be tested through its state assessment instrument.[156]

Content of the Policy

This was an official creationist victory on a scale not seen in many years around the country. What, precisely, did the new standard say, and what did it mean for schoolchildren in the state of Kansas? How different was it, first, from the original twenty-seven-member science committee's recommendations and, second, from Abrams's original proposed revision? According to an analysis conducted in late 1999 by an organization called Kansas Citizens for Science, a pro-evolution group, the overall language of the new standards bore a striking resemblance to the standards that Abrams and the Creation Science Association of Mid-America had hammered out earlier that year (referred to as the Willis / Abrams revisions in previous sections).[157] Just as in that initial anti-evolution proposal, there was no mention in this policy of what creationists call "macroevolution," or the origin of species and the process of change from one species to the next, except in the glossary. The body of the standards, however, did approve the teaching of "microevolution," or the genetic adaptation and natural selection within a species (the kind of evolutionary change that creationists approve of). This part of the policy was standard "intelligent design" fare.

Second, in keeping with a "young earth" orientation, the compromise standards also deleted all references to the big bang theory, which holds that the universe was born from a vast explosion of matter.[158] In so doing, the board removed references to radioactive dating of rocks and continental drift, as well.[159] In their place, the approved standards referred to Mount St. Helens, the volcano that erupted in Washington state in 1980, and Mount Etna, the live volcano in Sicily, Italy. The standard pointed to both of these active volcanoes as case studies that "suggest alternative explanations to scientific hypotheses or theories."[160] By deleting the theory of an expanding universe, initiated by an explosive moment of creation, and replacing it with modern events of geographical change, like active volcanoes, the standards questioned the old age of the earth and universe, and thus, the possibility of evolution over long expanses of time.[161]

But the Abrams / Voth compromise version was less explicit regarding the concept of divine creation, per se, than the original Willis / Abrams draft had been. Whereas the original Willis / Abrams document included the words, "The design and complexity of the cosmos requires an intelligent designer," the version passed in August did not.[162] All together, Kansas's new standards were something of a cross between "intelligent design" creationism and the older "young earth" creationism. They also included familiar language from Vista and the California science standards, when they stated, "Nothing in science or in any other field of knowledge should be taught dogmatically," as well as "No evidence or analysis of evidence that contradicts a current science theory should be censored."[163]

Finally, the new standards did not *prohibit* the teaching of evolution, as the advocating school board members were quick to point out. But by removing the topic of evolution from the state assessment tests, it did allow the state's 304 local school districts to decide on their own how they would like to handle the teaching of origins. The potential consequences of this removal were many, as both supporters and detractors indicated. The first and most obvious implication of the new policy was that it "freed" local school systems and individual teachers to decide whether they wanted to spend time on evolution in their districts and classrooms. According to an article in the *New York Times* the day following the vote, the decision was "likely to embolden local school boards seeking either to remove evolution from their curricula, to force teachers to raise questions about its validity, or to introduce creationist ideas," through the use of creationist textbooks.[164]

The changes in the standards were designed to take effect as early as school year 2000–2001.[165]

Board Vote Fallout

NEGATIVE MEDIA. Not surprisingly, most mainstream media writers couldn't find enough column inches to denigrate the board vote to their satisfaction. Kansas was deemed the "Land of Odds," by one editorialist, in a riff on Kansas's fame for "The Wizard of Oz."[166] It was reported to be a "national laughingstock," whose "six advocates of ignorance" brought shame and embarrassment to the state.[167] It was now a place imagined by non-Kansans where people "pick banjos with their bare feet."[168] It was, in short, a place for "hicks."[169] The *New York Times* ran a story about the board decision on its front page; the state took its licks on Comedy Central; board members even appeared on the *Today* show. Chinese journalists had called the school system inquiring about the vote, as had the Canadian and the French, upon hearing the news.[170]

Besides the ubiquitous "embarrassed-for-my-state" rhetoric used to disparage the vote, media writers and public spokespeople took the board to task for a variety of other reasons. Some wrote about economic issues, suggesting that national corporations would refuse to bring their business to Kansas: "Honchos," wrote one columnist, "may think twice about holding conventions here. High-tech companies may take a harder look before moving to the prairie."[171] One article reported that high-skilled employees were loath to move to Kansas for fear of the education their children would receive. A Kansas State University professor reported that he was having trouble "recruiting candidates for two openings in the biology [department]." The president of an out-of-state research university, it was reported, "said she would discourage students from working in Kansas, since their children would go to schools where science education might not include evolution."[172] Meanwhile, others predicted that students in the state would be disadvantaged when they took college entrance exams, "scratch[ing] their heads [when they] run across questions about evolution."[173] Still others, as expected, pointed to the religious basis of the decision, and they warned of constitutional abridgments built into the ruling. In fact, as soon as the outcome of the 6 to 4 vote was announced, the American Civil Liberties Union of Kansas and Western Missouri sent a letter to Kansas school districts warning them that they could face legal action if they began teaching creation science.[174]

Those in the scientific community, naturally, used equally harsh arguments to criticize the compromise standards. Bruce Alberts, president of the National Academy of Sciences, said the board's decision was "an unfortunate setback for all those attempting to prepare our young people for a century in which science and technology will play an ever-increasing role."[175] And a spokesperson at the National Center for Science Education, Molleen Matsumura, said that "trying to make [evolution] optional is like trying to make it optional to talk about gravity in a physics class. . . . The real losers are the children of Kansas."[176] John Staver, cochair of the original science committee appointed by the board, reported that all of the members of the science writing committee he had talked to insisted on now having their names removed from the standards.[177]

POSITIVE MEDIA. Having just described the negative media response rained down on the board vote, it is enlightening also to examine the positive press reactions the board enjoyed in Kansas City, the state's major metropolitan center. It is especially informative, given the relative dearth of such positive media response in either California or Vista, where the local newspapers, judging by the sheer numbers of critical articles published, were clearly opposed to the creationist measures being proposed. In the *Kansas City Star*, it was also clear that the newspaper's editorial board opposed the board's vote, but those same editors were much more likely to give space in their newspaper to pro-board voices than were the California papers. Perhaps out of a sense of fairness, perhaps out of a feel for their more conservative constituency, the Kansas papers provided an ample forum for the board's supporters.

It is not difficult to guess what the content of these positive pieces looked like, just as there were few surprises in the press from the negative camp. But again, it is less the *quality* of the response that is striking than the *quantity* in the Kansas case. Not once, but several times, the paper published articles in which arguments were presented about the weaknesses of Darwinian theory, the illegitimate hegemony of Darwinian evolution in the classroom, the weakness of the fossil record in support of "macroevolution," and the idea that children should learn about the "debates in science." These arguments appeared in both opinion columns devoted to these positions and in descriptive news articles discussing opposing points of view.[178] Phillip Johnson, the anti-evolution law professor from the University of California, Berkeley, visited Kansas City shortly after the vote, and commended the board members for being "courageous people" who issued the "shot heard 'round the world."[179]

A Reversal of Fortune

Indeed, the vote was a shot heard 'round the world, but among those taking note of the shock waves were many groups and individuals institutionally empowered to impede creationism's advance. Scientists, educators, and special interest groups were intent on making this vote but a temporary victory and to turn the state around in its deemphasis of evolution. In keeping with this effort to reverse the tide, the next major piece of news to strike Kansas concerning its standards came from the three national science groups whose work had been used as models for the original science committee—the National Academy of Sciences, the National Science Teachers Association, and the American Association for the Advancement of Science. Upon learning that the new Kansas science standard borrowed a good deal of language unrelated to evolution from their documents (they had been alerted to this fact by one of the original science committee members), the three groups denied the state permission to use *any* wording that their teams had developed. They issued a statement that disparaged the standards for "not embrac[ing] the vision and content" of the national documents, and that "by deeming that only certain aspects of the theory of evolution should be taught, the state board of education adopted a position that is contrary to modern science."[180] The three groups demanded that the Kansas board remove *all* passages from the current science standards that had originated in, or referred to in any way, their own three documents, under threat of copyright litigation. Authorities in the science world were not about to allow a group of policymakers in Kansas to adapt their scientific language to what they considered illegitimate ends.

If the strategy of the National Academy of Sciences and the two other science groups was partially to punish the Kansas Board of Education for what they considered to be its misdeeds, and partially to stall it from further action (by forcing it to rewrite huge swaths of its document), then they were acting in concert with the state's department of education, whose oppositional tactic was delay. According to reports in the newspaper, professional educators in the state had decided to deal with the political fallout of the board's vote by fending off implementation of the new policy in the schools until the following summer, when the 2000 primary election would be held, and the board members who had voted in the disastrous policy could be voted out by an embarrassed and / or enraged public. Nothing fancy, nothing unusual: no recall elections and no suits in court. Just make the conservative board members pay for their folly with their elected seats, and make sure that no implementation of the policy could be accomplished by the time they were voted out.

With this tactic in mind, moderate board members and concerned scientists around the state seized any opportunity they could to delay the integration of the new standards into teaching routines. The copyright suits threatened by the national science groups was one example of this foot-dragging, insofar as it provided for both a time-consuming sixth rewrite of the standards in the state and another round of external reviews to ensure the document's legality. Said one member of the original science committee, Steve Case, "I think it pushes everything back to February or March before they even can get an external review and can act. Then what are we—five months from the primary?"[181] Clearly, the idea of at least some education professionals associated with the state's department of education was to keep the issue at the forefront of voters' minds without giving the policy a chance to be fully implemented and institutionalized in the state.

The state's premiere newspaper was sympathetic to this strategy and, as most of its writers had been doing since 1996, the *Kansas City Star* sought, generally, to keep readers informed about the conservative slant on the board and to encourage them to vote out the members who had brought shame to the state. So were many private citizens aligned with this cause, and they formed volunteer organizations to recruit and campaign for candidates to run against the conservative members.[182] New community-outreach groups called Save Our Schools and the Mainstream Coalition joined forces with the educators' group, Kansas Citizens for Science, which held workshops for teachers and distributed fliers in its quest to replace the current board. But would they be successful? Could they mobilize enough of the state's citizenry to eject the conservative officials? Would moderate education professionals and other concerned citizens reject their representatives, or would they face defeat in the "Land of Odds"?

A Familiar Outcome

In a Republican primary election that concerned little but the creation-evolution issue, and which attracted many more thousands of dollars in campaign contributions and spending than any previous board election in the state, Kansas voters turned their backs on all of the conservative incumbents except one. In the primary election held in August 2000—just one year, to the month, since a majority of the board had voted to deemphasize evolution in the state—voters indicated that they were tired of the attention the Kansas science standards had been attracting from across the land, and they removed from office those who had brought them to these infamous crossroads. Of the five seats up for election in 2000, four of them were occupied by conservatives who had voted for the revised science standards—Linda Holloway, Mary Douglass Brown, Steve Abrams, and Scott Hill (although Hill had decided to not run for reelection). The fifth seat up for election that year was held by a moderate Democrat, Bill Wagnon, who was a vocal opponent of the standards. In the Republican primaries, voters did in Kansas what they had done in other places that had gone creationist before (and which had suffered the public condemnation that followed): they turned against creationism's champions. Of the four seats that were held by conservatives going into the August 1 election, just one remained: only Steve Abrams was able to best his moderate Republican primary challenger that year in his rural district. The outcome of the primary election meant that control of the school board would be certain to return to a moderate majority in the general election, when either moderate Republicans or Democrats would pick up those seats and take office in January 2001. The action that the conservatives had taken on behalf of "anti-Darwinism" had been repudiated by popular referendum. One month after the January general elections, in February 2001, the newly constituted Kansas Board of Education voted 7 to 3 to restore evolution (as well as the big bang theory) to the statewide science standards and, by extension, to the statewide assessment tests.[183]

The combination of many factors contributed to this outcome, from the constant barrage of media coverage of the issue (in one year, more than 200 articles concerning the science standards appeared in the *Kansas City Star* alone, not to mention the national attention it also received); to the state education department's opposition to the changes, followed by its stalling techniques surrounding implementation; to voters' fatigue of ridicule. Despite the fact that creationism's advocates in Kansas adopted transitional intelligent-design rhetoric in their policy—in that they deleted reference to a supervising creator, and that they, thus, made it more difficult for the ACLU and other like-minded organizations to challenge their victory in court—creationists lost because American education professionals and voters are not willing to tolerate the widespread institutionalization of creationism. At least, not in Kansas.

Conclusion

As it was for Kansas—in which supporters of scientific creationism were handed out ultimate defeat by voters and by the education establishment—so had transpired the historical denouements of the Louisiana, Vista, and California state cases, as well.[184] Even when creationism's advocates could take advantage of the political winds and win significant political victories from professional educators, ultimately, creationists attained no meaningful or lasting concessions from public school systems. Try as they might to represent their goals as ensuring balance, fairness, and / or the sanctity of "honest" science in the public schools, creationists were unable to convince education officials that they should extend curricular legitimacy to them. This was so even in cases where creationists had been able to secure political majorities.

This is a different scenario from educators' responses to Afrocentrists—where education officials in some locations were willing to work with their challengers, at least in the short term. This variation deserves close analysis. The following chapter is devoted both to studying the arsenal with which creationists, and their adversaries in the schools, fought for their positions and to understanding the outcomes that they obtained in the four cases.

Six

Cultural, Political, and Organizational Factors Influencing Creationist Outcomes

IN CHAPTER 4, I argued that Afrocentrists were in possession of three rhetorical resources that they used to their advantage in debates with public schools. Culturally, Afrocentrists had a compelling assertion that educators could not deny (schools' historical failure to educate black children well) and a set of deeply resonant principles with which to stake their claims for black children: the arguments for equality and liberty.[1] Afrocentrists also could use an effective charge of discrimination against reluctant school officials, arguing that their foes were "racist" if white, and "race traitors" if black. Finally, Afrocentrists were contesting a discipline—history—that was generally regarded by the culture at large, and by many educators in particular, to be negotiable and less than entirely insulated from shifting social concerns. Afrocentrists relied heavily on each of these frames to try to move educators to act in their interest.

Creationists tried to tap into a similar set of rhetorical resources to use in their own battles with schools, but unlike Afrocentrists, creationists were bereft of culturally resonant frames. They, therefore, had a much more difficult time convincing professional educators of the reasonableness of their cause. First, they could not present a compelling *problem* of Christian children's failure in the schools. Unlike African American children who had clearly suffered for decades in substandard schools, Christian students were not perceived by educators to have historically endured inadequate academic preparation. On the matter of *bias*, although creationists argued that Christian children were facing discriminatory teaching at the hands of secularists, their claims about "anti-Christian" educators fell flat—most people in this country simply seemed disinclined to believe that America's educators were openly hostile to Christianity. Unlike Afrocentrists' relatively successful claims about history's *negotiability*, creationists had a much harder time convincing their audiences that science was elastic enough to tolerate anti-Darwinian teaching. And, as if these relative disadvantages were not enough, creationists faced a fourth hurdle that Afrocentrists were completely unhindered by. Whereas Afrocentrists never had to defend themselves against questions of legality, creationists battled the charge of unconstitutionality—in the form of separation of church and state—at each and every turn. Having their challenge called *illegal*—on top of illogical—ultimately thwarted the campaign's progress in every school system I studied. Even though creationists constantly attempted to readapt their rhetoric to the claims educators made against them, with cultural encumbrances like the four I have listed above, Christian conservative challengers had a much more difficult time convincing educators that science curricula should be revised. Professional administrators and staff simply drew their curriculum boundaries more tightly against creationist intrusion than they had in any of the Afrocentric challenge cases, even in New York.

And yet, as we saw clearly in chapter 5, despite these cultural handicaps, creationists were sometimes able to breach the boundaries of curriculum decision making when they or their supporters were elected to governing bodies. Faced with the very public opposition of education staff members in their states or districts, creationism's advocates went straight to voters for referenda on their proposals, and they sometimes won, as we saw in Vista and in Louisiana and Kansas. Voted onto school boards and into state legislatures, creationists occasionally were able to assume political power and enact their creationist-friendly policies.

But, as we know, those victories were short-lived, halted by the courts, voters, or professional educators—and sometimes all three. Able to ascend to *political* power in three of the four school systems in the study, creationists were unable to make their policies stick, or to get professional educators to *institutionalize* their revisions. One of the most important findings I obtained in this study is that different sets of powerful actors in school systems possess different types of authority in central educational decision making: there is a difference between *elective* power in schools and *professional bureaucratic* authority there. As I will explain in both this chapter and the next, it was less elected school board members and legislators who held ultimate decision-making power in these struggles. Rather, professional educators—those who occupied the permanent, salaried, deeply institutionalized positions in all four school systems—were the power holders with the final say on curriculum. Creationists in the four cases I studied for this book were always unable to convert their political positions into institutional power, and they were therefore always unable to have lasting impact on the governing bodies to which they were elected. When all was said and done, institutional power was able to reassert itself in all cases, and the creationist challenge was stopped in its tracks.

Upon describing these findings, I will end the chapter with a consideration of creationists' current strategy for victory.

Cultural Constraint 1: "What Problem?"

We saw in chapter 4 that Afrocentrists gained adherents, or at least played on educators' vulnerabilities, when they argued about the *problem* of African American children's educational failure. When we look more systematically at the four creationist cases, will we see comparable levels of resonance with this type of claim, and subsequent support for the creationist critique? I will first examine how creationists framed their problem and then look methodically at how educators responded to those arguments.

Creationists from all positions on the spectrum—from what I am calling the literalist scientific creationists to the intellectual corps of the movement—argued that teaching evolution exclusively in the public schools was damaging to children and contributed, ultimately, to the deterioration of society. John Tyndall, the conservative Christian elected to the Vista school board from 1992 to 1994, issued this lament over American education:

> Ultimately, I think there is a philosophy . . . of socialism that is coming through our educational system. That, I think, we are successfully educating a generation that will vote in socialism. . . . I think we are creating kids to become dependent on the system. The lip service is out there that we want them to be "independent" but, in actual fact, I think we are putting them back in a dependency situation. A dependency on the government, the state, for direction in their lives. And taking away from the family unit, which is where the direction should come from.[2]

Helping to advance this general political agenda for socialism, according to Tyndall, is the teaching of evolution. In the absence of any instruction challenging the idea of natural selection, or suggesting that the universe may have been divinely created, children are losing their faith in authority—*all* authority: that of religious leaders, elders, and, especially, parents. When children lose respect for their parents and other elders, they are at the mercy of secular institutions, and irreparable damage is done—all at the hands of a "theory" that has never been proven.

A variation on this expression of the problem was presented to me by John Wiester, the chairman of the Science Education Commission of the American Scientific Affiliation (ASA), an organization of what I am calling the intellectual, or elite, anti-Darwinists. Wiester painted a picture of the confusion and difficulty encountered by observant Christian parents and their children when evolution is taught in public schools.

> Look at the poor mom, okay? You're in a religious home. A theistic home. Kid comes home and says, "Mom, today we were taught that

we were created by evolution, and evolution is an unsupervised, undirected, without-plan-or-purpose thing. And it sounds like we're just
accidents. I thought we were created by a loving God. You've always
told me that I was made in the image and likeness of God, and that I
ought to be responsible to Him."

That's a major conflict, okay [laughs]? And it's a *religious* conflict.
The statement that evolution is "without plan or purpose"; and is an
"unsupervised process"; and that "it created you.". . . It's pure ideology! And we need to get that out of the science classroom.[3]

Both Wiester's and Tyndall's complaints about the oppressive presence
of evolutionary teaching in the public schools—instruction that points
children away from truth—sounds similar to Afrocentrists' complaints
about the harmful indoctrination that African American children have
suffered in schools over the past century. According to both accounts, in
the place of a balanced curriculum that clearly lays out the contributions
of different perspectives on scientific knowledge or on history (in the cases
of creationist and Afrocentric scholars, respectively), there has been, instead, the wholesale disregard in American classrooms for the scholarly
contributions made by establishment outsiders. Schools have systematically withheld verifiable truths from pupils, while simultaneously perpe-
trating misleading falsities dressed up as fact. Generations of students
have paid the consequences.

In the three Afrocentric cases, we saw that school officials supported,
at least to some extent, Afrocentrists' contention that there was a problem
of this type in schools' historical treatment of African and African Americans' contributions, and that this treatment has had dire consequences
for African American children. Did the same type of acknowledgment
occur among educators in their responses to creationists?

The answer is no. When creationist challengers confronted any one
of the four school systems, the education staff of those systems did not
acknowledge the validity of creationists' claims of exclusion. Although
several education officials and their allies in academic science reported
that they felt *badly* about creationists' belief that schools were in crisis,
these same educators were unwilling to acknowledge that Christians had
been *damaged* by the teaching of evolution. Kevin Padian, the paleontologist at Berkeley who served as a member of the science curriculum committee for California's science framework, described how he was both
cognizant of creationists' belief that harm had been done to their children,
but forthright in battling them when the chips were down, lending no
support in their claims:

I, personally, really have to feel sad sometimes. I mean, what is the
world like for them? They are consistently facing a secularism that is

"threatening," "godless," "misguided," "warped," and undermining everything that they do, everything that they believe in, everything that they are trying to teach their children. It's a very wrenching position for somebody to be put into on a daily basis. Every time they turn on the television, open the newspaper, a book, a comic book, see a movie . . . they feel very much more strongly than most people about what's going on.

[Asked what responsibility educators have to respond to creationists, given their sense of disenfranchisement,] I hope that part of what we were doing [in California] was saying to people, "You know, you don't *have* to believe us. All we ask is that you let us explain to you what the world is like to people who comprise the vast majority in the world, regardless of race, religion, national origin, creed, or anything like that." I know scientists in my field who are Jews, Presbyterians, elders in the Presbyterian church, bishops in the Mormon church, Catholic priests. I mean, active scientists who are Catholic priests. People who are Hindus, Buddhists. They all work around the world in different countries, and they all work on evolution. They have no problem with evolution as a paradigm. They all see the same facts of nature. They all draw the same inferences.

And to see people [creationists] who are not even versed in this tell us that it is not possible—"you can't do this, you can't know this"—and to tell all these different kinds of people, "You can't believe this. . . ." I mean, that, to me, is the height of shutting the world out. Which is okay if you want to shut the world out. . . . But to tell the *rest* of the world that they can't put this in front of their *own* children with public funds or at the public level: that is a selfishness that is not part of twentieth-century systems.[4]

Others of my interviewees also shed light on the sympathy that educators and scientists sometimes felt for their creationist foes, but which ran far short of compelling them to concede that there is a "problem" that they were obligated to solve. Eugenie Scott, director of the National Center for Science Education, the group active in trying to defang the creationist challenge, said this about creationists' experience:

Evolution is an evil idea. If your child learns evolution, then your child will give up his faith. If a child gives up his faith, many bad things will happen. Certainly he will be lost to Salvation, and that is something that is very serious. Secondly, he will become a source of all of those "isms.". . . They are very happy to point out that Hitler thought evolution was great, that Marx wrote letters of congratulations to Charles Darwin, etc., etc. So, from that they make the fantasy that evolution was the source of Marx*ism*, and commun*ism*, and radical femin*ism*. . . . You pick the "bad stuff," and evolution is the cause of it.

So, by fighting against evolution, by keeping their kids from learning evolution, they are making society a much better place. There will be far fewer racists and communists and Nazis and so forth. But also, you're protecting souls from damnation, and this is a very strong motivator for these people.[5]

However compassionate toward her adversaries Eugenie Scott may have felt, when I asked her later if conservative Christian parents' concerns deserved accommodation, she quickly shot down the suggestion saying, "creation science is not science."

A third adversary to the creationist movement, Barbara Donovan of the Vista school board (formerly, leader of the recall campaign), said this about the creationists' sense of injury, at the same time that she dismissed Christian conservatives' demands for change in the science classroom:

The Radical Right has some points about public education that are true. Not everything is as it seems: We, in this district, [for example], are great proponents of parental involvement. But the reality of it is that parents who want to be involved are not always welcomed in with open arms. They are looked at as annoyances because they get in the way of how people are doing things. That's one of the cries of the Radical Right: that they are not involved enough, or that they are not wanted enough. And I am not saying that I think that is wrong. I think they have a valid point there.

Even though I had a philosophical difference with the members of the Radical Right, I could respect what they were going through. The only problem I had was the forum that they were trying to use. . . . The people who are really Radical Right are not just people who are Christians and have a certain moral concept that they abide by. The real hardcore Radical Right people: it's a political agenda. They use religion like we would use "motherhood." It's a ruse. It's a facade.

Their religious beliefs, I have no problem with. I've never had a problem, nor has anybody that I have worked with on the recall [election in Vista], had a problem with them being Christians. I'd say 98.9 percent of this community is Christian. It's a very tiny, tiny, tiny minority who are not. As I say, the only thing I didn't like was the use of the public schools as the forum. I mean, that's not where you express religion! The public school is the venue that our country has decided will be the one for our children to grow up in—each one—not having to deal with persecution because they are not a particular religion; that everyone can have their religion. But the public school is not the place where you would do it.[6]

In this quote we see board member Barbara Donovan nodding at creationists' sense of alienation from a system that they think is harmful, but we also see her rejecting the notion that their isolation has been the result of inappropriate instruction in the schools. The "Radical Right" in her school district was composed of political opportunists, she claimed, who could not be allowed to get a foothold in the public school system: not on the issue of creationism, not on any other issue that was part of their political agenda. Despite her sympathy, then, for their feelings of social isolation and educational danger, this community activist would not acknowledge that creationists had a legitimate "problem" that the school system should address. Creationists received far less understanding than Afrocentrists did in their struggles.

Donovan's quote gives us insight into a corollary disadvantage suffered by creationists, and another reason why the claims of this challenge did not resonate as well with educators as the Afrocentric problem did. Donovan constructed the creationist challenge as one undertaken by members of the "Radical Right," a term Donovan chose carefully, she reported. Elsewhere in our interview, Donovan explicitly stated that she refused to call this group either the "Religious Right" or "Christian conservatives" (the terms creationists generally use to refer to themselves) because each of these labels is too "mainstream." She rejected the idea that their project had a religious component to it at all, saying that the Radical Right was purely a political organization. In choosing her language so mindfully, this Vista citizen used all the resources in her power to delegitimate her opponents. To the degree that defenders of evolution, like Donovan, could construe their opponents as the "far right," they owed them nothing, since groups on the "radical fringe" are understood to deserve no concessions in the public square. They have little right to even demand political attention because they exist on the far reaches of the spectrum, according to this argument.[7]

Certainly, creationists recognized the power of this rhetorical turn, and several of my interviewees drew attention to this treatment. In chapter 5, we heard Vista's John Tyndall complain bitterly about his opponents' use of the label, "extreme right," to tarnish his image among voters. He understood that this label was a political weapon in his adversaries' arsenal, even when those opponents "knew better" than to associate his activities with a larger political movement. Phillip Johnson, professor of law at the University of California, Berkeley, and a leader in elite creationist circles, sounded the same theme when he argued that educators strategically used the label "creationist" to denote all those with whom they disagreed, lumping in the most scientific of theistic evolutionists with the most literalist of scientific creationists to discredit them all as "religious fanatics."[8]

Donovan, Padian, and Scott are representative of how educators and their consultants responded to creationists' claims that the system had failed to educate their children well. Unlike administrators who ended up compromising with Afrocentrists because those educators, too, were concerned about the problem of African American children's performance, professional educators and their supporters were willing to offer no concessions. This was true even when the creationists' sense of alarm elicited some sympathy among their opponents. The creationists' deficit was that they did not present a problem that motivated education officials to act on their behalf. Instead, they seemed to educators to be parochial and intolerant and, therefore, illegitimate.

What are we to make of educators' greater vulnerability to the Afrocentrists' problem than to the creationists'? As we can see, a large component of this vulnerability stemmed from administrators' greater sense of rapport with the problem that Afrocentrists presented, even if they did not also lend their support to Afrocentrists' solution. But another reason why educators responded more hospitably in the Afrocentric cases can be found in a second resource Afrocentrists had in their repertoire: the charge of racism and race betrayal that was used against those who opposed their efforts. Could creationists lob similarly successful complaints of bias and discrimination against educators, goading them into action with this claim? Would professional educators accommodate creationists who condemned schools for years of increasing social secularism and judicial decisions that had created a "hostile environment" for religious practice in public schools? As we will see in the next section, the frame of "bias" also fell on deaf ears.

Cultural Constraint 2: "Who's Biased?"

In chapters 3 and 4 we saw that Afrocentrists sometimes were able to push school systems into action when they called otherwise reluctant educators "racist" or "race traitors" (as witnessed in New York and Washington, D.C.). Just like Afrocentrists, creationist challengers charged that their adversaries discriminated against them: that secularists, atheists, and arrogant bureaucrats were forcing them out of any say at all in the school system.

One description of this bias was presented to me by Phillip Johnson, the law professor at Berkeley, who spoke of the arrogance and discrimination that he and others in the creationist movement had suffered at the hands of the public school and scientific communities:

You know, it's really offensive when the texts say we're not going to say anything about "religion," and [then they say,] "Now we are going to tell you that you were created by this purposeless material, mechanical process, and that's all there is." You know? So I say that the educators outright lie on that topic.

And they also are covering up, or suppressing, the problems with the [Darwinist] theory. The effort of the education [system] is to instill belief. That's really what it's all about. . . . You see, because they realize that if people outside that community of belief get a picture of the facts, then it's going to make them into doubters. Because people who do not want to believe are going to have their disbelief reinforced by that. So, what we are getting is a tremendous propaganda barrage which is really aimed not at educating, but at instilling belief. And that is what I am opposing.[9]

State Senator Bill Keith, the Balanced Treatment Act's champion in the Louisiana legislature, succinctly stated his criticism of schools' bias when he said, "The question here is whether students will be given a choice or will be given only one model of the origin of man. That's censorship."[10] Echoing this same theme of First Amendment abridgments nearly twenty years later, a Kansas creationism activist named Celtie Johnson and her husband put homemade fliers on cars at malls, with such phrases as "The theory of evolution is just a theory, yet our public schools' texts do not mention the significant amount of scientific evidence against it. Why the censorship?"[11] In summing up these feelings of discrimination, John Wiester of the American Scientific Affiliation said,

That's what makes me very unhappy here, that politics and this polemical propaganda immediately [move] into [the issue]. But that also has got to tell you something. What are the Darwinists scared of? Why do they have to do this?

[Asked, "What *are* they scared of?" Wiester responded,] Because I think they know. In their heart of hearts, I think they know what they are doing. [Asked "What?" Wiester said,] Propaganda. They have got their *own* religion going. And they view theists—by that I include Jews, Muslims, and Christians—as "deluded." And they need to be "straightened out." They need to be—to use a euphemistic word—"educated."[12]

Propagandists? Liars? Abridgers of constitutional rights? Would educators be pushed into action by this kind of rhetoric? Again, the answer is no. Educators shrugged off accusations that they were engaged in indoctrination and insisted, instead, that it was the Christian conservatives, not they, who were intolerant. Eugenie Scott had this to say about creationists' charges that scientists were out to indoctrinate children:

[Sarcastically] Oh yeah, evolution is a big religion. Even Phillip Johnson gets into that, and he should know better. It's very amusing to me that people will think that evolution is a religion because if it *is* a religion, it certainly is an awfully uninspiring one [laughs]. It has no places of worship. It has no creed. It has no liturgy. It has no professionals who administer solace to believers. I mean, it's pretty difficult to say that this is a religion.

Now, this is not to say that there are not individuals who have taken science—and even have taken evolution within science—and used this as a stimulus for developing a philosophy which is nonsupernatural, anti-supernatural. I have a difficulty calling that a religion. Because, as an anthropologist, the word "religion" to me requires some sort of interaction with the supernatural, or recognition of the supernatural, anyway. And if you have a belief system which denies the supernatural: it's kind of tough to call that a religion. So, I prefer to call that a philosophy, or a worldview, if you will. Now, this is not to say that there are not people who have made worldviews out of science and out of religion. Johnson talks about this a lot in his book. He calls it naturalism, or materialism. And those people exist. But, you know, if you wanted to, you could make a philosophy out of photosynthesis. That doesn't mean we stop teaching it. And this is a major flaw on the part of the people who are criticizing [evolution].[13]

A second strategy for dealing with the creationists' call for "fair," "non-discriminatory" treatment was to acknowledge the absolute legitimacy of teaching creationism in the public schools—just not in science classes. Eugenie Scott said this on the subject:

Oh, I think creationism should be taught! I will now pause for dramatic effect and clarify that. I think we are not only—and this is a little sound bite I came up with the other day—we are not only *scientifically illiterate*, we are also *theologically illiterate* in this country. I think it would be of positive value to have kids in this country and in this state learn more about religion. In all of its forms. I think that we *should* have comparative religion courses taught, where different views would be presented. The biblical literalist view could be presented. The Catholic view could be presented. The mainline Protestant view could be presented. . . . There are a lot of different ways that just Christians and Jews look at creation, much less the difference between the Hopi and the Navajo, right? Much less between the Brazilian rain tribe Indians, much less the ancient Norse. I mean, there's a lot of different stuff going on here. I think it would be very useful for students to understand the role of mythology. Mythology is more important than science in this society any day. Science just helps us get through the day; mythology is what makes life real. . . . And I think it would be very worthwhile for students to learn about this.

Hegemony?
Dominance

Now, that's different from saying that students should be taught—*falsely*—that there is scientific evidence to support a biblical literalist view. *Bzzzt . . . wrong . . . tilt*! [using game show and pinball signals for illegal plays].[14]

Elites in the creationist circles, like Phillip Johnson, responded to expressions of derision like Scott's, above, by adopting an even more sophisticated argument about ideological oppression than just censorship. In a rather lengthy quote, we can see Johnson tapping into contemporary academic debates—about authority and hegemony—to argue that he and his associates have been subjected to academic despotism at the hands of the very people who theorize so rhapsodically about "resistance." Michel Foucault may have argued about the will to power of societal elites, but it is academics like Foucault, himself, and others who support radical politics, according to Johnson, who should apply the terms of the debate to themselves. In his 1996 interview with me, Johnson said:

> I've learned a lot. I'm no post-modernist, as you know, no follower of Foucault. . . . but I've learned a lot from being intimately familiar with that debate in academia. Of how people read texts as filtered through their cultural situation. And, boy, is that true of science educators and elite reporters!
>
> [Asked if Foucault's arguments about authoritarian discourses resonated with him]: Oh, yeah, that's what I mean when I say "I've learned." But you see, what I find ridiculous about the postmodernists is that they apply it to all the wrong situations. I mean, Foucault, himself, was a pampered intellectual, laden with honors. I mean, he's part of the oppressor class, from my point of view, who does this sort of thing.
>
> Did you read about this *Social Text* hoax? . . . The writers in *Social Text* use these ideas of empowerment and resisting authority in such a narrow, tendentious, political agenda, when it is really much more broadly applicable to *themselves*. So, yes, you are right: I read that stuff with a great deal of interest. I just apply it differently.
>
> And that's one of the things that is very funny about my intellectual method. Because while [my] conclusions are considered outlandish in the academic world—you know, "natural selection can't really create, and all that"—the message it generates, though, is dead-bang mainstream academia these days. You know, [I'm] looking for the *hidden assumptions*, the *power relationships* . . . it's a very fashionable method, it's just that nobody ever dreamed that it would be applied to this particular sacred cow, [evolution].

Claims of injustice based on the oppression that creationists feel they face in the public sphere make for a fascinating adoption of rhetoric. To be sure, these claims form an elite argument that most people on the frontlines of the creationist challenge had no exposure to. But despite its aims at convincing education insiders of the persecution faced by creationists, the wider academic community (both in school systems and in universities that were involved in these four cases) rejected Christian conservatives' claims of bias. The creationists' discrimination charge (unlike that of the Afrocentrists) landed with a dull thud—that is, when it was not being openly mocked by academics, scientists, the media, and public school educators. Education officials in the four creationist cases I studied apparently did not suffer from the threat of being "not Christian enough" as compared with African American administrators and teachers being held to be "not black enough" in their school systems, or white administrators being considered "not racially sensitive enough."

Cultural Constraint 3: The Nonnegotiability of Science

Creationists suffered from a third cultural handicap that Afrocentrists did not. Whereas Afrocentrists were challenging concepts taught in history and social studies—two disciplines that are seen to be reasonably contestable—creationists were challenging *science*, a discipline that is considered far more objective. As suggested in chapter 4, history and the rest of the social sciences are now understood to be more flexible than scientific truths.

Notwithstanding theoretical movements of the past couple of decades that have led some theorists to take issue with the concept of "science" as a privileged type of knowledge,[15] Americans—from lay citizens to trained scientific experts—are generally impressed with the integrity of the scientific endeavor. According to polling data from the General Social Survey, an annual poll taken by the National Opinion Research Center, since the 1970s, American adults have consistently reported higher levels of confidence in the scientific community as an institution than in any other institution besides medicine (also a science related field, it should be noted). In 1998, for example—a date I selected because that year's survey also included a related question about the *trust* people have for science—respondents were told "I am going to name some institutions in this country. As far as people running these institutions are concerned, would you say you have a great deal of confidence, only some confidence, or hardly any confidence in them?" For the scientific community, 43.0 percent of the respondents reported "a great deal of confidence" (while only 8.5 percent reported "hardly any") compared to 45.0 percent who reported a great deal of confidence for medicine (8.9 percent hardly any), 27.2 percent for education (16.7 percent hardly any), 27.8 percent for organized religion

(19.4 percent hardly any), 26.3 percent for banks and financial institutions (16.4 percent hardly any), 14.4 percent in the executive branch of federal government (36.4 percent hardly any), 10.9 percent for Congress (31.0 percent hardly any), and 9.5 percent for the press (43.4 percent hardly any).[16] Meanwhile, when asked that same year whether "we trust too much in science and not enough in religious faith," only 31.2 percent of respondents agreed or strongly agreed with the statement, while 68.8 percent answered that they "neither agreed nor disagreed," "disagreed," or "strongly disagreed."[17] I would like to suggest that this relative appreciation for science and the scientific community has had a strong impact on recent creationist challenges.

Kevin Padian, the Berkeley paleontologist, laid out the bases for science's credibility vs. creationism's when he had this to say about his foes:

> What we have tried to point out is that a scientific proposition cannot be true in New Jersey, but not true in Alameda [County, California]. It just doesn't work that way. Our issue is that we can only tell people what is understood in science and received wisdom, and we can tell them what is *not* received wisdom that is going around in textbooks and is being advocated by certain people in the community. They can pick and choose, but if they *want* to misrepresent science, if they *want* to pretend [these subjects] are controversial, if they *want* to waste taxpayers' money, if they *want* to make their kids stupid and uncompetitive for going out into the real world. . . . I mean, that's certainly up to them, but our stance is: why would they want to do that?[18]

With regard for science relatively high in this country, one could make a reasonable guess that the average American citizen—not to mention educators—would be apt to agree with the ideas set forth here by Kevin Padian.

Supporters of creationism, of course, understood the power that the idea of science occupies in teachers' and lay citizens' minds, and we have witnessed time and again their attempts to align their goals with those scientific frames. Again, John Tyndall provided a good example of science's regard when he talked about the specifically scientific balance (and *not* religious) that he sought in Vista classrooms:

> I never looked to propose another model of origins into the classroom. I don't have any problem with accepting that, in California, evolution has a monopoly on origins theory in the classroom. I can accept that. Let's just do *science* in that theory then. Let's not propose another model out there, but let's do a *scientific theory*, or let's do *scientific testing* on this model. Let's let children—students—look at the evidence by which people are saying that this is accepted scientific fact. Let them

look at the evidence and let them make their own decision in a crit-
ical-thinking way and determine whether or not they believe evolution
has or has not happened. If they conclude that evolution has happened,
that's fine with me. If they conclude that evolution has not happened,
they are in a bind in California because there is no alternative model
in science classes. [But] I'm willing to leave it there. . . . That's the
California system. That's science teaching in America today. It does not
develop the critical thinking skills in science that other countries
would do.[19]

Part of the scientific community's effort in keeping science protected
from what they perceived as a different epistemological basis for truth
claims was to make it very clear what counts as science and what does
not. Scientists were particularly concerned with this boundary-building
when science was seen to be under attack from outside forces, like religious belief, although of course in the quote above, John Tyndall is clearly
stating that he is willing to abide by science's rules. In the following discussion, Kevin Padian, again, gives a remarkably clear account of the
grounds on which religion must not be confused with science. As one
reads the account, it is worthwhile to think about whether foes of Afrocentrism had the resources to attempt as convincing a case for rejecting
Afrocentric claims as foes of creationism had for turning back creationist
arguments:

Everything in science is testable. But nothing in religion is testable. And
if that isn't the simplest thing right away, I don't know what is. I can
visualize a world in which evolution can be modified, rejected. But it
must be replaced by something that uses natural mechanisms to explain
observed phenomena. No one can say that about the Immaculate Conception! If you look at the end of Phil [Johnson]'s book on naturalism,
he says you can throw out all this philosophy, and all you need to know
is this phrase—and he quotes from the Bible the part about Jesus dying
for your sins.

Well, there it is! Phil is a creationist. Once you get the legal[ism] and
the rhetoric and the misrepresentation of science and all the wordplay
[out of the way], . . . this is what he believes, and that is Step One of
his entire argument.

But we all knew that. . . . You have to understand that Phil has never
studied science. He has never taken a course. I have offered repeatedly
to let him come and look at our specimens: "Come by and I'll show
you why we know what we know in science." He refuses. And he won't
submit his ideas to peer-reviewed journals. He insists on publishing in
conservative presses like Regnery-Gateway. Well, scholarship in our
field, as you know, is peer-reviewed work. . . .

It's really funny because these people [creationists] are constantly claiming [that scientists] are really closed-minded and not listening to anybody else. Excuse me, science is open-minded, but it's not empty-headed. We go on the basis of hundreds of years of built-up theories, hypotheses, inferences, facts, observations, or whatever you want to call them. There is a body of work in science, and the business is to test what we think we know and to falsify it if we can. So, we are always challenging what we do. *But we just don't challenge it on grounds that are not scientific* [emphasis added].[20]

With aggressive defenses like these, the scientific community intended to be taken seriously when it warned of intrusions on facts. That community's relatively high esteem made life difficult for creationists.

Cultural Constraint 4: Legal Precedent

Finally, creationists in Louisiana, Vista, the state of California, and Kansas faced an obstacle in their debates with educators that Afrocentrists never encountered in their challenges to school curricula: the argument that their efforts were not only intellectually questionable, but patently illegal as well. Such a reputation proved impossible to escape, and it represented the last, debilitating cultural component of creationists' defeats. In fact, the impact of the *legal precedent* counterclaim on the creationist movement may have been so devastating that it could be said to form a kind of first-order strike against creationist challenges—culturally, politically, and structurally (although I will tend to its political-structural aspects later in the chapter). Even if creationists had been able to line up other rhetorical resources in their corner, legal precedent was probably powerful enough to have obviated their might. We saw the legal argument used time and again by creationism's opponents, from Louisiana, to the two cases in California, and to the case in Kansas.

As outlined in chapter 2, the modern era of anti-creationist activity in the courts began in 1968, when the Supreme Court ruled in *Epperson v. Arkansas* that anti-evolution laws violated the First Amendment. This case drew on earlier decisions, including the 1963 ruling in *Abington v. Schempp*, regarding prayer and the separation of church and state, which deemed unconstitutional any practices promoted by public institutions that did not have "a secular legislative purpose and a primary effect that neither advances nor inhibits religion." Decisions following the precedent-setting *Epperson* case continued through 1987, when the *Edwards v. Aguillard* decision stated that the creationist Balanced Treatment Act passed in Louisiana intended to advance religious beliefs.

In response, as we have seen, creationists have imported more "science" into their arguments and less overt "religion." When they have done so, creationists have argued against the Court's interpretation of their projects as abridgments to the Constitution's establishment clause. Their refrain has been that they simply want a chance to present the "whole picture" of what is known in science about origins, and that Darwinian evolution is but "one theory" on the topic. Challengers argued that Darwinists and humanists have arrogantly grabbed control of science education and have been unwilling to reveal bona fide scientific evidence that contradicts evolutionary dogma. Creationists were charging scientific and legal malfeasance.

Educators, their supporters in the academy (including the seventy-two Nobel laureates who submitted the amici curiae brief in the Louisiana case), the American Civil Liberties Union, and popularly known scientists like Stephen Jay Gould counterargued using both a science-based discourse and legal assertions. Eugenie Scott, of the National Center for Science Education, was also clear about her disdain for the creationist project both in its legal and scientific claims. Asked why she and other scientists rejected creationism, she said,

> Number one, by analysis of scientists and teachers and courts, creationism is clearly a sectarian religious view. This is the view that God created everything all at one time, which is not the view of all religions, by any stretch of the imagination. It is a religious view, no matter what. So, advocating this point of view is unconstitutional. And there is a difference between teaching *about* a point of view in a comparative sense, and *advocating* it. And what creation science is, is advocacy. They are saying not "some people believe this," they are saying, "this happened; and we have scientific evidence to support that this happened." That is the claim that they are making. So that's advocacy. And that is unconstitutional. The public schools need to remain neutral toward religion.
>
> The second reason that scientists complain about the teaching of creation science is that *it's not science*. . . . The consensus view of science is that evolution happened. We don't argue about that. We argue about how it happened: how important is natural selection vs. other mechanisms. . . . We argue a whole lot about that. And that's fun [laughs]! That's what makes it a science, right? But, we don't question whether evolution took place any more than we question whether the earth goes around the sun, or the sun goes around the earth. So to a scientist, to have some of these equal-time laws come up saying, "We're going to give the scientific evidence for evolution, and then we are going to be fair and give the scientific evidence for special creation," just generates

a big, "Huh?" Because to us it's like, "We're going to give the scientific evidence for heliocentrism and the scientific evidence for geocentrism." Sorry, nobody really takes geocentrism seriously. Why are you wasting the kids' time? I mean, I can find you some wonderful scientific arguments as to why the earth is the center of the universe. This is wonderful stuff, but, I mean, it's all bogus. And it's all wrong. And you know, we shouldn't be giving kids a bunch of wrong stuff.[21]

As we can see in this quote, one of the most recent waves of creationism in this country, scientific creationism, received little different reaction from science organizations, First Amendment organizations (like the ACLU), or the courts than did prior campaigns for creationism. Even though creation science leaders tried to adapt their rhetoric to the courts' ever stricter First Amendment interpretations, according to critics like Eugenie Scott, these adaptations were merely variations on a theme. When creationists called attention to the *scientific* aspects of their efforts, or to the idea that they were seeking *balance* in the curriculum (rather than the older call for excluding evolution), critics interpreted these new arguments as efforts aimed toward the same end: to minimize evolutionary instruction in the curriculum.

But what about "intelligent design," the most recent version of creationist challenge, whose advocates claimed that they were merely seeking to have science taught honestly, and who have even stopped insisting that any specific intelligent designer be mentioned at all in science classrooms? Has this newest branch of the argument fared better with educators, such as those in Kansas? Having distanced themselves from the literalist camp of creation-science challengers, have intelligent-design proponents received the respect and concessions they have fought so hard for? Molleen Matsumura, also of the National Center for Science Education, has urged school districts to see through what she regards as transparent bids for legitimacy and to recognize them for what they are, no matter how strenuously intelligent design advocates claim otherwise:

> Proposals to teach "creation science" may be disguised by euphemisms such as "arguments against evolution" or "alternative theories," "balanced treatment," "intelligent-design theory," "abrupt appearance theory," or "irreducible complexity.". . . By avoiding the term "creation science" and calling instead for "alternatives to evolution," anti-evolutionists hope to avoid legal entanglements. . . . These phrases are code words for an attempt to bring nonscientific, religious views into the science curriculum; no matter what it's called, it is illegal for public schools to advocate religious views of any kind.[22]

No one, said critics, should be tricked into missing the link back to creationism, particularly not anyone associated with science teaching in American public schools.

The legal discourse, which was used to counter creationist claims, hinted at concrete action, too. The American Civil Liberties Union and People for the American Way were abundantly clear that they would sue any school district that recognized creationism in any form in its science classes. Many financially strapped systems—whether at the state or district level—were persuaded by the threat and withdrew their own "anti-Darwin" proposals after court decisions reiterated their unconstitutionality. This kind of state and local system retraction occurred immediately following both the Supreme Court action concerning Louisiana's Balanced Treatment Act and the recall of the two board members in Vista, California.

The other challengers in this study, the Afrocentrists, didn't face a legal hurdle. While Afrocentrists, like creationists, were forced to defend themselves against accusations of scholarly sloppiness and other intellectual deficits, proponents of African-centered curriculum never had to defend themselves against the charge that their efforts were illegal. Afrocentrists fended off charges of misdirected goals and of "playing the race card," but they did not have to argue over the lawfulness of their effort. Preposterous, outrageous, wrong—indeed, Afrocentrists were called all of these at various times. But unlawful and unconstitutional—no. The complete absence of such a counterattack available to their opponents must clearly go into the assets column for Afrocentrists, as compared to creationists.

Consequences of Constrained Challenge

On each and every one of these cultural dimensions, creationists bore serious disadvantages, and their outcomes in the four locations suffered because of them. Educators were able to counter creationists' multiple arguments by evoking four cultural "givens": (1) a historical record of providing Christian children with quality education; (2) the fairness with which Christians historically have been treated by the education system; (3) the sanctity of science; and (4) legal precedent. When creationists tried to change curricula at the institutional level in these four locales—that is, at the level of official curriculum rather than in individual schools or classrooms—education officials ultimately turned them away on the basis of these arguments.

This was the finding I had obtained in 1998, having studied only the three earlier cases, Louisiana, Vista, and California. By the time I began writing the first draft of this book, however, the year was 1999, and the Kansas Board of Education had just voted 6 to 4 to delete evolution from statewide assessment tests. Remember what 1999 was like for creationists across the country after the Kansas school board voted for this change in the science standards: in Phillip Johnson's words, it was the "shot heard 'round the world."[23] For creationists, it was an unmitigated, unsurpassed victory. For my purposes as a researcher, the Kansas vote appeared to be a potentially positive case of creationist challenge after I had looked at so many cases with negative ultimate outcomes. Creationists had scored a major victory in Kansas, and since the language used in that state's framework reflected a hybrid of intelligent-design goals with the more literalist objectives of the earlier cases, I found studying events in Kansas to be irresistible. But in 2001, just eighteen months after the school board voted to delete both evolution and the big-bang theory from the state tests and had endured intense media and professional scrutiny, the newly constituted school board reversed its predecessor's action. This act represented yet another public defeat for the creationist movement. Challengers in Kansas were impeded by the same set of counterarguments that their like-minded colleagues had suffered in the previous cases.

So, the way it looks now for creationists is that the only victories that have "stuck" at the statewide or district-wide level are the inserts that now appear in science textbooks in two southern states. As I discussed in the previous chapter, in 1995, the Alabama Board of Education ordered its state's school personnel to paste a disclaimer onto the front page of all biology textbooks stating that evolution is a "controversial" theory that "some" scientists believe but that, since no one was there to observe it, "should be considered as theory, not fact."[24] In 1999, Oklahoma state education officials ordered the inclusion of the same statement in its state's science textbooks, using word-for-word the Alabama disclaimer.[25]

But what do the Alabama and Oklahoma victories really represent, especially when placed in the context of creationists' devastating defeats in Louisiana, the state of California, Vista, and the state of Kansas? Does this textbook front matter have any real impact on how students learn science in those states—as much as, say, providing side-by-side instruction on evolution and creation, or deleting the concept of evolution from state-wide tests? Do sentences that insist on science's observability and falsifiability (as were also the linchpins of the Kansas framework) actually lead students to doubt evolutionary processes? Can the inclusion of textbook disclaimers, or of scientific jargon in framework glossaries, really achieve creationists' objectives?

Without measures for students' understandings of science in Alabama and Oklahoma (before and after the disclaimers were added), it is hard to say for certain. But I can make some observations about what I think these paths represent for the creationist movement. Left with bitter disappointment over the failure of creationists' major reform efforts, John Wiester of the American Scientific Affiliation, in my 1996 interview with him, promoted the Alabama and Oklahoma textbook inserts as bona fide victories. Meanwhile, the ACLU and other pro-evolution advocates regarded the inserts as the first steps down a slippery slope toward the teaching of creationism. I wonder how sanguine or worried, respectively, these groups really should be about the future. Even if we are witnessing anew creationists' long-term strategy of adapting the rhetoric and demands of their battle to the legal realities of the day, what I think we are also witnessing is creationists' willingness to pare down their demands to any level necessary in order to achieve a "win." They, too, are looking for "symbolic victories," just like Afrocentrists, and they are willing to take them where they can.

Having been rejected when they have stated their demands and desires forthrightly, creationists are now keeping their curriculum demands ambiguous, resorting to the technicalities of their preferred "empirical, not theoretical" scientific method to cast doubt on evolution. In Kansas, for example, the anti-evolution board members agreed to strike all references to a creator from the framework in order to achieve compromise, and neither "creationism" nor "creation" appeared in the framework's glossary. Replacing the demand for creationist instruction was what I would consider to be a case of vague semantics about scientific concepts and methodology. Definitions of testability, falsification, and verifiability were provided, but God was out, as was any explicit mention of designed and supervised creation.[26] And yet, creationists still considered the new framework a resounding victory. They did, anyway, until voters across the state voted out of office all but one of the framework's proponents (of those who were up for reelection), and evolution was eventually restored as a concept to be tested on statewide tests.

Desperate to end the days of evolution's "hegemonic" grip on public school students, but faced with defeat in all grand attempts, creationists have decided to fight for progressively less explicit "creationist" content in the public schools as they proceed with their cause.

Should professional educators and their supporters, meanwhile, be concerned when creationists win any concessions, even if those victories are based on the obtuse concept of falsifiability, for example? Although I concur with Molleen Matsumura of the National Center for Science Education that any policy aimed at "deemphasizing evolution" *is* code for creationism, and that creationists are eager to build on any foothold in any systems they can find, I am not convinced that these victories represent creationist success that can be further built upon, realistically. It is not clear to me that students in the classroom are a keen enough audience to pick up on the code that is written into these statements of empirical evidence and verifiability, to divine the importance of the creationist points being made. These small changes—even if they were to be adapted in a more permanent way—hardly seem to be in the same ballpark as telling African American students in history class, for example, that their ancestors were kings and queens in Egypt, or that America has a history of oppressing its black citizens. The kinds of concessions that conservative Kansas school board members won temporarily, and that John Wiester and Phillip Johnson are arguing for, and even that the Alabama and Oklahoma science textbook inserts represent—all of these have to be understood as highly diluted outcomes that have emerged from the greatly reduced demands that creationists are now making. They are symbolic victories, at most, rather than real victories. Those fighting for the legitimacy of creationism have expressed satisfaction at making *any* inroads in the curriculum, even those that clearly are miles away from their ultimate objective—the discussion of a creator in science classrooms. Besides the fact that such diluted demands exasperate the ACLU and scientists, and evoke visions of slippery slopes, it is difficult to see how the victories that emerged out of these demands could seriously threaten the teaching of evolution in schools.

Now, this is not to suggest that the scientific, legal, and educational communities in this country are incorrect to think that evolutionary teaching requires stubborn defense and periodic reinforcement if evolution is to remain in the classroom. And their victories over creationists are not only ceremonial or a foregone conclusion. In 1998, for example, the National Academy of Sciences (the same prestigious science group that ordered Kansas to remove its copyrighted language from the state's revised science framework) determined that teachers in many parts of the country continue to face pressure from parents and other conservative citizens to scale back the teaching of evolutionary theory.[27] Across the country, a number of school boards still order their personnel to give equal time to scientific creationism and, as I write this chapter, a teacher in Faribault, Minnesota, is appealing a court decision that bars him from using intelligent-design arguments in his public school biology class.[28] On a related note, according to an article in the *Los Angeles Times*, surveys in Texas, Ohio, and Kansas have shown that 25 percent of biology teachers in these three states ascribe to the creationist account of human origins, rather than evolution.[29] And, when the People for the American Way (PAW) conducted a national poll concerning creationism and evolution in 1999 (following the Kansas school board action), the organization found that 29 percent of Americans thought that creationism should be taught as "scientific theory" in science courses, while an additional 29 percent thought that creationism should be taught alongside evolution in science classes as a "belief" about origins.[30] Given that a major barrier to creationism over the past two decades has been judicial, and that the election of President George W. Bush may very well change the makeup of the court in the coming years, the level of support that PAW found among the electorate may encourage a potentially more conservative judiciary to assist creationism's path.

What I want to emphasize, though, is that educators—in all meaningful respects in the large meaningful cases—have found a variety of different ways to turn back the creationist proposals advanced in their school systems. They have used crushing oppositional rhetoric, concerned voters, consistently negative federal courts, and organizational procedures to negate creationist content, even in those cases where creationists gained electoral power. Despite the fact that creationists' substantive demands have diminished over the years (adapting to cultural and political changes on the social, cultural, and political landscape), school systems' counterclaims have remained aggressive, and professional educators on the bureaucratic inside of school systems have beaten back their Christian conservative foes.

This finding has made for a fascinating comparison with the results discovered in the Afrocentric cases. It is now time to think about both types of challengers together to see what more sense can be made of these outcomes.

Seven

Making More Institutional
the Study of Challenge

 AFTER SIX chapters of description and analysis, what do we now know about these seven cases of Afrocentric and creationist challenges to American public schools? We have learned that both sets of challengers attempted to sway school systems to act on their behalf using rhetoric about the welfare of children, the purported lack of justice found in school classrooms, the intellectual bankruptcy of educational curricula, and the need for pluralism in the classroom, among other arguments. We have seen that Afrocentrists had an easier time advancing these arguments in the schools than creationists did, and that Afrocentrists, at least for some time in their three different locations, enjoyed recognition as people who had rights to make demands on schools. We know, conversely, that professional educators regarded creationists with deep skepticism, publicly labeling them as representatives of the Radical Right. In short, what we have learned from this part of the comparison is that challengers' differential access to resonant frames influenced their ability to gain outward support in the school systems that they challenged.

We know, however, that cultural resources were not the only factors contributing to outcomes in these cases: we have seen that political and organizational factors also influenced results—even among cases fought for the same cause. Despite their similar access to rhetoric about injustice, for example, New York's Afrocentric challengers bumped into a different set of political conditions and organizational constraints in their targeted school system than did Afrocentrists in Atlanta or Washington D.C., and these conditions and constraints shaped the New York challengers' ability to make headway in their locale. Kansas's creationist challengers, similarly, found a different set of political opportunities to exploit in their state than did John Tyndall and his colleagues in Vista, California, or than pro-creationist legislators did in Louisiana, or than conservative lobbyists did in the California science framework debate. These political opportunities led to different processes of challenge in the Midwestern location than in the Western or Southern cases—even though professional educators had enough power in all four of these cases to beat back creationist gains.

Finally, we also have seen evidence suggesting that members of the education establishment were adept at determining when they could eliminate an opponent with heavy rhetorical and organizational artillery (calling challengers' claims "dangerous" and, their curriculum "illegitimate"), and when they had to make concessions to challengers' demands—and then minimize gains later. In all four creationist cases, school system professionals dug deep trenches from which to battle their challengers and made a public show of being committed to defeating them—even when creationists gained political entry onto some of their decision-making bodies. Meanwhile, there was considerably more conflict among professional educators in the three school systems challenged by Afrocentrists, concerning what should be done about challengers. But, in each and every case, school systems figured out how to grant Afrocentrists only token, or symbolic, victory—even over the complaints of some Afrocentric devotees among school officials.

What does all of this mean? In the preceding chapters I have analyzed challenge events from the perspectives of culture, politics, and organization. Now, in this final chapter, I want to look more closely at the study's most interesting implications along these three dimensions and examine the overlaps that exist among them. To this end, I want to clarify three specific areas that can add nuance to what we think about as the cultural, political (structural), and organizational bases for action in challenge events.

First, I will review the *targets* of challengers' rhetorical arguments, and compare them to the targets that social movements research traditionally has described. This review of targets will reveal that Afrocentrists and creationists often directed their arguments for change directly at establishment insiders—and not just at other outsiders, like a mobilizable public— and that sometimes these arguments resonated with those school officials. Upon consideration of this phenomenon, we will see that there is greater interplay between the cultural aspects of challenger frames and the structural locations of their occasional advocates than much previous scholarship has documented.

Second, I want to look at the roles that insiders and outsiders played in these school challenges, generally, and ask how we should conceptualize these different locations in the institutional field. Once we have taken note of the fact that insiders are sometimes the targets of challenger frames and even occasionally, they, themselves, become challenge advocates, then we have to recognize that the old line separating "insiders" from "outsiders" in challenge events is suspect. When we consider the possibility that challenge proponents and leaders may come from positions of authority inside the school systems, clear implications emerge for reconsidering the cultural and structural boundaries previously described for challengers and the institutions they challenge.

Third, I will continue to examine the relationship between *political* power and *institutional* power in American school systems, which I began in the last chapter. I will look at how both sets of challengers—Afrocentrists and creationists—could often tap into the former system of authority (political), but less often the latter (institutional). In this investigation we will see implications for distinguishing between what is a political aspect of challenge and what is organizational, and we will see the power of institutional logics to supercede political authority—at least in this one American institution, American public schools.

Finally, I will attempt to provide a theoretical model for making sense of these three previous issues. I will end the chapter with a consideration of whether the seven cases can speak to larger issues in the study of contentious politics.

Resonance with Establishment Insiders: An Overlooked Site of Successful Framing Activities?

The best entry point for launching a consideration of these questions is to begin with the social movements concepts that I laid out briefly in chapter 1, and upon which I have drawn throughout the description and analysis of the seven cases. As we now know at the tail end of looking at these two challenges, Afrocentrists and creationists were rather poor examples of the phenomenon "social movements," at least in the material sense of the word "poor." Neither Afrocentrists nor creationists had access to a wealth of organizational assets, such as natural leaders or extensive mobilizable networks of people. Indeed, the two challenges remained small since they both represented "fringe" groups of two more popular movements on the cultural landscape—multiculturalism and Christian conservatism, respectively. Neither challenge's spokespeople had significant control of mass media, as we saw in the wholly negative press received by six of the seven challenges. And except for the funding from Christian conservative organizations that creationists were able to raise in Louisiana, neither challenge was able to amass a large war chest for entering into battle, an especially important point for the creationists, whose struggle was opposed by well-funded organizations like the American Civil Liberties Union and People for the American Way. Generally lacking serious financial and organizational resources, Afrocentric and creationist challengers relied largely on appeals to cultural beliefs to make headway in their school systems—impassioned arguments that were meant to move their struggle forward. Interestingly, both movements turned to the powerful cultural frames of pluralism and inclusion to lobby for curricular change in the schools.

Not long ago, researchers trained to think about the material resources of social movements might have been stumped if confronted with challenges like these, which were largely constructed around discourse, without the backup of material resources. It was not until the 1980s—following the preeminence of resource mobilization and political process models, two approaches that emphasized the structural elements of movement viability—that several movements researchers reintroduced ideational factors as a matter of primary importance in the analysis of contentious politics.[1] Analyzing cultural factors like "symbols and ideas, and related processes of signification or framing," scholars such as William Gamson, David Snow, Robert Benford, and their collaborators provided the conceptual means for understanding the projects that challengers like Afrocentrists and creationists waged in schools.[2] These challengers were "making meaning" about what it felt like to be a subjugated race or religious group, they were claiming that fairness in schools was absent, and they were appealing to Americans' commitment to justice and to educators' commitment to pluralistic instruction to amend these slights. Following the lead of Snow, Gamson, and others, the social movements field now has the tools to make better sense of challengers' meaning making.

For the past fifteen years or so that scholars have increasingly examined the cultural terrain, they have concentrated mostly on how culture operates in constituent mobilization, where the sharing of movement goals and symbols occurs most overtly. According to numerous studies, social movements leaders explicitly strategize which frames to use in their mobilization efforts at different times and places, taking into consideration the composition of the movement organization, the nature of the movement's opposition, and the combination of actors involved in the institutional field.[3] Because they represent the actions of savvy actors, these framing strategies differ depending on the group that the challenger is targeting.

To think about this point, let's take the leaders of the creationist movement as an example. In the context of their own churches and even in their cyberspace communications, where they presume that potential followers make up the bulk of their audience, scientific creationists strategically frame their goals as devout *religious* commitments, and as a dedication to keeping the word of God foremost in all their endeavors. In the opening sentence of its web site, for instance, the Institute for Creation Research (ICR)—the young earth creationist research organization located outside San Diego—states that the organization "is a Christ-focused creation ministry where science and the Bible live in harmony,"[4] as we will recall from chapter 5. Directing rhetoric at their core constituency, which is made up of religious believers, ICR leaders bet that this "Biblical science" frame will most successfully mobilize and sustain adherents' support for the cause. But when ICR has taken its challenge public, as it did most prominently in Louisiana, the group knew that its target audience would include the media, the courts, and educators, and it altered its rhetoric accordingly, downplaying the religious foundations of its challenge and emphasizing the pluralistic and pedagogical goals of the movement. The stated goal no longer was to meld science with religion; rather, it was to allow all children to feel welcome in publicly paid-for schools and to offer "balanced" scientific instruction in science classrooms for the good of *science*. The point of their proposal, creationists argued, was to be more inclusive, to make schools fair again, and to return objectivity to the scientific enterprise.

Movements research over the years has demonstrated that challengers tailor their arguments to different audiences, as in this case of ICR's message, in the hopes that their frames will *resonate* with different listeners' understandings. Resonance between social movements and their audiences is said to occur when the movement's frames strike a deep responsive chord among prospective adherents.[5] The supreme indicator of a resonant frame, according to studies in the field, is its ability to mobilize constituents to contribute time and energy to the movement. The mobilization of constituents then puts pressure on authorities, who are more likely to act in accordance with challenger frames than if there were no mobilization. By this account, social movements use potentially resonant frames to mobilize and persuade two central target audiences: (1) possible adherents in the broader public and (2) the media, both of which then put pressure on the established system to change. Movements' ultimate targets, according to this approach, may be policymakers, but in order to reach them, challengers must mobilize people and resources in the greater society to influence this authoritative elite.[6] Outcomes are determined by the disruptive force challengers can bring to bear on reluctant power holders.

Targets of Framing Activities: A Mobilizable Public and Institutional Authorities

I have found some evidence for this standard social movements account of frame targets—described, again, as being potential adherents in the public at large—in several of the cases I studied. Some challengers in this set of seven did, indeed, attempt to gain support among lay citizens. We saw, for example, that in their struggle to maintain a strong "anti-dogma" statement in the California state science framework, leaders of the conservative Traditional Values Coalition vowed to bring citizens' wrath down on unsympathetic school board members. And we observed that in Washington, D.C., leaders of the organization called Operation Know Thyself, among others, mobilized parents to lobby for African-centered education.

But while this standard account aptly describes some of the framing activities I witnessed in these two cases, there are a few important elements of this description that do not entirely square with the processes that occurred most frequently throughout all seven. Because the subject I was studying was challenge waged against *institutional power*, and not political power—a difference I will explain in more detail shortly—what I observed most prominently in all of these cases was that challengers aimed their discourse predominantly at educators, or *establishment insiders*, and not at the public at large. When I say that challengers directed their arguments at insiders, I mean that they tried to persuade those in the field who were positioned to enjoy "routine access to government agents and resources"—as many in the movements literature have defined insiders.[7] In other words, I observed that Afrocentrists sought to change the minds, directly, of those vested with decision-making power in these school systems.

Now, having elected to study challenges aimed at institution-level processes (i.e., schools) rather than at a more narrowly defined political structure (like the governmental arm of state), it is not surprising to have discovered that Afrocentrists and creationists directed their demands at education decision makers rather than at the public, since different political logics operate in schools than in governmental structures. As Kelly Moore has indicated in her own work on institutional challenges, power in institutions (like schools) is frequently more diffuse than power in political institutions, insofar as authority is spread among professional bureaucrats, which insulates them from direct pressure. Under such circumstances, challengers sometimes have a difficult time determining how they would even use supportive adherents from the general public to put pressure on institutional authorities.[8] In addition, challengers to institutions may find that it is not always desirable to expend energy on potential mobilizable constituents, since the public's attitudes are frequently dismissed anyway by institutional insiders as "naive," "nonexpert," and unwelcome in an arena where it is de rigeur for professionals to exercise decision-making authority. Understanding both that it was education officials who held decision-making power in these organizations *and* that the public had relatively little suasion with these officials—as compared to the public's potential power to assert its will in the political realm— challengers sought to change educators' (and not the public's) minds about curriculum content.[9]

What I am arguing here is that we must pay careful attention to all targets of framing activity in challenge events. To date, the movements literature has largely ignored—empirically, anyway—how challengers may pitch their arguments directly to insiders, and how those frames interact with, and sometimes may very well resonate with, the frames produced by the establishment insiders whose actions the challengers seek to influence. While the literature rightly reminds readers that social movements must address themselves to various audiences in a multiorganizational field,[10] researchers often have sidestepped their own insights when it has come to describing those multiple audiences: they have neglected establishment insiders' potential centrality as targets of those frames and as prospective allies to the challenge. Considering the establishment to be an always oppositional force, social movements research has had a harder time accounting for the occasions when challengers' frames resonate with establishment insiders' common sense, a resonance that potentially renders their institutions vulnerable to change. Instead of viewing challengers' efforts as invariably aimed at "*recruit[ing]* members, *persuad[ing]* bystanders, and *neutraliz[ing]* opponents," as one scholar describes movements' goals, we would do well to recognize occasions when "opponents" might also be recruited, persuaded, or perhaps even mobilized, to the cause.[11] As we consider challengers' success in a particular institutional arena, we should examine whether its framing of the issues might "work" ideologically not only with potential constituents, but also with insiders located in the organization, or establishment, itself.[12]

The resonance that I discuss here goes beyond the gaining of "elite allies" that others in the literature have talked about, and it does so in two ways.[13] First, I am describing members of the subject bureaucracy itself—school officials—as persons whose ideas about the challenge changed substantially, and not just members of outside funding sources or interest groups who then acted on behalf of the challenge. Second, I wish to be very clear that I am describing ideological shifts here, rather than more instrumental *political* shifts, on the part of institutional insiders. When I describe challengers' frames as "working" with insiders' frames, I mean that these insiders decided to align with challenger goals because they came to believe in those goals, not only because they gained some political benefit from supporting the challenge.

Having just made the theoretical claim that challengers sometimes aim their rhetoric directly at establishment insiders, and that these power holders sometimes act in concert with challengers' frames because their cultural beliefs are aligned, it's a good time to ask a simple question: do we have any empirical evidence from these cases that either Afrocentrists or creationists (1) partook of these activities or (2) benefited from "insider resonance"? Specifically, have we seen examples of challengers who managed to frame their demands to resonate with the frames of targeted insiders, rather than with only those of the public at large?

I would argue that we do have such evidence, and that in all three of the Afrocentric cases, challengers directed their arguments toward educators; those arguments resonated with some number of influential organiza-

Afrocentrism yes

tional insiders; and the challengers won some "voice" in the proceedings, if only rarely any concrete reform in those systems. Even in New York, yes where there was an obviously negative outcome for Afrocentric challengers, there was an early period in the challenge when Afrocentrists' frames about bias and its correction "made sense" sufficiently to the state commissioner and his deputies, such that they appointed a task force to investigate the schools' treatment of African Americans and other minority groups. Even in this most adversarial of Afrocentric cases, the New York education department did not just cast aside Afrocentrists' claims as spurious, as they might have done with some other curricular investigators (like creationism, say). To be sure, much of the impetus for action in New York came from Commissioner Sobol's attempts to be *politically* sensitive to outraged members of his constituency (who had expected the appointment of an African American or Latino commissioner), and not just from challengers' success in evoking his common-sense understandings about race, education, and justice. But while Sobol acknowledged that there was a political dimension to his decision to appoint the task force, in an interview with me, he also insisted that the *problem* that his minority constituents were complaining about seemed to him to be a genuine educational crisis.[14] Challenger framing worked to move this institutional insider. In Atlanta and Washington, occurrences of resonance with school officials were even more obvious.

Creationism

Using this same analytical tool, let's turn now to the creationist challenges to see if their frames resonated with school officials. As we know, creationists, too, spoke of the problem of miseducating children, and of discrimination and bias at the hands of oppressive teachers. Over the years, they even had increasingly withdrawn the specifically "Godly" parts from their curricular demands in an attempt to win educators' support for their classroom objectives as scientific and methodologically legitimate. But presented with creationists' miseducation claim, educators had no available experiences or beliefs to which the allegations of mistreatment and discrimination could attach and seem credible. And when educators were faced with creationists' *scientific* assertions, they called them irregular and suspect. In fact, the very route by which creationist rhetoric had traveled over the years had invited educators' increasing skepticism. School officials criticized their challengers' constant voyages into foreign framing territory—venturing first from an emphasis on the literal truth of the Bible, then to a focus on the scientific basis for divine origins, then to a concentration on creationism's pluralist goals. What next? To educators and, especially, to interest groups like the National Center for Science Education, this path appeared to be an effort at rhetorical manipulation. In their efforts to suit an ever-changing legal/cultural/scientific terrain, creationists set themselves up only to seem more devious in their adversaries' eyes. There were no frames available to creationists that could convince education authorities.

This discussion of the degree to which each group of challengers' arguments resonated with institutional authorities (as opposed to a mobilizable public) should not be seen as splitting hairs. In fact, if we overlooked the fact that challengers' frames sometimes connected with insiders' frames (and that, consequently, insiders fought for the good of the movement in some challenges), then we would have missed one of the most important features differentiating the Afrocentric challenge from the creationist movement. Culturally, Afrocentrists were relatively endowed. During the years of this study, they could take their arguments directly to education decision makers and get them acted upon—never with a complete victory at the end of the line, and sometimes only to the degree that their complaints received a formal hearing, which resulted in a critique of the status quo, not in solutions. But in all three cases, Afrocentrists ended up achieving some modicum of symbolic concession, some acknowledgment from schools that their concerns were important. By appealing to the common sense of those actors in the field who were structurally able to make policy decisions, Afrocentrists used their cultural resources to open up opportunities for their reform demands. Even though school officials and Afrocentric challengers were separated by institutional boundaries, Afrocentrists found a way to bridge those structural differences by invoking cultural beliefs. Creationists simply did not have the same options or results; they had a track record that was at odds with the legal and pedagogical business of this country, according to their education opponents, and they were treated with less respect and less progress in the system because of it.

The Importance of Insider Resonance: A Departure Point for Adding Further Complexity to the Insider / Outsider Boundary

In addition to the resonance that Afrocentrists were able to strike strategically with establishment insiders is a second area in which the boundaries between the institutional "inside" and "outside" also blurred—an ambiguity largely unrecognized in the movements field. In one of the Afrocentric cases—Atlanta—a subset of establishment insiders was not only *recruited as allies* by challengers' successful framing campaigns, they were actually *initiating members* of the challenging group. With few exceptions, this is not how movements scholars have portrayed "challengers." Movements researchers have traditionally described challengers as those social actors who lack routine access to government agents and resources, and who may, only under favorable political circumstances, be able to recruit elites to their positions as allies. They have *not* been depicted as people who may potentially hold positions of authority within the targeted institution, and who then *commence* a challenge—to be the superintendent of the school district, for instance, or the director of curriculum. Because of the discrepancy between prior research accounts and the reality I found in this challenge, it seems that we need to reconsider the line between "institutional insiders" and "challenging outsiders"—at least for some specific sites in some movements.

Mary Katzenstein is another scholar whose work calls for a more complex understanding of these seemingly oppositional structural locations. In *Faithful and Fearless*, Katzenstein has documented that the feminist gains made in the traditionally male-dominated institutions of both the U.S. military and the Catholic Church would not have been possible if activism had been initiated only from the "outside" of the institution banging in. Instead, she has found that many women who have sought to change both the military and the church have done so from the "inside"— that is, from within positions of authority in the organization. Accustomed to thinking about challengers as those who lack representation in established institutions, who are politically unmobilized,[15] or who use disruptive movement tactics,[16] we are simply not inclined to think of people in positions of power and authority as willfully adopting and advancing protest claims. Challenger calls for change, on the one hand, and access to routine levers of power, on the other hand, have seemed for too long to be contradictory.

But through the use of compelling data, Katzenstein shows that we must see through this "contradiction," relax the strict intellectual division between insider and outsider status, and open our eyes to the fact that even within "total," or "greedy," institutions—institutions that are hugely demanding of time and loyalty[17]—people in positions of some power and authority, such as female officers or Catholic sisters, push for institutional change. These insiders may even initiate activities to alter the institution. Whether fighting for what Katzenstein labels "interest group" politics—concrete demands for material resources like fair pay or job equality—or "discursive" politics—demands that the institution "reinterpret, reformulate, rewrite, and rethink the norms and practices of society and state"[18]—some members of the established institution actively identify and act as challenge agents.

Katzenstein's insights obviously mirror the nature of the relationships I found in the Afrocentric cases, particularly in Atlanta, where arguments for justice and self-esteem compelled several consummate insiders to initiate the challenge. And there were other insiders in these three school systems, vested with various forms of routine access to resources, who were sympathetic to Afrocentric goals, or who were among the first to identify change as a desirable objective. Education insiders in these challenges were not just coerced into supporting Afrocentrism through the pressure they received from mobilized protesters outside the institution (of whom there were quite few), or even through the threat of being called "racist" or "race betrayers." Rather, the "ideational centrality" of the Afrocentric challenge also led some administrators in these systems to believe in the movement's goals, to pick up the mantle of the movement, and to fight for its success.[19] When this happened, the boundary between inside and outside blurred.

Expanding Katzenstein's Insights to Capture "Insider" Variability: The Difference between Political and Institutional Authority

The careful reader should be able to anticipate the next question. Can Katzenstein's theory about the blurring of inside / outside boundaries aid our understanding of the four creationist cases, as well? We know that creationists were less able than Afrocentrists to frame their demands so that they resonated with education officials and, so, they did not find professional educators' support for their objectives like Afrocentrists did (at least symbolically). But as we saw so clearly in chapters 5 and 6, creationists often did find their way onto what should be considered to be the "inside" rungs of educational decision making. They and their supporters became members of the Vista and Kansas state school boards, as we will recall, and they occupied House and Senate seats in the Louisiana legislature—enough supporters did so, anyway, to pass the Balanced Treatment Act in 1981. In three of the four creationist cases in this sample—in every case except the California framework battle—Christian conservatives were able to force their issue onto the legal agenda or onto the school board program. They were able to vote 71–19 and 26–12 in the Louisiana House and Senate, respectively; they were able to win 3–2 in Vista, California; and they were able to muster a vote of 6–4 in Kansas in support of creationist-friendly policy. It certainly seems as though challengers were able to find their way to the inside of these institutions, and to make decisions from those seats of power.

How should we understand creationists' ability to make *political* gains and to obtain access to inside positions like school board seats, even as they were unable to forge a *cultural* connection with permanent education staff in their schools systems? How helpful were these "inside" positions of power, in the final analysis? Should creationists in these cases really be counted as having gained access to the "inside"?

Up to this point in this chapter, when discussing the inside / outside boundary, I have lumped all education policymakers into a single, unified group, and I have called them "insiders." I have done this to illustrate two points—that challengers frequently target insiders as well as the general public in their framing activities, and that the traditional line social movements researchers have used to demarcate defensive "insiders" from challenging "outsiders" lacks empirical support, at least in these seven cases. But from evidence presented in previous chapters, we should regard such lumping with skepticism. Not all school system "insiders" were equally likely to adopt challengers' frames and, even more importantly, not all insiders possessed the same authority to accept or reject challenger revisions over the long run.

Katzenstein's insights about the blurring of inside and outside can help us see that both the creationist and Afrocentric challenges were fought partially from within education circles as well as from without. But her blurring of the inside / outside boundary does not assist us very much with this last batch of observations, which requires that a distinction be made between political authority and bureaucratic / professional authority as two different kinds of "insider" status. For, what is apparent in the creationist cases is that we need to go beyond just a blurring of locations "internal" or "external" to the school organization, since gaining access to the putative "inside" ultimately bought creationists very little. We have to complicate the very definition of these terms. As we look at these activities in greater detail, I think it becomes clear that assigning creationist board members or legislators the label "insider," without saying anything more about the actual *types* of power they held, is misleading. Although current social movements concepts make no distinctions among insiders once they win decision-making authority, there is reason to believe that in these cases, the categorization requires greater sophistication. While it is true that creationist challengers gained "routine access to government resources" like having a vote on educational policy, these elected officials should not be confused with insiders who came by their positions through professional systems of learning and credentialing, and who held bureaucratic authority in the school systems. Elected onto these educational governing bodies, creationists did gain a vote on school policies. But they did not penetrate to the core of educational practices.

Rather, creationism's champions won something else: they gained political power. But this political power frequently did not come with accompanying institutional power. Creationists in these systems may have been located in inside positions, and sometimes, they may have even wielded authority over bureaucratic / professional educators—such as when they served on school boards and were, technically, the bosses of system administrators. But, because creationist board members and legislators were not professionalized in the same institutions as educators, because they did not occupy positions in the routine education system, and especially because they made decisions that were far outside the fold of routine education decision making, they simply were not regarded as legitimate decision makers when it came to crafting educational policy. As operatives of "the will of the people," these elected officials may have been tolerated by administrators in their jurisdictions, and may have received some ceremonial respect—as we saw in the case of Vista's Associate Superintendent Bill Loftus, who reported that there was not much he could do, professionally, about the creationist-friendly school board, once its majority members drafted policy. But in all three cases where creationists attained political power, education professionals could ultimately vanquish creationist content once it crossed the line of "legitimate education principles." Educators ridiculed creationists as buffoons; they lambasted creationists as dangerous threats to the Constitution's guarantee of the separation of church and state; they argued that creationists should not be mistaken for professionals when they made policy that was offensive to educational officialdom.

When we look at both the Afrocentric and creationist cases in this degree of detail, we understand that challengers could reach the inside of the institution and, yet, still not have what was defined as a legitimate voice there. These political insiders could work to aid their challenger brothers and sisters on the outside of the system (as Katzenstein's institutional activists did), but for us simply to know this fact does not tell us enough about how and when their efforts would be beneficial, or irrelevant, or even a hindrance to the struggle. Creationists, like Afrocentrists, may have benefited from the efforts of numerous establishment insiders (like school board members), but the eventual outcomes of those efforts were dependent on a second factor having to do with establishment position: those actors' actual location on the inside of the establishment. Certain insider positions have greater capacity to advance challenges and draft revisions than do others. By this statement I do not mean that getting superintendents to go along with the challenge proved more fruitful than getting janitors' support—an all-too-obvious observation of organizational authority structures. What I mean, instead, is that certain seats of power in an organization may have great authority—to make policies, to change curricula, perhaps—but that if bureaucratic / professional insiders, or those who are learned in the routines of the organizational ideology, do not also align with the challenge, then outcomes are likely to be far less successful than at first they appeared. Political power in school systems often does not translate to bureaucratic power in that same organization.

The larger point is that some of the current modes of analyzing institutional challengers are in need of review. Political "insider" status, or "polity membership," is one of these concepts begging to be revamped. As it stands now, it is simply too blunt an instrument to discern who has authority in a system, what kind of authority they actually have, and whether they have the clout to effect real, concrete change. Even when we expand our understanding to include Katzenstein's inside-outside boundary overlap, to say that some party exists on the institutional "inside" still obscures more complex relationships. There are analytically distinguishable forms of insider status—positions of political power and positions of institutional power. This is not to say that the same person couldn't be in possession of both types of power; indeed, some of the insiders we have observed in the seven cases did possess both. It is to say, however, that we have to distinguish between the two types of authority to see the discrete effects of each on challenger outcomes. Merely obtaining inside access may be insufficient to changing organizations.

Adopting an Institutionalist Approach to Studying Challenge Processes and Outcomes

This line of thinking about the eventual outcomes in Afrocentric and creationist cases has taken us quite a distance from most descriptions of the relationship between those who challenge and those who are challenged in movement events. First, there is the possibility that cultural resonance might be struck between challengers and inside decision makers. Second, we have seen that these locations in the field of challenge are sometimes far more continuous than the dichotomous inside / outside line would indicate.[20] Third, we have evidence that simply winning political access to the inside of the institution does not guarantee institutional power for challengers. Where does this leave us in our consideration of Afrocentrism and creationism, and of social movements, generally? These agenda items point us in the direction of a more complex understanding of how culture, politics, and organization operate in challenge events—particularly in the type of contentious, institutional events that I have studied in this book. Having already described the empirical realities of these challenges in chapters past, and having just given a fairly lengthy review of the cultural aspects of these challenges, it is now important to define precisely what is meant by "political processes" and "organizational routines," and to map out how these two interacted in the challenges. This will constitute the final theoretical piece of the project's puzzle.

Political Processes

First, let's consider the political side. As we have seen in the sections of the book that examine challengers' "political opportunity structures," when researchers describe the impact that the broader political system has on social movements, they are, in effect, turning the analysis of challenge away from factors internal to movements—such as cultural claims and material resources—and turning it toward the political conditions that shape the timing and formation of social movements.[21] Scholars using the political process model argue that the emergence and spread of collective action and protest must be traced to the possibilities created by the practical politics of the system, as well as to the ideologies of those systems, and they have observed the special occasions when challengers are able to take advantage of these structural conditions.[22] Such occasions occur, according to Doug McAdam, a key figure in this field, when (1) there is a relative openness of the institutionalized political system, (2) intra-elite conflict is present, (3) challengers find allies among elites, and / or (4) there are alterations in the level of state oppression. McAdam has called these the "informal structure of power relations" present in a system under challenge, which can make the system vulnerable to change.[23] Research in this area has focused on the extant structures in the political environment, on the strategies challengers develop to confront that environment, and on the dynamics that proceed from this interaction.[24]

This description of political opportunities is helpful for thinking about the dynamics that were present and influential in the Afrocentric and creationist challenges. As we saw in both types of challenge, political cracks and cleavages frequently occurred among school system members in these cases. When challengers could figure out how to capitalize on these rifts, they did, indeed, render the systems more vulnerable to their demands. Knowledgeable of political conflict that divided administrative elites in Atlanta into a more "proactive" faction vs. an "old timer status quo" faction, for example, perceptive Afrocentric challengers exploited these divisions to win the support of the system's younger, activist faction. Although even among this faction most administrators were personally committed to multicultural change rather than to Afrocentric revision, members of this administrative group were willing to back the African-centered education initiative (among other proposed policy initiatives) as part of their larger campaign to overcome the intransigence of their adversaries within the system.[25] Some of these allied insiders even led the Afrocentric charge. In this situation, Afrocentrists' claims were advanced at the right place at the right time, such that some of the most dissatisfied personnel among the system's elite aligned with the challengers' agenda in order to gain an advantage over other administrative elites, while also satisfying their own desire for change in the system. This is a clear example of what McAdam has called intra-elite conflict, and its ability to make an institution vulnerable to challenge.[26]

And in another example of the influence of political opportunities—this time from two of the creationist cases—in both Vista and Kansas, creationists took advantage of their school systems' formal political openness when they exercised their right to run as candidates for their school boards. Competing in races that do not generally capture the public's attention, creationism-friendly candidates found it quite easy in both of these locales to be democratically elected to school boards. Strategizing to maximize their mobilized constituencies' power of the vote, challengers in these school systems traveled the institutionalized route to victory by using a political opportunity written into law: candidates with either a majority of the vote (Kansas) or a plurality of the vote (Vista) won seats on these school boards.

These examples demonstrate the ability of the political opportunities model to explain each of these systems' initial vulnerability to challenger activities. But because the model is oriented toward the *origins* of contention, the political process approach is limited in its capacity to fully capture events that *subsequently* took place in these three locations (indeed, in any of the seven locations). For, as we know, despite their ability to take advantage of political opportunities such as these, and despite their ability to use these opportunities to reach the inside rungs of institutionalized decision making, neither Afrocentrists nor creationists were able to achieve full victory in any of the seven locations I studied. Organizational practices, employed by establishment insiders, stopped them.

Let's look, first, at how these organizational practices worked in the Afrocentric challenges. Even in those systems where Afrocentrists did win concessions—sometimes through their cultural appeals (racial injustice, a stated support for pluralistic education) and sometimes aided by political opportunities (particularly if there was an African American majority in the district who could be said to be demanding the reforms)—challengers did not have enough influence with enough professional educators, administrators or teachers—for those political nods to withstand institutional power. Once education officials granted curriculum space to Afrocentric content in their systems, this content was then subject to any number of institutional routines. Education officials relied on these routines to safeguard curricula from change. Oppositional administrators and teachers could virtually ignore mandatory reforms, even if challengers had succeeded in getting professional educators to acknowledge their demands, or even to implement them, in the system. One example of this organizational containment took place in Washington, D.C., where

Abena Walker's African-centered program was highly restricted to just one school-within-a-school setting, despite Walker's (and supportive parents') keen desire to expand. Through the use of district-wide tests, which showed that students in Walker's program were performing at par with other district school children, the superintendent made the case that the program should be maintained, but not expanded. Due to this decision to contain, Walker's program was taught to only about 120 children out of the district's total 80,000 students.

We witnessed another example of keeping challenger gains in check in Atlanta, where Georgia's use of the Iowa Test of Basic Skills could be relied on to free teachers from having to teach new district-specific revised curriculum (that is, Afrocentric curriculum), if they so desired. In both of these cases, what had been acceptable as a political concession to constituents and to other administrators fighting for Afrocentric revisions, was not, ultimately, acceptable to many as an educational consideration. School system decision-makers simultaneously manufactured success for the challengers (thereby pleasing their vocal constituency) *and* defeat (thereby pleasing many of their own in the teaching and administrative ranks of the district). They manufactured this "token victory" using resources from an institutional tool kit characteristic of educational practices, a tool kit that had been decades in the making, and one that was unique to schools. So, despite the inroads that Afrocentrists were able to make in these school systems, administrators and teachers still found behind-the-scenes processes for protecting curricula to a considerable degree from too much overhaul, thereby demoting challenger victory from what seemed to be a sure bet.

Creationists, meanwhile, could not even extract symbolic concessions in their school systems, once educators brought organizational practices to bear on the situations. First, I would argue that the separation of church and state—the force that acted so conclusively against creationists—was not only a cultural belief that educators held dearly, but also an organizational imperative on which they could rely. Following federal court decisions that have prohibited religious content in schools, administrators attempted to protect their science curricula from the demands of creationists by arguing strenuously that their schools were not *permitted* to incorporate creationism in any form. Using the double weapons of financial burden and shame brought to the community, school officials warned of impending legal suits that litigants would bring against the school system, were creationism to be allowed into the curriculum. This was an especially valued tool when creationists claimed that they—not professional educators—represented constituents' interests. Certainly, schools' access to such a script represented a far more efficient way of closing off schools to challenge than if such an unambiguous rule were unavailable.

But as we have seen, legal precedent was not foolproof, and creationists sometimes managed to achieve political power in school districts. And yet, even in these circumstances, challengers' political gains were lost when administrators and other powerful actors in the school systems used organizationally derived practices to stop the challenge. What sorts of organizational practices were these? When professional education staff did not succeed at immediately stopping creationist advances using legal precedent (their preferred first line of defense), school officials became adept at using *delay*, for example, to obstruct creationist policy. As we witnessed in both Louisiana state and in Kansas, educators who were outraged by the imposition of creationist-friendly content on their systems dragged their feet when it came to implementing actual change in the curricula.

While delay, itself, may not be an institutionally sanctified routine in education settings, the ends to which educators applied this practice in all systems where it was used most certainly were. In Kansas, educators insisted that they were required to delay development of the board's new science standards since several national science organizations (including the National Academy of Sciences and the American Association for the Advancement of Science), whose language had been used in those standards, had demanded that the framework excise any and all portions of their terminology. And in Louisiana, educators who had been instructed by the legislature—against their will—to develop the actual "balanced" science framework, had stalled such activity until an ACLU suit could be settled. Although education bureaucrats in both Louisiana and Kansas labeled their actions as money- and labor-saving measures, we should also interpret them as strategic organizational obstructions to legislative and board actions.

As we know, the delay strategy worked, and for no time between 1981 and 1987, while the Balanced Treatment Act traveled through the court system, did Louisiana schoolchildren learn about creationist theory of origins (at least not officially). And in Kansas, for the one year between 1999 and 2000 that the policy was on the books, evolution remained staunchly on the statewide assessment tests as a concept to be evaluated. Educators' delay tactic worked just as planned. While creationists on the school board and in the legislature complained that education officials were frustrating the public's will, there was nothing that these political insiders could do to get professional insiders to move more quickly.

Actions such as these—in which educators relied on a statewide system of testing to minimize the impact of a new policy, or when they stalled implementation of legislation—are not political, exactly, in the sense that "political" refers to power struggles. Rather, these features are embedded in the culture of organizational decision making and are part of the every-

day understandings of "the way things are done" in this particular institution. These organizational features may be accounted for in a power
model, I suppose, and they may be made to fit the label of "political opportunities and constraints." But I think that these organizational factors
are sufficiently different from the political as to require a unique analysis
that draws on institutional insights to understand them. Particularly if contentious politics are taking place more and more in institutions like schools
in our current "social movements society"—and not as frequently against
entrenched political authority like the broader state apparatus—we simply
need to know more about the common-sense understandings and pat-
terned sets of practices of those actors who reside in schools to make sense
of officials' protective stance toward extant curricula and the tools they
use to preserve them.[27] We need a theory of institutional cultures and structures that can give us some parameters on what "reasonable" concessions
might look like, according to a particular set of practices, or when school
systems might, instead, attempt "outright rejection." If we do not understand something about how these targeted school systems depended on
institutional logics for their day-to-day workings—particularly concerning
the protection of boundaries and normal routines—then we will be at a
loss for understanding how educators could have conceded only as much
authority to their Afrocentric challengers as they absolutely had to (implementing change mostly at the symbolic level), but could afford to delay
and ultimately provide nothing to their creationist opponents, and still be
considered a legitimate public institution.

Organizational Opportunities Arising from Internal Conflict and from Inclusion in an Institution

So, there is one more level beyond culture and politics that I believe
shaped outcomes in the Afrocentric and creationist battles. We are able
to map the precise contours of challenger results only if we think about
what I am calling the *organizational practices* located in the system, not
just the cultural and political opportunities and constraints found there.
By this, I mean that challenger outcomes depended on the effects of the
more routinized characteristics of the organization, in addition to the
more unusual circumstances and politics that sporadically arose and the
cultural beliefs that challengers could tap in school systems.

I have already described four of these organizational routines in the
previous section (containment, testing, reliance on legal precedent, and
delay), and I have discussed several others at the end of chapter 4. But I
have not yet addressed the question of *why* these organizational routines
should have been so influential in the school systems where they were

used. Why did organizational routines exert such power in these challenge events, enough to overcome the considerable political power that challengers sometimes managed to attain? This is an area of inquiry to which social movements research has paid too little attention, although it is beginning to attract consideration. Sidney Tarrow has gestured toward the "more stable structural elements" that help or hinder institutions' ability to withstand challenge, and Doug McAdam, John McCarthy, and Mayer Zald have written that any informative analysis of challenger movements must couple (1) efforts to study how movements seek to influence established institutions with (2) an assessment of *how those same established institutions seek to "control, channel, repress, or facilitate movements* [emphasis added]."[28] And yet, despite these signals, the influence of the subject organization on challengers—with the organization's systems of legitimacy and authority built into its everyday workings—has remained in something of a black box.

ORGANIZATIONAL COMPONENT 1: CONFLICT (REDUX). As I wrote in chapter 1, there are a couple of directions in which the study of contentious politics can be pushed by organizational theory.[29] The first that I have chosen to look at, as explained briefly in chapter 1, is the *conflict* that is always found in organizations like school systems, even in the absence of outside agitators.[30] The rifts that occurred in Atlanta, Vista, and Kansas (which allowed entrée for challengers), for example, may not have been as extraordinary or infrequent as political opportunities researchers have understood them to be. School systems' members are rarely, if ever, committed to exactly the same set of goals or, for that matter, to the same set of methods for attaining similar goals. Even more fundamentally, organizations, such as school systems, simply are not the always-rational, goal-oriented, purposive entities of our rational actor colleagues' imaginations. They possess limited rationality; they attribute solutions to problems that, before the solutions were concocted, had not yet been imagined as "problems"; and they have contested and uncertain goals.[31] Given this level of nonconsensus in organizations, it is no wonder that Afrocentric and creationist challengers were able to make headway in various parts of school systems, as they mobilized with various other insider and outsider members in the field.

ORGANIZATIONAL COMPONENT 2: INSTITUTIONAL PRACTICES. But focusing on conflict among school officials demonstrates only a fraction of the insights that organizational theory can add to the study of contentious politics. A more profound way for organizational theory to contribute to this analysis of Afrocentric and creationist challenges—and to institutionalized contentious politics, more generally—is to elucidate the relationship that existed between the local organizational structures under challenge, on the one hand (the school systems), and the larger institutional world to which those local structures belonged, on the other (such as the network of schools of education, state credentialing agencies, similarly situated school systems, and the like) that shaped professional educators' beliefs and practices. By coaxing us to look at the multiple levels that make up the education world, organizational theory opens up new ways of thinking about power and its sources, so that we go beyond thinking about the influences of just broad cultural beliefs or political circumstances on outcomes. New institutionalist theory encourages us to think, for example, of local school systems and their decision makers as being located in a large web of expectations, knowledge, expertise, practices, and routinized ways of doing things that are particular to this institution, known as "the American education system." This network, home to ideas about "legitimate" educational practices—like curriculum content—then influences action in the local school systems. Educators may refer explicitly or implicitly to these practices and understandings as the "appropriate" modus operandi for dealing with curricular challenges like Afrocentrism or creationism, and they may also explicitly or implicitly seek to reinforce these models in their home districts. Whatever the level of articulation, though, these institutional practices shape school personnel's perceptions of challenges and how they choose to handle them.

As implied in the foregoing, a central notion developed in the new institutionalist literature is that institutions should be understood not as formal organizational structures defined by official mission statements but, instead, as the cultural understandings, rules, scripts, and constraints that shape the activities of actors who fall within a particular area of activity—in this case, public schools. In its concern with how reality is constructed within a particular domain, or field, new institutionalist theory charts "the ways in which action is structured and order made possible by shared systems of rules."[32] These shared systems of rules set parameters on actions that will be considered to be legitimate or illegitimate in the schools.

Stressing "order" and "shared systems of rules," this understanding of institutions provides a means for thinking about why professional educators sought to maintain their positions as legitimate authorities in their systems, even when faced with culturally resonant demands for change, or with pressure from challengers who had made it to political centers of power in their school systems. Over time, the ideas and practices that have constituted legitimate history and science curriculum content have ceased to be seen as one of many possible instructional alternatives and, instead, institutional members have assumed that these ideas and practices are the most effective and beneficial way of educating their students (although, as we know, there is more "stretch" in what is considered legitimate in the social sciences than in the "hard" sciences). In other words, over time, the institutional world of schools has consolidated around a set of ideas for the "correct" way of instructing children in their classrooms, and its members—from New York to Kansas to California—have developed strong commitments to those ideas.

There are two major explanations outlined in the new institutionalist literature for why members of school systems (or other organizations) become committed to such prevailing definitions of "how things are correctly done"—even in the face of client demands for change. The first is a more instrumental conception of adherence, which argues that school systems and their members conform to these classifications of legitimate history and legitimate science because it is adaptive for them to do so: their survival and resources depend on their congruity with institutional curriculum expectations.[33] Funding from government sources, ability to use mainstream publishers' textbooks, ease of finding teachers trained in conventional curricular content—all of these bear on school systems' decisions to minimize challengers' revision attempts. Not only that, but survival also clearly implies a power dynamic: once administrators and other professional educators find themselves in positions of authority, they are inclined to invest a great deal of energy to reconfirming their right to occupy those positions in their school systems.

The second explanation for why professionals conform to institutional scripts has less to do with acting instrumentally, and more to do with the ethnomethodological basis of their action. This means that educators in school systems, as an example, adhere to institutional beliefs about what constitutes "reasonable instruction" in order to reduce their own uncertainty about the historical or scientific content that children should be taught, and to boost their own experiences of order. These institutional guideposts are especially useful, in fact, in times of conflict, when order and certainty about curriculum content are threatened. The scripts for legitimate curriculum might be used to close off certain avenues of action that seem suddenly to open during unsettled times—like compromising with challengers to buy some peace in the school system.[34] Neil Fligstein has written that once an organizational field has formed, there is a strong element of the taken-for-granted in these institutional rules, which easily allows organizational actors like professional educators to act appropriately as they follow their unwritten, but widely understood, scripts.[35] If political scientist Mary Katzenstein is also correct, then educators in these seven cases relied on these rules, as well, to give them a sense of the *value* of their participation in their school systems (like their role in protecting core curricula), and to figure out *who they are* and *what is important to them*.[36]

In sum, the institutional concept, described here, helps explain the *structuration* of public schools—that is, the establishment and mainte- nance of this world.[37] As such, it gives us a solid foundation for under- standing why school systems at some point in all seven of these challenge events tried to minimize—or even, outrightly reject—Afrocentric and cre- ationist curriculum changes. Both of these challenges threatened to create chaos in the routine patterns of educational life (even while they insisted that they would not) and, in response, bureaucratic authorities attempted to minimize both.

Demands for Change and Institutional Responses to Those Demands

And yet, while administrators may have preferred constancy in their school systems, they were also expected to take community demands into serious consideration and sometimes, even, respond favorably to those constituents. Part of the reason why schools are expected to respond to outside interests is because, as a public institution, the boundary separat- ing clients from "experts" is not as clearly defined as it is in other fields, and the clients in school systems expect to have some input into schools' operations. Afrocentrism and creationism certainly were not the first chal- lengers ever to make demands on American public schools, and innumera- ble earlier challenge attempts have resulted in concrete change at various levels of the institution. In the not so distant past, there have been demands in American schools for the abandonment of organized prayer (and now, struggles to reintroduce it); efforts to include multicultural curricula in social studies classes from coast to coast; demands for a back-to-basics curriculum; calls for phonics; and campaigns for Sex Respect. The list goes on. Each one of these efforts represented a challenge to schools that threat- ened to shake up the normal practices of the educational process, and school officials were called upon to make decisions about how to handle these sometimes politically and culturally volatile issues.

What do these occasions of challenge tell us? They tell us that as much as professional educators may take the present structure for granted, as much as they may rely on institutional scripts to limit change, as much as they may perceive it to be in their interest to resist reform: external and internal challengers still do make demands on established institutions, and reluctant administrators must deal with those demands. Preserving routines is not easy for institutions that are expected to have more porous boundaries, and maintaining these routines calls for the imaginative work of educators who wish to dispatch their challengers.

In sum, this is a system in constant interaction with its many constituents—internal and external—and public schools must adapt to survive. They cannot and do not stand still. And yet, they also, obviously, do not wish to respond positively to every challenge that their constituents mount and that some insiders may support. Particularly because schools are seen to transmit a common stock of knowledge (history, science, values, and national identity), these organizations face a multitude of clients who are unlikely to agree on what that common culture should look like, not to mention a number of their own staff who are in disagreement over such matters. Making decisions about history and science curricula places schools squarely in the middle of cultural and political conflicts. Determining what type of content to teach students is potentially explosive because everybody has an idea about what children should know and how they should be taught. The constituents of this benevolent organization believe they deserve to have input over the content that is delivered to their offspring. And while most educators would like to keep these constituents away from curriculum decisions—or at the very least, to keep them distant from any lasting decision-making authority—there is conflict among organizations about when, how, and if to concede to community demands in particular situations.[38] Other researchers, like Larry Cuban and David Tyack, have found that educators are generally willing to "tinker" around the edges of school reform, granting to challengers marginal reforms in areas at the periphery of the educational enterprise.[39] School staff stop challengers, however, when the efforts are aimed at the "core activity" of their jobs: curriculum development, particularly in central curricula like history and science. This is an institutional imperative, built up in education, where bureaucratic professionals are mandated to be responsive, at least to some degree, to their constituents: concede to reformers what is necessary; encourage them to think they have made gains, if possible; but in the final analysis, protect the inner core of the organization's functions.

In the case of Afrocentric and creationist challengers, we have seen variation in whether education professionals fortified their borders and fought to the death for the status quo, or whether they negotiated with challengers, giving on some ground and remaining steadfast on other terms. They have been seen to differ in their strategies, depending on who the challengers were, what the nature of their claims were, and whether the challengers had been able to marshal political resources. But in all seven cases, educators succeeded in protecting their core—whatever the compelling cultural claims and political strengths that challengers could generate.

Conclusion

As we can see from this discussion, we simply need to know about the organizational structure and culture of school systems that affected challenges. If we had looked only at the cultural beliefs that motivated education professionals or only at the structure of political opportunities that were created in school systems, and not the organizational exigencies and pressures that also acted on them, we would now understand only a portion of the story of these challengers' outcomes.

The social movements literature on culture, framing, and resonance, until recently, has failed to consider subject bureaucracies' organizational structures in a serious way, and when political opportunity scholars have taken structure seriously, they have focused on sporadic opportunities for challengers, stemming from elite cleavages, economic shifts, or war;[40] or on the contradictions and gaps in dominant ideologies, which trigger opposition.[41] But they have not paid enough attention to the logics that are implicit in the everyday workings of the organization. Perhaps this absence in the literature has three causes.

The first reason, as I mentioned in chapter 1, is that social movements researchers have primarily studied challenges to political systems, like the state, and not to subunits of the state, like its education system. Over the past twenty years, social movements scholars have focused on climactic, rebellious movements that "take place in the street," and that are aimed at established political authority—movements such as civil rights, women's rights, and Operation Rescue. But in this focus, they have overlooked the kind of struggles that I study in this book—contentious politics that target institutional authorities, that are nonviolent and nondisruptive. According to some in the field, these smaller, institutional challenges are becoming the archetypal form of contentious politics affecting Western democracies today—a sign of the "social movement society" in which we live.[42] If this theory is correct—and I believe it is—then to understand these kinds of struggles, we must redirect our gaze at how and where these challenges occur. Only when we bring the analysis down to the level of identifiably organizational units like school districts will we be better positioned to observe the everyday institutional and organizational practices that typify that setting, and to get a handle on this form of contention. Additionally, once we are better able to describe the mundane organizational practices used by institutions battling challengers, we may also be better equipped to see these same types of practices used by states, in the rarer events that challengers confront them.

The second reason why organizational exigencies have gone missing in the past two decades of social movements research is that movements theorists have privileged the study of national movements to the exclusion of local challenger movements. Often this is a practical matter, as McAdam, Tarrow, and Tilly acknowledge in their recent theoretical overview of contentious politics.[43] To simplify their analysis, researchers have focused on national, as opposed to local or regional, contention since national conflicts generally tend to generate greater amounts of scholarly materials than do localized events.

But we should not allow the availability of materials to influence our practice of oversampling national movements, for studies of local challenges can tell us something useful, and they are long overdue. Think of what is learned from the comparison of Afrocentric and creationist challenges to local school systems. If I had looked only at national challenger movements during this same historical period (1980–2000), my sights would have fallen predominantly on the success of conservative movements and issues of the time: anti-abortion, the back-to-basics movement in education, and the move to curtail welfare benefits, among others. But in examining the local level of movement activity at this point in history, I found something quite different: a racial-identity movement that was able to make some headway in some school systems (at least initially in some locations), and a conservative creationist challenge that was eventually overturned in each instance of its expression. These challenges to schools didn't make much of a blip on movements researchers' radar screens, but they did have the potential to shape the educational lives of millions of people. We can only see such action at the local level.

Finally, social movements research may simply be suffering from methodological routine. Because it has traditionally been case-study based, particularly in the United States, and not comparative across challengers that confront the same institution, researchers may simply have missed occasions to see that the organization of the institution matters greatly to the outcomes of challenges.[44] But when research does compare different challenges to the same institution, as reported here, then these organizational logics come into focus.

This project integrates some of the features of an organizational analysis into the study of challenger movement outcomes. I have demonstrated why it makes sense to reject the increasingly untenable assumption that the institution being challenged is a unified, consensual, purposive, goal-directed entity that knows precisely how to do away with challengers. In so doing, I have demonstrated that some members of some school systems acted on behalf of their challengers, while others in the same system fought to limit gains.

I also have demonstrated how educators' conformity to implicit rules and conventions contributed to the stability of established systems, and how such conformity was an attempt to seal off schools from reform-minded challengers. But while the project suggests the power of established institutions generally to resist challenges, it also demonstrates that the process of defending these borders is variable. The particular form of institutional response to a challenge depends on several factors: the cultural resources the challenger has available to it (including whether the challenger can tap into the meaning system that shapes institutional members' expectations) and the type of political and organizational structures that compose the institution under challenge—from the power it exerts to the ideas that structure that power.

All of this is to say, then, that wider cultural logics, political opportunities, and organizational practices affect challengers' perceived legitimacy and, thus, efficacy, in opening up institutions to change—whether it is in the public schools as I describe here, or in other organizations that are part of different institutions. Larger systems of legitimacy—which both the social movements literature and the new institutionalist literature teach us to pay attention to—enter the established institution (in this case, public schools) by these three different routes.

The first route is the larger cultural system, which is home to beliefs about race, opportunity, the relationship of state and religion, and the like. Challengers and the challenged institution, alike, make meaning out of the circumstances they find themselves in, they interpret those circumstances, and they develop solutions for ameliorating their condition while devising strategies and framing techniques for achieving those ends.

The second route is through political maneuvers—whether it is the challenger exploiting rifts among institutional insiders, taking advantage of power vacuums, or some other strategic action to capitalize on institutional weakness. Furthermore, as Aldon Morris and Doug McAdam have argued separately, there is a strong interaction loop that links challengers' cultural repertoires and political opportunities.[45] Social construction, or creative cultural work, almost always shapes "political" opportunities. Sometimes in these cases of Afrocentric and creationist challenge, political opportunities presented occasions for challengers to exploit, as political process theorists have long demonstrated. But at other times, challengers used cultural arguments, symbols, and beliefs to open up those political opportunities in the first place—such as when Afrocentrists led potential fellow travelers in the Atlanta administration to see that they could achieve their political goals by advocating Afrocentric reform rather than multiculturalism. Challengers both create and respond to opportunities.[46]

The third route by which challengers may (or may not) gain legitimacy is through the organizational practices that are located in the institution. Challengers may bump into the organization's efforts to protect its boundaries, into systems of teacher professionalization, into testing protocols. All of these factors represent the everyday practices used by the organization. They differ from traditional "political opportunities" in that they are relatively constant in the system, and inadvertently benefit some challengers while disadvantaging others. Only if we examine how challengers achieve legitimacy in light of all of these logics—cultural, political, and organizational—can we understand why certain insurgent movements (even when they are marginal) may wield some power in the institutional setting while others do not. While the school curriculum movements I examined in this study were engaged in significantly narrower struggles than those studied in the contentious politics field—struggles centered mainly, but not exclusively, on state and local school boards—the principles of analysis that I am using arguably can be applied at broader levels. My hope is that, once sensitized to the kinds of organizational and institutional factors that also operate in fields of contention, other researchers will seek to explore these factors in their own studies.

Appendix

I. Interview Respondents

Atlanta

D. F. Glover, former school board member of the Atlanta Public School System, and professor in the Department of Social Science, Morris Brown College

Mae Kendall, former director of Program Planning and Curriculum Development in the Atlanta Public School System

Cathy Loving, district archivist for the Atlanta Public School System

Murdell McFarlin, former public information officer, Superintendent's Office, Atlanta Public School System

Midge Sweet, former school board member of the Atlanta Public School System

Gladys Twyman, project coordinator of the African American Infusion Program in the Atlanta Public School System

Betsy White, former education reporter for the *Atlanta Journal-Constitution* anonymous school board member of the Atlanta Public School System

Washington, D.C.

Russell Adams, professor and chair of African American Studies at Howard University

Constance Clark, deputy superintendent for educational programs and operations, District of Columbia Public Schools

Betty Topps, executive assistant to the superintendent, District of Columbia Public Schools

Abena Walker, founder and principal of the African-Centered School at Webb Elementary School, District of Columbia Public Schools

New York

Linda Biemer, former dean of the School of Education, State University of New York, Binghamton, and co-chair of the New York State Curriculum and Assessment Committee

Walter Cooper, member of the New York State Board of Regents

Hazel Dukes, director of the New York chapter of the NAACP and former chair of the New York State Task Force on Minorities: Equity and Excellence

Nathan Glazer, professor in the School of Education, Harvard University, and former member of the New York State Social Studies Syllabus Review and Development Committee (the "Diversity Committee")

Leonard Jeffries, professor and former chair, Black Studies Department, City College of New York and consultant to the New York State Special Task Force on Minorities: Equity and Excellence

Ali Mazrui, professor of the humanities, State Universiy of New York, Binghamton, and former member of the New York State Social Studies Syllabus Review and Development Committee (the "Diversity Committee")

Diane Ravitch, professor in the School of Education, New York University and former U.S. assistant secretary of education

Virginia Sanchez Korrol, professor and chair of Puerto Rican Studies at Brooklyn College and former member of the New York State Social Studies Syllabus Review and Development Committee (the "Diversity Committee")

Thomas Sobol, professor at Teacher's College at Columbia University and former commissioner of education for the state of New York

California

Bill Honig, former superintendent of public instruction, California Public Schools

Phillip Johnson, professor in the Boalt School of Law at the University of California, Berkeley

Kevin Padian, associate professor of Integrative Biology and curator of the Museum of Paleontology at the University of California, Berkeley, and former member of the Science Subject Matter Committee of the State of California

Eugenie Scott, director of the National Center for Science Education

Elizabeth Stage, executive director of the California Science Project, University of California, and former chair of the Science Subject Matter Committee of the Curriculum Development and Supplemental Materials Commission of the State of California

John Wiester, chairman of the Science Education Commission of the American Scientific Affiliation

Vista, California

Tom Conry, math teacher in the Vista Unified School District and president of the Vista Teachers Association

Barbara Donovan, "Recall" organizer and school board member of the Vista Unified School District

Jack Gyves, superintendent, Vista Unified School District

Bill Loftus, assistant superintendent for instruction, Vista Unified School District

Pete McHugh, associate superintendent for instruction, Vista Unified School District

Henry Morris, president emeritus of the Institute for Creation Research

Linda Rhoades, school board member of the Vista Unified School District

Rene Townsend, former superintendent of the Vista Unified School District and current superintendent of the Coronado School District

John Tyndall, director of accounting for the Institute for Creation Research and former school board member of the Vista Unified School District

II. Media Sources

The Atlanta Journal-Constitution
The New York Times
The Washington Post
The New Orleans Times-Picayune
The Kansas City Star
The San Diego Union Tribune
The Los Angeles Times

Notes

Preface

1. From about 1990 to 1995, both academics and journalists wrote impassioned tracts warning that the country had become engulfed in "culture wars," in a battle between "progressives" and "traditionalists" said to be shaping the lives of all citizens (see for example James Davison Hunter's *Culture Wars* (New York: Basic Books, 1991), as well as William Bennett's *The Devaluing of America* (New York: Summit Books, 1992); Dinesh D'Souza's *Illiberal Education: The Politics of Sex and Race on Campus* (Toronto: Collier Macmillan, 1991); and Robert Bork's *Slouching towards Gomorrah* (New York: Regan Books, 1996). By 1998, the disturbing cries had quieted somewhat when other social scientists demonstrated that the warnings had been exaggerated. For these critiques, see Rhys Williams' edited volume called *Cultural Wars in American Politics: Critical Reviews of a Popular Myth* (New York: Aldine de Gruyter, 1997); Paul DiMaggio, John Evans, and Bethany Bryson's article "Have Americans' Social Attitudes Become More Polarized?" *American Journal of Sociology* 102 (1996): 690–755; and for a more recent critique, Paul DiMaggio and Bethany Bryson's "Public Attitudes towards Cultural Authority and Cultural Diversity in Higher Education and the Arts" in *The Arts, of Democracy: The State, Civil Society, and Culture*, ed. Casey Blake (Princeton: Woodrow Wilson Center Press, 2000).

2. The most celebrated Ebonics case, of course, occurred in Oakland, California, in December 1996, when the school board of that district voted to educate children in their "African American language," in part to improve their fluency in Standard English.

Chapter One
Introduction to Afrocentrism and Creationism, Challengers to Educational "Injustice"

1. David Tyack and Larry Cuban, *Tinkering toward Utopia* (Cambridge: Harvard University Press, 1995), p. 4.

2. See Nicola Beisel's description of the antivice movements made on behalf of students in the nineteenth century in *Imperiled Innocents: Anthony Comstock and Family Reproduction in Victorian America* (Princeton: Princeton University Press, 1997). See, also, work that I have done previously, especially "Constructing Racial Rhetoric: Media Depictions of Harm in Heavy Metal and Rap Music," *American Sociological Review* 58 (1993): 753–67, which compares the mass media's warnings of the harm posed to children by rap and heavy metal. Scott Davies also draws attention to the strength of child-centered rhetoric in curricular reform efforts; see "The Changing Meaning of Progressive Pedagogy: Justifying School Reform in Three Eras," unpublished paper, 2000.

3. Both Molefi Asante, "Multiculturalism: An Exchange," *The American Scholar* 60 (1991): 267–76, and Bayo Oyebade, "African Studies and the Afrocentric Paradigm: A Critique," *Journal of Black Studies* 21 (1990): 233–38, make this point.

4. Asa Hilliard, an Afrocentric scholar at Georgia State University, made this argument, as cited in G. Putka "Curricula of Color: Course Work Stressing Blacks' Role Has Critics but Appears Effective," *Wall Street Journal*, July 1,1991. Alan Singer also writes about Afrocentrism's objectives in "Multiculturalism and Afrocentricity: How They Influence Teaching U.S. History," *Social Education* 57 (1993): 283–86.

5. While administrators are just one faction of the education establishment— policymakers and practitioners are the others—I am primarily concerned with administrators' responses to challenge in this project.

6. Michael Olneck writes about multiculturalism as an "identity movement" in his "Terms of Inclusion: Has Multiculturalism Redefined Equality in American Education?" *American Journal of Education* 101 (1993): 234–60.

7. Mary Katzenstein discusses the differences between "interest group" and "discursive" politics in her book *Faithful and Fearless* (Princeton: Princeton University Press, 1998). The distinction will be made clearer in chapter 7.

8. This form of investigation echoes work being done by Michèle Lamont on symbolic boundaries in *Money, Morals, and Manners: The Culture of the French and American Upper-Middle Class* (Chicago: University of Chicago Press, 1992) and in a volume she edited, *The Cultural Territories of Race: Black and White Boundaries* (Chicago: University of Chicago Press; New York: Russell Sage Foundation, 1999). It also is similar to a study Josh Gamson conducted on ACT-UP, the AIDS activist organization, in his article "Silence, Death, and the Invisible Enemy: AIDS Activism and Social Movement 'Newness.'" *Social Problems* 36 (1989): 351–67.

9. See, for example, Doug McAdam, Sidney Tarrow, and Charles Tilly, *Dynamics of Contention* (Cambridge: Cambridge University Press, 2001).

10. For more information on the social movement society concept, see David S. Meyer and Sidney Tarrow's *A Movement Society: Contentious Politics for a New Century* (New York: Rowman and Littlefield, 1998).

11. Comments made by Kim Voss at the annual meetings of the American Sociological Association, Washington, D.C., 2000.

12. For an important exception, see Marco Giugni, Doug McAdam, and Charles Tilly, eds., *How Social Movements Matter* (Minneapolis: University of Minnesota Press, 1999) and Fabio Rojas's "Social Movement Outcomes and Organizational Decision Making: An Analysis of the Establishment of the Black Studies and Women's Studies Programs," manuscript, Department of Sociology, University of Chicago, 2000. Language about the absence of this kind of work is taken from Marco Giugni's introduction to *How Social Movements Matter*— the idea that we know little about target organizatgions' ability to change is found in Rojas.

13. Tyack and Cuban, *Tinkering toward Utopia*.

14. This is Sidney Tarrow's description of contentious politics in *Power in Movement: Social Movements and Contentious Politics* (Cambridge: Cambridge University Press, 1998).

15. See also Donatella Della Porta's chapter called "Protest, Protesters, and Protest Policing: Public Discourses in Italy and Germany from the 1960s to the 1980s," in *How Social Movements Matter.*

16. Daniel Cress and David Snow have studied individuals and institutions they call "benefactors," who are sometimes targeted by social movements to advance their causes [see "Mobilization at the Margins: Resources, Benefactors, and the Viability of Homeless Social Movement Organizations," *American Sociological Review* 61 (1996): 1089–1109]. Benefactors differ from the institutional insiders I discuss, insofar as they do not reside in the home institution under challenge.

17. Tarrow, *Power in Movement.*

18. Kelly Moore is one researcher who has not overlooked the work that "fellow traveler" institutional members do for the challenging movement, as described in her chapter, "Political Protest and Institutional Change: The Anti-Vietnam War Movement and American Science," in *How Social Movements Matter.* She calls individuals who are members of a movement, and also professional members of an institution, "mediators" (p.104).

19. The specifics of these works will be described in chapter 7.

20. See McAdam, Tarrow, and Tilly, *Dynamics of Contention.*

21. See W. E. Douglas Creed and Maureen Scully, "More than Switchpersons on the Tracks of History: Situated Agency and Contested Legitimation during the Diffusion of Domestic Partner Benefits," unpublished paper.

22. Paul Burstein, "Social Movements and Public Policy" in *How Social Movements Matter.*

23. Kelly Moore, "Political Protest and Institutional Change."

24. This quote comes from Walter Powell's discussion of academic presses, *Getting into Print: The Decision-Making Process in Scholarly Publishing* (Chicago: University of Chicago Press, 1985), pp. 98–99.

25. Mary Katzenstein demonstrates contentiousness in the military and the Catholic church (*Faithful and Fearless*); Calvin Morrill describes contentiousness among the upper executives of business firms [*The Executive Way: Conflict Management in Organizations* (Chicago: University of Chicago Press, 1995)]; Kelly Moore shows how New Left politics entered what might have been considered the neutral territory of science organizations ("Political Protest and Institutional Change").

26. Tyack and Cuban, *Tinkering toward Utopia.*

27. See Rojas for an explanation of this in terms of universities' decisions to implement black studies and women's studies departments ("Social Movement Outcomes and Organizational Decision Making: An Analysis of the Establishment of the Black Studies and Women's Studies Programs").

28. Rojas (ibid.) provides a clear articulation of the differences between old and new institutionalism.

29. Katzenstein, *Faithful and Fearless.*

30. Rachel Moran distinguishes between these two strands of multiculturalism in her article "In the Multicultural Battle, Victory Is to the Weak," *Public Affairs Report*, published by the Institute of Governmental Studies, University of California, Berkeley, 1996.

31. Scott Davies also notes Christian conservatives' adoption of multicultural rhetoric in "From Moral Duty to Cultural Rights: A Case Study of Political Framing in Education," *Sociology of Education* 71 (1999): 1–23.

32. Michael Schudson has been instructive in theorizing "how culture works." For example, see his important article, "How Culture Works: Perspectives from Media Studies on the Efficacy of Symbols," *Theory and Society* 18 (1989): 153–80.

33. See Doug McAdam, John D. McCarthy, and Mayer Zald's edited volume, *Comparative Perspectives on Social Movements: Political Opportunities, Mobilizing Structures and Cultural Framings* (Cambridge: Cambridge University Press, 1996); Mario Diani, "Linking Mobilization Frames and Political Opportunities: Insights from Regional Populism in Italy," *American Sociological Review* 61 (1996): 1053–69; and Sidney Tarrow, *Power in Movement* for multiple examples of this call to researchers.

34. In "Framing Political Opportunity," William Gamson and David Meyer argue that challengers often *create* political opportunities; they do not just sit back and wait for them to occur (in *Comparative Perspectives on Social Movements*).

35. Elizabeth Clemens used this phrase while serving as a discussant on a panel on "institutional change" at the annual meetings of the American Sociological Association, Washington, D.C., August 2000.

36. I am very fortunate to be writing about these challengers and this challenged institution at a time when many others are doing parallel work—not on these particular challengers, per se, but in the study of both contentious politics and institutional change. Indeed, issues like those that I am considering in this project are "in the air" these days, animating studies in and out of the province of sociology. Whether begun as theoretical projects aimed at mapping the field, or as empirical studies that simply require more sophisticated tools for understanding challenger outcomes and institutional change, there is exciting work being done that addresses the topics of challenge processes and challenge outcomes. What makes this time especially productive for work in this area, I think, is that these many people—trained in different approaches for studying these issues—are expanding the tight boundaries of each subfield's purview.

37. Greg Thomas, "The Black Studies War: Multiculturalism versus Afrocentricity," *The Village Voice*, January 11–17, 1995.

38. For more information on the conflicts between the orthodox and progressives, see the disputed *Culture Wars* by James Davison Hunter; on creationist legal battles see Edward J. Larson, *Trial and Error: The American Controversy over Creation and Evolution* (New York: Oxford University Press, 1985); on the rise of the Religious Right, see Jerome Himmelstein, *To the Right: The Transformation of American Conservatism* (Berkeley: University of California Press, 1990); Stephen Bates, *Battleground: One Mother's Crusade, the Religious Right, and the Struggle for Our Schools* (New York: Henry Holt, 1993); and Joan DelFattore,

What Johnny Shouldn't Read: Textbook Censorship in America (New Haven: Yale University Press, 1992), among many others.

Chapter Two
The Challengers

1. Michael Dawson, *Black Visions: The Roots of African-American Political Ideologies* (Chicago: University of Chicago Press, forthcoming).

2. Ali Mazrui, Professor of Humanities at the State University of New York at Binghamton, has gone on record in support of *multicultural* revisions to curriculum, not Afrocentrism. But his attitude toward Afrocentrism is deeply respectful in that he seeks a synthesis between what he sees as Afrocentrism's full-scale African assault on Eurocentrism and multiculturalism's broader emphasis on universal challenges to European hegemony. I interviewed Ali Mazrui in 1995.

3. Thomas describes this history in "The Black Studies War."

4. Oyebade, "African Studies and the Afrocentric Paradigm," p. 233.

5. Ali Mazrui, "Afrocentricity versus Multiculturalism? A Dialectic in Search of a Synthesis." Paper delivered at the University of California, Los Angeles, May 5, 1993.

6. Bayo Oyebade, "African Studies and the Afrocentric Paradigm," p. 234.

7. Molefi Kete Asante, *Kemet, Afrocentricity, and Knowledge* (Trenton, N.J.: Africa World Press, 1990), 14.

8. Oyebade, "African Studies and the Afrocentric Paradigm."

9. Asante, *Kemet, Afrocentricity, and Knowledge*, p. 15.

10. Kariamu Welsh-Asante 1985, cited in Molefi Asante's *Kemet, Afrocentricity, and Knowledge*, p. 12.

11. Thomas, "The Black Studies War," p. 26.

12. For a critique of this enterprise, see Paul Gilroy's *The Black Atlantic: Modernity and Double Consciousness* (Cambridge: Harvard University Press, 1993).

13. See George James, *Stolen Legacy* (New York: Philosophical Library, 1954) on the stolen theories; *African-American Baseline Essays* (Portland, Ore.: Multnomah School District, 1987) for materials on astronomy and flight; and Ivan Van Sertima's "Future Directions for African and African-American Content in the School Curriculum," in *Infusion of African and African American Content in the School Curriculum: Proceedings of the First National Conference*, ed. Asa Hilliard III, Lucretia Payton-Stewart, Larry Obadele Williams (Chicago: Third World Press, 1990) on the Sphinx's nose. For a critique of this scholarship, see Bernard Ortiz de Montellano's "Afrocentric Pseudoscience: The Miseducation of African Americans" in *The Flight from Science and Reason*, ed. Paul R. Gross, Norman Levitt, and Martin W. Lewis (New York: New York Academy of Sciences, 1996); and Mary Lefkowitz' *Not Out of Africa: How Afrocentrism Became an Excuse to Teach Myth as History* (New York: Basic Books, 1996).

14. Interview with Abena Walker, founder and principal of the African-Centered School at Webb Elementary School, District of Columbia Public Schools, October 5–6, 1995.

15. Howard Winant, *Racial Conditions: Politics, Theory, Comparisons* (Minneapolis: University of Minnesota Press, 1994). "Ebonics," a relatively recent ini-

tiative concerning the use of black English in the instruction of students, can be thought of as another contemporary educational "racial project."

16. This is a point made in Manning Marable and Leith Mullings, "The Divided Mind of Black America: Race, Ideology, and Politics in the Post Civil Rights Era," *Race and Class* 36 (1994): 61–72.

17. Ibid. Marable and Mullings' is just one possible categorization of extant black ideologies. Another approach is offered in Dawson's *Black Visions*.

18. Marable and Mullings, "The Divided Mind of Black America," p. 67.

19. Michael Dawson, *Black Visions*.

20. Marable and Mullings, "The Divided Mind of Black America," p. 69.

21. Ibid.

22. Ibid., p. 70.

23. For data on African Americans' frustration in current times, see Howard Schuman, Charlotte Steeh, and Lawrence Bobo's book *Racial Attitudes in America* (Cambridge: Harvard University Press, 1985); Cornel West, "The Postmodern Crisis of Black Intellectuals," in *Cultural Studies*, ed. Lawrence Grossberg, Cary Nelson, and Paula Treichler (New York: Routledge, 1992); and Joe Feagin and Melvin Sikes, *Living with Racism: The Black Middle Class Experience* (Boston: Beacon Press, 1994).

24. In a personal communication, Michael Dawson told me that he had found that African Americans are divided in their allegiance to black nationalism: approximately 50 percent of black respondents to a recent national survey supported a mild form of black nationalism, while about 25 percent could be considered hardcore supporters. Respondents were not questioned about Afrocentrism, per se.

25. Molefi Kete Asante, "Racing to Leave the Race: Black Postmodernists Off-Track." *The Black Scholar* 23 (1993): 50–51.

26. Algernon Austin, "The Effect of Multicultural Education on the Academic Achievement of Black Students," unpublished paper, Center for Urban Affairs and Policy Research, Northwestern University, 1995, p.1.

27. Mazrui, "Afrocentricity versus Multiculturalism?" p. 1.

28. Joseph Raz, "Multiculturalism: A Liberal Perspective," *Dissent* 41 (Winter 1994): 73.

29. Mazrui, "Afrocentricity versus Multiculturalism?"

30. For a critique of the liberal-pluralist's "common culture" argument, see Henry Giroux, "Post-Colonial Ruptures and Democratic Possibilities: Multiculturalism as Anti-Racist Pedagogy," *Cultural Critique*, no. 21 (Spring 1992).

31. Moran, "In the Multicultural Battle."

32. Ibid., p. 1.

33. Ibid., p. 1. Also see Mazrui, "Afrocentricity versus Multiculturalism?" p. 2.

34. Making such rigid distinctions between Afrocentrism and multiculturalism, as I have done above, serves to describe the theoretical divide that separates the two movements. And yet, not surprisingly, on the ground level—e.g., in the school districts, where real reform efforts take place—this division becomes much murkier. Before endeavoring into this practical terrain, it is important to clarify terminology. When I refer to "multiculturalists" I mean one thing only: advocates of a broadened curriculum that includes the contributions of all previously neglected race and ethnic groups. By "Afrocentrist," on the other hand, I actually

include two types of challengers. There is, first, the ideal typical advocate of Afrocentrism: the self-identified Afrocentrist who concentrates on the needs of the African American student exclusively, not the Hispanic, Asian, Native American, etc. The second type of Afrocentrist I refer to are those people who may *philosophically* align themselves with the broader goals of multiculturalism (e.g., people who believe in including the contributions of all cultures in a reformed curriculum), but who, because of the context they find themselves in (for example a 90 percent or more black school system), choose to champion the Afrocentric reforms being waged in their districts. This latter group is generally typified by the "insider" supporter of the challenge, as I described in earlier sections: people who might not otherwise be recognized as a member of the challenging movement.

35. For more information on the identity conflicts that occur between Afrocentrists and multiculturalists, see Amy Binder, "Friend and Foe: Boundary Work and Collective Identity in the Afrocentric and Multicultural Curriculum Movements in American Public Education," in *The Cultural Territories of Race: Black and White Boundaries*.

36. Larson, *Trial and Error*.

37. Christopher P. Toumey, *God's Own Scientists: Creationists in a Secular World* (New Brunswick, N.J.: Rutgers University Press, 1994), p. 56, quoting Tim LaHaye, "The Religion of Secular Humanism," in *Public Schools and the First Amendment*, ed. S. M. Elam (Bloomington, Ind.: Phi Delta Kappa 1983), p. 3.

38. See Toumey's *God's Own Scientists*, for an example.

39. For more information on this, see the National Center for Science Education web site, "The Creation / Evolution Continuum," http://www.natcenscied. org/continuum.html (2000c); and Ronald Numbers's book *The Creationists* (New York: Alfred A. Knopf, 1992).

40. Numbers, *The Creationists*.

41. This is an explanation given by Keith Miller, an evangelical Christian and geologist at Kansas State University, who is not a young-earth creationist but who understands the movement. He explained these relationships in an interview he gave to the *Kansas City Star*, "Woman's Creationism Crusade Shakes Up Public Education," November 27, 1999, p. A1.

42. The young-earthers' ideas are laid out in such books as Henry Morris's own *The Troubled Waters of Evolution* (San Diego: Creation Life, 1974) and John Woodmorappe's publication *Noah's Ark: A Feasibility Study* (El Cajon, Calif.: Institute for Creation Research, 1996). In the latter, the author speculates on (and provides hypothesized calculations for) multiple technical requirements of the ark, including feeding schedules of all animals on board (taking into consideration the special needs of carnivores and herbivores, for example), the problem of waste disposal, and the labor power required for such tasks.

43. See Numbers' *The Creationists*, and the National Center for Science Education, "The Creation / Evolution Continuum."

44. National Center for Science Education, "The Creation / Evolution Continuum."

45. For more information on the concept of irreducibly complex systems, see the friendly descriptions by Michael Behe in *Darwin's Black Box: The Biochemical Challenge to Evolution* (New York: Touchstone, 1996), and by William

Dembski, "Origins" web site, http://www.origins.org/offices/dembski/docs/
bd-idesign.html (2000). For a critique of the concept, see the National Center
for Science Education, "The Creation / Evolution Continuum." Defining a system
that is too elaborate to have been formed randomly, Behe writes,

> "By *irreducibly complex*, I mean a single system composed of several well-matched,
> interacting parts that contribute to the basic function, wherein the removal of any one
> of the parts causes the system to effectively cease functioning. An irreducibly complex
> system cannot be produced directly (that is, by continuously improving the initial func-
> tion, which continues to work by the same mechanism) by slight successive modifica-
> tions of a precursor system, because any precursor to an irreducibly complex system
> that is missing a part is by definition nonfunctional. An irreducibly complex biological
> system, if there is such a thing, would be a powerful challenge to Darwinian evolution.
> Since natural selection can only choose systems that are already working, then if a
> biological system cannot be produced gradually it would have to arise as an integrated
> unit, in one fell swoop, for natural selection to have anything to act on" (39).

46. See the web site of the Access Research Network, http://www.arn.org/
arn (1997).

47. The most liberal statement of this view was most recently seen supported
in an October 1996 statement delivered by Pope John Paul II, which read that
"the theory of evolution [is] more than just a hypothesis." See Ronald Bailey,
"Origin of the Specious," *Reason* 29 (1997): 27.

48. John Wiester of the American Scientific Affiliation was helpful in explaining the meaning of this difference to me. Interview with John Wiester, December 4, 1996.

49. Both Larson, *Trial and Error*, p. 84, and Toumey, *God's Own Scientists*,
p. 26, describe this era of science teaching.

50. Toumey, *God's Own Scientists*.

51. Numbers, *The Creationists*.

52. National Center for Science Education web site, "Facing Challenges to
Evolution Education," http://www.natcenscied.org/tenchal.html (2000b).

53. *Epperson v. Arkansas* 1968 393 US 97; National Center for Science Education web site, "Seven Significant Court Decisions Regarding Evolution / Creation
Issues," http://www.natcenscied.org/courtdec.html (2000a).

54. Interview with Phillip Johnson, Professor at the Boalt School of Law, University of California, Berkeley, October 9, 1996.

55. Thomas McIver, "Creationism: Intellectual Origins, Cultural Context, and
Theoretical Diversity," Ph. D. diss., Department of Anthropology, University of
California, Los Angeles, 1989.

56. Larson, *Trial and Error*, pp. 126, 134.

57. Although I would have liked to have interviewed a random sample of teachers from each school system, as well, to examine how practitioners were handling
these controversies in their classrooms, I did not have the resources or time to
engage in such discussions.

58. While, ideally, I would have conducted interviews with many more central
actors in all of my sites, the nature of the project limited the amount of time

that I could devote to this endeavor. With seven cases in the comparison and vast numbers of activists, administrators, parents, teachers, legislators (in Louisiana), school board members (in Kansas, Vista, Atlanta, and Washington), state regents (in New York), and journalists in each case figuring into the decision making and opining, I decided to limit the number of interviews I would conduct. As noted above, I was not able to collect interview data in Louisiana because of the difficulty of locating people who had been involved in this case and were willing to talk about it with me. I attribute this reluctance to the time that has passed since the events took place (almost twenty years). Meanwhile, I decided to forego interviews in Kansas because of the late addition of this case to the project. While I am convinced that interviews would certainly be valuable for understanding this case, I do not believe they were necessary for explaining events there.

59. See McAdam, McCarthy, and Zald, *Comparative Perspectives on Social Movements*, and McAdam, Tarrow, and Tilly, *Dynamics of Contention*, for a description of the first; and Diani, "Linking Mobilization Frames and Political Opportunities," for an example of the latter.

60. Marco Giugni, "How Social Movements Matter: Past Research, Present Problems, Future Developments," in *How Social Movements Matter*.

Chapter Three
History of the Three Afrocentric Cases: Atlanta, Washington, D.C., and New York State

1. This is the way that Scott Davies talks about frames in "The Changing Meaning of Progressive Pedagogy: Justifying School Reform in Three Eras," paper presented to Political Sociology Workshop, Department of Sociology, Stanford University, October 2000.

2. Nathan Glazer, *We Are All Multiculturalists Now* (Cambridge: Harvard University Press, 1997).

3. Interview with Abena Walker, founder and principal of the African-Centered School at Webb Elementary Schools, District of Columbia Public Schools, 1995.

4. "Curriculum Seeks to Lift Blacks' Self-Image," *New York Times*, March 8, 1989, p. A1.

5. "Portland, Ore., Schools Lead Way in Teaching Black Culture 'In Every Classroom,'" *Atlanta Journal-Constitution*, January 29, 1989, p. A14.

6. Portland Public Schools web site, http://www.pps.k12.or.us/district/depts/mc-me/essays.shtml.

7. *African-American Baseline Essays*, p. ii.

8. Ibid., p. iv.

9. Portland Public Schools web site, http://www.pps.k12.or.us/district/depts/mc-me/essays.shtml.

10. Ibid.

11. For an example, see Lefkowitz, *Not Out of Africa*.

12. Interview with Murdell McFarlin, former public information officer, Superintendent's Office, Atlanta Public School System, 1995.

13. Interview with Mae Kendall, former director of Program Planning and Curriculum Development in the Atlanta Public School System, 1995.

14. Ibid.

15. Ibid.; "City Schools Skim Over Black History," *Atlanta Journal-Constitution*, January 29, 1989, p. A1.

16. "Expert Calls on Black Educators to Stop Blaming Woes on Others," *Atlanta Journal-Constitution*, December 4, 1988, p. A2.

17. Ibid.

18. One account of this story is found in "City Schools Skim Over Black History," p. A1. I also heard this version of events in an interview with Gladys Twyman, project coordinator of the African American Infusion Program in the Atlanta Public School System, 1995.

19. "Expert Calls on Black Educators to Stop Blaming Woes on Others," p. A2.

20. Ibid.

21. Ibid.

22. I learned this in an interview with Mae Kendall, 1995.

23. Interview with Cathy Loving, district archivist for the Atlanta Public School System, 2000.

24. Interview with Gladys Twyman, 1995.

25. Interview with Murdell McFarlin, 1995.

26. My interviewees who recalled whites' reservations were Mae Kendall and Murdell McFarlin (interviews with each respondent, 1995). Others who recall enthusiastic support for the proposal include Midge Sweet, a board member of the Atlanta Public Schools (interview 1995), and a past board member who prefers anonymity (interview 1995). An article called "Taking Pride in Their Heritage" (*Atlanta Journal-Constitution* February 1990, p. C6) describes the massive teacher training in the district, and quotes one white teacher who expressed reservations about "being blamed for something I didn't do."

27. "City Schools Skim Over Black History," p. A1.

28. "Portland, Ore., Schools Lead Way in Teaching Black Culture 'In Every Classroom,'" p. A14.

29. "Taking Pride in Their Heritage," p. C6.

30. Interview with Betsy White, former education reporter for the *Atlanta Journal-Constitution*, 1995.

31. Communication with Betsy White, 2001.

32. Interviews with Murdell McFarlin, 1995, and Cathy Loving, 2000. Unfortunately, I was not able to look at the board minutes for this meeting.

33. In fact, there is yet a fourth account of the program's origins, related to me by school board member D. F. Glover, who claimed that *he* had introduced the idea of Afrocentrism in Atlanta. On the school board from 1981 to 1993, Glover was frequently criticized for being antagonistic toward whites, generally; hostile toward other board members, black or white; and in many other ways an embarrassment to the board. For a number of reasons, Glover's account of the program's beginnings seems less credible than the other three. Interview with D. F. Glover, professor in the Department of Social Science, Morris Brown College, former board member of the Atlanta Public Schools, 1995.

34. Interview with Gladys Twyman, 1995.

35. "From K to 12, Afrocentrism Has Made the Grade in Atlanta," *Washington Post*, October 17, 1993, p. B1.

36. Interview with Mae Kendall, 1995.

37. This trainer asked to remain anonymous.

38. Interview with Betsy White, 1995.

39. Interview with Murdell McFarlin, 1995.

40. "From K to 12, Afrocentrism Has Made the Grade in Atlanta," p. B1.

41. Interview with Midge Sweet, 1995.

42. "Black History Month: Lessons in Cultural Awareness; Schools' Observances Taking On a New Look," *Atlanta Journal-Constitution*, February 24, 1992, p. C2.

43. "D.C. Schools Seek To Rekindle Flame of Pride in Black Heritage," *Washington Post*, April 23, 1989, p. B1.

44. "Grant Furthers Afro-Centric Solution in D.C. Schools," *Washington Post*, December 21, 1989, p. J3.

45. Ibid.

46. Interview with Betty Topps, executive assistant to the superintendent, District of Columbia Public Schools, 1995.

47. "By Picking Smith, the School Board Finally Gets Its Outsider," *Washington Post*, April 25, 1991, p. J3.

48. "D.C. School Board Discusses Plan to Oust Jenkins," *Washington Post*, July 3, 1990, p. B1.

49. Interview with Betty Topps, 1995.

50. "Schools Urged to Adopt Afro-Centric Curriculum," *Washington Post*, February 2, 1989, p. J7.

51. "D.C. Schools Seek to Rekindle Flame of Pride in Black Heritage," p. B1.

52. "'Afrocentrism' and the Tribalization of America; The Misguided Logic of Ethnic Education Schemes," *Washington Post*, September 23, 1990, p. B1.

53. Interview with Russell Adams, professor and chair of African American Studies, Howard University, 1995.

54. "A Time for Learning," *Washington Post*, December 3, 1990, p. D3, and "Toward a New Curriculum; Seminar Focuses on Effort to Make Studies Afro-Centric," *Washington Post* December 14, 1989, p. J1.

55. Interview with Abena Walker, 1995.

56. "Afrocentric Education Would Benefit All," *Washington Post*, November 19, 1990, p. B3.

57. "A Center of Controversy: Sketchy Plans, Racial Issues Mire Afrocentric Project, *Washington Post*, September 13, 1993, p. B1.

58. At the same time that the district committed resources to the Walkers' Afrocentric curriculum, according to an article in the *Washington Post*, "Participants Laud Afrocentric Program, Blast Media" (September 23, 1993, p. B1), it spent another portion of the $750,000 on developing a different arm of the program. With these funds, the district brought in several of the nation's best-known Afrocentric scholars to lecture in 1989 and 1990. These seminars gave the scholars an opportunity to discuss a variety of potential projects with district administrators and school principals. Just as he had taken part in the Portland and Atlanta pro-

grams, Asa Hilliard came to Washington, D.C., as one of the earliest visitors to the district, arriving in December 1989 to meet with 200 district personnel (see "Toward a New Curriculum: Seminar Focuses on Effort to Make Studies Afro-Centric" in the *Washington Post* (December 14, 1989, p. J1). Constance Clark, then a curriculum director, also remembers that several district personnel also traveled to Atlanta at district expense to meet one-on-one with Hilliard, and curriculum directors made a trip to Portland to become acquainted with the implementation of Hilliard's *Baseline Essays* in that school system (interview with Constance Clark, deputy superintendent for educational programs and operations, District of Columbia Public Schools, 1995).

59. "Jenkins to Stay On for Final Year; Board Backs Down Under Pressure, Superintendent's Resolve," *Washington Post*, July 13, 1990, p. A1.

60. "D.C. School Board Discusses Plans to Oust Jenkins," p. B1.

61. "Jenkins to Stay On for Final Year," p. A1.

62. Ibid.

63. "Reform or Political Football? Afrocentrism in Spotlight in Jenkins Firing," *Washington Post*, December 6, 1990, p. C1.

64. "Jenkins Aides Mobilize Fight To Keep D.C. School Chief," *Washington Post*, November 30, 1990, p. B1.

65. Ibid.

66. Ibid.

67. "Reform or Political Football?" p. C1.

68. Ibid.

69. "A New View from the Top; Franklin Smith's Agenda," *Washington Post*, August 29, 1991, p. J6.

70. Interviews with Abena Walker, 1995, and Constance Clark, 1995.

71. "Smith Gives Afrocentric Program Less Than a Passing Grade," *Washington Post*, September 2, 1993, p. C1.

72. "D.C. Afrocentric Program In Trouble as Term Nears; Deadline Is Today for Curriculum Revisions," *Washington Post*, September 3, 1993, p. B3.

73. "Smith Gives Afrocentric Program Less Than a Passing Grade," p. C1.

74. "Unlicensed College Provided D.C. Afrocentric Training," *Washington Post*, August 14, 1993, p. A1.

75. "Smith Gives Afrocentric Program Less Than a Passing Grade," p. C1.

76. Ibid.

77. Interview with Constance Clark, 1995.

78. "Smith Gives Afrocentric Program Less Than a Passing Grade," p. C1.

79. Ibid. Smith added that the only reason why Walker had withheld more information about her well-developed curriculum, in the first place, was her concern that other people might steal her teaching ideas and methods if she were to make them public ("Afrocentric Program Gets Go-Ahead; Schools Chief Says He Trusts Consultant," *Washington Post*, September 4, 1993, p. A1).

80. "Afrocentric Program Gets Go-Ahead," p. A1.

81. "The Year in Review: 1993," *Washington Post*, December 30, 1993, p. J1.

82. "District to Expand Afrocentric Classes, Superintendent Plans To Open Similar Program at 2nd School" *Washington Post*, July 25, 1994, p. B1.

83. Just as Smith announced his plan to expand the Webb school-within-a-school program by one classroom in 1994, other school officials were dispatched to announce that the district soon would be opening its preferred African-centered program that fall in one of the district's high schools. This program was to be called the African Centered / Multicultural High School at Spingarn High School. It would teach approximately eighty ninth-grade students, and the district made clear that it would be totally unrelated to the Webb program or to Abena Walker. This point was made explicit in press releases and conferences issued by the school district. Juxtaposing the new program to the Webb program, officials announced that the Spingarn curriculum "is grounded in sound research and practice," and had been developed with the help of the Smithsonian Institution and Howard University, two of the most prestigious and respected institutions in the city. (See "District to Expand Afrocentric Classes," p. B1, and "Specialist Favors Expansion of District's Afrocentric Curriculum," *Washington Post*, September 22, 1994, p. A17.)

84. District of Columbia Public Schools, web site, http://www.k12.dc.us/DCPS/curriculum/stanford9/stanford9_intro.html (1998).

85. Interview with Abena Walker, 1995.

86. Thomas Sobol, former commissioner of education for the state of New York, talked about his decision in an interview I conducted with him in 1995. Another account of this story can be found in Catherine Cornbleth and Dexter Waugh, *The Great Speckled Bird: Multicultural Politics and Education Policymaking* (New York: St. Martin's, 1995).

87. "Education Watch; From Scarsdale to Albany," *New York Times*, March 29, 1987, section 4, p. 6.

88. Interview with Linda Biemer, former dean of the School of Education, State University of New York, Binghamton, and co-chair of the New York State Curriculum Assessment Committee, 1995.

89. "Education Commissioner Confounds His Critics," *New York Times*, February 14, 1990, p. B1.

90. Thomas Sobol quoted in "Lessons," *New York Times*, February 7, 1990, p. B5.

As in many other states, New York's curriculum guides, or frameworks, provide information on the general skills and knowledge that its students are expected to acquire during their public school careers in each curriculum area (such as science, social studies, mathematics, etc.). Generally, frameworks consist of multiple parts and guidelines, including a "rationale or platform" for the curriculum area (description of the values, assumptions, and principles used to draft the framework); the "scope and parameters of the curriculum area; the broad goals and purposes of subjects within the curriculum area; guidelines for course design; content; teaching and learning principles; [and] guidelines for evaluation of subjects," among others (see Colin Marsh, *Key Concepts for Understanding Curriculum* [London: Falmer, 1992]). Although it is only advisory, the content of the guidelines is sometimes interpreted to be a symbol of various constituencies' relative power in the system, and so, from time to time, it is at the center of controversy throughout the state.

91. For examples of this critique, see the following articles from the *New York times*: "New York Education Chief Seeks New Stress on Nonwhite Cultures," February 7, 1990, p. A1; "Now the Critics Must Decide If History Will Be Recast," February 11, 1990, section 4, p. 5; "A Tough Test for the Regents, April 27, 1990, p. A34; and "Education Chief: At Eye of Diversity Storm," August 1, 1991, p. B1. In an interview I conducted in 1995, Diane Ravitch, a professor in the School of Education at New York University, and former assistant secretary of education in the first Bush administration, stated the same criticisms.

92. "New York Education Chief Seeks New Stress on Nonwhite Cultures," p. A1, and "Lessons," p. B5.

93. Interview with Linda Biemer, 1995.

94. Interview with Thomas Sobol, 1995.

95. For a discussion of this negotiability, see also Glazer, *We Are All Multiculturalists Now*, and Steven Brint, *Schools and Societies* (Thousand Oaks, Calif.: Pine Forge Press, 1998).

96. Interview with Hazel Dukes, director of the New York chapter of the NAACP and chair of the New York State Task Force on Minorities: Excellence and Equity, 1995.

97. From "Curriculum of Inclusion," 1989, p. 4. See New York State Education Department Social Studies Committee, "Curriculum, Instruction, and Assessment Preliminary Draft Framework," 1995.

98. Interview with Leonard Jeffries, professor and former chair in the Department of Black Studies, City College of New York, 1995; and consultant to the New York State Special Task Force on Minorities: Equity and Excellence, "Curriculum of Inclusion," 1989.

99. Interview with Leonard Jeffries, 1995.

100. John Leo, "Multicultural Follies," *U.S. News and World Report*, July 8, 1991, p. 12.

101. New York State Special Task Force on Minorities: Equity and Excellence, "Curriculum of Inclusion," 1989.

102. When asked years later whether that report should be considered "Afrocentric," respondents gave a variety of responses ranging from an adamant yes to an equally indignant no. Tom Sobol, who ultimately was hurt badly by his connection with that report, said in his 1995 interview with me, "I think it was [Afrocentric] in many ways, and I'm not surprised by that. If you ask a group of people to tell you what they think, and they are not a group of people whose opinion is ordinarily solicited by people in officialdom—as this was not—then what you are apt to get . . . is not only what they think, but what they feel. And what came out was a great deal of pent-up anger at the way they *felt*."

According to others, however, the "Inclusion" report should *not* be seen as Afrocentric, since "the African American section of that document makes up [only] one-fourth" of the entire document, said Virginia Sanchez Korrol, professor and chair of Puerto Rican Studies, Brooklyn College, New York, in our 1995 interview. Unlike Asa Hilliard's *Baseline Essays*, to which Sanchez Korrol readily attached the Afrocentric label, "Inclusion" did not deserve to be called Afrocentrism, she said.

103. Interviews with Virginia Sanchez Korrol, 1995; and Diane Ravitch, 1995.

104. Interview with Virginia Sanchez Korrol, 1995.

105. Interview with Diane Ravitch, 1995.

106. Ibid.

107. Adelaide Sanford is quoted in "Education Chief: At Eye of Diversity Storm," *New York Times*, August 1, 1991, p. B1; Diane Ravitch recounted her response in our 1995 interview.

108. Interview with Walter Cooper, Member of the New York Board of Regents, 1995.

109. "Lessons," p. B5.

110. See Glazer, *We Are All Multiculturalists Now* (p. 24) for an account of the letter.

111. Interview with Thomas Sobol, 1995.

112. "Regents Approve Panel on New Ethnic Studies," *New York Times*, April 28, 1990, section 1, p. 29.

113. Glazer, *We Are All Multiculturalists Now*.

114. Interview with Thomas Sobol, 1995.

115. Interview with Linda Biemer, 1995.

116. Diane Ravitch based her skepticism surrounding the ability of the group to produce a credible report on three observations. She argued, first, that "the existing history curriculum [was] not biased against any race or ethnic group; no doubt it [could have been] improved, but it [was] not biased; second, the recommendations were based on a task force report that contain[ed] a good deal of deeply objectionable anti-white and anti-Western rhetoric; and third, the proposals of the task force would [have] encourage[d] particularism, rather than critical thinking." The last quote can be found in a letter to the editor Ravitch sent to the *New York Times* (February 28, 1990, p. A26). The content from the rest of the paragraph was obtained in an interview with Diane Ravitch in 1995.

117. Cornbleth and Waugh, "The Great Speckled Bird"; interviews with Virginia Sanchez Korrol, 1995, and Ali Mazrui, Professor of the Humanities, State University of New York, Binghamton, 1995.

118. Follow-up interview with Virginia Sanchez Korrol, 2001.

119. Interview with Nathan Glazer, 1995.

120. Nathan Glazer, *We Are All Multiculturalists Now*.

121. Nathan Glazer's ambivalence is not hard to discern. In his own written account of the New York commission on which he served, he writes that the "quality" of the report . . . "was not distinguished." He goes on to say that the "report wended its way in educationese through various uncontroversial themes, as is typical of all educational curricular reports, and avoided inflammatory writing" (*We Are All Multiculturalists Now*).

122. See Arthur Schlesinger, Jr., "Report of the [New York State] Social Studies Syllabus Review Committee: A Dissenting Opinion," in "One Nation, Many Peoples: A Declaration of Cultural Interdependence," 1991, pp. 45–47; and Kenneth Jackson, "A Dissenting Comment," in "One Nation, Many Peoples," pp. 39–40.

123. "Arguing about America; A Common Culture or a Land of Diversity? That Is the Curriculum Debate in New York," *New York Times*, June 21, 1991, p. A1.

124. Thomas Sobol and the New York State Education Department, "Understanding Diversity" memo, 1991, p. 12.

125. Interview with Thomas Sobol, 1995.

126. Interview with Leonard Jeffries, 1995.

127. Jeffries also paid dearly for having made this speech. Following its delivery, the City College of New York stripped Jeffries of his chairmanship of the black studies department, and hired Edmund Gordon away from Yale to take his place. This was the same Edmund Gordon, of course, who had headed the New York State Social Studies Syllabus Review and Development Committee, or "Diversity Committee." After losing the position of chair, Jeffries did remain in the department as full professor.

128. Interview with Virginia Sanchez Korrol, 1995.

129. Interview with Linda Biemer, 1995.

130. Interview with Ali Mazrui, 1995.

131. Personal correspondence with Virginia Sanchez Korrol, 2001.

132. Interview with Diane Ravitch, 1995.

133. Interview with Leonard Jeffries, 1995.

Chapter Four
Cultural, Political, and Organizational
Factors Influencing Afrocentric Outcomes

1. Scott Davies has written about the "master frame" of progressivism in the public education arena in his paper "The Changing Meaning of Progressive Pedagogy: Justifying School Reform in Three Eras."

2. Gamson and Modigliani, "Media Discourse and Public Opinion on Nuclear Power"; David Snow and Robert Benford, "Master Frames and Cycles of Protest" in *Frontiers in Social Movement Theory*, eds. Aldon Morris and Carol McClurg Mueller (New Haven: Yale University Press, 1992).

3. In *We Are All Multiculturalists Now*, Nathan Glazer writes that all of us seem to be "ranged along a spectrum of greater or lesser enthusiasm or acceptance of the new reality" of multiculturalism, even multiculturalism's critics. "Those who truly stand against it, the true advocates and prophets of assimilationism, are so miniscule in American public and intellectual life that they can barely be discerned in public discussion" (p. 97). This is an obvious argument for the power of the Afrocentrists' rhetoric that "something must be done" along more multicultural lines.

4. It also drew upon the frame of progressivism. As Scott Davies has written persuasively in "The Changing Meaning of Progressive Pedagogy," the "master frame" of progressive pedagogy pervades the public education arena, such that challengers of many different stripes now argue that their reform falls under the progressivist label. Afrocentrists used the theme of progressivism to tap into educators' underlying assumptions about teaching children content that is meaningful to them—not just teaching by rote; treating them like unique individuals, not just undifferentiated tabulae rase. Progressives since John Dewey, Davies argues, have "championed their pedagogy as necessary for keeping pace with an ever-changing society, while claiming that traditionalists, lacking developmental sensitivity, have

been outmoded by new social realities." Afrocentric champions picked up on this rhetoric, presenting their solution to the problem of black children's miseducation as sensitive, humanistic, and caring.

5. Kris Parker, opinion-editorial, "A Survival Curriculum for Inner-City Kids," *New York Times*, September 9, 1989, section 1, p. 23.

6. Interview with Mae Kendall, 1995.

7. Interview with Gladys Twyman, 1995.

8. Interview with Betty Topps, 1995.

9. Interview with Nathan Glazer, 1995.

10. Glazer, *We Are All Multiculturalists Now*, p. 77. Ali Mazrui shared a similar thought during our interview (1995). He said that quintessentially "economic" and "political" remedies had already been tried in this country to correct African Americans' low relative status: affirmative action and civil rights, respectively. Afrocentrists were presenting a remedy that was different: a *cultural* solution.

11. Interview with Abena Walker, 1995.

12. Interview with Thomas Sobol, 1995.

13. Interview with Murdell McFarlin, 1995.

14. Interview with Abena Walker, 1995.

15. Interview with Walter Cooper, 1995.

16. Interview with Hazel Dukes, 1995.

17. Interview with Thomas Sobol, 1995.

18. For the conservative stance, see D'Souza, *Illiberal Education*; Bennett, *The Devaluing of America*; Gross, Levitt, and Lewis, eds., *The Flight from Science and Reason*; Paul Gross and Norman Levitt, *Higher Superstition: The Academic Left and Its Quarrel with Science* (Baltimore: Johns Hopkins University Press, 1994).

19. The factors that I discovered coincide remarkably well with the list of factors that Michael Fullan and others in the "reform implementation" literature have developed to describe the implementation of reform in school systems. See Michael Fullan, *The Meaning of Educational Change* (Toronto: OISE, 1982); Michael Fullan and Allan Pomfret, "Research in Curriculum and Instruction Implementation," *Review of Educational Research* 47 (1977): 335–97; Colin Marsh, *Key Concepts for Understanding Curriculum*. Fullan and other authors have found four types of factors that combine to determine an "innovation's" success in getting implemented in schools: attributes of the innovation, itself; characteristics of the school system; characteristics of the school as a unit; and factors external to the local school system, such as the political winds of the time. I focus on just two of these factors: "characteristics of the school system" and "factors external to the school system"; and of these two, I place the weight of my analysis on Fullan's "characteristics of the school system," or what I am calling the system's local organizational particularities. Remember that I do not have to deal with the "attributes of the innovation" here since this factor is being held constant across all three cases (the cultural arguments for Afrocentrism), and Fullan's third factor (the school as a unit) is not applicable in my project as a factor to investigate, since I look at only *system-wide* adoption, and not at *school-by-school* implementation.

20. U.S. Department of Education, web site, 1999 at http://nces.ed.gov/pubs/digest97/d97t045.html.

21. Colin Marsh, Christopher Day, Lynne Hannay, and Gail McCutcheon, *Reconceptualizing School-Based Curriculum Development* (London: Falmer, 1990).

22. Karen Diegmueller comments on several of these in "Controversy Predicted over New York Social Studies Framework." *Education Week on the Web*, http://www.edweek.org/ew/1995/39social.h14 (June 21, 1995).

23. An anonymous reviewer helped me recognize this point.

24. Fullan and Pomfret, "Research in Curriculum and Instruction Implementation."

25. The idea of educational charters is explored in Carolyn Hodges Persell and Peter Cookson, Jr., "Chartering and Bartering: Elite Education and Social Reproduction." *Social Problems* 33 (1985): 114–29.

26. Again, Howard Winant's writing about "racial projects" is instructive (*Racial Conditions*, 1994).

27. Interview with Russell Adams, professor and chair of African American Studies, Howard University, 1995.

28. Some outside critics have come to see Smith's decision, itself, as a "miscalculation." I attribute these insights to Russell Adams, ibid.

29. Bork, *Slouching towards Gomorrah*.

30. For a discussion of the variety of multicultural forms and implementation processes, see Olneck, "Terms of Inclusion: Has Multiculturalism Redefined Equality in American Education?"

31. Glazer, *We Are All Multiculturalists Now*, p. 27.

32. Doug McAdam, "Conceptual Origins, Current Problems, Future Directions" in *Comparative Perspectives on Social Movements*, p. 33.

33. See, for example, the article in the *Atlanta Journal-Constitution* "Portland, Ore., Schools Lead Way in Teaching Black Culture in Every Classroom," p. A14.

34. John Meyer and Brian Rowan use the term "loose coupling" to describe the relationship between formal rules and everyday practices in institutions such as schools; see "Institutional Organizations: Formal Structure as Myth and Ceremony," *American Journal of Sociology* 83 (1977): 340–63.

35. For information on teachers' aversion to change, see Dan Lortie's *Schoolteacher* (Chicago: University of Chicago Press, 1975); for evidence of teachers' willingness to change when their own performance is evaluated, see Marsh, *Key Concepts For Understanding Curriculum*.

36. Interview with Mae Kendall, 1995.

37. Interview with Murdell McFarlin, 1995.

38. Interview with Betsy White, 1995.

39. Communication with Betsy White, May 4, 2001.

40. New York State Social Studies Syllabus Review and Development Committee, "One Nation, Many Peoples: A Declaration of Cultural Independence," 1991, p. 15.

41. Interview with Linda Biemer, 1995.

42. "Portland, Ore., Schools Lead Way in Teaching Black Culture 'in Every Classroom,'" p. A14.

43. Interview with Betsy White, 1995.

44. Articles from the *Atlanta Journal-Constitution*, in order of reference: January 31, 1989, p. A10; February 19, 1990, p. C1; May 27, 1990, p. G2; February 2, 1991, p. C1; and March 1, 1991, p. A18.

45. Aldon Morris makes a similar point in "Reflections on Social Movement Theory: Criticisms and Proposals," *Contemporary Sociology*, 29 (2000): 445–54.

Chapter Five
History of the Four Creationist Cases: Louisiana State, California State, Vista, California, and Kansas State

1. "American Civil Liberties Union Takes the Theory to Court in Arkansas," *New Orleans Times-Picayune*, December 6, 1981, p. 16.

2. Wendell Bird quoted in "Creation Theorists Monkey in Science," *New Orleans Times-Picayune*, December 18, 1978, p. 6.

3. "Reagan Swipes at Darwin," *New Orleans Times-Picayune*, September 3, 1980, p. 17.

4. This account of the Arkansas bill is found in Toumey, *God's Own Scientists*, p. 40.

5. "Scientists Gear Up for Fight To Halt Spread of Creationism," *New Orleans Times-Picayune*, May 16, 1982, section 7, p. 10.

6. This is the statement that appeared on the ICR website, October 10, 2000, http://www.icr.org/.

7. "Creationism Teaching Bill Becomes Law," *New Orleans Times-Picayune*, July 22, 1981, p. A1.

8. Ibid.

9. "Equal Time for Creationism Passes House," *New Orleans Times-Picayune*, July 7, 1981, p. A1; and "Creation Bill Goes to Treen," *New Orleans Times-Picayune*, July 9, 1981, p. A1, respectively.

10. "Louisiana To Teach 'Creation,' " *New York Times*, July 22, 1981, p. A5.

11. National Center for Science Education web site, "Seven Significant Court Decisions Regarding Evolution / Creation Issues" http://www.natcenscied.org/courtdec.html (2000a).

12. This is the same John Whitehead of the Rutherford Institute who would later offer to help pay for any lawsuits arising in Vista, California, following the school board's decision to institute the Sex Respect sex education program. It is also the same John Whitehead whose institute later footed many of Paula Jones's legal bills in her sexual harassment case against President Bill Clinton in the late 1990s.

13. "2 Area Lawmakers Prefile Bill To Repeal Law on Creationism," *New Orleans Times-Picayune*, February 3, 1982, p. A22; "One Battle Lost, Creationists Regroup for Second Round," *New York Times*, March 7, 1982, section 4, p. 20.

14. According to an article, "Creationism Suit Trial Pushed by Guste," in the *New Orleans Times-Picayune* (May 4, 1982, p. A13), the ACLU made two motions to dismiss the suit, both of them on technical grounds. The first of these motions was made by the State Board of Elementary and Secondary Education (BESE), which claimed that the state legislature had no authority, according to the Louisiana constitution, to determine public school curricula. BESE claimed

that the authority to determine curriculum belonged to it, and only it. The second motion for summary judgment was made by another defendant—a local school district represented by the ACLU—which argued that state law was at issue in this case, not federal law. It was this argument that ended up persuading the judge in Baton Rouge and that led him to dismiss the case.

15. "Public Schools Board Switches, Asks End of Creationism Law," *New Orleans Times-Picayune*, October 7, 1982, p. B6.

16. "Education Board Takes Sides against Law on Creationism," *New Orleans Times-Picayune*, January 29, 1982, p. A4.

17. "Public Schools Board Switches, Asks End of Creationism Law," p. B6.

18. "Education Board Takes Sides against Law on Creationism," p. A4.

19. The state Supreme Court's decision is quoted in "Louisiana Court Upholds Law on 'Creationism,'" *New York Times*, October 18, 1983, p. A16.

20. Ibid.

21. Du plantier's quote can be found in "Creation Law Invalid, Judge Rules," *New Orleans Times-Picayune*, January 11, 1985, p. A1.

22. "La. Creationism Law Won't Get Rehearing," *New Orleans Times-Picayune*, December 13, 1985, p. A38; "High Court Will Review Creationism," *New Orleans Times-Picayune*, May 6, 1986, p. A17.

23. "Creationists Assert They Hold a Scientific View," *New York Times*, September 2, 1986, p. C8; see also Joan DelFattore, *What Johnny Shouldn't Read*.

24. Gould's quote is found in "Nobel Laureates Fight against Creationism Law," *New Orleans Times-Picayune*, August 19, 1986, p. A1.

25. "Creationists Assert They Hold a Scientific View," p. C8; amici curiae brief 1985, submitted to the U.S. Supreme Court in support of the appellants in *Edwards v. Aguillard*, 482 U.S. 578.

26. Toumey, *God's Own Scientists*, p. 46.

27. "Suit over Creationism Reaches Supreme Court," *New Orleans Times-Picayune*, December 10, 1986, p. B1.

28. "Creationists Assert They Hold a Scientific View," p. C8.

29. "Creationist Law Aired before Supreme Court," *New Orleans Times-Picayune*, December 11, 1986, p. A1.

30. Ibid.

31. "High Court Voids Curb on Teaching Evolution Theory," *New York Times*, June 20, 1987, p. A1.

32. "La.'s Creationism Law Struck Down," *New Orleans Times-Picayune*, June 20, 1987, p. A1.

33. "High Court Voids Curb on Teaching Evolution Theory," p. A1.

34. "La.'s Creationism Law Struck Down," p. A1.

35. Lawrence Tribe, "Despite Defeats, Fundamentalists Vow To Press Efforts To Reshape Schools," *New York Times*, August 29, 1987, p. A6.

36. Stephen Jay Gould, "The Verdict on Creationism," *New York Times*, Sunday Magazine, July 19, 1987, p. 32.

37. "Revised Science Textbooks Win State Board Approval," *Los Angeles Times*, December 14, 1985, p. A1.

38. "Publishers Adapt to Meet State's Evolution Criterion," *Los Angeles Times*, November 10, 1985, p. A3. California's adoption process has several steps,

and involves a number of parties: specially appointed panels, state education department staff, the state board of education, and textbook publishers, among others. First, an Instructional Materials Evaluation Panel, made up of teachers, master teachers, professors, and curriculum experts in each of the disciplines (e.g., science, math, history) reads new textbooks proposed for the next seven-year cycle and considers their correspondence with the curriculum frameworks currently in place. They then make recommendations to an appointed Curriculum Commission regarding which books should be used in California classrooms, and which should not. The Curriculum Commission, then, proposes to the state board of education a list of five to fifteen texts in each subject area to be used in each grade. Finally, the board votes to approve or reject the recommendation, ordinarily voting with the recommendation it has received from the Curriculum Commission. At that point, the framework is distributed to textbook publishers to make alterations, if they wish for California to use their books.

39. Toumey, *God's Own Scientists*.

40. For more on this, see ibid., p. 37.

41. To read more about this case, see Joan DelFattore, *What Johnny Shouldn't Read*.

42. "Coast School Policy Upheld on Teaching of Evolution," *New York Times*, March 7, 1981, p. A9.

43. "Education Chief's Bandwagon Rolling; Feverish Pace By Honig Builds a Wide Consensus," *Los Angeles Times*, November 3, 1985, p. A1. George Deukmejian served as governor of California from 1983 to 1991.

44. "Panel Urges Rejection of Texts Short on Evolution," *Los Angeles Times*, August 25, 1985, p. A3.

45. This piece of information was contained in an editorial, "Survival of the Fittest," *Los Angeles Times*, August 29, 1985, p. B4.

46. Ibid.

47. "State Orders More Stress on Evolution in Textbooks; Rejects Seven Books as Inadequate," *Los Angeles Times*, September 13, 1985, p. A6.

48. Although, as the *Los Angeles Times* noted, two board members—one from Long Beach and another from San Pedro—believed that the books contained "too much evolution already." But after urging the book panel to scren out "dogmatic" statements on behalf of evolution, both voted with other members to have the books revised. See "State Orders More Stress on Evolution in Textbooks," p. A6; "Textbooks' Treatment of Man's Origin Spawns Debate," *Los Angeles Times*, September 13, 1985, p. A23; See "State Board of Education Rejects New Science Books," *Los Angeles Times*, September 14, 1985, p. A1.

49. "Publishers Adapt To Meet State's Evolution Criterion," p. A3.

50. "Revised Texts Inadequate on Evolution, Scientists Say," *Los Angeles Times*, December 7, 1985, p. A1.

51. Padian quoted in the article "Revised Texts Inadequate on Evolution, Scientists Say," p. A1.

52. "Revised Science Textbooks Win State Board Approval," *Los Angeles Times*, December 14, 1985, p. A1.

53. Ibid.

54. Honig is quoted in "Revised Science Textbooks Win State Board Approval," p. A1.

55. Interview with Kevin Padian, associate professor of Integrative Biology and curator of the Museum of Paleontology at the University of California, Berkeley, 1996. He is also a former member of the Science Subject Matter Committee of the State of California.

56. "Panel Oks Strengthening of Science Curriculum," *Los Angeles Times*, January 6, 1989, p. A3.

57. "State Board Oks New Science Teaching Policy," *Los Angeles Times*, January 14, 1989, p. A27.

58. Ibid.

59. "Textbook Panel Bolsters Stand on Teaching Evolution," *Los Angeles Times*, September 29, 1989, p. A3.

60. "Textbook Panel Defends Teaching Evolution as Fact," *Los Angeles Times*, July 22, 1989, p. A30. The Curriculum Commission oversees each of the disciplines' framework committees. The commission makes recommendations to the board.

61. "Textbook Panel Bolsters Stand on Teaching Evolution," p. A3.

62. "Textbook Guideline Urged To Alter View of Evolution," *Los Angeles Times*, November 5, 1989, p. A1.

63. This change was described in an editorial, "The Facts of Life," *Los Angeles Times*, November 8, 1989, p. B6.

64. "Textbook Guideline Urged To Alter View of Evolution," p. A1.

65. Interview with Elizabeth Stage, executive director of the California Science Project, University of California, and former chair of the Science Subject Matter Committee of the Curriculum Development and Supplemental Materials Commission of the State of California, 1996.

66. People for the American Way was started by writer-producer-director Norman Lear in 1980 to protect free speech and challenge ultraconservative influence on public policy. It is a watchdog group on the issues of scientific creationism and school prayer. For Sheldon's and Hudson's quotes, see "Textbook Guideline Urged To Alter View of Evolution," p. A1.

67. This is how Robert A. Jones described Sheldon's role in the "framework" debate in his unflattering article on Lou Sheldon, "On California: Heady Days for a Bible Thumper," *Los Angeles Times*, November 12, 1989, p. A3.

68. "Compromise on Texts Reluctantly Backed," *Los Angeles Times*, November 8, 1989, p. A3.

69. Interview with Kevin Padian, 1996.

70. Interview with Bill Honig, former superintendent of public instruction, California Public Schools, 1996.

71. The Christian Coalition is a conservative advocacy group formed in the 1980s by televangelist and later presidential candidate, Pat Robertson.

72. "Christian Activists Using 'Stealth' Campaign Tactics; Voting: Conservative Religious Groups Try to Capitalize on Gains Using Methods Shielded from the Public," *Los Angeles Times*, April 5, 1992, p. A1.

73. "Religious Right Shifts Focus to Schools," *San Diego Union Tribune*, September 30, 1991, p. A1.

74. "Christian Activists Using 'Stealth' Campaign Tactics," p. A1.

75. "Vista School Chief May Move to Smaller, Quieter Coronado," *San Diego Union Tribune*, May 21, 1994, p. B3.

76. Interview with Pete McHugh, associate superintendent for instruction, Vista Unified School District, 1996.

77. Interview with Bill Loftus, associate superintendent for instruction, Vista Unified School District, 1996.

78. Interview with Pete McHugh, 1996.

79. Interview with Linda Rhoades, school board member of the Vista Unified School District, 1996.

80. Interview with Tom Conry, president of the Vista Teachers Association, 1996.

81. "Church Coalition Challenging Christian Right," *San Diego Union Tribune*, May 23, 1992, p. B2.

82. Interview with Linda Rhoades, 1996.

83. In 1992, John Tyndall and Joyce Lee did not run stealth campaigns. Tom Conry, president of the teachers' union and an opponent of Lee's and Tyndall's candidacies, sardonically described these candidates as satisfied with running "a more typical American campaign: they *lied* to the voters" by withholding from them their more "extremist" goals (interview with Tom Conry, 1996).

84. Interview with John Tyndall, former school board member of the Vista Unified School District, and director of accounting, Institute for Creation Research, 1996.

85. I will be consistent in labeling the two sides "Christian conservative" and "moderate," since these are the labels each side prefers. More pejorative labels, of course, were available in Vista. The Christian conservatives were frequently called the "Radical Right" and "social extremists," for example, while the mainstream members were often accused of being "liberals."

86. Interview with Tom Conry, 1996.

87. The crowd at this meeting segregated itself into a pro-conservative-majority section and an anti-conservative-majority section of the gymnasium, such that it looked like a wedding, with a bride's side and a groom's side, according to my interviews in 1996 with Barbara Donovan (a community member at that time) and Linda Rhoades (a board member).

88. Interview with Rene Townsend, former superintendent of Vista Unified School District, 1996; see also an article called "Battle Lines Drawn over Vista School Board; Now War of Words," *San Diego Union Tribune*, January 30, 1993, p. B1.

89. Interview with John Tyndall, 1996.

90. "Vista Controversy Brews over Recommended Text Called Veiled Creationism," *San Diego Union Tribune*, March 9, 1993, p. B3.

91. Interview with John Tyndall, 1996.

92. It is interesting to note that Tyndall was an employee of the young-earth ICR, but that he was promoting use of a book from an intelligent-design perspective, the more "elite" version of creationism described in chapter 2.

93. "Flap over Biology Book Evolves in Vista; Critics Claim It Promotes Creationism," *San Diego Union Tribune*, May 2, 1993, p. B3.

94. *Vista Unified School District Science Supplementary Book Review*, 1993.

95. This quote is from an editorial, "Keep Them Separate: Religion, Science Don't Mix in Schools," *San Diego Union Tribune*, March 15, 1993, p. B8.

96. "Are Things 'Evolving'? Not in Vista; Fundamentalist School Board Amends Science Curriculum," *San Diego Union Tribune*, April 16, 1993, p. B1.

97. Interview with John Tyndall, 1996.

98. This information is found in an opinion article, "Creationists Are at It Again; Vista School Board Pushes Religious Beliefs," *San Diego Union Tribune*, May 19, 1993, p. B6.

99. "A Call for Non-Evolution Theories; Vista Trustee Holliday Wants Alternatives Mandated by the Board," *San Diego Union Tribune*, May 14, 1993, p. A1.

100. "2 Vista School Trustees Reignite Creationism Debate," *San Diego Union Tribune*, May 21, 1993, p. B1.

101. Ibid.

102. During our interview in 1996, John Tyndall read this letter aloud to me.

103. "Teachers' Leader Is Unworried by Policy," *San Diego Union Tribune*, August 14, 1993, p. A1.

104. Interview with John Tyndall, 1996.

105. The board objected to the free breakfast component of this last program because it was thought to interfere with family values, according to a story called "Foes Threaten Suit over Sex Respect Program," *Los Angeles Times*, March 22, 1994, p. A3.

106. "Vista School Chief May Move to Smaller, Quieter Coronado," p. B3. The Sex Respect curriculum sparked debate because it promoted chastity until marriage, ignored discussion of birth control (since it assumed abstinence among unmarried couples), and restricted discussions of homosexuality and masturbation.

107. "Friction Escalates in Vista's Schools; Some Teachers Say Board Opposes Them," *San Diego Union Tribune*, July 25, 1993, p. B1.

108. Just as in districts elsewhere, administrators in the Vista Unified School District are, in the final analysis, hired to advise citizen-elected boards and to cooperate with them. Unlike teachers, who have tenure, are insulated in their classrooms, and are more remote from the authority of the board, management is the "right arm" to boards of trustees, and is paid to follow the policy that the school board writes, according to administrators I spoke with. Administrators' jobs, in fact, depend on the perception that they are being cooperative with the board, according to Jack Gyves, who, at the time I spoke with him, was the superintendent of the Vista Unified School District.

Making matters worse for the administrators in Vista is that they were hired on year-to-year contracts by the board, and had no safety net like tenure to protect them from the will of their bosses, the school-board members. Although it would have been highly unlikely for the board to have removed an administrator from the district altogether, there was always the threat that a targeted administrator could have been moved back into the classroom at the board's will. This was very clearly the threat looming over at least two high-level administrators during the Holliday-Tyndall-Lee-majority board. Holliday was known to despise both associate superintendents for instruction in the district, Pete McHugh and Bill Loftus, and it was quite clear that all three Christian conservative board members regarded the superintendent, as well, with deep suspicion.

109. Interview with Barbara Donovan, 1996.

110. "Move to Recall Vista Trustees Pushed Back," *San Diego Union Tribune*, February 14, 1994, p. B1.

111. Interview with Rene Townsend, 1996.

112. Ibid. See also "Vista Trustee Rules Out Re-election Bid; Carter Adds She's Tired of Fighting Extreme Right," *San Diego Union Tribune*, May 11, 1994, p. B1; and "Battle Fatigue: In a Dismaying Loss for Vista, Trustee Carter Calls It Quits," *San Diego Union Tribune*, May 12, 1994, p. B13.

113. "Trustees' First Goal Is To Heal Old Schism," *San Diego Union Tribune*, November 10, 1994, p. B1.

114. "Ex-Trustee Pulls 4 Kids Out of Schools; Ousted Vistan Loses Faith in District He Led," *San Diego Union Tribune*, December 10, 1994, p. B1.

115. Interview with Pete McHugh, 1996.

116. Interview with John Tyndall, 1996.

117. Interview with Barbara Donovan, 1996.

118. Interview with Linda Rhoades, 1996.

119. In the title of this section, I am quoting Steve Kraske, "Want To Toss Your Hat in the Ring?" *Kansas City Star*, August 15, 1999, p. B2.

120. [London] *Guardian*, May 11, 1996, p. 2.

121. "Next Conflict for Board of Education: Evolution," *Kansas City Star*, April 12, 1999, p. A1.

122. I found the copy of the Alabama textbook insert in a publication called *Education or Indoctrination? Analysis of Textbooks in Alabama* (1995) which was written by Norris Anderson and published by the pro-creationism organization called Access Research Network; see its web site http://www.arn.org/arn (2000).

123. See "Kansas Board Kills New Plan for Math Education Standards," *Kansas City Star*, June 11, 1998, p. C3 for the math issue; "Meek for Kansas Schools," *Kansas City Star*, July 30, 1996, p. B6 for the sex education issue; "State Group Plays Key Role in Vote," *Kansas City Star*, August 3, 1996, p. C1 for the Quality Performance Accreditation issue; "State Group Plays Key Role in Vote," p. C1, and "At Odds over Education," *Kansas City Star*, May 9, 1999, p. A1 for the federal funding issue.

124. "State Group Plays Key Role in Vote," p. C1.

125. I gathered this information from "State Group Plays Key Role in Vote," p. C1, and in "Keep Eye on State School Board Races," *Kansas City Star*, August 2, 1996, p. C5.

126. See the editorial "Choices in State Races," *Kansas City Star*, November 2, 1996, p. 2, urging Kansans to vote against the KEW-NET endorsed candidates.

127. "Board Election Seen as Pivotal," *Kansas City Star*, October 22, 1998, p. C1, carries information on the Bacon-Gilmore friendship.

128. "Neuenswander, Waugh for Kansas Education Board," *Kansas City Star*, July 15, 1998, p. C6, and "John Davidson for Education in 3rd District," *Kansas City Star*, October 28, 1998, p. 34.

129. Kansas Curricular Standards for Science Education web site, http://www.ksbe.state.ks.us/outcomes/science_12799.html, (1999).

130. *New York Times*, August 25, 1999, p. A1.

131. "Focus Is on State Science Standards; Board Member Is Proposing Some Changes," *Kansas City Star*, May 11, 1999, p. B1, and "No Decision on Science Standards; Kansas School Board Remains Divided on Question of Creation vs. Evolution," *Kansas City Star*, May 13, 1999, p. B1.

132. "Debate over Evolution Plays Out in Classrooms," *Kansas City Star*, May 20, 1999, p. A1. Interestingly, this move by the board went completely unnoticed by the *Kansas City Star* at the time of the committee's appointment. I have been able to find no media documentation of the committee's selection until well after the decision had had serious consequences for the teaching of evolution. This leads me to believe that the editorial writers at the newspaper were concerned about a large number of potential issues the board might make policy on, but changing science pedagogy in the state did not appear to writers to be among the priorities of the board.

133. "Focus Is on State Science Standards," p. B1.

134. Ibid.

135. "Next Conflict for Board of Education: Evolution," p. A1; and "Creation, Evolution Class Role Is Argued; Kansas Board Will Debate Issue Today," *Kansas City Star*, May 12, 1999, p. B1.

136. Kansas science education standards, cited in "Creation, Evolution Class Role Is Argued," p. A1.

137. "Next Conflict for Board of Education: Evolution," p. A1.

138. "Focus Is On State Science Standards," p. B1.

139. Ibid., and "Woman's Creationism Crusade Shakes Up Public Education," *Kansas City Star*, November 27, 1999, p. A1.

140. "At Odds over Education," p. A1.

141. "Focus Is on the State Science Standards," p. B1.

142. "Creation, Evolution Class Role Is Argued," p. A1.

143. "No Decision on Science Standards," *Kansas City Star*, May 13, 1999, p. B1; "Officials Hold Off on Evolution Dialogue," May 27, 1999, p. B1.

144. "Next Conflict for Board of Education: Evolution," p. A1.

145. Ibid.

146. "Setback Looms for Darwinists," *Kansas City Star*, August 9, 1999, p. B1.

147. "Earth to Board: It's 1999," *Kansas City Star*, April 14, 1999, p. B1.

148. "Creation, Evolution Class Role Is Argued," p. A1.

149. "Kansas Evolution Debate Put Off; Science Standards Talks Set for August," *Kansas City Star*, July 1, 1999, p. B3.

150. Ibid.

151. Ibid.

152. Ibid.

153. Ibid.

154. At about this point in the board's deliberations, the governor of the state, moderate Republican Bill Graves, began commenting on the board's actions and lobbing barbed critiques about the wisdom of its decision making. According to

the *Kansas City Star*, he called the fight over creationism and evolution counter-productive to good education policy-making, and he, perhaps hopefully, predicted that the citizens of the state and the legislature would in the near future support his proposal to change the way the board is selected ("Continuing Deadlock Suggests Need for Reform," *Kansas City Star*, July 5, 1999, p. B4)—by gubernatorial appointment, for example, a method voters had only recently rejected in 1990 ("Elected Board Again a Target; Some Lawmakers Talk of Abolishing Education Panel," *Kansas City Star*, August 18, 1999, p. B1). In "Continuing Deadlock," the governor is quoted as having made a pointed comment about Abrams's proposal, in particular, saying that it had caused "great consternation and concern" among scientists and educators, while junking "a well-conceived proposal by a committee of science educators appointed by the board to do that job."

While many moderates in the state certainly agreed with the governor's assessment and were likely to support nearly any proposal that would rid the state of this particular panel of members, it is important to note here the *political* dimensions of Graves's comments. Graves, a moderate Republican who supported abortion rights, among other issues, was hardly a favorite of Christian conservatives across the state, in the GOP party, or on the board, and they were no favorites of his. In fact, in an article in the *Star* long predating the science standards melee ("Conservative Republicans Discuss Challenging Graves," *Kansas City Star*, March 29, 1998, p. B3), Abrams, who was the former chairman of the state GOP party, was reported to have thrown his hat in the ring for a future contest for the governor's seat. Clearly, the issue of science teaching had political resonance across the state, and all parties were willing to try to exploit it. The same continues to this day.

155. There is actually fine irony in the fact that it was Harold Voth who cast the deciding vote in favor of the "compromise" standards, for Voth, known on the board as a relative moderate Republican (see "Evolution Question Left to Schools," *Kansas City Star*, August, 12, 1999, p. A1), had been encouraged to run for the board in 1998 in order to thwart a "conservative" bid for that open seat.

156. Information on the standard's review by the Council for Basic Education is found in an article called "New Review of Science Standards; Kansas Guidelines that Prompted Evolution Debate to Undergo Study," the *Kansas City Star*, December 8, 1999, p. B1.

157. "Pro-Evolutionists Raise More Issues in Science Debate," *Kansas City Star*, January 12, 2000, p. B1.

158. "Kansas Votes to Delete Evolution from State's Science Curriculum," *New York Times*, August 12, 1999, p. A1.

159. "Focus on Science, Chancellor Urges," *Kansas City Star*, September 9, 1999, p. B1.

160. "Kansas Votes to Delete Evolution," p. A1.

161. According to a profile of a creationism activist, the *Kansas City Star* reported that the importance of Mount St. Helens to the creationist belief in the earth's young age is as follows: "The eruption of Mount St. Helens in 1980 produced 25 feet of finely layered sediment and gouged canyons in one afternoon, which shows that millions of years are not required to form rock layer." This lends credence to the global flood and other catastophic events in the Bible, cre-

276

ationists say ("Woman's Creationism Crusade Shakes Up Public Education," p. A1).

162. "Kansas Votes to Delete Evolution," p. A1; *Kansas City Star*, May 11, 1999, p. B1.

163. Kansas Curricular Standards for Science Education, web site, http://www.ksbe.state.ks.us/outcomes/science_12799.html (1999) and "Holloway Defends Evolution Decision," *Kansas City Star*, April 14, 2000, p. B1.

164. "Kansas Votes to Delete Evolution," p. A1.

165. "Evolution Vote Puts Retired Educator in Spotlight," *Kansas City Star*, August 14, 1999, p. A1.

166. "Want To Toss Your Hat into the Ring?" p. B2.

167. "Evolution Blunder Opens Up Kansas to Ridicule," *Kansas City Star*, August 13, 1999, p. B6.

168. "Johnson County Is To Blame," *Kansas City Star*, August 13, 1999, p. B1.

169. "Want To Toss Your Hat into the Ring?" p. B2.

170. "Kansas, Evolution in Headlines; Board of Education Vote Makes News around the World," *Kansas City Star*, August 14, 1999, p. B3; "Want To Toss Your Hat into the Ring?" p. B2.

171. "Want To Toss Your Hat into the Ring?" p. B2.

172. Both of these quotes are found in the article called "Reaction to Kansas Evolution Decision Vocal, Varied," *Kansas City Star*, August 28, 1999, p. A1.

173. "Want To Toss Your Hat into the Ring?" p. B1.

174. "Kansas, Evolution in Headlines," p. B3.

175. "P.S.: Evolution Fallout," *Kansas City Star*, August 21, 1999, p. B1.

176. "Evolution Question Left to Schools," p. A1.

177. Ibid.

178. For pro-creationism columns, see "Darwin vs. 'Intelligent Design'; Three Views on the Kansas Controversy over Teaching Evolution in Public Schools: The Fossil Record Has Yet To Validate His Theory," *Kansas City Star*, August 22, 1999, p. L1, and "A New, Improved Theory of Earth's Origin," *Kansas City Star*, August 25, 1999, p. B7. For a news article stating these positions, see "Evolution Question Left to Schools," p. A1.

179. "Evolution Critic Cheers Board Vote," *Kansas City Star*, August 27, 1999, p. B3.

180. "Science Groups Rebuff Kansas; Evolution Issue Again in Focus," *Kansas City Star*, September 24, 1999, p. A1.

181. "New Review of Science Standards," *Kansas City Star*, December 8, 1999, p. B1.

182. "Ballot in Spotlight for Kansas; Opposing Camps Gearing up for State School Board Races," *Kansas City Star*, January 19, 2000, p. A1.

183. "Evolution Returns to Kansas Schools," *Los Angeles Times*, February 15, 2001, p. A5.

184. And this result is not limited to school systems in the United States. Recently, events in Calgary, Alberta, and Abbotsford, British Columbia, show parallels to this outcome. In these Canadian cities, Christian conservatives were elected to the provinces' governing boards, they made some changes copacetic with

their ideological and religious beliefs and were, shortly thereafter, rebuffed by inside authorities.

Chapter Six
Cultural, Political, and Organizational Factors
Influencing Creationist Outcomes

1. Glazer (*We Are All Multiculturalists Now*, p. 19) argues that "behind the victory of multiculturalism, whatever the discomforts it brings, lie these two great principles, equality and liberty, and few want to be in the position of opposing their claims."

2. Interview with John Tyndall, 1996.

3. Interview with John Wiester, 1996.

4. Interview with Kevin Padian, 1996.

5. Interview with Eugenie Scott, 1996.

6. Interview with Barbara Donavan, 1996.

7. James Davison Hunter (*Culture Wars*, p. 47) argues this point in a similar vein: "By labeling the opposition an extremist faction that is marginal to the mainstream of American life, each side struggles to monopolize the symbols of legitimacy. This is seen most clearly in the effort of each side to depict themselves as defenders of the institutions and traditions of American life while depicting the opposition as the foes."

8. Interview with Phillip Johnson, 1996.

9. Ibid.

10. Sen. Bill Keith, quoted in "Evolution Battle Revving Up Again," *New Orleans Time Picayune*, December 17, 1980, section 1, p. 30.

11. This information was found in *Kansas City Star*, "Woman's Creationism Crusade Shakes Up Public Education," p. A1.

12. Interview with John Wiester, 1996.

13. Interview with Eugenie Scott, 1996.

14. Ibid.

15. For an example of the scientific enterprise under a constructivist lens, see Steve Woolgar, *Science: The Very Idea* (London: Tavistock, 1988).

16. These data can be found on http://www.icpsr.umich.edu/GSS/rnd1998/merged/indx-sub/confiden.htm.

17. These data can be found on http://csa.berkeley.edu:7502/cgi-bin12hsda3.

18. Interview with Kevin Padian, 1996.

19. Interview with John Tyndall, 1996.

20. Interview with Kevin Padian, 1996.

21. Interview with Eugenie Scott, 1996.

22. National Center for Science Education, "Facing Challenges to Evolution Education," web site, 2000b.

23. Phillip Johnson quoted in "Evolution Critic Cheers Board Vote," *Kansas City Star*, August 27, 1999, p. B3.

24. See Norris Anderson, *Education or Indoctrination? Analysis of Textbooks in Alabama*. Colorado Springs: Access Research Network, 1995.

25. "Creationist Captain Sees Battle 'Hotting Up,'" *New York Times*, December 1, 1999, p. A15.

26. The framework's entry for "falsification" is a good example of creationists' arguments for an intelligent designer (Kansas Curricular Standards for Science Education web site (http://www.ksbe.state.ks.us/outcomes/science_12799.html, [1999]). For a theory to be a valid scientific explanation, states the framework, it must withstand attempts at falsification.

- To be falsifiable a theory must be testable, by others, in such a way that, if it is false, the tests can show that it is false. Repeatability is an inadequate criterion and is supplemented with falsification. The reason for falsifiability may not be intuitively obvious. It is fine to make statements like "this theory is backed by a great body of experiments and observations," but often overlooked is the fact that such claims are meaningless. Experiments and observations do not verify theories, they must be evaluated by human reason to determine the degree of verification they provide.
- As a result of the weakness of repeatability as a sole criteria for the validity of scientific explanations, Karl Popper, the famous twentieth-century British philosopher of science, and countless others, have insisted that, to be called a "test" of a theory, the test must be designed in such a way that, if the test fails, the theory can be considered false! This criterion is reasonable. How can you call an experiment a "test" of a theory if failure of the test has no meaning? In the United States, falsifiability in science can even be considered "the law of the land," because of the decision of a federal judge (William Overton) in a famous trial.
- A concomitant criteria, as stated by Popper, Overton, and others, is that the theory itself must be "falsifiable," i.e., it must be possible to design a test that will fail if the theory itself is false. This is a very difficult position to establish, but that is the nature of good science. Unfortunately, lost in all this discussion is what used to be taught in most science colleges: experimental design. The key here is that "testing" a theory and "falsification" are more associated with the attributes of the test and its interpretation than they are with the theory itself. Another point is that experimental design is critical to theory verification. Critical analysis of the weaknesses (known or potential) of experimental tests of hypotheses, is critical to any ability to make informed decisions based on science education. Therefore, sound science teaching must include the logic of experimental design and evaluation.

27. In response, the National Academy of Sciences published a guidebook to encourage teachers to remain committed to good science, and to provide teachers with answers for refuting skeptics (*Teaching about Evolution and the Nature of Science*; see web site, http://www.nap.edu/catalog/5787.html (1998).

28. For information on the Minnesota case, see "Teacher Awaits Appeal on Evolution Education," *Minneapolis Star Tribune*, August 14, 2000, p. A1.

29. John Richard Schrock, a professor at Emporia State University in Kansas, and a member of the Kansas Science Education Standards Writing Committee, cites five surveys of biology teachers, in an article called "Evolution Returns to

Kansas Schools," in the *Los Angeles Times*, February 15, 2001, p. A5. Information on Schrock's service on the Kansas Standards committee can be found at http://www.kcfs.org/scidraft5.html.

30. The People for the American Way found the following results in a 1,500 person, randomly selected national poll conducted in 1999 (see web site, http://www.pfaw.org/issues/education/creationism-poll.pdf):

- 20 percent of Americans think that evolution should be taught in public schools without any creationism mentioned at all.
- 17 percent think that only evolution should be taught in science class, but that religious explanations of origins (creationism) can be discussed in another class outside of science.
- 29 percent say that creationism can be discussed in science class, but discussed as a "belief," not as a scientific theory (while evolution should be taught as a "scientific theory" in science class).
- 13 percent think that both evolution and creationism should be taught as "scientific theories" in science class.
- 16 percent think that only creationism should be taught in science classes, with no mention of evolution.
- 5 percent are not sure.

Chapter Seven
Making More Institutional the Study of Challenge

1. See, for example, William Gamson, "Introduction" to *Social Movements in an Organizational Society: Collected Essays*, ed., Mayer Zald and John D. McCarthy (New Brunswick, N.J.: Transaction Books, 1987); Carol McClurg Mueller, "Building Social Movement Theory," in *Frontiers in Social Movement Theory*; Sidney Tarrow, "Mentalities, Political Cultures, and Collective Action Frames: Constructing Meanings through Actions," in *Frontiers in Social Movement Theory*; Steven Buechler, "Beyond Resource Mobilization? Emerging Trends in Social Movement Theory." *The Sociological Quarterly* 34 (1993): 217–35; Mary Bernstein, "Celebration and Suppression: The Strategic Uses of Identity by the Lesbian and Gay Movement," *American Journal of Sociology* 103 (1997): 531–65; Stephen Ellingson, "Understanding the Dialectic of Discourse and Collective Action: Public Debate and Rioting in Antebellum Cincinnati," *American Journal of Sociology* 101 (1995): 100–44; Doug McAdam, John McCarthy, and Mayer Zald, Introduction to *Comparative Perspectives on Social Movements;* Mario Diani, "Linking Mobilization Frames and Political Opportunities;" Brian Donovan, "Political Consequences of Private Authority: Promise Keepers and the Transformation of Hegemonic Masculinity. *Theory and Society* 27 (1998): 817–43, to name a few.

2. This quote is taken from Snow, review of *Social Movements in an Organizational Society: Collected Essays*, in *Contemporary Sociology* (1987): 603.

3. Bernstein, "Celebration and Suppression."

4. Institute for Creation Research, web site, http://www.icr.org (October 10, 2000).

5. Among others, the following authors have discussed resonance at some length: Gamson and Modigliani, "Media Discourse and Public Opinion on Nuclear Power" Snow and Benford, "Master Frames and Cycles of Protest"; Binder, "Constructing Racial Rhetoric."

6. John McCarthy, Jackie Smith, and Mayer Zald, "Accessing Public, Media, Electoral, and Governmental Agendas" in *Comparative Perspectives on Social Movements*.

7. In *Dynamics of Contention*, McAdam, Tarrow, and Tilly have introduced this area of research as one to question further.

8. Kelly Moore ("Political Protest and Institutional Change") studied the effects of Vietnam protest on scientific research in the United States. For two different discussions of the public's relative power in the political realm vs. other institutional realms, see this chapter by Moore and a separate chapter by Paul Burstein ("Social Movements and Public Policy") in the same volume (*How Social Movements Matter*).

9. While the temptation may exist in the face of this information to write off these challenges as mere "interest groups" or as examples of intragroup conflict (a temptation I rejected in chapter 1), my objective, instead, is to use these scenarios to push harder against current social movements concepts to see if my findings coincide with work being done at the frontiers of the discipline. As one among a group of scholars trying systematically to extend social movements concepts beyond the confines of political challenge to institutional challenge—and to look at the interplay of culture, politics, and organizational factors in those challenges—the findings may point a partial way for future research paths.

10. See, for example, Bert Klandermans, "The Social Construction of Protest and Multiorganizational Fields," in *Frontiers in Social Movement Theory*; Doug McAdam, John D. McCarthy, and Mayer Zald, "Social Movements" in *Handbook of Sociology*, ed. Neil Smelser (Newbury Park, Calif.: Sage, 1988); McCarthy, Smith, and Zald, "Accessing Public, Media, Electoral, and Governmental Agendas" in *Comparative Perspectives on Social Movements;* Robert Benford, "An Insider's Critique of the Social Movement Framing Perspective," *Sociological Inquiry* 67 (1997): 409–30. Among those multiple audiences whose vulnerability to framing has been described are "benefactors"—organizations or individuals whose resources can help challengers (see Daniel Cress and David Snow's "Mobilization at the Margins"). But insider elites have largely been overlooked.

11. Rhys Williams describes the goals of movements in these terms in "Constructing the Public Good."

12. The following authors have discussed this concept of culture "working": Michael Schudson; "How Culture Works," Nicola Beisel, "Morals Versus Art: Censorship, the Politics of Interpretation, and the Victorian Nude," *American Sociological Review* 58 (1993): 145–46; Amy Binder, "Constructing Racial Rhetoric." Meanwhile, Cress and Snow ("Mobilization at the Margins") approach the issue of insider resonance when they study social movement organizations' relationships with "benefactor" organizations. Benefactor organizations are outside the movement and they provide resources and support for the challenge, but they are not the same as institutional insiders. The authors do not explore what

happens when challengers' rhetoric resonates with the actual insiders of the establishment under challenge.

13. See Doug McAdam's *Political Process and the Development of Black Insurgency, 1930–1970* (Chicago: University of Chicago Press, 1982) as an example of this description of elite allies.

14. Interview with Thomas Sobol, 1996.

15. Katzenstein (*Faithful and Fearless*) citing Paul Burstein, Rachel Einwhoner, and Jocelyn Hollander, "The Success of Political Movements: A Bargaining Perspective," in *The Politics of Social Protest: Comparative Perspectives on States and Social Movements*, ed. J. Craig Jenkins and Bert Klandermans (Minneapolis: University of Minnesota Press, 1995), 275–96.

16. Katzenstein citing McAdam's *The Political Process and the Development of Black Insurgency.*

17. Katzenstein quoting Erving Goffman, *Asylums: Essays on the Social Situation of Mental Patients and Other Inmates* (Garden City, N.Y.: Anchor, 1961).

18. Katzenstein, *Faithful and Fearless*, p.17.

19. Snow and Benford define resonant frames as empirically credible, experientially commensurable, and ideationally central to their audiences. See their articles, "Ideology, Frame Resonance, and Participant Mobilization" and "Master Frames and Cycles of Protest."

20. This is language borrowed from Katzenstein's *Faithful and Fearless*.

21. Kiyoteru Tsutsui has written elegantly about this distinction in an as yet unpublished work "Global Dimensions of Contemporary Social Movements: The Case of a Social Movement for 'Comfort Women,'" Department of Sociology, Stanford University, October 2000. Among the most important texts in this area of research are Charles Tilly's *From Mobilization to Revolution* (Reading, Mass.: Addison-Wesley, 1978); McAdam's *Political Process and the Development of Black Insurgency*; Sidney Tarrow's *Power in Movement*.

22. Mario Diani has written specifically of the "practical politics" that exist in conflict events (see his "Linking Mobilization Frames and Political Opportunities").

23. Doug McAdam, introduction to *Comparative Perspectives on Social Movements*.

24. McAdam, Tarrow, and Tilly, *Dynamics of Contention*.

25. Murdell McFarlin, the public information officer in Atlanta, told me about this politicized situation among school district administrators (interview with Murdell McFarlin, 1995).

26. It is also a case that calls for a reconsideration of political opportunities along cultural lines. Political opportunities, that is to say, are not only structural, but also cultural in nature—a point that is beginning to be addressed by scholars of contentious politics. If challengers actively and strategically try to get their arguments to "work" with institutional insiders, as in this Atlanta example, then we should be paying closer attention in our studies to the interaction that frequently occurs between cultural resonance and political opportunities. Our assumption of a simple binary relationship between opposition and establishment is already shaky the moment we speak of elite divisions as a source of political opportunity. A close look at the sources of such divisions and the ways in which contending groups might exploit them is in order.

In this case, challengers' strategic use of rhetoric and symbols concerning the need for change actually created a political opportunity for Afrocentrists, when some of the establishment's insiders recognized that Afrocentrism coincided with their own efforts to change the system. Challengers often forge that recognition; they do not merely wait for political opportunities to crop up. Again, this is not the way social movements scholars customarily have understood political opportunities to operate. Political opportunities, by the standard description, arise thanks to no special effort of challengers. Then they are simply consumed, or used up, by challengers. But this conceptualization of political opportunities is beginning to change, and we are beginning to appreciate the "agentic" nature of challengers' interactions with structural elements. In "Reflections on Social Movement Theory: Criticisms and Proposals," recently published in *Contemporary Sociology* (29 [1000]: 445–54) Aldon Morris argues strongly that we must begin describing those instances when challengers use cultural action to create political opportunities.

27. Robert Wuthnow, *Meaning and Moral Order: Explorations in Cultural Analysis* (Berkeley: University of California Press, 1987).

28. See Tarrow's *Power in Movement* and McAdam, McCarthy, and Zald's "Social Movements," p. 719.

29. In fact, there are more than a couple directions, although I cannot address them all in the body of this work.

New ideas about the relationship between challengers and the organizations they challenge, as well as about the conditions shaping institutional stasis and change, are occurring in a variety of academic disciplines of late. This new body of theory starts with the assumption that challenge processes occur in many different sorts of institutions—not just against seats of political power as social movements theory has traditionally addressed—and that these challenges rightfully should be considered to be members of a broadened family called "contentious politics." Contentious politics may be located within arms of the government, in churches, on executive boards, in school systems, and so forth. Their targets may be organizations, the larger institutions to which organizations belong, or the state.

As we have seen in Katzenstein's work, some scholars in this new area of research have gone from studying new *settings* in which contests occur to recognizing that the relationship between the so-called "establishment" and its "challenging movements" is more continuous than it is dichotomous; meaning that the boundary between "challenger" and "challenged" is more fluid than once was considered. From another group of scholars comes the call to question the division frequently made between "institutionalized" and "non-institutionalized" politics, which, it is argued, overemphasizes the differences between contention that occurs routinely and contention that arises outside of conventional politics. McAdam, Tarrow, and Tilly (*Dynamics of Contention*) represent these new strides. From others comes the (related) resolution to contextualize investigations of challenger activities in their larger historical and institutional fields than has traditionally been done, so that we see the historical *dialogue, accommodation*, and *redirection of demands* that occurs between challengers and institutions, rather than a static image of adversarial relations (see W. Trexler Proffitt and Marc Ventresca, "A New Type of Fieldwork: Ideology, Mobilization, and U.S. Shareholder Activism," unpublished manuscript, 2000, for an example). Each one of these areas of innovative thought opens up fascinating avenues for the future study of the relationships between challengers and organizations.

30. For a recent account of conflict in corporations (this one at the executive level), see Calvin Morrill, *The Executive Way.*

31. See James March and Herbert Simon on "limited rationality," in their classic text, *Organizations* (New York: Wiley, 1958); see Karl Weick on "garbage can theory" in *The Social Psychology of Organizing* (Reading, Mass.: Addison Wesley, 1969) ; see Charles Perrow on organizations' contested goals in "The Analysis of Goals in Complex Organizations," *American Sociological Review* 26 (1961): 854–66; see Walter Powell for an empirical and theoretical tour de force that brings these aspects of organizational decision making into focus in his *Getting into Print.*

32. Paul DiMaggio and Walter Powell, introduction to *The New Institutionalism in Organizational Analysis*, eds. Walter Powell and Paul DiMaggio (Chicago: University of Chicago Press, 1991), pp. 9–10.

33. Meyer and Rowan, "Institutional Organizations: Formal Structure as Myth and Ceremony"; John Meyer and Brian Rowan, "The Structure of Educational Organizations" in *Environments and Organizations*, ed. Marshall W. Meyer et al. (San Francisco: Jossey-Bass, 1978).

34. This is similar to Ann Swidler's description of culture being used as a tool box, action that becomes particularly noticeable during "unsettled times" ("Culure in Action: Symbols and Strategies," *American Sociological Review* 51 [1986]: 273–86).

35. Neil Fligstein, "Social Skill and Institutional Theory," *American Behavioral Scientist* 40 (1997): 397–405.

36. Katzenstein, *Faithful and Fearless.*

37. See DiMaggio and Powell, introduction to *The New Institutionalism in Organizational Analysis.*

38. In *Key Concepts for Understanding Curriculum*, Colin Marsh writes about educators' protection of core activities.

39. Tyack and Cuban, *Tinkering toward Utopia.*

40. Tilly, *From Mobilization to Revolution*; McAdam, *Political Process and the Development of Black Insurgency.*

41. Francesca Polletta, "Culture and Its Discontents: Recent Theorizing on the Cultural Dimensions of Protest," *Sociological Inquiry* 67 (1997): 431–50.

42. See Meyer and Tarrow, introduction to *A Movement Society: Contentious Politics for a New Century.*

43. McAdam, Tarrow, and Tilly, *Dynamics of Contention.*

44. See McAdam, McCarthy and Zald on the limits of the single case-study method in their introduction to *Comparative Perspectives on Social Movements.*

45. Aldon Morris, "Reflections on Social Movement Theory: Criticisms and Proposals"; McAdam, *Political Process and the Development of Black Insurgency*; McAdam, Tarrow, and Tilly, *Dynamics of Contention.*

46. Gamson and Meyer, "Framing Political Opportunity," *Perspectives on Social Movements*; and Brian Donovan, "Political Consequences of Private Authority."

References _____

Abington v. Schempp. 1963. 374 US 203.

Access Research Network. 1994. Web site, http://www.arn.org/arn. Phillip Johnson vs. William Provine debate at Stanford University, April 30.

Adams, Hunter Havelin, III. 1987. "African and African-American Contributions to Science and Technology." In *African-American Baseline Essays*. Portland, Ore.: Multnomah School District.

Adams, Russell, professor and chair of African American Studies, Howard University. 1995. Interview by author, October 6, Washington, D.C. Tape recording.

African-American Baseline Essays. 1987. Portland, Ore.: Multnomah School District.

Amici curiae brief submitted to the U.S. Supreme Court in support of the appellants. 1985. Submitted by John Whitehead and Larry Crain; Edwards v. Aguillard, 482 U.S. 578.

Anderson, Norris. 1995. *Education or Indoctrination? Analysis of Textbooks in Alabama*. Colorado Springs: Access Research Network.

Anonymous Atlanta School Board Member. 1995. Interview by author, November 29, Atlanta, Ga. Tape recording.

Asante, Molefi Kete. 1990. *Kemet, Afrocentricity, and Knowledge*. Trenton, N.J.: Africa World Press.

———. 1991. "Multiculturalism: An Exchange." *The American Scholar* 60:267–76.

———. 1993. "Racing to Leave the Race: Black Postmodernists Off-Track." *The Black Scholar* 23:50–51.

Austin, Algernon. 1995. "The Effect of Multicultural Education on the Academic Achievement of Black Students." Unpublished paper, Center for Urban Affairs and Policy Research, Northwestern University.

Bailey, Ronald. 1997. "Origin of the Specious." *Reason* 29:22–8.

Bates, Stephen. 1993. *Battleground: One Mother's Crusade, the Religious Right, and the Struggle for Our Schools*. New York: Henry Holt.

Behe, Michael. 1996. *Darwin's Black Box: The Biochemical Challenge to Evolution*. New York: Touchstone.

Beisel, Nicola. 1993. "Morals Versus Art: Censorship, the Politics of Interpretation, and the Victorian Nude." *American Sociological Review* 58:145–46.

———. 1997. *Imperiled Innocents: Anthony Comstock and Family Reproduction in Victorian America*. Princeton: Princeton University Press.

Benford, Robert. 1997. "An Insider's Critique of the Social Movement Framing Perspective." *Sociological Inquiry* 67:409–30.

Bennett, William. 1992. *The Devaluing of America*. New York: Summit.

Bernstein, Mary. 1997. "Celebration and Suppression: The Strategic Uses of Identity by the Lesbian and Gay Movement." *American Journal of Sociology* 103:531–65.

Biemer, Linda, dean of the School of Education, State University of New York, Binghamton, and co-chair of the New York State Curriculum and Assessment Committee, 1995. Interview by author, October 30, Binghamton, N.Y. Tape recording.

Binder, Amy. 1993. "Constructing Racial Rhetoric: Media Depictions of Harm in Heavy Metal and Rap Music," *American Sociological Review* 58:753–67.

———. 1999. "Friend and Foe: Boundary Work and Collective Identity in the Afrocentric and Multicultural Curriculum Movements in American Public Education." In *The Cultural Territories of Race: Black and White Boundaries*. Edited by Michèle Lamont. Chicago: University of Chicago Press and New York: Russell Sage Foundation.

———. 2000. "Why Do Some Curricular Challenges 'Work' While Others Do Not? The Case of Three Afrocentric Challenges: Atlanta, Washington, D.C., and New York State." *Sociology of Education* 73:69–91.

Bird, Wendell. 1978. "Freedom of Religion and Science Instruction in Public Schools." *Yale Law Journal* 87:515–70.

Bork, Robert. 1996. *Slouching towards Gomorrah*. New York: Regan.

Brint, Steven. 1998. *Schools and Societies*. Thousand Oaks, Calif.: Pine Forge.

Buechler, Steven. 1993. "Beyond Resource Mobilization? Emerging Trends in Social Movement Theory." *The Sociological Quarterly* 34:217–35.

Burstein, Paul. 1999. "Social Movements and Public Policy." In *How Social Movements Matter*, edited by Marco Giugni, Doug McAdam, and Charles Tilly. Minneapolis: University of Minnesota Press.

Clark, Constance, deputy superintendent for educational programs and operations, District of Columbia Public Schools. 1995. Interview by author, August 22, Washington, D.C. Tape recording.

Clemens, Elisabeth, and James Cook. 1999. "Politics and Institutionalism: Explaining Durability and Change." *Annual Review of Sociology* 25:441–66.

Conry, Thomas, president of Vista Teachers Association. 1996. Interview by author, October 16, Vista, Calif. Tape recording.

Cooper, Walter, member of the New York State Board of Regents. 1995. Interview by author, October 29, Rochester, N.Y. Tape recording.

Cornbleth, Catherine, and Dexter Waugh. 1995. *The Great Speckled Bird: Multicultural Politics and Education Policymaking*. New York: St. Martin's.

Creed, W. E. Douglas, and Maureen Scully. 2000. "More than Switchpersons on the Tracks of History: Situated Agency and Contested Legitimation during the Diffusion of Domestic Partner Benefits." Unpublished paper.

Cress, Daniel, and David Snow. 1996. "Mobilization at the Margins: Resources, Benefactors, and the Viability of Homeless Social Movement Organizations." *American Sociological Review* 61:1089–1109.

Davies, Scott. 1999. "From Moral Duty to Cultural Rights: A Case Study of Political Framing in Education." *Sociology of Education* 71:1–23.

———. 2000. "The Changing Meaning of Progressive Pedagogy: Justifying School Reform in Three Eras." Paper presented to Political Sociology Workshop, Department of Sociology, Stanford University, October.

Davis, Percival, and Dean H. Kenyon. 1993 [1989]. *Of Pandas and People: The Central Question of Biological Origins*. 2nd. ed. Dallas: Haughton.

Dawson, Michael. Forthcoming. *Black Visions: The Roots of African-American Political Ideologies*. Chicago: University of Chicago Press.

DelFattore, Joan. 1992. *What Johnny Shouldn't Read: Textbook Censorship in America*. New Haven: Yale University Press.

Della Porta, Donatella. 1999. "Protest, Protesters, and Protest Policing: Public Discourses in Italy and Germany from the 1960s to the 1980s." In *How Social Movements Matter*, edited by Marco Giugni, Doug McAdam, and Charles Tilly. Minneapolis: University of Minnesota Press.

Dembski, William. 2000. "Origins." Web site, http://www.origins.org/offices/dembski/docs/bd-idesign.html.

Diani, Mario. 1996. "Linking Mobilization Frames and Political Opportunities: Insights from Regional Populism in Italy." *American Sociological Review* 61:1053–69.

Diegmueller, Karen. 1995. "Controversy Predicted over New York Social Studies Framework." *Education Week on the Web*, http://www.edweek.org/ew/1995/39social.h14, June 21.

Dillingham, Gerald. 1981. "The Emerging Black Middle Class: Class Conscious or Race Conscious?" *Ethnic and Racial Studies* 4:432–51.

DiMaggio, Paul, and Walter Powell. 1991a. Introduction to *The New Institutionalism in Organizational Analysis*. Edited by Walter Powell and Paul DiMaggio. Chicago: University of Chicago Press.

———. 1991b. "The Iron Cage Revisited: Institutional Isomorphism and Collective Rationality in Organizational Fields." In *The New Institutionalism in Organizational Analysis*, edited by Walter Powell and Paul DiMaggio. Chicago: University of Chicago Press.

DiMaggio, Paul, and Bethany Bryson. 2000. "Public Attitudes towards Cultural Authority and Cultural Diversity in Higher Education and the Arts." In *The Arts of Democracy: The State, Civil Society, and Culture*, edited by Casey Blake Princeton: Woodrow Wilson Center Press.

DiMaggio, Paul, John Evans, and Bethany Bryson. 1996. "Have Americans' Social Attitudes Become More Polarized?" *American Journal of Sociology* 102:690–755.

District of Columbia Public Schools. 1998. Web site, http://www.k12.dc.us/DCPS/curriculum/stanford9/stanford9_intro.html.

Donovan, Barbara, "Recall" organizer and school board member of the Vista Unified School District. 1996. Interview by author, October 14, Vista, Calif. Tape recording.

Donovan, Brian. 1998. "Political Consequences of Private Authority: Promise Keepers and the Transformation of Hegemonic Masculinity." *Theory and Society* 27:817–43.

D'Souza, Dinesh. 1991. *Illiberal Education: The Politics of Sex and Race on Campus*. Toronto: Collier Macmillan.

Dukes, Hazel, director of the New York chapter of the NAACP and Chair of the New York State Task Force on Minorities: Excellence and Equity. 1995. Interview by author, November 7, New York, N.Y. Tape recording.

Edwards v. Aguillard. 1987. 482 US 578.

Ellingson, Stephen. 1995. "Understanding the Dialectic of Discourse and Collective Action: Public Debate and Rioting in Antebellum Cincinnati." *American Journal of Sociology* 101:100–44.

Epperson v. Arkansas. 1968. 393 US 97.

Feagin, Joe, and Melvin Sikes. 1994. *Living with Racism: The Black Middle Class Experience.* Boston: Beacon.

Fligstein, Neil. 1997. "Social Skill and Institutional Theory." *American Behavioral Scientist* 40:397–405.

Focus on the Family. 1995. "The Defamation of Two Cities." *Citizen*, October 16 (article written by Scott DeNicola).

Fullan, Michael. 1982. *The Meaning of Educational Change.* Toronto: OISE Press.

Fullan, Michael, and Allan Pomfret. 1977. "Research in Curriculum and Instruction Implementation." *Review of Educational Research* 47:335–97.

Gamson, Josh. 1989. "Silence, Death, and the Invisible Enemy: AIDS Activism and Social Movement 'Newness.'" *Social Problems* 36:351–67.

Gamson, William. 1987. Introduction to *Social Movements in an Organizational Society: Collected Essays.* Edited by Mayer Zald and John D. McCarthy. New Brunswick, N.J.: Transaction.

———. 1992. *Talking Politics.* New York: Cambridge University Press.

Gamson, William, and David Meyer. 1996. "Framing Political Opportunity." In *Comparative Perspectives on Social Movements: Political Opportunities, Mobilizing Structures and Cultural Framings*, edited by Doug McAdam, John McCarthy and Mayer Zald. Cambridge: Cambridge University Press.

Gamson, William, and Andre Modigliani. 1989. "Media Discourse and Public Opinion on Nuclear Power: A Constructionist Approach." *American Journal of Sociology* 95:1–37.

Gilroy, Paul. 1993. *The Black Atlantic: Modernity and Double Consciousness.* Cambridge: Harvard University Press.

Giroux, Henry. 1992. "Post-Colonial Ruptures and Democratic Possibilities: Multiculturalism as Anti-Racist Pedagogy." *Cultural Critique* 21 (Spring).

Giugni, Marco, Doug McAdam, and Charles Tilly, eds. 1999. *How Social Movements Matter.* Minneapolis: University of Minnesota Press.

Glazer, Nathan, professor in the School of Education at Harvard University and former member of the New York State Social Studies Syllabus Review and Development Committee (the "Diversity Committee"), 1995. Interview by author, November 10, Cambridge, Mass. Tape recording.

———. 1997. *We Are All Multiculturalists Now.* Cambridge: Harvard University Press.

Glover, D. F., former school board member of the Atlanta Public School System, and professor, Department of Social Science at Morris Brown College. 1995. Interview by author, December 1, Atlanta, Ga. Tape recording.

Gross, Paul, and Norman Levitt. 1994. *Higher Superstition: The Academic Left and Its Quarrel with Science.* Baltimore: Johns Hopkins Press.

Gross, Paul, Norman Levitt and Martin Lewis, eds. 1996. *The Flight from Science and Reason.* New York: New York Academy of Sciences.

Gyves, Jack, superintendent of Vista Unified School District. 1996. Interview by author, October 15, Vista, Calif. Tape recording.

Harris, Michael. 1992. "Africentrism and Curriculum: Concepts, Issues, and Prospects." *Journal of Negro Education* 61:301–16.

Himmelstein, Jerome. 1990. *To the Right: The Transformation of American Conservatism.* Berkeley: University of California Press.

Honig, Bill, former superintendent of public instruction, California Public Schools. 1996. Interview by author, October 8, San Francisco, Calif. Tape Recording.

Hunter, James Davison. 1991. *Culture Wars: The Struggle to Define America.* New York: Basic Books.

Institute for Creation Research. 2000. Web site, http://www.icr.org.

Jackson, Kenneth, 1991. "A Dissenting Comment." In "One Nation, Many People: A Declaration of Cultural Interdependence," by the New York State Social Studies Syllabus Review Committee," pp. 39–40.

James, George. 1954. *Stolen Legacy.* New York: Philosophical Library.

Jeffries, Leonard, professor and former chair, Department of Black Studies, City College of New York; consultant to the New York State Special Task Force on Minorities: Equity and Excellence. 1995. Interview by author, November 8. New York, N.Y. Tape recording.

Johnson, Phillip, professor in the Boalt School of Law, University of California, Berkeley. 1996. Interview by author, October 9, Berkeley, Calif. Tape recording.

Kansas Curricular Standards for Science Education. 1999. Web site, http://www.ksbe.state.ks.us/outcomes/science_12799.html.

Katzenstein, Mary Fainsod. 1998. *Faithful and Fearless: Moving Feminist Protest Inside the Church and Military.* Princeton: Princeton University Press.

Kendall, Mae, former director of Program Planning and Curriculum Development in the Atlanta Public School System. 1995. Interview by author, November 30, Atlanta, Ga. Tape recording.

Klandermans, Bert. 1992. "The Social Construction of Protest and Multiorganizational Fields." In *Frontiers in Social Movement Theory*, edited by Aldon Morris and Carol McClurg Mueller. New Haven: Yale University Press.

Kliebard, Herbert. 1986. *The Struggle for the American Curriculum.* Boston: Routledge & Kegan Paul.

LaHaye, Tim. 1983. "The Religion of Secular Humanism." In *Public Schools and the First Amendment*, edited by S. M. Elam. Bloomington, Ind.: Phi Delta Kappa.

Lamont, Michèle. 1992. *Money, Morals, and Manners: The Culture of the French and American Upper-Middle Class.* Chicago: University of Chicago Press.

———, ed. 1999. *The Cultural Territories of Race: Black and White Boundaries.* Chicago: University of Chicago Press and New York: Russell Sage Foundation.

Lamont, Michèle, and Marcel Fournier, eds. 1992. *Cultivating Differences: Symbolic Boundaries and the Making of Inequality.* Chicago: University of Chicago Press.

Larson, Edward J. 1985. *Trial and Error: The American Controversy over Creation and Evolution.* New York: Oxford University Press.

Lefkowitz, Mary. 1996. *Not Out of Africa: How Afrocentrism Became an Excuse To Teach Myth as History*. New York: Basic Books.

Leo, John. 1991. "Multicultural Follies." *U.S. News and World Report*, July 8, p. 12.

Loftus, Bill, associate superintendent for instruction, Vista Unified School District. 1996. Interview by author, October 14, Vista, Calif. Tape recording.

Lortie, Dan. 1975. *Schoolteacher*. Chicago: University of Chicago Press.

Loving, Cathy, district archivist for the Atlanta Public School System. 2000. Email interview with author, September 6.

Marable, Manning, and Leith Mullings. 1994. "The Divided Mind of Black America: Race, Ideology, and Politics in the Post Civil Rights Era." *Race and Class* 36:61–72.

March, James, and Herbert Simon, 1958. *Organizations*. New York: Wiley.

Marsh, Colin. 1992. *Key Concepts for Understanding Curriculum*. London: Falmer.

Marsh, Colin, Christopher Day, Lynne Hannay, and Gail McCutcheon. 1990. *Reconceptualizing School-Based Curriculum Development*. London: Falmer.

Mazrui, Ali. 1993. "Afrocentricity versus Multiculturalism?: A Dialectic in Search of a Synthesis." Paper delivered to the University of California, Los Angeles, under the sponsorship of the James S. Coleman African Studies Center, May 5.

———, professor of the humanities, State University of New York, Binghamton. 1995. Interview by author, October 30, Binghamton, N.Y. Tape recording.

McAdam, Doug. 1982. *Political Process and the Development of Black Insurgency, 1930–1970*. Chicago: University of Chicago Press.

———. 1996. "Conceptual Origins, Current Problems, Future Directions." In *Comparative Perspectives on Social Movements: Political Opportunities, Mobilizing Structures and Cultural Framings*, edited by Doug McAdam, John D. McCarthy, and Mayer Zald. Cambridge: Cambridge University Press.

McAdam, Doug, John D. McCarthy, and Mayer Zald. 1988. "Social Movements." In *Handbook of Sociology*, edited by Neil Smelser. Newbury Park, Calif.: Sage Publications.

———. 1996. Introduction to *Comparative Perspectives on Social Movements: Political Opportunities, Mobilizing Structures and Cultural Framings*. Edited by Doug McAdam, John D. McCarthy, and Mayer Zald. Cambridge: Cambridge University Press.

McAdam, Doug, Sidney Tarrow, and Charles Tilly. 2001. *Dynamics of Contention*. Cambridge: Cambridge University Press.

McCarthy, John D., Jackie Smith, and Mayer Zald. 1996. "Accessing Public, Media, Electoral, and Governmental Agendas." In *Comparative Perspectives on Social Movements: Political Opportunities, Mobilizing Structures and Cultural Framings*, edited by Doug McAdam, John D. McCarthy, Mayer Zald. Cambridge: Cambridge University Press.

McClurg Mueller, Carol. 1992. "Building Social Movement Theory." In *Frontiers in Social Movement Theory*, edited by Aldon Morris and Carol McClurg Mueller. New Haven: Yale University Press.

McFarlin, Murdell, former public information officer, Superintendent's Office, Atlanta Public Schools. 1995. Interview by author, November 29, Atlanta, Ga. Tape recording.

McHugh, Pete, associate superintendent for instruction, Vista Unified School District. 1996. Interview by author, October 14, Vista, Calif. Tape recording.

McIver, Thomas. 1989. *Creationism: Intellectual Origins, Cultural Context, and Theoretical Diversity*. Ph. D. diss., Department of Anthropology, University of California, Los Angeles.

McLean v. Arkansas Board of Education. 1982. 529 F. Supp. 1255 (E.D. Ark.).

Meyer, David S., and Sidney Tarrow. 1998. Introduction to *A Movement Society: Contentious Politics for a New Century*, edited by David Meyer and Sidney Tarrow. New York: Rowman and Littlefield.

Meyer, John, and Brian Rowan. 1977. "Institutional Organizations: Formal Structure as Myth and Ceremony." *American Journal of Sociology* 83:340–63.

———. 1978. "The Structure of Educational Organizations." In *Environments and Organizations*, edited by Marshall W. Meyer et al. San Francisco: Jossey-Bass.

Miller, Kenneth. 1999. National Center for Science Education web site. http://biocrs.biomed.brown.edu/Oklahoma/Oklahoma-Disclaimer.html.

Moore, Kelly. 1999. "Political Protest and Institutional Change: The Anti-Vietnam War Movement and American Science." In *How Social Movements Matter*, edited by Marco Giugni, Doug McAdam, and Charles Tilly. Minneapolis: University of Minnesota Press.

Moran, Rachel. 1996. "In the Multicultural Battle, Victory Is to the Weak." *Public Affairs Report*, published by the Institute of Governmental Studies, University of California, Berkeley.

Morrill, Calvin. 1995. *The Executive Way: Conflict Management in Organizations*. Chicago: University of Chicago Press.

Morris, Aldon. 2000. "Reflections on Social Movement Theory: Criticisms and Proposals." *Contemporary Sociology* 29:445–54.

Morris, Aldon, and Cedric Herring. 1987. "Theory and Research in Social Movements: A Critical Review." *Annual Review of Political Science* (edited by Samuel Long).

Morris, Henry. 1974. *The Troubled Waters of Evolution*. San Diego: Creation-Life.

———, president emeritus of the Institute for Creation Research. 1996. Interview by author, October 16, El Cajon, Calif. Tape recording.

National Academy of Sciences. 1998. *Teaching about Evolution and the Nature of Science*. Web site, http://www.nap.edu/catalog/5787.html.

National Center for Science Education (NCSE) 2000a. "Seven Significant Court Decisions Regarding Evolution / Creation Issues." Web site, http://www.natcenscied.org/courtdec.html.

———. 2000b. "Facing Challenges to Evolution Education." Web site, http://www.natcenscied.org/tenchal.html.

———. 2000c. "The Creation / Evolution Continuum." Web site, http://www.natcenscied.org/continuum.html.

New York State Education Department Social Studies Committee. 1995. "Curriculum, Instruction, and Assessment Preliminary Draft Framework."

New York State Social Studies Syllabus Review and Development Committee. 1991. "One Nation, Many Peoples: A Declaration of Cultural Interdependence."

New York State Special Task Force on Minorities: Equity and Excellence. 1989. "A Curriculum of Inclusion: Report of the Commissioner's Task Force on Minorities: Equity and Excellence."

Numbers, Ronald. 1992. *The Creationists*. New York: Alfred A. Knopf.

Olneck, Michael. 1993. "Terms of Inclusion: Has Multiculturalism Redefined Equality in American Education?" *American Journal of Education* 101:234–60.

Olson, Daniel. 1997. "Dimensions of Cultural Tension among the American Public." In *Culture Wars in American Politics: Critical Reviews of a Popular Myth*, edited by Rhys Williams. New York: Aldine de Gruyter.

Ortiz de Montellano, Bernard. 1996. "Afrocentric Pseudoscience: The Miseducation of African Americans." In *The Flight from Science and Reason*, edited by Paul R. Gross, Norman Levitt, and Martin W. Lewis. New York: New York Academy of Sciences.

Oyebade, Bayo. 1990. "African Studies and the Afrocentric Paradigm: A Critique." *Journal of Black Studies* 21:233–38.

Padian, Kevin, associate professor of integrative biology and curator of the Museum of Paleontology at the University of California, Berkeley. 1996. Interview by author, October 9, 1996. Tape recording.

Perrow, Charles. 1961. "The Analysis of Goals in Complex Organizations." *American Sociological Review* 26: 854–66.

Perry, Theresa, and Lisa Delpit, eds. 1998. *The Real Ebonics Debate: Power, Language, and the Education of African American Children*. Boston: Beacon.

Parker, Kris. 1989. "A Survival Curriculum for Inner-City Kids." *New York Times*, September 9, section 1, p. 23.

Persell, Carolyn Hodges, and Peter Cookson, Jr. 1985. "Chartering and Bartering: Elite Education and Social Reproduction." *Social Problems* 33:114–29.

Polletta, Francesca. 1997. "Culture and Its Discontents: Recent Theorizing on the Cultural Dimensions of Protest." *Sociological Inquiry* 67:431–50.

Portland Public Schools. n.d. Web site, http://www.pps.K12.or.us/district/depts/mc-me/essays.shtml.

Powell, Walter. 1985. *Getting into Print: The Decision-Making Process in Scholarly Publishing*. Chicago: University of Chicago Press.

Proffitt, W. Trexler, and Marc Ventresca. 2000. "A New Type of Fieldwork: Ideology, Mobilization, and U.S. Shareholder Activism." Unpublished manuscript.

Putka, G. 1991. "Curricula of Color: Course Work Stressing Blacks' Role Has Critics but Appears Effective." *Wall Street Journal*, July 1.

Ravitch, Diane, professor in the School of Education, New York University, and former U.S. assistant secretary of education 1995. Interview by author, November 8, New York, N.Y. Tape recording.

Raz, Joseph. 1994. "Multiculturalism: A Liberal Perspective." *Dissent* (Winter) 41:67–79.

Rhoades, Linda, school board member of the Vista Unified School District. 1996. Interview by author, October 16, Vista, Calif. Tape recording.

Rojas, Fabio. 2000. "Social Movement Outcomes and Organizational Decision Making: An Analysis of the Establishment of the Black Studies and Women's Studies Programs." Unpublished manuscript, Department of Sociology, University of Chicago.

Rowan, Brian. 1982. "Organizational Structure and the Institutional Environment: The Case of Public Schools." *Administrative Science Quarterly* 27: 259–79.

Sanchez Korrol, Virginia, professor and chair of Puerto Rican Studies, Brooklyn College, and member of the New York State Social Studies Syllabus Review and Development Committee. 1996. Interview by author, November 8, New York, N.Y. Tape recording.

———. 2001. Follow-up email interview with author, May 15.

Schlesinger, Arthur, Jr. 1991. "Report of the New York State Social Studies Syllabus Review Committee: A Dissenting Opinion." In "One Nation, Many Peoples: A Declaration of Cultural Interdependence," pp. 45–47.

———. 1992. *The Disuniting of America: Reflections on a Multicultural Society.* New York: W. W. Norton.

Schudson, Michael. 1989. "How Culture Works: Perspectives from Media Studies on the Efficacy of Symbols." *Theory and Society* 18:153–80.

Schuman, Howard, Charlotte Steeh, and Lawrence Bobo. 1985. *Racial Attitudes in America.* Cambridge: Harvard University Press.

Scott, Eugenie, director of the National Center for Science Education. 1996. Interview by author, October 7, Berkeley, Calif. Tape recording.

Selznick, Philip. 1948. "Foundations of the Theory of Organization." *American Sociological Review* 13:25–35.

Sewell, William. 1992. "A Theory of Structure: Duality, Agency, and Transformation." *American Journal of Sociology* 98:1–29.

Singer, Alan. 1993. "Multiculturalism and Afrocentricity: How They Influence Teaching U.S. History." *Social Education* 57:283–86.

Snow, David. 1987. Review of *Social Movements in an Organizational Society: Collected Essays,* edited by Mayer Zald and John D. McCarthy, in *Contemporary Sociology* 603–4.

Snow, David, and Robert Benford. 1988. "Ideology, Frame Resonance, and Participant Mobilization." *International Social Movement Research* 1:197–217.

———. 1992. "Master Frames and Cycles of Protest." In *Frontiers in Social Movement Theory,* ed. Aldon Morris and Carol McClurg Mueller. New Haven: Yale University Press.

Snow, David, E. Burke Rochford, Steven Worden, and Robert Benford. 1986. "Frame Alignment Processes, Mobilization, and Movement Participation." *American Sociological Review* 51:464–81.

Sobol, Thomas. 1991. "Understanding Diversity." Memo written to the New York Board of Regents to accompany the report "One Nation, Many Peoples: A Declaration of Cultural Interdependence" by the New York State Social Studies and Syllabus Review and Development Committee.

Sobol, Thomas, former commissioner of education for the state of New York and currently professor of education, Teachers' College, Columbia University. 1995. Interview by author, November 7, New York, N.Y. Tape recording.

Stage, Elizabeth, executive director of the California Science Project, University of California, and chair of the Science Subject Matter Committee of the Curriculum Development and Supplemental Materials Commission of the State of California. 1996. Interview by author, October 11, Oakland, Calif. Tape recording.

State University of New York and the State Education Department. 1991. "A New Compact for Learning: Improving Public Elementary, Middle, and Secondary Education Results in the 1990s."

Sweet, Midge, school board member of the Atlanta Public School System. 1995. Interview by author, November 29, Atlanta, Ga. Tape recording.

Swidler, Ann. 1986. "Culure in Action: Symbols and Strategies." *American Sociological Review* 51:273–86.

Tarrow, Sidney. 1992. "Mentalities, Political Cultures, and Collective Action Frames: Constructing Meanings through Actions." In *Frontiers in Social Movement Theory*, edited by Aldon Morris and Carol McClurg Mueller. New Haven: Yale University Press.

———. 1998. *Power in Movement: Social Movements and Contentious Politics.* Cambridge: Cambridge University Press.

Thomas, Greg. 1995. "The Black Studies War: Multiculturalism versus Afrocentricity." *The Village Voice*, January 11–17.

Tilly, Charles. 1978. *From Mobilization to Revolution.* Reading, Mass.: Addison-Wesley.

Topps, Betty, executive assistant to the superintendent, District of Columbia Public Schools. 1995. Interview by author, August 21, Washington, D.C. Tape recording.

Toumey, Christopher P. 1994. *God's Own Scientists: Creationists in a Secular World.* New Brunswick, N.J.: Rutgers University Press.

Townsend, Rene, former superintendent of the Vista Unified School District, and current superintendent of the Coronado School District. 1996. Interview by author, October 15, Coronado, Calif. Tape recording.

Tsutsui, Kiyoteru. 2000. "Global Dimensions of Contemporary Social Movements: The Case of a Social Movement for 'Comfort Women.' " Unpublished paper, Department of Sociology, Stanford University.

Twyman, Gladys, project coordinator, African American Infusion Program, Atlanta Public School System. 1995. Interview by author, November 30, Atlanta, Ga. Tape recording.

Tyack, David, and Larry Cuban. 1995. *Tinkering toward Utopia: A Century of Public School Reform.* Cambridge: Harvard University Press.

Tyndall, John, former school board member of the Vista Unified School District and director of accounting, Institute for Creation Research. 1996. Interview by author, October 16, Vista, Calif. Tape recording.

U.S. Department of Education. 1999. Web site, http://nces.ed.gov/pubs/digest97/d97t045.html.

Useem, Bert, and Mayer Zald. 1982. "From Pressure Group to Social Movement: Efforts to Promote Use of Nuclear Power." *Social Problems* 30:144–56.

Van Sertima, Ivan. 1990. "Future Directions for African and African-American Content in the School Curriculum." In *Infusion of African and African-American Content in the School Curriculum: Proceedings of the First National Conference*, edited by Asa Hilliard III, Lucretia Payton-Stewart, Larry Obadele Williams. Chicago: Third World Press.

Veblen, Thorstein. 1994 [1899]. *The Theory of the Leisure Class*. New York: Dover Publications.

Vista Unified School District Science Supplementary Book Review. 1993.

Walker, Abena, founder and principal of the African-Centered School at Webb Elementary School, District of Columbia Public Schools. 1995. Interview by author, October 5 and 6, Washington, D.C. Tape recording.

Weick, Karl. *The Social Psychology of Organizations*. Reading, Mass.: Addison Wesley.

Welsh-Asante, Kariamu. 1985. "Commonalities in African Dance: A Foundation for an African Aesthetic." *Journal of Black Studies*, 15.

West, Cornel. 1992. "The Postmodern Crisis of Black Intellectuals." In *Cultural Studies*, edited by Lawrence Grossberg, Cary Nelson, and Paula Treichler. New York: Routledge.

Whitcomb, John, and Henry Morris. 1961. *The Genesis Flood*. Philadelphia: Presbyterian & Reformed Publishing.

White, Betsy, education reporter for the *Atlanta Journal-Constitution*. 1995. Interview by author, December 1, Atlanta, Ga. Tape recording.

———. 2001. Follow-up email interview with author, May 7 and 9.

Wiester, John, chairman of the Science Education Commission of the American Scientific Affiliation. 1996. Phone interview by author, December 4. Tape recording.

Williams, Rhys. 1995. "Constructing the Public Good: Social Movements and Cultural Resources." *Social Problems* 42:124–44.

———. 1997. Introduction and afterword to *Cultural Wars in American Politics: Critical Reviews of a Popular Myth*, edited by Rhys Williams. New York: Aldine de Gruyter.

Winant, Howard. 1994. *Racial Conditions: Politics, Theory, Comparisons*. Minneapolis: University of Minnesota Press.

Woodmorappe, John. 1996. *Noah's Ark: A Feasibility Study*. El Cajon, Calif.: Institute for Creation Research.

Woolgar, Steve. 1988. *Science: The Very Idea*. London: Tavistock.

Wuthnow, Robert. 1987. *Meaning and Moral Order: Explorations in Cultural Analysis*. Berkeley: University of California Press.

Zald, Mayer, and John D. McCarthy, eds. 1987. *Social Movements in an Organizational Society: Collected Essays*. New Brunswick, N.J.: Transaction Books.